D0003503

Made in the USA
Middletown, DE
02 December 2015

PRAISE FOR THE
JONATHAN CLEMENTS MONEY GUIDE

"It's hard to imagine a finer place to begin your search for financial peace of mind than with *Jonathan Clements Money Guide*. Yes, it's long. But so is the list of financial challenges faced by American families. Don't be intimidated. He's made it easy to navigate through these challenges, identify those where you need help, and successfully deal with them. Don't just scan this fine, readable, and insightful guide. Keep it by your desk and return to it as your circumstances change, as financial markets change, and as the world turns."
– John C. Bogle, founder, The Vanguard Group

"A comprehensive financial guide ranging from navigating health insurance alternatives to forming sensible investment portfolios. Clements is a first-rate financial writer who is a genius at making sophisticated advice accessible to everyone and a delight to read."
– Burton G. Malkiel, author of *A Random Walk Down Wall Street*

"Since the early 1990s, Jonathan Clements's columns taught his readers, profited them, and made them smile. Trouble was, you needed to have read all his *Wall Street Journal* articles. Until now, that is. His *Money Guide* wraps this bounty, and then some, into a tidy package, destined to be enjoyed and referred to over and over by readers for decades to come."
– William J. Bernstein, author of *The Investor's Manifesto*

"How do you get nearly 30 years of personal-finance wisdom and advice in an engaging, entertaining and easy-to-use format? Keep Jonathan Clements's *Money Guide* on your desk or tablet for instant answers to your essential money questions."
– Consuelo Mack, anchor, *Consuelo Mack WealthTrack*

"Would you like to have a friend who knew a lot and would share the straight scoop with you on any investment topic at any time in clear language, with candor and a wry sense of humor? Well, here it is. What a break!"
– Charles D. Ellis, author of *What It Takes* and *Winning the Loser's Game*

"As someone who has read just about every personal-finance book ever published, I can honestly say this is the best money manual ever written—period! Jonathan Clements's *Money Guide* offers readers a host of brilliant insights on how to grow their money. It's required reading for anyone striving for financial independence."
– Allan Roth, author of *How a Second Grader Beats Wall Street*

FOR NICHOLAS, ANDREW AND VICTORIA

CONTENTS

ACKNOWLEDGMENTS

Putting out this second edition of the *Jonathan Clements Money Guide* has been a less frenetic and less stressful affair, for which my doctor is grateful. Part of the credit goes to readers. Many of you wrote, pointing out a few errors and offering suggestions for the 2016 edition. Have further ideas for how to improve the *Money Guide*? Write to ClementsGuide@gmail.com.

I use the *Money Guide* in the college course I teach, and I was pleasantly surprised to learn that other professors do the same. If you assign the book to your students and there's any supporting material or additional content that would be helpful, let me know. I have also heard from folks interested in licensing the book's content for their websites or other uses. If you want to discuss that possibility, please get in touch.

Once again, David Glaubke designed the cover of the *Money Guide* and Prudence Crowther copyedited the manuscript. Many, many thanks. The day-to-day angst of revising this book was borne by my family, especially poor Lucinda. Along the way, she learned more about personal finance than she ever wanted to know.

Finally, this year's edition of the *Money Guide* is dedicated to my three siblings, Nicholas, Andrew and Victoria, with whom I have fought, laughed, cried, had childhood adventures (and a few adult ones), drunk too much, driven too fast, bicycled countless miles and (many, many decades ago) even taken a few baths.

PART I

INTRODUCTION
START HERE,
GO ANYWHERE

Welcome to the *Jonathan Clements Money Guide 2016*. This year's edition is roughly 25 percent larger and substantially revised, with a host of new features added:

Great Debates. In these sections, you'll get a quick look at seven of the great financial arguments, including when to take Social Security, whether to buy term or cash value life insurance, and whether it's possible to beat the market.

My Story. Scattered throughout the book, you will find seven sections where I detail my own financial experiences. What worked for me might not work for you—but I hope these sections will give you food for thought.

Dos and Don'ts. Here, you'll find a list of financial steps you ought to take in 2016—and some you should avoid.

Investment Math. I realize that many readers will approach this new chapter with trepidation. But I hope it provides a painless introduction to the topic, even for the mathematically phobic.

Your Financial Plan. This new final chapter pulls together core ideas from the *Money Guide* and shows how to create your own financial plan with relative ease.

Key Concepts. This appendix grew out of a college course I teach on personal finance. These are the concepts I insist my students understand, and I figure the list may be of interest to others.

From here, you might quickly peruse the first section, which is devoted to navigating this book. Next, consider heading to the sections devoted to today's economy, your human capital—and your goals. That's where your journey will begin in earnest. In this chapter, you can also learn a little about my biases.

Be warned: This is not a get-rich-quick book. You won't find a forecast for stock and bond returns in 2016. You won't find me proclaiming that some single investment—real estate, cash-value life insurance, gold—will answer all of your financial prayers. If that's what you are looking for, please ask for a refund.

Next year, I will be back with the *Jonathan Clements Money Guide 2017*. Wish the book had more details on a particular topic? Let me know at ClementsGuide@gmail.com.

1. NAVIGATING THIS BOOK

You could studiously work your way through the *Money Guide* from the first page to the last. But I've tried to design it so you can quickly zero in on the information you want.

Got a specific issue you need help with? While this year's *Money Guide* contains much new material and I have rewritten many parts, the basic format remains the same. The book is divided into 419 sections, each typically 250 to 350 words. This is section 1. At the end of Part XIV, you'll find section 419. The sections are listed in the detailed table of contents, which is located at the back of the book and is akin to an index. Got a particular topic that's on your mind? See if you can find it listed there.

While we tend to think of financial issues in different buckets—retirement, taxes, estate planning—one topic is often connected to another. When that's the case, I've tried to make it clear, and then direct readers to other relevant parts of the *Money Guide*.

You will also find a slew of websites listed in the book, where you can find additional information and helpful calculators. Throughout, I have incorporated the latest numbers on the economy, markets and tax rates. In addition, I have included statistics on how the typical American is faring financially, so you can see how you stack up against your neighbors.

Finally, I have strong views on financial issues, and I realize not everybody shares my opinions. When I want to emphasize particular points or I figure my views may raise a few eyebrows, I have inserted them in a paragraph or two labeled "JONATHAN'S TAKE."

2. DECEMBER 2015: WHERE WE STAND

The financial crisis of 2008 may be fading from memory. But as we assess where America stands financially, we invariably think back to that turbulent time.

- The unemployment rate, which hit a high of 10 percent in October 2009, was 5 percent in October 2015.

- The U.S. economy grew 2.2 percent, after adjusting for inflation, over the 12 months through 2015's third quarter. That's a vast improvement from 2008 and 2009, when the economy contracted, though growth continues to disappoint compared to the 2.9 percent average for the past 50 years.

- Inflation ran at just 0.2 percent over the 12 months through October. Because inflation has been so subdued, Social Security retirement benefits weren't increased for 2016 and there were only modest changes in federal tax thresholds.

- The savings rate in 2015 was running at just over 5 percent of disposable personal income. That's better than 2005's low of 2.6 percent, but the savings rate remains far lower than financial experts recommend.

- Total borrowing by Americans, including mortgage debt, hit a peak of $12.7 trillion in the third quarter of 2008. By 2015's third quarter, it was down to $12.1 trillion. That's equal to $46,150 per household.

- Home prices rose 4.9 percent in the 12 months through September 2015, but remain 5 percent below their mid-2006 peak, as measured by the S&P/Case-Shiller U.S. National Home Price Index.

- The Standard & Poor's 500-stock index was up 1 percent in 2015 through Nov. 30, bringing the bull market gain since the March 2009 low to 207.5 percent. Despite that robust rally, the S&P 500 has climbed just 36.2 percent since its March 2000 peak—a modest 2 percent annual price gain for the past 15-plus years.

- The benchmark 10-year Treasury note stood at 2.21 percent as of Nov. 30, 2015, versus 2.17 percent at year-end 2014, as bond yields defy the pundits and remain stubbornly low.

- Buyers of certificates of deposit and savings accounts should see higher yields in 2016, as the Federal Reserve lifts short-term interest rates.

- As of mid-2015, U.S. households were 4.7 percent wealthier than a year earlier, according to the Federal Reserve. This reflects the value of all real estate, financial accounts and other household assets, minus mortgages and other money borrowed.

- Congress put a halt to a popular strategy for claiming Social Security, which involved one spouse delaying retirement benefits even as the other spouse collected spousal benefits. There's more on this in Part II.

• Rewriting the tax code has moved to the front of the political agenda. Nothing happened in 2015 or is likely to happen in 2016, but big changes could lie ahead.

3. YOUR HUMAN CAPITAL

As you consider what financial steps to take in 2016, you might begin with your most valuable asset—yourself. Economists refer to our income-earning ability as our human capital. It should figure into many of our financial decisions, including how much debt we take on, how much emergency money we need, what insurance we purchase, and what mix of stocks and bonds we buy.

For instance, if you're a government worker with a steady job and a traditional pension upon retirement, you may not have huge lifetime earnings, but your paycheck doesn't involve much risk. That means you can probably take a fair amount of risk elsewhere in your financial life, including investing heavily in stocks and using an adjustable-rate mortgage to buy your home. But if you're a small-business owner, you are taking a lot of risk with your human capital—and you may want to favor bonds in your portfolio, keep your debts modest and build up a large emergency fund.

You will also want to protect your human capital, which means buying health and disability insurance, and perhaps also life insurance if you have a family that depends on you financially. Maybe more important, you will want to save part of the income generated by your human capital, so that one day you will no longer need a paycheck and you can retire.

In the pages ahead, I'll encourage you to think about your human capital as you tackle four goals many of us share: paying for retirement, buying a home, putting the kids through college and protecting our family. Those four goals are the subject of the *Money Guide*'s next four parts.

As we pursue these goals, we'll do all manner of spending, saving, investing, taxpaying, borrowing and giving, which are discussed in the chapters that follow. I have also included chapters on financial markets and investment math for those who don't mind a little complexity. Not everything fits neatly into these various categories. That's why I have a chapter on life events. To wrap up things, there's a chapter on how to draw up your own financial plan, plus an appendix that recaps key concepts.

4. YOUR GOALS

While most of us have four key goals—retirement, college for the kids, owning a home and protecting our family—that leaves plenty of room for interpretation. The house I dream of owning is no doubt quite different from the one you're imagining.

That is both good and bad. It's good because, if we can visualize our goals in great detail, we'll be more motivated to make the necessary sacrifices to achieve them. It is worth spending considerable time pondering our goals, so we strive for things we truly want.

That's where the bad part comes in. We just aren't very good at figuring out what we want. Maybe we hanker after a luxury sedan. But then the sedan turns out to be a disappointment. When we were kids, our parents always owned luxury cars and we remember our childhood as a happy, carefree time. But maybe it's the happy, carefree time we miss—and the expensive sedan is just a symbol in our air-brushed recollection.

How can you avoid such costly mistakes? Take your time before making major financial decisions. Don't impulsively buy the timeshare during the wonderfully relaxing vacation. Think hard about why you want something. Do you truly believe the pricey private school will give your children a better education—or are you drawn to the prestige or compensating for your perceived failings as a parent? Think about the potential headaches. The luxury sedan may be alluring. But what about the car payments?

Leading a thoughtful financial life can help you get the most out of your money. We all have limited means. If we waste money on goals that aren't important to us, we may not have enough for those that matter.

5. JONATHAN'S TAKE

I like to think of this *Money Guide* as an encyclopedia with attitude. Here are just some of the attitudes that permeate the pages that follow:

• It's a big mistake to view our homes, investment accounts, life insurance and other parts of our financial lives in isolation. Instead, we should take a broad view of our finances that encompasses our human capital, debts, stocks, bonds, real estate, financial obligations to family and more. This can help us to earn higher returns, avoid unnecessary risks and make sensible financial tradeoffs.

• All too many people hunt for the big win, whether it's with stocks, rental properties or lottery tickets. Many are disappointed. If your goal is financial success, a much surer path is managing risk, holding down investment costs and taxes, and saving diligently. Indeed, a healthy savings habit is the greatest of the financial virtues.

• Complexity might suggest sophistication. But in the financial world, it usually means high fees and befuddled investors. I would limit how many financial accounts you have and stick with simple investments that you truly understand, with a special emphasis on mutual funds and exchange-traded funds. What about individual company stocks? I don't think they should play a major part in the typical investor's portfolio.

• Money supposedly buys happiness—and yet many folks lead lives of financial anxiety and regret. They worry about having enough to pay the monthly bills and whether they're saving enough. They fret over their investments. They lust after new purchases, only to find themselves later disappointed. Want to be a contented investor and a happy consumer? You need to think hard about what unnerves you and what gives you a lasting sense of satisfaction.

6. ABBREVIATIONS

I strongly believe that sensible money management doesn't have to be complicated and, indeed, that simpler is usually better. Wall Street may try to bamboozle investors with jargon and needless complexity in an effort to justify its hefty fees. But in this guide, I have endeavored to avoid such nonsense and instead make the financial world understandable to the interested layperson.

With that in mind, I have avoided a lot of abbreviations. In each of the 419 sections, I try to spell out the full name on first reference, and only abbreviate on second and subsequent references.

But when it came to exchange-traded index funds, individual retirement accounts and Standard & Poor's (as in S&P 500), this started to seem silly because there are so many references. So be prepared: You'll see a lot of mentions of ETFs, IRAs and S&P—and, fingers crossed, you'll remember what those initials stand for.

PART II

RETIREMENT
IT MAY COME LAST, BUT YOU SHOULD PUT IT FIRST

If you just entered the workforce, it's time to start preparing for retirement. Over the next four decades, you might pull in tens and perhaps hundreds of thousands of dollars every year. An October 2012 Census Bureau study estimates that those with a bachelor's degree have average lifetime earnings of $2.4 million, figured in today's dollars.

Of course, it's lucky you will have all that income coming in, because ahead of you lies life's toughest financial task: amassing enough money so you can retire in comfort. In dry economic terms, your working career is about accumulating enough financial capital, so that one day you'll no longer need the income from your human capital. This is, alas, a task that most Americans are not good at.

Want to do better? To get you started, check out this chapter's dos and don'ts for 2016. As you dig deeper and ponder how to pay for retirement, it's helpful to think about your life in three stages—your 20s, 30s and 40s, your 50s and early 60s, and age 65 and beyond—which is how the rest of this chapter is divvied up. Readers under age 50 might stick with the initial sections of the chapter and those already retired might head straight to section 25. What about those who are within 15 years of retirement? You should probably read both the part devoted to your 50s and early 60s and the sections geared to folks age 65 and beyond.

7. A WOBBLY THREE-LEGGED STOOL

Experts sometimes talk about the three-legged retirement stool, consisting of Social Security, traditional defined benefit pension plans and personal savings. The latter includes money stashed in 401(k) plans, individual retirement accounts and regular taxable accounts.

Cutting Social Security is a constant topic of conversation in political circles, with some Republican presidential candidates proposing to raise the age at which you can claim Social Security, while also reducing benefits for high-income earners. Even without those changes, benefits are getting scaled back. The age at which retirees can claim full Social Security retirement benefits is gradually climbing. The full Social Security retirement age is 66 for those born between 1943 and 1954. It rises for those born in subsequent years, eventually hitting age 67 for those born in 1960 or later.

Meanwhile, traditional defined benefit pensions continue to disappear. These pensions, which pay eligible employees income every month throughout retirement, remain relatively common among public sector workers, despite recent cutbacks. Instead, the big falloff has occurred in the private sector. According to a Bureau of Labor Statistics study, just 18 percent of private-sector workers had pensions as of 2011, down from 35 percent in the early 1990s.

What about personal savings, the third leg of the retirement stool? Given the cutbacks elsewhere, this needs to be the strongest leg of the stool—but it also looks extremely wobbly.

8. TODAY'S RETIREMENT READINESS

How are Americans doing when it comes to retirement savings? Solid numbers are hard to come by. But the available statistics aren't encouraging. According to the Employee Benefit Research Institute's 2015 Retirement Confidence Survey, 52 percent of workers age 55 and older reported having savings of less than $50,000. This figure excludes the value of their home, Social Security and any defined benefit pension plan.

What if you include those items? For households approaching retirement age, the typical net worth is $598,700, calculates Boston College's Center for Retirement Research. That sounds more impressive—but 50 percent of this figure is represented by the value assigned to Social Security benefits, and another 26 percent by traditional pension plans, which are fast disappearing.

You can also get a glimpse of America's retirement readiness from the Federal Reserve's 2013 Survey of Consumer Finances. Among households headed by someone age 65 to 74, 85.8 percent owned their home. But 42.2

percent also had a mortgage, while 66.4 percent were carrying some kind of debt. Meanwhile, just 48 percent of this group had an IRA or similar retirement account.

Even if most folks aren't in good shape for retirement, presumably some are. How many? Each year, Phoenix Marketing International calculates how many U.S. households have $1 million or more in investable assets. Based on a 4 percent portfolio withdrawal rate, $1 million would give you $40,000 in first-year retirement income, on top of whatever you might receive from Social Security and any pension plans. That should be enough for a comfortable, though hardly lavish, retirement.

Phoenix calculates that 5.2 percent of U.S. households had $1 million or more in investable assets as of 2014. Maryland, Connecticut and New Jersey had the highest concentration of millionaire households, at more than 7 percent, while Mississippi was at the bottom of the table, with less than 4 percent.

9. DOS AND DON'TS FOR 2016

Saving enough for retirement, and then turning those savings into a reliable stream of retirement income, is our life's great financial task. Want to check on your progress? Here are some "to dos" for 2016:

• Do a little daydreaming. Think about what you might do with your retirement that would make your final decades especially fulfilling.

• Run the numbers to check whether you're on track to have enough saved by retirement.

• Hold a fire drill. If you are retired and we got a repeat of the 2007–09 stock market collapse, when the S&P 500-stock index fell 57 percent, how would you cope financially?

And here are some things not to do:

• Don't miss out on free money by failing to invest enough in your employer's 401(k) plan to earn the full matching contribution.

• Don't automatically claim Social Security at age 62, which is when almost half of all retirees claim benefits. Often, it makes sense to delay Social Security, so you get a larger monthly check.

• Don't abandon stocks when you retire. You could easily live 25 or 30 years in retirement, which is plenty of time to earn healthy gains in the stock market. You may need those gains, because 25 or 30 years is also plenty of time for inflation to do hefty damage.

• Don't rule out buying an income annuity. These aren't a popular product—but they could be the key to a more comfortable, less financially stressed retirement.

10. WOMEN AND MONEY

Wall Street firms often direct marketing pitches at women, claiming that they have distinct financial needs. But in truth, women's financial needs aren't all that different from those of men, though there are five differences that are worth bearing in mind as you save and invest for retirement. First, women typically live longer than men, so it's helpful if you have a somewhat larger nest egg and it may make even more sense to delay Social Security benefits to get a larger monthly check.

Second, there's a greater chance you will end up in a nursing home. Thanks to their longer life expectancy, women typically outlive their husband or partner, and often there's no one to provide care when they are ailing. You can learn more about nursing home costs, and how to handle them, in Part V.

Third, women often earn less than men, making it more difficult to save for retirement. In addition, there's a fourth factor: Their careers may be interrupted by raising children, denting their total lifetime earnings and delaying their next promotion.

Finally, women tend to be less inclined to take investment risk than men. This is both good and bad. Women seem less drawn to high-risk investments—betting big on individual stocks, trading listed options, buying aggressive mutual funds—that often wreak havoc with men's investment returns.

But women also appear to be less comfortable owning stocks generally, which can hurt their long-run results. If women can overcome this reluctance, however, they often make great investors, because they're less inclined to buy the high-risk investments that can torpedo men's results.

11. YOUR 20s, 30s AND 40s

Most of us have all kinds of financial desires, including a nice home, a fancy car, a good education for the kids and a fun trip next summer. But retirement should take precedence. Think of it this way: You can take out a loan to buy a house or car, and your kids can borrow to pay for college, and then slowly pay the money back. But when it comes to retirement, you'll need to start out with a heaping stack of dollar bills.

Moreover, retirement is significantly more expensive than these other goals, in part because you need to be so cautious when spending down your savings. Financial experts often talk about a 4 percent withdrawal rate. Translation: For every $100,000 you have saved by the time you quit the workforce, you can reasonably expect to pull out $4,000 in the first year of retirement. Want $60,000 in portfolio income during retirement? You will likely need to sock away something like $1.5 million. To amass that sort of money, you will probably have to save diligently starting soon after you enter the workforce.

Even if you're a good saver, that still leaves lots of decisions—including which accounts to stash those savings in, precisely how much to save every year and what investments to buy.

12. PUT RETIREMENT FIRST

Our hunter-gatherer ancestors were focused on surviving until tomorrow. We need to focus on retiring decades from now. Not surprisingly, this isn't something that comes naturally.

Our inclination is to deal with life's goals consecutively, rather than concurrently. In other words, we might save for the house down payment in our 30s, pay for the kids' college in our 40s and then finally turn our attention to retirement in our 50s. But if we do that, we could find ourselves in financial trouble. It's awfully tough to amass enough for retirement if we start saving in our 20s, let alone beginning at age 50.

Indeed, even as your attention is drawn to more immediate goals, don't shortchange retirement. Maybe you can't save 12 to 15 percent toward retirement in your 20s and 30s. But try to save at least some money every month.

The earlier you start saving, the longer your time horizon will be. In addition to having more years of saving regularly, you can take the risk of investing more in stocks and potentially earn higher returns. You may also get the chance to fund your employer's 401(k) plan and collect a matching employer contribution. That's free money—and you don't want to miss out.

Moreover, if you save a healthy sum from your 20s onwards, you will give yourself options. You may reach your late 40s or early 50s and discover that you are comfortably on track for retirement. At that point, you might opt to work fewer hours or switch to a less lucrative but perhaps more fulfilling career.

13. ARE YOU SAVING ENOUGH?

As a rule of thumb, you should probably save 12 to 15 percent of your pretax income toward retirement. If your employer has some sort of traditional defined benefit pension plan, which will pay you income every month in retirement, you can likely save less.

Similarly, if your employer makes a fixed or matching contribution to its 401(k) or 403(b) plan, you might be able to trim your savings rate. Suppose your employer matches your 401(k) contributions at 50 cents on the dollar up to 6 percent of pay. To hit a 12 percent savings rate, you only need to sock away 9 percent, because you'll get 3 percent from your employer.

A 2015 study by Financial Engines found that roughly a quarter of employees fail to contribute enough to get the full matching contribution, thus passing up the chance to get free money from their employer. Among participants in retirement plans overseen by Vanguard Group, a third don't contribute enough to get the full match.

If you want a better sense for how much you ought to save every month, by factoring in how far you are from retirement and how much you have already saved, try playing around with one of the many online financial calculators. But given all the uncertainty about market returns, take these projections with a grain of salt.

JONATHAN'S TAKE: While I'm not advocating a life of self-imposed poverty, I would strongly suggest saving as much as you reasonably can whenever you can. In today's turbulent job market, you don't know when your ability to save may be disrupted by a bout of unemployment or if you might be forced to retire earlier than planned.

According to the Employee Benefit Research Institute's 2015 Retirement Confidence Survey, workers on average expect to retire at age 65. But it turns out the actual retirement age is 62. Many of those retirements aren't voluntary, with folks leaving the workforce because of ill health or layoffs. It might be ideal to save just enough every month for the retirement we want. But the reality is considerably messier: We retire with whatever we have managed to amass by that juncture—and the more we have, the easier our retirement will be.

14. FINANCIAL CALCULATORS

Are you saving enough for retirement? To find out, try the Retirement Planner at Dinkytown.net (named after a neighborhood in Minneapolis). You can quibble that the calculator is overly simplistic and easily abused: It presumes you earn the same return year after year, which is unrealistic, and delusional folks can make everything look rosy by assuming an absurdly high rate of return. Still, it offers a quick look at your retirement readiness. If you have something akin to a 60 percent stock–40 percent bond portfolio, override the default investment returns: For the period both before and during retirement, plug in a 5 percent annual return and 3 percent for inflation.

What's the problem with assuming the same return year after year? Check out FIRECalc.com, which drives home a key concept every retiree needs to grasp: sequence-of-return risk. The bottom line: If you get rotten returns early in retirement, you can quickly end up in financial trouble, even if average returns over your retirement are just dandy.

Looking to dig deeper into retirement or other financial issues? TRowePrice.com has an impressive collection of retirement tools, including its Retirement Income Calculator, which uses something called Monte Carlo analysis to see how you might fare in a host of different market scenarios. Also check out the Retirement Income Calculator at Vanguard.com.

15. WHERE TO STASH YOUR SAVINGS?

You are saving diligently for retirement—but where should you invest those savings? You'll want to give careful thought to your so-called asset allocation, which is your basic mix of stocks, bonds and other investments. You will also want to consider whether to stash your savings in a taxable account, your employer's 401(k), a Roth IRA or elsewhere. You can get detailed help with these two issues in Part VIII, which is devoted to investing, and Part XI, which discusses taxes.

You might start by thinking about your human capital. When you have a paycheck to cover your daily living expenses, there's less need to buy conservative, income-generating investments. That frees you up to invest for the long haul by buying stocks, which can offer wretched short-term performance but healthy long-run gains. Because you won't need to spend all your savings on the day you quit the workforce, your investment time horizon if you're in your 20s might be six decades or more, which should be plenty of time to ride out a few rough spells in the stock market.

Your long time horizon also means you can make full use of retirement accounts. These involve a long-term commitment: There are typically tax penalties if you withdraw money before age 59½. But in return for that commitment, you can enjoy some great tax advantages, as well as a potential matching contribution if you fund your employer's retirement plan.

16. YOUR 50s AND EARLY 60s

If you're within 10 or 15 years of retirement, the financial "to do" list can be daunting. This is your last chance to use the income from your human capital to prep your finances for life without a paycheck.

Between now and retirement, you probably want to save as much as you can and get all debt paid off. You need to decide whether to stay in your current home and, if you'll move, whether it makes sense to move now, while you have a paycheck to cover the costs involved. If you retire before you become eligible for Medicare at age 65, you have to figure out how to cover health care costs. You should also consider how you will cope if you end up needing long-term care. Health care issues are covered in Part V.

Pay particular attention to two key questions. First, will you have enough retirement income, and where will this income come from? That means assessing how much you will have saved by retirement, and considering what portfolio adjustments and other steps you should take to turn these savings into a reliable income stream. You should also weigh when to claim Social Security and whether it makes sense to continue working part-time once you leave your fulltime job.

Second, give some thought to what you will do with your retirement. This might seem laughably easy as you imagine sleeping late, lingering over the newspaper, heading out for lunch, taking a nap and so on through the day. But this is unlikely to make for a fulfilling retirement.

17. A FULFILLING RETIREMENT

We spend decades saving for retirement, but we often give scant thought to what we'll do with all that free time. This can be a huge mistake.

We might imagine that what we want is more time to relax. But we aren't built to relax. Rather, thanks to our hunter-gatherer ancestors, we're built to strive. We are here today because they never let up in their quest for survival. Result: We're often happiest when engaged in activities that we think are important, we're passionate about, we find challenging and which give us that pleasant sense we're making progress.

We also tend to be happiest when we feel we are part of a community— another inherited instinct. Studies have found that people are more satisfied and tend to live longer if they have a robust network of friends and family.

What does this mean for your retirement? The answer will be different for all of us. But as you contemplate what you might do with your final 20 or 30 years, try thinking back to the times in your life when you were happiest. What was it about those times that made them so happy? Maybe it was the friends you were with or the projects you were engaged in. If you can figure out what you find most fulfilling, you could have the roadmap for a great retirement.

18. WILL YOU HAVE ENOUGH TO RETIRE?

Are you on track for a comfortable retirement? Here's how to get a quick sense for where you stand:

• Add up the savings you have for retirement. Plug this number into the Retirement Planner at Dinkytown.net, along with how much you expect to save in the years ahead and when you expect to retire. Override the default investment returns, inserting 5 percent as your expected portfolio performance and 3 percent for inflation.

• Use the Retirement Estimator at SocialSecurity.gov to calculate your likely benefit. For a fast but less accurate estimate, try SocialSecurity.gov's Quick Calculator.

• Find out how much you will receive from any traditional employer pensions. For many folks, the number will be zero because these plans, unfortunately, are now relatively rare.

On track? You might have the option of retiring early. Falling short? You'll need to play catch-up. Either way, you may want to make some portfolio adjustments, while also getting a firm grip on your living expenses.

19. ADJUSTING YOUR PORTFOLIO

In your 20s, 30s and 40s, you might have invested heavily in stocks because you had a paycheck to cover your living expenses. When you retire, you give up that paycheck—and that has big implications for your portfolio. Suddenly, you want not just growth from your investments, but also income.

Later in this chapter, when we talk about issues facing those age 65 and older, we'll discuss how you might generate income from your savings while fending off the threat from both short-run market declines and long-run inflation. But to prepare your portfolio and make sure your impending retirement isn't derailed by a stock market crash, you should probably scale back your investment risk over the last 10 or 15 years before you quit the workforce. An example: While you may have had 80 percent of your money in stocks in your early 40s, you might move toward a mix of perhaps 50 percent stocks and 50 percent conservative investments by the time you retire.

The precise percentages will depend on a host of factors. For instance, if Social Security and any pension income will cover a large portion of your retirement living expenses, you might take more risk with your portfolio. On the other hand, if the bulk of your retirement income will come from savings or you have little stomach for market swings, you might be somewhat more conservative.

20. THE 80 PERCENT RULE

One rule of thumb suggests that, to retire in comfort, you need 80 percent of your preretirement income. Why the 20 percent drop? You are no longer saving 10 percent or so every year toward retirement and you're no longer paying an employee's 7.65 percent payroll-tax contribution to Social Security and Medicare. In addition, you won't have to buy work clothes or pay commuting costs. Your income tax bill should also go down, in part because a portion of your retirement income will likely come from Social Security benefits, which are always at least partly tax-free.

It turns out, however, that many retirees are living on far less than 80 percent of their final salary. For instance, a 2014 T. Rowe Price Group survey of relatively affluent recent retirees found that these retirees were, on average, living on 66 percent of their preretirement income—and they reported being quite content.

This isn't a huge surprise, for three reasons. First, many folks save much more than 10 percent in the run-up to retirement, so they're already used to living on a lot less than 80 percent of their income. Second, many homeowners aim to get their mortgage paid off by retirement, which eliminates a major expense. Finally, by retirement, the kids are usually through college and in the workforce, which also greatly reduces the parents' spending. Add it all up, and you may find you can comfortably retire on 50 or 60 percent of your final salary.

21. ESTIMATING EXPENSES

Think about how much you spend during a one-week vacation. Now, imagine being on vacation 52 weeks a year. The implication: You'll likely find ample opportunities to spend whatever retirement income you have.

Your ability to splurge on travel, entertainment and eating out will depend not only on your after-tax income, but also on how much of that income gets chewed up by fixed costs, so you might take a shot at estimating what those will be. We're talking here about expenses such as utilities, groceries, car payments and insurance premiums. Potentially, your two biggest fixed costs will be housing and debt payments. You may want to spend your final years in the workforce getting those two under control.

To that end, consider whether you ought to trade down to a smaller home, which may cut your maintenance expenses, utility bills, homeowner's insurance and property taxes. It may also allow you to pay off any remaining mortgage debt and perhaps free up home equity that can then be added to your retirement savings.

For many folks, eliminating their mortgage is the sign that retirement is finally affordable. What if there's no way you can get your mortgage paid off by the time you quit the workforce—and you foresee carrying the loan for many years after that? You might refinance your existing loan balance with a new 30-year mortgage. That could slash your monthly payments, because you're extending the loan's repayment over a much longer period.

22. EARLY RETIREMENT

If you take early retirement, there are three key issues you need to worry about. First, and most important, do you really have enough saved? In this chapter, we've talked about a 4 percent portfolio withdrawal rate. But if you're quitting the workforce in your 50s, you might play it a little safer and assume not a 4 percent withdrawal rate, but 3 percent instead.

Second, if you retire before age 59½, you could potentially face tax penalties if you tap your retirement accounts. There are ways around that, as you'll learn in Part XI. Still, if your goal is early retirement, you may want to sidestep potential problems by building up your regular taxable account.

Third, if you retire before you turn age 65 and become eligible for Medicare, you'll likely need to buy your own health insurance. That's become easier, thanks to the health care exchanges launched as part of the Affordable Care Act. You might also cover yourself for 18 months by taking advantage of the so-called COBRA coverage that may be offered by your employer. For more on both topics, head to Part V.

23. PLAYING CATCH-UP

Doesn't look like you'll have enough saved for retirement? Here's how you could get back on track:

• Save like crazy. You might take advantage of catch-up contributions to 401(k) plans and IRAs. You can learn more in Part XI.

• Slash your expenses. Get all debts paid off. Trade down to a smaller home now rather than waiting for retirement.

• Delay retirement. Suppose you put off retirement from, say, age 65 to 67. That will give you two more years to save and two more years to earn investment returns. You can also put off claiming Social Security and buying an income annuity for two additional years, which will give you extra income.

• Annuitize more of your savings. The best annuity available is Social Security. Already planning to delay Social Security until age 70, so you get the largest possible monthly check? If you want more guaranteed income, you might buy an immediate fixed annuity when you quit the workforce.

Retirees are often reluctant to buy income annuities. But this can be a good strategy if your goal is to squeeze maximum lifetime income out of your savings.

• Work part-time in retirement. Suppose you can make $10,000 a year working part-time. That is like having an investment portfolio that is $250,000 larger, assuming a 4 percent withdrawal rate.

One warning: Don't try to compensate for your modest savings by gunning for outsized investment returns. That risky approach may backfire or you might panic during a market decline, thus ruining any chance of a comfortable retirement. What if your situation seems hopeless? In the next section, check out one possible strategy for those in rough financial shape.

24. WHEN ALL ELSE FAILS

Let's suppose you have little or nothing saved for retirement. What to do? You might focus on one overriding goal: not claiming Social Security retirement benefits until age 70.

Social Security is a wonderful income stream: It's government guaranteed, at least partly tax-free, it rises every year with inflation, you get it for as long as you live and your spouse may receive your benefit as a survivor benefit. By delaying until age 70, you ensure that you will get the maximum possible monthly benefit. With any luck, that monthly check will allow you to retire in moderate comfort.

Of course, you might lose your job or your employer might compel you to retire before age 70. If that happens, look to continue working, even if it's at a modest wage, so you can delay Social Security.

Meanwhile, save what you can. Also look to slash your cost of living. In particular, consider trading down to a less expensive home and try to get all debts paid off by the time you retire. With maximum Social Security benefits, some savings and low living costs, you may be able to enjoy a modest retirement.

25. AGE 65 AND BEYOND

If amassing enough savings to retire is life's toughest financial task, managing that money in retirement is the trickiest. Consider the juggling act ahead: You need your money to last at least as long as you do, while fending off the threat from long-run inflation and short-term market declines. You also need to be prepared for unexpected expenses—and perhaps the biggest is long-term care, which we discuss in Part V.

No single financial product will accomplish all of these tasks. Instead, you'll want to figure out the best combination of Social Security, pension and annuity income, as well as the right mix of stocks, bonds and cash investments. To that financial toolkit, you might add part-time work, long-term-care insurance and the equity in your home.

Once retired, you'll also have a few other financial tricks at your disposal. For instance, you could temporarily cut back your spending if there's a major market decline. In addition, as a retiree, you have a great opportunity to manage your annual tax bill. You no longer have a regular paycheck coming in. Instead, you're creating your own paycheck. Each year, you can decide whether to take money from a taxable source, such as traditional IRAs, or from accounts that won't have any tax consequences, such as cashing out part of your savings account or Roth IRA. You can read more about this in Part XI.

26. LIFE EXPECTANCY

What is retirement's biggest financial risk? Simply put, you don't want to run out of money before you run out of breath. Therein lies the great conundrum: You don't know how long you'll need to make your savings last.

To get a handle on the issue, don't look at life expectancies as of birth. Those are dragged down by all the folks who die before reaching retirement age. Instead, you might consider life expectancies as of age 65. According to the Social Security Administration, a 65-year-old man's life expectancy is age 84, while a 65-year-old woman can expect to live until 87. Bear in mind that these are medians. Half of retirees will die before these ages and half will live longer.

How much longer? Social Security estimates that a quarter of today's 65-year-olds will live beyond age 90 and 10 percent will live beyond age 95. If you're a couple, you have two tickets to the life-expectancy lottery—and there's a good chance that at least one of you will live to a ripe old age.

The Society of Actuaries estimates that there is a 51.8 percent chance that one member of a couple will survive to age 90 and an 8.7 percent chance that both will survive to that age. The Society notes that this may underestimate the odds, because there's evidence that married couples live longer than those who are single, divorced or widowed. Want to check out your life expectancy as of your current age? Try the Life Expectancy Calculator at SocialSecurity.gov.

27. INFLATION

Short-term market declines get all the attention. But long-run inflation can prove far more threatening.

In recent years, inflation has been relatively subdued. Over the 12 months through October 2015, consumer prices—as measured by CPI-U, the most popular inflation measure—climbed just 0.2 percent, while inflation over the past decade has clocked in at 1.8 percent. Imagine annual inflation continued to run at 1.8 percent during a retirement that lasted 30 years. By the end of three decades, the purchasing power of $1 would be reduced to less than 59 cents.

Moreover, CPI-U may underestimate how much seniors are affected by rising prices. The Bureau of Labor Statistics has a separate measure, known as CPI-E, which is designed to gauge inflation as experienced by households with folks age 62 and up. CPI-E assigns greater weight to housing and medical care. Both items tend to eat up more of the income of older Americans. Over the 32 years through September 2015, CPI-E rose 2.9 percent a year, versus 2.7 percent for CPI-U.

It gets worse. Even if retirees can generate an income stream that rises with inflation, they will likely find themselves lagging behind their neighbors who are still in the workforce. Why? The standard of living rises not with inflation, but with per capita GDP, which in the U.S. has grown 1.9 percentage points a year faster than inflation over the past 50 years.

The implication: Even as you strive to generate current income, you need to prepare for higher prices down the road. That might mean looking for income streams that are indexed to inflation, seeking capital gains by investing part of your portfolio in stocks, and possibly setting aside a portion of each year's investment income to spend in future years.

28. MARKET DECLINES

While you had a job, it might have been unnerving when the stock market declined. But there was no immediate impact on your standard of living. You had a paycheck to cover your daily living expenses, so it wasn't like you needed to sell stocks to buy groceries.

In fact, a market decline represented an opportunity. You could funnel part of your paycheck into stocks, thus taking advantage of the lower prices. Want to amass a healthy retirement nest egg? If you're a rational investor who is unperturbed by market turmoil, you should hope for lousy returns while you are saving for retirement, followed by a huge bull market as you approach the day you will quit the workforce. That way, you would buy investments when they are cheap and sell when they're expensive.

What if you aren't so lucky, and you retire and get hit with a bear market? You aren't saving regularly anymore, so tumbling markets no longer represent a great buying opportunity. True, you could take advantage of the decline by shifting some of your money from bonds to stocks. But instead of buying, you are far more likely to be selling as you seek to generate income.

Indeed, now that your human capital has stopped providing you with a paycheck, you'll need your portfolio to play that role instead. That means designing a financial strategy that focuses less on growth and more on income—and which can limit the damage done by sinking markets.

29. YOUR RETIREMENT INCOME

Where will your retirement income come from? You will likely rely on some combination of six key sources:

Savings. You will want to think carefully about how you'll extract income from your portfolio—and how much you can safely withdraw each year. To get a quick check on your plan, try the Nest Egg Calculator at Vanguard.com.

Social Security. When should you claim Social Security? Many folks opt for benefits at the earliest possible age. But relying solely on savings during your initial retirement years, while delaying Social Security to get a larger monthly check, is often the smarter strategy.

Pension plans. Not many people have traditional defined benefit pension plans anymore. Consider yourself lucky if you do. But also give some thought to the threat from rising living costs, because your pension is probably fixed rather than growing along with inflation.

Income annuities. Don't have a pension plan but like the idea of predictable monthly income? In addition to delaying Social Security, you might look into buying an income annuity.

Part-time work. Working a few days each week could greatly ease any financial strain, while adding richness to your retirement.

Home equity. Tapping your home's value to pay for retirement can be as simple as trading down to a less expensive place, or it could involve the hefty cost of a reverse mortgage.

This list isn't exhaustive: You might also receive income from rental properties, installment payments from the sale of a business and perhaps even an inheritance. You'll want to consider what role each of the above six income sources will play, and how their role may evolve over time. For instance, part-time work might be important early in retirement, while home equity could be your financial backstop if you live longer than you planned for.

30. PORTFOLIO WITHDRAWALS

Financial experts often suggest retirees use a 4 percent portfolio withdrawal rate. For instance, if you retire with $400,000 in savings, that would mean $16,000 in pretax first-year portfolio income. You might be able to generate that income by purchasing a collection of bonds that yield 4 percent. Problem is, that would leave you vulnerable to inflation, which will reduce the purchasing power of your bond interest with every passing year.

To fend off the threat from inflation, you might allocate part of your savings to stocks, which have the potential to deliver long-run inflation-beating gains. But that creates a new set of headaches, because you will likely have to cope with nasty short-term market declines.

What to do? Instead of investing for yield, try aiming for a healthy total return through a combination of interest, dividends and share-price gains. To generate that return, you might have perhaps 50 percent in stocks and 50 percent in bonds. Every year, to get your 4 percent portfolio withdrawal, you could spend your dividends and interest, while also cashing in some of your stock market and bond market winners. What if you don't have any winners to sell because you just got hit with a big market decline? As a precaution, consider rigging up a robust financial safety net.

31. YOUR SAFETY NET

It's a retiree's worst nightmare: Your stocks are hammered by a market crash. Your bonds are battered by rising interest rates. Yes, you have your dividends and interest. But to get more income from your portfolio, you might be compelled to sell stocks and bonds at the worst possible time.

To avoid that nightmare scenario, which many retirees faced in 2008 and early 2009, try dividing your portfolio in two. You might allocate 80 percent to a mix of stocks and riskier bonds designed to deliver healthy long-run growth. Meanwhile, consider earmarking 20 percent for a cash cushion that's stashed in savings accounts, certificates of deposit, short-term bonds and similar investments. That 20 percent is equal to five years of portfolio withdrawals, assuming a 4 percent withdrawal rate.

Every year, you would pull spending money from the cash cushion. In good years for the market, you could replenish your cash cushion by selling winners from the growth portion of your portfolio. In bad years, you wouldn't do any selling. Thanks to the five years of portfolio withdrawals in your cash cushion, you could ride out a long bear market without selling stocks and bonds at distressed prices.

To bring added predictably to this approach, you might ladder shorter-term bonds or certificates of deposit to cover your living expenses over the next five years. As you approach retirement, you would buy bonds or CDs that mature in each of the first five years of your retirement, thus providing you with the spending money you need. Thereafter, as you take gains from the growth portion of your portfolio, you might use the proceeds to buy new five-year bonds or CDs to replace those that have matured.

Don't like the cash cushion approach? Alternatively, you might again invest for long-run growth, but ensure you have enough income from dividends, interest, annuities, pensions, Social Security and other sources to cover at least your fixed living costs. If markets crash, you might cut out discretionary spending and live solely off this income stream until you can, once again, sell stocks and bonds at reasonable prices.

32. FOUR PERCENT WITHDRAWAL RATE

By the late 1990s, with almost two decades of robust investment returns under their belts, investors would talk about 6, 8 and even 10 percent as a reasonable rate at which to draw down a retirement portfolio. But researchers begged to disagree—and the financial markets provided brutal confirmation, hitting stock investors with back-to-back bear markets in 2000–02 and 2007–09.

Today, 4 percent is considered a safe withdrawal rate (though even that number has been called into question). What does that 4 percent represent? Let's say you retired with $500,000. A 4 percent withdrawal rate suggests you would pull out $20,000 from your portfolio in the first year of retirement and thereafter step up that sum each year with inflation. For instance, if inflation ran at 3 percent a year, you would withdraw $20,600 in year two, $21,218 in year three and so on.

Any dividends and income you receive would count toward the annual sum withdrawn. Also, this 4 percent is pretax. After all those years of tax-deferred growth in 401(k) plans and IRAs, the tax bill comes due in retirement. Once Uncle Sam takes his cut, you will have less than 4 percent to spend.

Here's another way to look at that 4 percent withdrawal rate: If you know how much retirement income you want from your portfolio, you should aim to amass 25 times that sum by the time you retire. Need $20,000 in first-year retirement income from your portfolio? To generate that sum using a 4 percent withdrawal rate, you'd want 25 times $20,000, or $500,000, saved by retirement.

According to studies, a 4 percent initial withdrawal rate coupled with annual inflation adjustments should allow you to make it through a 30-year retirement without depleting your savings. This might seem like a meager income stream. But it's necessary because of a major danger: sequence-of-return risk.

33. SEQUENCE-OF-RETURN RISK

Consider this hellish scenario: You retire with what you imagine is plenty of money—and you're immediately hit with a brutal market decline, even as you pull out a growing sum from your portfolio each year to cover rising living expenses. You quickly deplete your savings. A few years later, the markets bounce back. But you don't benefit much because, by then, your portfolio has been whittled down by your need for spending money.

This is a key reason researchers have suggested a 4 percent withdrawal rate. In most financial situations imaginable, you should be able to withdraw that much initially, step up the annual sum withdrawn with inflation and still make your savings last through a 30-year retirement.

Problem is, a 4 percent withdrawal rate may not give you enough retirement income. Moreover, the whole premise seems a little absurd—that you would not simply withdraw the same sum each year, but robotically increase it along with inflation, no matter how terribly the financial markets perform.

What's the alternative? You might initially spend closer to 5 percent. But if the markets turn against you, you should stand ready to slash your portfolio withdrawals.

34. VARYING YOUR SPENDING

When we think about the financial tools available to us, we often overlook a key lever: our ability to control how much we spend. It is typically a lot easier to cut our spending than to increase our income. That is especially true once we are retired and no longer pulling in a paycheck.

No matter what, you'll always have to cover your fixed monthly costs. That is why it's important to know what that number is and keep it at a reasonable level. By contrast, it is pretty easy to cut out discretionary spending—things like eating out, going to the movies and taking vacations. This is discussed further in Part VI, the chapter on spending.

That brings us to your retirement-income strategy. While a 4 percent withdrawal rate is a good guideline, you might potentially spend more, but with one proviso: If the markets have a major downturn, you immediately slash your spending and hence your portfolio withdrawals.

In fact, you might try a variation on the 4 percent withdrawal rate, which assumes you increase the sum withdrawn each year along with inflation. As an alternative, you could simply withdraw a sum each year equal to 5 percent of your beginning-of-year portfolio balance. Any dividends and interest payments would count toward the 5 percent.

In good markets, your annual withdrawals will automatically go up along with your portfolio's value. In bad years, your withdrawals will go down. Because you're always withdrawing a percentage of whatever you have left, you would never run out of money, though a string of bad years could leave you with drastically reduced income.

In Part XI, which is the chapter on taxes, we discuss required minimum distributions, or RMDs. This is the sum those age 70½ and older must pull from their retirement accounts each year. Instead of using a 4 percent withdrawal rate or a similar strategy, some retirees base their annual spending on RMDs. This works pretty well as a rough-and-ready strategy and it does indeed force you to raise or lower your withdrawals, based on your retirement account's performance. Still, just because the government says you have to withdraw a certain sum from your retirement accounts doesn't mean that's the right amount to be spending—and it could be that you're safe spending even more.

35. INTRODUCTION TO SOCIAL SECURITY

In 2014, 43 percent of men and 49 percent of women claiming Social Security retirement benefits were age 62, the youngest possible age. (This calculation excludes those on Social Security disability benefits who were automatically converted over to retirement benefits.) If these 62-year-olds were in poor health, claiming benefits right away might have been the right choice. But many were likely making a mistake.

You can claim Social Security as early as age 62 or as late as age 70. The longer you delay, the larger your benefit will be. The amount of the increase will depend on the year you were born and hence your full Social Security retirement age. But waiting carries a cost, because you don't get benefits during the intervening years. The big risk: You die early in retirement and get nothing back after a lifetime of paying Social Security payroll taxes. Still, delaying Social Security will make sense for many retirees for three reasons:

• It provides insurance against living a surprisingly long time—and the later you claim benefits, the more insurance you'll have. Remember, Social Security payments are stepped up every year with inflation and paid for as long as you live. By delaying, you buy yourself more of this income, which could prove invaluable if you live longer than expected and run through your other savings.

• It can provide spousal benefits to your husband or wife, who may also want to delay, thereby getting more income.

• It can provide a survivor benefit to your spouse. By waiting, you can ensure more income for your husband or wife after your death. In fact, it may be worth delaying Social Security even if you're in poor health, because your benefit could live on after your death.

JONATHAN'S TAKE: Social Security is such a wonderful source of retirement income that most folks, I believe, should delay benefits so they get a larger monthly check. Retirement's big financial risk isn't dying young, with scant money collected from Social Security. Rather, the big risk is living so long that you deplete your savings—at which point a fat Social Security check could be your financial salvation.

36. SOCIAL SECURITY ELIGIBILITY

To be eligible for Social Security, you need to have worked and paid Social Security payroll taxes for 40 quarters, equal to 10 years. Your benefit is calculated based on your 35 years with the highest earnings. If you don't work for the full 35 years, you are still eligible for Social Security, but your benefit will be lower. The average retirement benefit is roughly $1,330 a month, while the average spousal benefit is $680 a month.

If you claim benefits before your full Social Security retirement age, which will be either age 66 or 67, your benefit will be reduced if you're still working and your earnings are above certain thresholds. This is the so-called retirement earnings test. At issue here are earnings from paid employment, not income such as interest from your bond portfolio or withdrawals from your retirement accounts.

In 2016, if you earn more than $15,720, you will lose $1 of Social Security benefits for every $2 you earn above this threshold. In the year you reach your full Social Security retirement age, the threshold is more generous. You will lose $1 of benefits for every $3 you earn above $41,880. The earnings test only applies up until the month you reach your full Social Security retirement age.

Sound bad? It isn't as bad as it seems: Once you reach your full retirement age, your monthly benefit will be increased to reflect the benefits that were lost because of the earnings test.

37. CLAIMING BENEFITS EARLY AND LATE

How much of a haircut will you take if you claim Social Security early? To find out, you need to know your full Social Security retirement age—a crucial piece of information, especially if you're married and trying to figure out the best strategy for claiming benefits.

If you were born between 1943 and 1954 and hence your full Social Security retirement age is 66, your benefit will be reduced by 25 percent if you claim benefits at age 62, 20 percent if you claim at 63, 13.3 percent at 64 and 6.7 percent at 65.

If you were born in 1960 or later and hence your full Social Security retirement age is 67, your benefit will be reduced by 30 percent if you claim benefits at 62, 25 percent if you claim at 63, 20 percent at 64 and so on. For those born between 1955 and 1959, the reduction will fall somewhere between these two numbers.

What if you claim benefits after your full retirement age? Your benefit will increase by 8 percentage points for every year you wait. These are known as delayed retirement credits. For instance, if your full retirement age is 66, at which point you would be eligible for $1,000 a month, you could receive $750 if you claim at 62 or $1,320 if you claim at 70—a difference of 76 percent. Similarly, if your full retirement age is 67 and you'll be eligible for $1,000 at that point, you could receive $700 at 62 or $1,240 at 70—a difference of 77 percent. These figures don't reflect any increases because of inflation.

If you live to an average life expectancy, you should—roughly speaking—find that you fare equally well no matter when you claim benefits. This "actuarial equivalence," however, doesn't take into account three valuable benefits that tilt the argument in favor of delaying: spousal benefits, survivor benefits and the financial safety net that Social Security provides in case you live longer than expected.

What if you claimed Social Security and then realize you took benefits too early? You have two options. First, once you reach your full retirement age, you can suspend your benefit and earn delayed retirement credits. Under new rules that kick in after April 2016, if you suspend your own benefit, you will also suspend any spousal or family benefits that are being paid based on your earnings record.

Second, you could withdraw your application for benefits. This is a onetime option that's available within 12 months of starting benefits. It can be used before or after your full retirement age. But there's a sizable price to be paid: You have to repay the benefits already received, including benefits collected by family members based on your earnings record.

38. BREAKING EVEN ON SOCIAL SECURITY

When should retirees claim Social Security? Let's dispense with a few preliminaries. If you have young children, it may be worth claiming at age 62, so your kids can receive family benefits. Meanwhile, if you're married and you were the main breadwinner, it's probably worth delaying benefits to age 70 to get the larger monthly check. This is true even if you are in poor health. The reason: Your benefit may live on as a survivor benefit for your spouse.

Instead, we're keeping it simple. We will assume you are single and your full Social Security retirement age is 66. You're trying to decide between a monthly benefit of $750 starting at 62, $1,000 at 66 or $1,320 at 70. Your plan is to take the money and invest it in high-quality bonds, and you want to know what the breakeven age is. In other words, if you take benefits later, at what age would the monthly checks you've collected be worth more than taking benefits at 62?

Social Security benefits rise each year with inflation, so you need to figure that into the calculation. To make things easy, let's think in terms of real (after-inflation) returns. For instance, if 10-year Treasury notes are yielding 2 percent and inflation is 2 percent, your real return is 0. We will look at three scenarios in which high-quality bonds deliver after-inflation annual returns of 0, 1 and 2 percent. Based on those three real returns, how long would you have to live to make delaying benefits worthwhile?

If you delay from age 62 to 66 and you're investing in bonds that deliver a 0 percent real return, you'll be ahead shortly after you turn age 78—and the longer you live after that, the greater the advantage grows. Meanwhile, at a 1 percent real return, delaying benefits to 66 will put you ahead if you live to age 80, while a 2 percent real return will put you ahead by age 81. What if you delay benefits from age 62 to 70? You're ahead at age 81 assuming a 0 percent real return, 82 assuming a 1 percent real return and 83 assuming a 2 percent real return.

What if you plan to invest in stocks, not bonds? That could raise the breakeven age, because the potential return is higher. But the risk is also vastly greater, and that messes up the analysis. You shouldn't make a straight comparison between a relatively sure bet (the government keeps paying Social Security) and something so uncertain (remember, stocks lost roughly half their value twice in the past 15 years) without factoring in the difference in risk.

39. SPOUSAL BENEFITS

If you are married, you can receive a spousal benefit equal to as much as half your husband's or wife's benefit as of his or her full retirement age. If you claim a spousal benefit before your own full retirement age, your benefit will be reduced.

The reduction can be severe. Check out the Benefits for Spouses calculator available at SocialSecurity.gov. If your full retirement age is 66, your spousal benefit will be reduced by 30 percent if you claim at 62, 25 percent at 63 and so on. What if your full retirement age is 67? The reduction at 62 would be 35 percent, while at 63 it would be 30 percent. On the other hand, don't claim spousal benefits any later than your full retirement age. Why not? You don't get any credit for delaying beyond that point.

Keep two key provisions in mind. First, if you file for benefits, you will be deemed to have filed for both spousal benefits and any benefit owed based on your own earnings record, and you'll get paid the higher of the two. There's a loophole for those who turn age 62 before year-end 2015, which we discuss in section 42, but the 2015 Budget Act closed this loophole for everybody else.

That said, if you file for benefits, you can always get benefits based on your own earnings record, but you may not be able to claim spousal benefits. That brings us to the second key provision: You can't receive spousal benefits until your husband or wife claims his or her benefit. Confused? It's helpful to look at different strategies that couples might use.

40. CLAIMING STRATEGIES FOR COUPLES

What's the best strategy for claiming Social Security benefits if you're married—and you can't take advantage of the loopholes closed by the 2015 Budget Act and discussed in section 42? For most couples, it will make sense for the spouse with higher lifetime earnings to delay claiming benefits until age 70. Let's be politically incorrect and assume that's the husband.

Delaying until 70 ensures not only the maximum possible monthly benefit for the husband, but also a handsome survivor benefit for his wife, assuming the husband dies first. Because the husband's benefit could live on after his death, it can make sense for him to delay Social Security, even if he's in poor health. Problem is, until the husband claims benefits, his wife can't receive spousal benefits, though she can receive benefits based on her own earnings record.

For instance, if the husband and wife are the same age and the husband delays benefits until age 70, the wife will miss out on eight years of spousal benefits and, to make matters worse, she won't receive any credit for delaying spousal benefits beyond her full retirement age of 66 or 67. Still, because the husband's benefit will be paid until both he and his wife have died—thanks to the survivor benefit—it will typically make sense for him to delay.

When shouldn't the husband delay? There are three factors that could prompt the husband to claim benefits earlier.

First, he might claim benefits earlier than age 70 if both he and his wife are in poor health. If only one of them is in poor health, it probably still makes sense for the husband to delay benefits, because his larger monthly check will be paid until both spouses have died.

Second, the husband might claim earlier if he's much younger than his wife. For instance, if the husband is four years younger than his wife and he delays benefits until age 70, his wife wouldn't collect spousal benefits until age 74—which means she would miss out on 12 years of benefits. In that scenario, it can still make sense for the husband to delay until age 70, but the case isn't as strong.

Third, the husband might claim earlier if his wife had little or no lifetime earnings. Remember, the wife receives the higher of either her spousal benefit or her own benefit based on her lifetime earnings. If the wife's own benefit is large, the extra from spousal benefits may not be worth much, if anything, so there's little cost in the husband delaying to age 70. But if the wife's own benefit is modest, the spousal benefit will be worth a lot—and the husband might want to claim benefits when his wife reaches age 66 or 67. That will allow his wife to claim spousal benefits at her full retirement age, at which point her spousal benefit will be as large as it will ever get, ignoring any adjustments for inflation.

If the higher-earning spouse delays benefits until age 70, when should the lower-earning spouse—the wife in our example—claim benefits based on his or her own earnings record? This is a less crucial decision, because the lower-earning spouse's benefit disappears when the first spouse dies. If one spouse is in poor health, the lower-earning spouse might claim at 62. If both spouses are in decent health, the lower-earning spouse might claim at his or her full retirement age of 66 or 67.

Need additional guidance? Check out SSAnalyze at BedrockCapital.com.

41. BENEFITS FOR DEPENDENT CHILDREN

When you claim Social Security retirement benefits, it isn't just your spouse who can receive benefits based on your earnings record. If you have dependent children, they too may receive Social Security.

Unmarried children are eligible to receive benefits if they are under age 18, up to age 19 if they're still in high school, and at any age if they become disabled before age 22. Your children may be eligible to receive a sum equal to as much as half of your benefit as of your full retirement age. Moreover, a spouse of any age may receive benefits if he or she is caring for a child who is under age 16 or who is disabled. A child can be a biological child, adopted, a stepchild and sometimes even a dependent grandchild.

There is, however, a limit to Social Security's generosity. The total amount paid out to you and your family is typically capped at between 150 and 180 percent of your full retirement age benefit. Spousal benefits paid to an ex-spouse don't count toward the family maximum.

If you are age 62 and have children who would qualify for benefits, you may want to claim benefits right away, despite the many sound reasons for delaying Social Security. After all, your children will only get older—and, if you delay claiming benefits, they might not receive any money from Social Security. But there is a cost. Your benefit will be permanently reduced, as will any survivor benefit that's paid based on your earnings record. One possibility: If your children are no longer eligible for benefits once you reach your full Social Security retirement age of 66 or 67, you might suspend benefits to earn delayed retirement credits from then until age 70—but this may cause your spouse to lose his or her spousal benefits for that length of time.

42. BUDGET ACT 2015

In the budget passed by Congress in October 2015, there were two key changes made to Social Security, which affected both the popular "file and suspend" strategy and the use of restricted applications. The latter was often used in conjunction with file and suspend.

Before the budget law was passed, if you opted to suspend benefits once you reached your full retirement age, your spouse and children could continue to receive benefits based on your earnings record. That remains true until April 2016—but once the new rules become effective, if you suspend benefits, you will also stop the flow of spousal and family benefits.

In other words, for those 66 or older, there's a small window of opportunity. The higher-earning spouse may want to file for benefits, so that the other spouse can claim spousal benefits. The higher-earning spouse would then immediately suspend benefits, so that his or her benefit can continue growing until as late as age 70.

What's the second change? Those under age 62 as of year-end 2015 can no longer file a so-called restricted application. This option, which was available once you reached your full retirement age, allowed a husband or wife to claim just spousal benefits, while leaving his or her own benefit to continue growing.

What if you reach age 62 by Jan. 1, 2016, and hence you can still file a restricted application? For these folks, it may make sense for the lower-earning spouse to claim benefits early. That will allow the higher-earning spouse to file a restricted application at his or her full retirement age of 66, requesting just spousal benefits. The higher-earning spouse would then delay his or her own benefit until age 70, thereby ensuring both a maximum monthly benefit while alive and also a maximum survivor benefit for the husband or wife.

43. SURVIVOR BENEFITS

If your spouse dies, you can receive his or her benefit as a survivor benefit. The larger your spouse's benefit, the more you receive.

Keep a few key details in mind. If you're at your full retirement age or later, you will be entitled to 100 percent of your spouse's benefit as a survivor benefit. If you claim earlier, there will be a reduction. There are slight differences between the full retirement age for regular Social Security benefits and the full retirement age for survivor benefits.

Unless you care for a child who is under age 16 or who is disabled, or you're disabled yourself, you can't claim survivor benefits before age 60. If you claim at age 60, your survivor benefit will be 28.5 percent less than your deceased spouse's benefit. Unmarried children may also be eligible for benefits, possibly up until age 19, or if they're disabled.

You can't receive both survivor benefits and a benefit based on your own earnings record at the same time, but you can switch between the two. One strategy: If you're in your 60s, you might claim survivor benefits right away—but put off claiming your own benefit until age 70, at which point it might potentially be larger than your survivor benefit, thanks to the credits you receive for delaying. Alternatively, you might claim benefits based on your own earnings record at age 62, while delaying survivor benefits until your full Social Security retirement age, which would be 66 or 67.

One modest financial item: A surviving spouse is eligible to receive a $255 onetime payment from Social Security.

44. DIVORCE AND SOCIAL SECURITY

You may be entitled to retirement benefits based on your ex-husband or ex-wife's earnings record, assuming your marriage lasted at least 10 years. If you remarry, however, you lose this right. Instead, you could potentially claim benefits based on your new spouse's earnings record.

Similarly, you may be eligible for survivor benefits based on your late ex-spouse's earnings record. Again, the marriage must have lasted at least 10 years. As with a married spouse, you need to be at least age 60 or older to receive survivor benefits. In this case, it's okay if you are remarried—as long as you didn't remarry until after age 60.

None of this should cause your ex-spouse any concern: If you claim benefits based on his or her earnings record, it won't affect either your ex-spouse's benefit or those of, say, his or her new wife or husband.

45. SOCIAL SECURITY'S FUTURE

Once again in 2015, there was talk of fixing Social Security so that the benefits paid out don't greatly exceed the Social Security payroll taxes that are collected. There are different fixes being bandied about, including changing the inflation measure used to increase benefits each year, raising the eligibility age for Social Security and even means-testing benefits.

Eventually, there will likely be some fix made, but you shouldn't be too alarmed by that prospect. First, Social Security's unfunded liability is considerably smaller than that for Medicare, and thus it could probably be addressed without action that's too drastic.

Second, any major changes to Social Security will likely only apply to those under age 50 or 55, so younger workers should have plenty of time to adjust and potentially compensate by saving more for retirement.

What if you are already retired? It's almost inconceivable that any politician hoping to get reelected would vote to cut benefits for those who have reached retirement age. The outcry would be deafening. One implication: If you're, say, age 62, you shouldn't rush to claim benefits now, fearing the government will slash your Social Security benefit.

46. GREAT DEBATES: WHEN TO CLAIM?

Among experts on Social Security, there's a strong consensus that most folks should delay benefits to get a larger monthly check—and yet almost half of retirees claim Social Security at 62, the earliest possible age.

No doubt many retirees take benefits right away because they need the money or they haven't given the issue much thought. What about those who have wrestled with the topic—and still insist that claiming at 62 is the right strategy? There appear to be three reasons people opt to take benefits right away.

First, they think the politicians will reduce Social Security or start means-testing benefits, so they should get whatever money they can now. It's hard to predict what politicians will do, though it seems unlikely that any cuts would apply to existing retirees, because it would cause so much financial distress. For 65 percent of Social Security recipients age 65 and up, Social Security accounts for more than half of their income.

Second, retirees claim Social Security early because they believe they can earn a higher return by taking benefits early and investing the money. That might be true if you invested in stocks. But given the greater risk involved, comparing stock returns and Social Security is like comparing apples and oranges. A more appropriate comparison is between Social Security and high-quality bonds. Based on that, you would be better off delaying Social

Security, assuming you live to an average life expectancy.

Third, those claiming at 62 reckon their spending will be higher early in retirement, when they're more active, so it makes sense to claim benefits right away. Even if that's the case, this is hardly a reason to claim Social Security early. If you want to spend more during your early retirement years, you could always draw more heavily from savings.

47. PENSION PLANS

If you're a participant in a defined benefit pension plan, ask yourself two questions. First, what happens if your pension plan doesn't pay as promised? Even if your employer seems committed to its pension plan today, much could change between now and when you retire—and perhaps even after you retire.

If you're a public sector employee, maybe a fiscal crunch will force big budget cuts, including cuts to the pension plan. If you're a private sector employee who works for a seemingly healthy company, maybe there are financial shenanigans you're unaware of. Perhaps the company will get hit with a business-crippling lawsuit. Maybe your employer will get taken over in a leveraged buyout, the resulting debt proves too burdensome and the company ends up in bankruptcy.

If that happens, the plan may be bailed out by the Pension Benefit Guaranty Corporation. You can find out whether your plan is covered at PBGC.gov. If an insured private pension plan is terminated, the PBGC will pay benefits up to the guaranteed maximum, currently around $5,000 a month for workers who begin benefits at age 65.

Given all this uncertainty, it's prudent to have other retirement savings. If the pension plan doesn't come through, those additional savings could salvage your retirement. If the plan pays as promised, you will no doubt be happy to have the extra savings.

That brings us to the second question: What about inflation? Most pensions pay monthly benefits that aren't indexed for inflation. That means the benefit you receive at age 65 could have substantially less purchasing power by the time you're 80 or 85. To ensure your standard of living doesn't suffer too much as you grow older, you might save part of each pension check during the early years of retirement—or, alternatively, take the precaution of building up a decent pool of savings during your working years.

48. PENSION VS. LUMP SUM PAYMENT

As companies look to reduce their pension liabilities, many are making this offer to former employees: Instead of paying you a regular pension in retirement, we'll give you a lump sum now.

The lump sum might seem sizable. But to see whether it's truly a good deal, find out how much income that lump sum would buy if you purchased a so-called deferred income annuity. These annuities pay regular income starting at some future date. In this instance, you'd probably want to know how much income you would receive as of age 65, which is when your pension would likely start paying. You can get quotes from sites such as Fidelity.com/gie, ImmediateAnnuities.com, IncomeSolutions.com and myAbaris.com. If your pension will be payable to your spouse, assuming you die first, be sure to get a quote for an annuity that pays income for both your lifetime and that of your spouse.

In all likelihood, you will find that the lump sum is less valuable than the pension income you're set to receive, and you shouldn't take the offer. Who should? If you are in poor health—and so is your spouse, assuming you're married—accepting the offer might make sense. The offer might also be appealing if you have serious doubts about the financial health of the pension fund.

49. INCOME ANNUITIES

Social Security, with its guaranteed stream of inflation-indexed income, is arguably the best income annuity available. This is why you should give serious thought to delaying Social Security, so you get the largest possible check.

Even if you delay benefits, you may want more lifetime income. That's where income annuities come in. Annuities have a reputation for being costly, complicated products pushed by aggressive salespeople. A January 2015 survey by TIAA-CREF found that just 28 percent of Americans had a favorable impression of annuities. But not all annuities are a bad investment. There are four types you might consider:

Immediate fixed annuities. These can provide a check every month for life, though—unlike Social Security—that check usually doesn't increase with inflation.

Charitable gift annuities. These are similar to immediate fixed annuities, except you buy from your favorite charity, not an insurance company. The downside: Charitable gift annuities typically pay less income. The upside: If you die early in retirement, your favorite charity stands to benefit, rather than an insurance company. Charitable gift annuities, along with charitable remainder trusts, are discussed in Part XIII.

Longevity insurance. This provides lifetime income starting at a future date, thus addressing the financial risk of living a surprisingly long time.

Variable annuities that generate income. These are complicated products that offer the chance to generate lifetime income, while still investing for long-run growth. Some allow you to add a so-called living benefits rider, while others can be converted into immediate variable annuities.

JONATHAN'S TAKE: Retirees are often reluctant to buy income annuities, just as they're reluctant to delay Social Security. I think this is a mistake. Delaying Social Security and buying income annuities can be the key to a more comfortable, less financially stressful retirement. Both strategies make particular sense for those looking to squeeze maximum income out of their savings. Intrigued by income annuities? I'd check out longevity insurance and plain-vanilla immediate fixed annuities.

50. POOLING RISK

Risk pooling is a great way to handle life's financial pitfalls, and we are happy to do it—most of the time. When we buy life insurance or we purchase a homeowner's policy, we're contributing to a pool of money that's overseen by an insurance company and to which many others are contributing. Those who see their homes burn down, and the families of those who die, collect big money from the pool. Those of us who remain standing—and whose homes remain standing—don't collect on our insurance policies. We are out of pocket, but you won't hear many complaints.

Unless, that is, we are talking about a form of risk pooling known as an income annuity. Income annuities come in all kinds of flavors. But the idea is basically the same: We throw in our lot with other retirees, so we can share risk. The insurance company that manages the pool is able to promise handsome income for life because it knows that, while some retirees will collect checks until they're age 95, others will only collect until 75.

Why do folks—who happily buy life, health, disability, auto and other insurance—balk at this type of risk pooling? Maybe it's the taint associated with the label "annuity." Most of the abuses over the years, however, have involved equity-indexed annuities and tax-deferred variable annuities, not income annuities.

Or maybe it's the double downside of income annuities: If we die early in retirement, not only do we fail to get much back from our big annuity investment, but also we're well and truly dead—and that thought just isn't palatable.

51. IMMEDIATE FIXED ANNUITIES

With an immediate fixed annuity, you hand over a wad of money to an insurance company and, in return, the insurer sends you a check every month for a specified period. You can purchase annuities that will pay income for, say, 10 or 20 years. But if your financial worry is living longer than expected, you'll want to buy an annuity that pays lifetime income.

To get a sense for how much income an annuity might generate, check out Fidelity.com/gie, ImmediateAnnuities.com and IncomeSolutions.com. Suppose a husband and wife are both age 70 and they use $100,000 of their savings to buy an annuity that pays the same income every year for life. According to ImmediateAnnuities.com, as of late November 2015, the annuity would pay $7,692 every year if the husband buys, $7,140 if the wife buys and $6,288 if the annuity pays income until the second spouse dies.

These payouts may not be as generous as you had hoped. If you delay Social Security, you get a big increase in benefits, because Social Security is designed to be fair based on the typical American's life expectancy. By contrast, insurers deal with a more select group: They know that income annuities tend to be bought by folks who think they will live longer than average, so they're priced accordingly. Still, the older you are when you buy an income annuity, the more income you can receive. If you buy when interest rates are higher, that should also mean a larger monthly check.

You can get an annuity that pays income just for your life or for the life of both you and your spouse. You can also get various guarantees, such as payments made for a minimum number of years, even if you die earlier. You almost always pay a price for these guarantees in the form of lower monthly income.

Still, the guarantees highlight the big fear with immediate fixed annuities—that you'll make a big investment and keel over a few months later, having received little income from your big annuity investment. You might address this fear by making smaller annuity purchases over the course of perhaps five or 10 years. This will also allow you to buy from a variety of insurers, thus reducing the risk that your retirement will be imperiled by any one insurer going bankrupt, and perhaps you'll be able to purchase at higher interest rates, should they rise from today's modest levels. Alternatively, you might explore a charitable gift annuity, where the beneficiary of your early demise would be your favorite charity. These are discussed in Part XIII.

52. LONGEVITY INSURANCE

Suppose you retired at age 65 and you knew it would all be over at 85. That would make generating retirement income relatively easy: You might spend 1/20th of your savings in year one, 1/19th in year two and so on. Problem is, there's a decent chance you will live beyond 85. That is where longevity insurance can help.

Longevity insurance, also called a deferred income annuity, is essentially an annuity that pays lifetime income starting at some future date. Because there's no guarantee that you will live that long, let alone collect a lot of income if you do, this has the potential to be a relatively low-cost way of dealing with longevity risk. For every $100 you invest in a deferred income annuity at age 65, you might receive $40 to $60 a year of income starting at age 85. For a precise quote, go to Fidelity.com/gie, ImmediateAnnuities.com, IncomeSolutions.com or myAbaris.com. You could use perhaps 15 percent of your savings to purchase longevity insurance that kicks in once you turn age 85. Meanwhile, you might spend down the other 85 percent of your savings between now and age 85 using the strategy described in the first paragraph.

You can buy pure longevity insurance that pays only if you live to the specified age. But many folks, fearful they will die without getting any money back from their insurance purchase, opt for various guarantees. These guarantees carry a cost, which is paid in the form of lower future income.

Don't like the idea of longevity insurance? You could designate 15 or 20 percent of your portfolio for the post-age 85 period. If you live that long and you're in good health, you might use this money to buy an income annuity. If your health isn't so good, you could simply spend down your remaining savings. What if you don't live until age 85? The money could make a handsome inheritance.

53. LIVING BENEFITS

Variable annuities are tax-deferred savings vehicles, not unlike IRAs but more costly. We'll talk more about them in Part XI. These variable annuities can be used to generate lifetime income, while still leaving you as owner of the account's assets, by adding a living benefits rider.

There are two types of rider that can provide lifetime income: a guaranteed lifetime withdrawal benefit (GLWB) and a guaranteed minimum income benefit (GMIB). With a GLWB, you might be assured annual income for life equal to 4 to 6 percent of your account's initial value, depending on your age when you begin withdrawals. If your investment choices perform well, and your account increases in value even after accounting for the annuity's investment costs and your own withdrawals, your annual income can rise.

With a GMIB, there might also be a 4 to 6 percent initial guarantee, which you can take as a withdrawal or use to increase your "income base," which is an accounting device that's distinct from the account's actual value. The increased income base will mean higher income in future years.

What if you add a GMIB rider and then deplete the annuity's actual value through some combination of withdrawals and bad investment performance? After a waiting period, which is typically 10 years from the time you added the GMIB rider, you can swap into an immediate fixed annuity. That annuity will give you regular income for life based on your income base. This immediate fixed annuity may pay less income than the amount you were initially receiving based on the 4 to 6 percent.

The big problem with living benefits: Not only are they complicated, but also the annual costs are high. Those costs crimp performance, so there's a risk your income won't increase over time and the account won't have much value upon your death. What to do? In an effort to boost performance, you might invest the annuity heavily in stocks. That way, you are also taking advantage of the downside protection that's costing you so much. If your investment bets go wrong, you can always fall back on the annuity's guaranteed minimum.

54. IMMEDIATE VARIABLE ANNUITIES

Instead of adding a living benefits rider, you can squeeze income out of a tax-deferred variable annuity by converting it to an immediate variable annuity. But there's a crucial difference between the two. A variable annuity with living benefits leaves you as owner of the account's assets and there may be money left over for your heirs. With an immediate variable annuity, you surrender ownership to the insurance company.

Indeed, immediate variable annuities are an odd beast: As with an immediate fixed annuity, you hand over a lump sum to an insurance company in return for lifetime income. But unlike with an immediate fixed annuity, you still get to call the shots on how the immediate variable annuity is invested. As with other variable annuities, there's a menu of investment options you can choose from.

Your goal: Pick investments that beat a hurdle rate of return, known as the "assumed interest rate," which might be 3 or 4 percent a year. The higher the AIR and the older you are when you buy the annuity, the more income you initially receive. But a high AIR has a drawback: For your income to grow, the investments you select within the variable annuity need to generate annual returns that outpace this hurdle rate. What if you fall short? Your monthly income will decline.

You also need to pay close attention to a variable annuity's costs. The higher those costs, the harder it will be for your investments to earn decent performance and thereby outpace the hurdle rate of return. Still, an immediate variable annuity should give you more initial income than a tax-deferred variable annuity with a living benefits rider—and, if the markets are kind, you could see your income rise over time.

55. MANAGED PAYOUT FUNDS

As an alternative to income annuities, some mutual fund companies have rolled out managed payout funds. Historically, mutual funds have been geared toward investors who are amassing money for financial goals, notably retirement. Managed payout funds represent an attempt by fund companies to cater to investors who are no longer saving and instead are looking to generate regular income.

For instance, Fidelity Investments offers a series of income replacement funds. The funds, when coupled with Fidelity's Smart Payment Program, aim to provide a stream of income that rises with inflation between now and the fund's horizon date, at which point your investment would be depleted.

A more common approach is taken by Vanguard Group, which offers a managed payout fund that aims to throw off 4 percent a year, with the income paid monthly—but with no fixed horizon date. The hope is that the income will climb over time with inflation, but it could be cut if the fund performs poorly. To generate steady and rising income, the Vanguard fund owns a traditional mix of stocks and bonds, but also allocates money to commodities, foreign bonds and low-volatility stocks. In addition, it has part of its money in a so-called market neutral fund, which aims to generate moderate returns no matter what happens to stock prices.

Like Vanguard, Charles Schwab aims to provide monthly income in perpetuity. But Schwab's lineup of monthly income funds comes in three flavors, each of which targets a different combination of income and growth. If you buy the fund that generates the most income, you should expect lower long-run growth.

Unsurprisingly, managed payout funds were roughed up during 2008's stock market collapse, forcing them to cut the income paid to shareholders. Those cuts hurt the reputation of managed payout funds, many of which had only just been launched. Still, such funds are an intriguing option for retirees who want to keep their finances simple. These funds don't provide guaranteed lifetime income, like Social Security or an income annuity. But they do offer a way to generate additional retirement income, while maintaining control over your assets and possibly allowing you to bequeath at least part of the money to your children or other family members.

56. SPENDING HOME EQUITY

If your retirement savings are on the skimpy side, you might tap into the value of your home. Consider three strategies.

The safest strategy is to trade down to a less expensive home. Selling one home and buying another can be both costly and a hassle. Still, this has the potential not only to free up home equity that you can then spend, but also it may lower your living costs, including property taxes, utilities, homeowner's insurance and maintenance expenses.

The least expensive but riskiest strategy is to refinance your home by taking out a 30-year mortgage for as much as the bank will let you borrow. Thereafter, you'll have to make regular mortgage payments again, presumably drawing on the money you got in the refinancing. But if you do the refinancing late in retirement and your life expectancy is 10 years or less, the refinancing should leave you with money for other expenses. The risk: If you live longer than expected or you spend too freely, you might end up without money to pay the mortgage—and you'd be in a heap of trouble.

Finally, you might take out a reverse mortgage. With all the fees involved, coupled with the need for you or your heirs eventually to sell the house, this has the potential to be the costliest strategy. But as long as you're careful, a reverse mortgage should allow you to stay in your home for the rest of your life.

57. REVERSE MORTGAGES

A reverse mortgage lets you borrow against the value of your home without paying back any of the loan during your lifetime. Instead, the loan is repaid when you move permanently or, more likely, after your death. At that juncture, the total amount owed, including all accrued interest, can't exceed your home's value. You can typically borrow more if you're older, interest rates are low or your house is appraised at a high value. The money received is tax-free.

The big downside is cost. To get a handle on the expenses involved, try playing with the calculator offered at ReverseMortgage.org, which is the website of the National Reverse Mortgage Lenders Association. At the bottom of the calculation, you'll see a figure for "Total Fees & Costs." This doesn't, however, tell the entire story. At the top of the estimate, check out the initial loan interest rate—which will likely be higher than on a conventional mortgage—and the charge for mortgage insurance that's layered on top of that.

In addition, keep in mind that you still have to handle the home's maintenance, property taxes and insurance. If those expenses prove too burdensome, you may be compelled to move, at which point the reverse mortgage has to be repaid. There have also been problems because just one spouse was listed on the reverse mortgage, that spouse dies or moves to a nursing home, and the surviving spouse has had to deal with demands to repay the loan.

One option for well-heeled families: Arrange a private reverse mortgage. To help their parents pay for retirement, adult children or other family members might provide a credit line that is secured by the parents' home. That gives the parents access to extra cash, while the adult children can be fairly confident they'll eventually get their money back, plus interest. The costs involved are far lower than with a conventional reverse mortgage, and it ensures the house stays in the family. For more information, head to NationalFamilyMortgage.com.

JONATHAN'S TAKE: Despite all the drawbacks, I wouldn't rule out a reverse mortgage. Let's face it: You get only one shot at retirement and you should make the most of it, even if it means spending assets you had hoped to bequeath to your children. That said, I would consider a reverse mortgage a last resort, not your first choice.

58. MY STORY: HOW I PLAN TO HANDLE RETIREMENT

In many ways, I feel like I am already semi-retired. I no longer have a fulltime job, though I'm working harder than ever, thanks to my teaching, freelance articles, blogging, updating this book every year, working on a new book entitled *How to Think About Money*, and more. All this, however, is by design: I might drop some of these activities as I grow older, but I'd like to keep one or two of them going. Partly, that's to give a sense of purpose to my days. But partly, it's to keep a little cash coming in, which can ease some of the financial strain of retirement.

To give me greater financial flexibility, I'm also endeavoring to keep my fixed monthly costs low. The monthly payment for my apartment's maintenance and property taxes is higher than I would like—a common complaint among those who live in or near New York City. But I don't have any debt and few other fixed monthly financial obligations. That makes for less stress and leaves me with spare cash for things I enjoy, like travel and eating out.

Because I still earn enough to cover my costs, I'm not yet dipping into savings, so I don't have a firm plan for generating retirement income. But my ideas are starting to take shape. At this juncture, I intend to delay Social Security until age 70, so that I get the largest possible monthly benefit.

As I scale back work and need money from savings, I plan to draw on both taxable and retirement accounts, with the goal of generating enough income each year to hit the top of the 25 percent tax bracket. If I am not quite at the top of the bracket, I'll probably seize the chance to convert more of my traditional IRA to a Roth.

I'm still debating whether to buy an immediate fixed annuity and, if so, how much to commit. I suspect I'll plunk down $200,000, which— depending on when I buy—might give me $12,000 a year or so to supplement what I receive from Social Security. The money I put into the income annuity will come from the bond side of my portfolio.

Currently, I have roughly 70 percent in stocks and 30 percent in conservative investments. I suspect I'll shift to 60 percent stocks and 40 percent bonds as I approach my mid-60s.

How much will I draw from savings each year? I'm not going to use the classic 4 percent strategy, where you withdraw 4 percent of your portfolio's value in the first year of retirement and thereafter robotically increase withdrawals along with inflation. Instead, I might simply aim to keep my annual withdrawals below 5 percent of my portfolio's beginning-of-year value. That way, if we get a bad spell in the markets, I'll be forced to curtail my spending.

PART III

HOUSES
A GREAT INVESTMENT, THOUGH NOT FOR THE REASONS YOU THINK

Despite the property market's 2006–12 downturn, many Americans remain firmly convinced of the virtues of homeownership. What underpins that faith? Here are five reasons most folks should aim to buy their own home.

First, with a fixed-rate mortgage, you lock in your housing costs and thereby protect yourself against a booming real estate market that drives up rents and property prices. An adjustable-rate mortgage doesn't offer the same degree of certainty, though typically there are caps on how much your monthly payment can increase.

Second, as you pay down your mortgage, you come to own a valuable asset outright. Think of a mortgage as forced savings, with a portion of every monthly payment going toward reducing your loan's principal balance.

Third, once your mortgage is paid off, you eliminate a major expense, making it easier to retire because you can now live "rent-free."

Fourth, home prices historically have increased slightly faster than consumer prices, thus acting as a hedge against inflation. Inflation also effectively trims the cost of your mortgage, because it allows you to pay off the loan with dollars that are less valuable.

Finally, Congress has showered homeownership with tax breaks. You can deduct your mortgage interest and property taxes. Up to $500,000 of your home's price appreciation may be tax-free when you sell. There's also a less obvious advantage: If you rented out your home, you would have to pay taxes on the rent you receive. But there's no tax owed when you rent to yourself.

Yet, even with these five advantages, things can go terribly wrong. In 2015, the housing market continued its recovery, with prices now up a cumulative 31 percent since 2012's market bottom. Still, the 2006–12 housing bust remains a harsh reminder that a home isn't a sure financial bet. Want to avoid major mistakes? Check out this chapter's dos and don'ts for 2016—and read about five housing myths you ought to avoid succumbing to.

59. TODAY'S REAL ESTATE MARKET

How did the property market perform over the past year? Let's look at the numbers:

• Home prices rose 4.9 percent over the 12 months through September 2015, as measured by S&P/Case-Shiller's U.S. National Home Price Index.

• The national median sales price for an existing home was $219,600 as of October 2015, reports the National Association of Realtors. This average disguises huge variations, with even modest homes in cities on the two coasts often costing three or five times as much. Sales of existing homes rose 3.9 percent over the past year, while the inventory of homes for sale declined 4.5 percent.

• As of late November 2015, a 30-year fixed rate mortgage cost 3.97 percent, barely changed from the 4.04 percent interest rate at year-end 2014.

• Housing has become less affordable over the past year, calculates the National Association of Realtors. Affordability is assessed by looking at the typical home price, typical family income and current mortgage rates.

• Homeownership remains widespread, with 65.2 percent of American families owning their home and 13.2 percent owning a place that isn't their main residence, according to the Federal Reserve's 2013 Survey of Consumer Finances. That 13.2 percent includes second homes, rental properties and time shares. The survey also found that, among homeowners, 65.9 percent have a mortgage or other debt that's secured by their home.

• Homes remain a major asset for American families. The Federal Reserve puts the value of U.S. households' real estate holdings at $21.6 trillion. For comparison, there's $4.7 trillion in 401(k) plans and $7.6 trillion in individual retirement accounts, according to the Investment Company Institute.

60. DOS AND DON'TS FOR 2016

Want to take a fresh look at your housing situation? Here are some "to dos" for 2016:

• If you're renting, run the numbers to see whether it's worth buying. Use the Mortgage Calculator at Bankrate.com to figure out how big a mortgage you could support with your monthly rent payments. That will give you a sense for whether homeownership is within reach.

• If you currently own, run the numbers to see whether it's worth refinancing your mortgage. There is more on mortgages in Part XII.

• If you are approaching retirement, consider whether it's worth downsizing to a smaller home, so you lower your maintenance costs and property taxes. Downsizing may also free up home equity that you can then add to your retirement stash.

And here are some things not to do:

• Don't buy a home unless you can see staying put for a minimum of five years, and preferably seven years or longer.

• Don't buy an excessively large house or undertake elaborate remodeling projects thinking you're making a great investment.

• Don't take out an excessively large mortgage, believing it's some sort of financial freebie.

61. HOUSING MYTHS

Housing is a source of endless confusion—which isn't surprising given that there are so many issues to consider, including attractive tax breaks, fluctuating property prices, leverage from any mortgage debt, and the monthly mortgage payment's shifting mix of interest and principal. Here are five common myths:

"You can't go wrong with real estate." You heard this often before and during the real estate bubble, but far less frequently since the brutal decline that saw homes lose more than a quarter of their value between mid-2006 and early 2012. The potential for another decline should factor into your decision about whether to rent or buy.

"My house is the best investment I've ever made." Paying down a mortgage forces people to save and owning a house gives them a place to live. But what about home price appreciation? Historically, that's been modest and largely offset by the costs of homeownership.

"The bank owns half my house." Not true. The bank merely lent you money. Unless you plan to go into foreclosure, you own 100 percent of your home—and benefit from any price increase and suffer any decline.

"You should take out the largest mortgage possible." Many homeowners think mortgage interest is some sort of financial freebie. Think again. If you're in the 25 percent federal income tax bracket, pay $1 of mortgage interest and itemize your deductions, you'll save just 25 cents in federal taxes—which means the other 75 cents is coming out of your pocket.

"Our new kitchen added $100,000 to our home's value." The home may have climbed in value. But the boost from the new kitchen was almost certainly less than its cost. Homeowners typically don't fully recoup the cost of remodeling projects.

62. BUY OR RENT?

Homeownership offers many advantages, which we detailed at the start of this chapter. But there's no guarantee you will make money, especially if you own a house for just a few years. Thinking of purchasing a home? Here are four caveats.

First, given the risk of declining property prices, you shouldn't buy unless you can see staying put for at least five years and preferably seven years or longer. Even now, more than nine years after the real estate market peaked, prices in some places are below the heady levels of mid-2006. While it's hard to imagine we will suffer another decline of similar magnitude any time soon, a smaller drop is entirely possible.

Second, homes are horribly expensive to buy and especially sell, which is another reason you need a long time horizon. There's the mortgage-application fee, home inspection, title insurance and legal fees when you buy—and the 5 or 6 percent real estate brokerage commission and local transfer taxes when you sell. Suppose your home's price rises a few percentage points a year, but you end up selling after just five or six years. Once you figure in all the costs of buying and selling, you may not make money.

Third, homeownership involves hefty ongoing costs. On top of the mortgage payments, you'll have property taxes, homeowner's insurance and regular maintenance.

Finally, if you can't make the regular payments on your home, your financial life can unravel fast. That's why, before you buy, it is important to have a strong sense that your job is secure and a backup plan in case you're wrong. That plan might include not only a healthy emergency fund, but also a list of expenses you'll slash if your income suddenly drops. Both topics are discussed in Part V.

63. REAL ESTATE RETURNS

Folks are fascinated by what their homes are worth. Along the way, they make all kinds of dubious claims about how much they've made—and they miss the big story. Want to get a better grip on your home as an investment? For the moment, forget about your mortgage and focus just on home price appreciation.

Historically, homes have not been a great source of price appreciation. According to Freddie Mac, U.S. home prices climbed 4.7 percent a year over the 40 years through September 2015, not much ahead of the 3.7 percent inflation rate.

Next, think about all the ongoing costs that homeowners incur, such as maintenance expenses, homeowner's insurance and property taxes. These costs will vary widely. Property taxes are much steeper in some parts of the country than others. Insurance can be significantly higher if there's a risk of extreme weather, flooding or earthquakes. Maintenance costs—not to be confused with home improvements—will be greater if you own an older home. While the land underneath your home should appreciate over time (as the saying goes, "they aren't making any more of it"), the dwelling itself will tend to lose value unless you're diligent about regular maintenance.

Add up these various expenses, and they might equal 2 or 3 percent of a home's value each year. Deduct the cost from a home's price appreciation and many homeowners will find they are lagging far behind inflation, and perhaps barely breaking even.

Unfortunately, the expenses don't end there. There are the costs to buy a home, including mortgage-application fees, lawyers, title insurance, home inspections and possibly private mortgage insurance. You'll pay even more when you sell, notably a substantial commission to the real estate agents involved.

All of this might be true, you concede. But what happens once you figure in the mortgage? That mortgage can potentially take even modest gains and leverage them into big money.

64. LEVERAGE

Suppose you purchase a $300,000 home. To avoid taking out private mortgage insurance, you make a 20 percent down payment, equal to $60,000. You borrow the other $240,000 using a 30-year fixed-rate mortgage with a 5 percent interest rate. Five years later, your home is worth $360,000, or 20 percent more than you paid.

Your gain, however, looks considerably larger. Your home equity, which was initially $60,000 thanks to your down payment, has grown to $120,000.

That's the wonder of leverage: A 20 percent rise in your home's value translated into a 100 percent increase in your home equity. In fact, your home equity would be closer to $140,000, because you would have whittled down the $240,000 mortgage balance to almost $220,000 with your first five years of monthly mortgage payments.

But leverage is not always so kind. From the mid-2006 peak to the early 2012 trough, home prices tumbled 27.4 percent, as measured by the S&P/Case-Shiller U.S. National Home Price Index. In the above example, that decline would have left you underwater, wiping out both your $60,000 down payment and the $20,000 you had trimmed from the mortgage balance with your five years of monthly payments.

Moreover, even if your home's value had climbed by 20 percent to $360,000, you would have paid a high price for that appreciation. Over those first five years, you would have coughed up almost $58,000 in mortgage interest, as well as homeowner's insurance, property taxes and maintenance expenses. Sound bad? It gets worse: If you tried to cash in your gain and paid a 5 percent real estate commission to sell your $360,000 home, you would immediately lose $18,000.

Yet none of this should dissuade you from buying a house. We're still missing the final piece of the puzzle: the so-called imputed rent.

65. IMPUTED RENT

Okay, real estate price appreciation is nothing to write home about. Okay, the benefits of leverage might be offset by the cost of the mortgage. In fact, once you figure in all the expenses involved in buying, owning and selling a home, there's a good chance you are losing money big-time. But you get to live in the place, right?

That is, indeed, the big payoff from homeownership. If you live in your own home, you are essentially renting the place to yourself. Think about how much you might pay each year if you didn't own your current home and instead had to make monthly payments to a landlord. While your home might appreciate just 3 percent a year in today's low-inflation environment, the annual value of this imputed rent could be equal to 7 percent of your home's value. That 7 percent is the big allure of investing in rental properties.

But if you're the person living in the house, nobody is paying you this 7 percent. In essence, your home is part consumption—you get to live there—and part investment, which is the price appreciation. And the consumption part is significantly more valuable than the investment part.

JONATHAN'S TAKE: Whether you're buying a principal residence or a vacation property for your own use, you need to keep in mind the crucial distinction between price appreciation and imputed rent. You are unlikely to make much from home price appreciation, once you factor in all costs. You will enjoy large sums of imputed rent, but you're the one consuming that imputed rent. The implication: You should focus on buying homes that you can comfortably afford and that'll give you a lot of pleasure—because that pleasure is the big return from owning real estate.

66. MY STORY: ADVENTURES IN REAL ESTATE

Since 1992, I have owned three homes. I bought a house in New Jersey in 1992 for $165,000 and sold it two decades later for $409,000. I next owned an apartment in Manhattan, bought in 2011 for $570,000 and sold in 2014 for $800,000. I used the proceeds to buy my current home, an apartment just north of New York City, for $730,000.

All this makes homeownership sound like a money-making endeavor—and it has been, but perhaps not in the way readers imagine. For instance, in the time I owned the New Jersey home, I paid $106,000 in mortgage interest (and it would have been much more, but I paid off the mortgage early) and $120,000 in property taxes, plus I spent $183,000 on home improvements. I also had homeowner's insurance, which might have averaged $500 a year. On top of all that, it cost me $9,000 in closing costs to buy the place and $32,000 in realtor commissions and other costs to sell.

To be sure, my mortgage interest and property taxes were tax-deductible. But even with that tax deduction, my total costs over the two decades were far greater than the profit I supposedly made when I sold my New Jersey home.

A bad deal? Not at all. For two decades, the house provided my family with a place to live. A quick back-of-the-envelope calculation suggests that this 20 years of imputed rent might have amounted to $400,000.

67. BUYING A HOME

Thinking of buying a home? Before you start bidding on properties, ask yourself six questions:

How long will you stay put? If you think you'll move within five years, perhaps because of your job or because the house you can currently afford won't really be big enough, buying may not be smart. It would likely be better to wait until you can purchase a place you'll be happy with for the long haul.

How much can you borrow? A mortgage lender may be willing to let you take on total monthly mortgage payments, including principal, interest, homeowner's insurance and property taxes, equal to 28 percent or so of your pretax monthly income. We have more on mortgages in Part XII.

How much can you put down? Ideally, you should save enough to put down 20 percent of the purchase price, so you avoid taking out private mortgage insurance, or PMI. Even if you can't scrape together 20 percent, the more you put down, the less you may have to pay in PMI. Coming up short? You might be eligible to make a $10,000 penalty-free withdrawal from your individual retirement account and, if married, your spouse could do the same. The $10,000 is a lifetime limit, and the provision can be used only by those who haven't owned a house within the past two years.

The down payment isn't the only cost you will incur. Mortgage application fees, legal costs, a home inspection and title insurance could easily amount to $3,000 to $6,000, and maybe more.

Where should you buy? In tackling that question, give particular thought to two issues. First, are the schools good? If not, you might find yourself paying for private schools, which is an expensive proposition. Even if you don't have children, good schools can bolster property prices. Second, how long will your commute be? Research suggests that a long commute is one of the biggest causes of unhappiness.

What other costs will you face? Beyond the down payment and closing costs, give some thought to other expenses you might incur. What are the property taxes? Will you need to spend substantial sums on remodeling, either immediately or within the first few years?

Should you use a real estate agent? While sellers typically use a real estate agent, there's less need if you are buying—and it could put you in a weaker bargaining position. Yes, by retaining a real estate agent, you may hear about properties before they hit the public listings.

But if you're negotiating with a seller, you may also find there's less wiggle room if you use a realtor. If a seller's agent is looking at earning the entire commission, he or she might shave the commission to bridge the difference between what a buyer is offering and what a seller will accept. But if the seller's agent will have to split the commission with a buyer's broker, the agent may be less willing to cut the commission.

68. SELLING A HOME

Prepping a home for sale can take months, so give yourself ample time. What needs to be done—and what shouldn't you do? Here are some pointers:

Skip the remodeling. Most home improvements are money losers, so you shouldn't undertake extensive remodeling with a view to turning a profit when you sell. On the other hand, smaller improvements—a fresh coat of paint, a tidier garden, refinishing the bathtub—could be worthwhile, because they may make your home easier to sell.

Go neutral. If you paint the bedrooms or retile the kitchen or bathroom, favor colors and patterns that are less likely to offend. No matter how tasteful you think your decorating is, many potential buyers will likely disagree. When you ready your home for sale, you should also remove personal pictures and get rid of clutter. The goal: Organize your home so buyers can see themselves living there, not you.

Negotiate the commission. The 6 percent real estate agent's commission, once standard, is fast becoming history. You should pay less than 6 percent unless there's something about your home that will make it extremely difficult to sell, such as the need for major repairs or an environmental problem.

Price realistically. To win your business, an agent might suggest your home is worth some fancy price. But do your own research, including checking listings for comparable homes.

If it's clear you are asking too much, move quickly to lower the price to a more compelling level, rather than making a series of small price drops that might make your home seem like tainted goods to potential buyers. That's especially true if your home is sitting empty. You aren't getting any use from the house, but you are incurring all the carrying costs, plus the equity tied up in the house could be invested elsewhere and earning gains.

69. SELLING YOURSELF

The precise number is a matter of some debate: Still, each year, it seems 10 to 20 percent of homes are sold directly by owners, rather than through a real estate agent. Should you, too, try selling your own home?

Sellers can list their homes using sites such as BuyOwner.com, ByOwner.com, ForSaleByOwner.com, Owners.com and Zillow.com. Many of these sites charge if you want more than a basic listing. Even so, with traditional real estate agents often taking 5 or 6 percent of the proceeds from a sale, the potential savings are huge.

The potential hassles, however, are also great. You need to be available to show your home at any time, often on short notice. Buyers are frequently suspicious of homes that are listed without an agent, fearful that the properties may have undisclosed problems. Many sellers also hurt their cause by pricing their homes too high. Before you list your home, be sure to study the local property market and carefully prepare your home for sale.

Among folks who endeavor to sell on their own, many throw in the towel and end up using an agent. But if you aren't in a rush, trying initially to find a buyer by yourself could be a smart move. Want to learn more?

You can find an extensive library of articles at BuyOwner.com, ForSaleByOwner.com and Owners.com.

70. REAL ESTATE AGENTS

Despite the cost involved, the vast majority of homeowners continue to use a broker when they sell. Real estate commissions were once a standard 6 percent of the proceeds from a home's sale. Today, 5 percent is increasingly common, with the commission set at perhaps 4 percent if the seller's agent also manages to find the buyer, without involving another agent. But whether it is 6, 5 or 4 percent, it's a lot of money, though maybe not as lucrative to the broker as you imagine.

Suppose you're selling your home and you have negotiated a 5 percent commission with your real estate agent. If the house sells for $400,000, the commission will nick $20,000 out of your proceeds. Your agent will have a big payday, but he or she won't be getting the full $20,000. The commission will have to be split with the buyer's agent. The real estate brokerage firms that employ the two brokers will also get a cut. Result: Your agent, especially if he or she isn't a high producer, might personally pocket just $5,000, or 1.25 percent of the gross proceeds.

Because the percentage is so small, your agent's greatest incentive isn't to garner the highest possible price, but rather to get the deal done as quickly as possible. Suppose you hold out for an extra $20,000 and it takes an extra six weeks to sell your home. You'll pocket perhaps $19,000 more, which you would no doubt be happy about. But your agent may collect just a few hundred additional dollars, despite weeks of extra work.

71. ASSESSING THE LOCAL MARKET

As 2015 ends, the national housing market appears to be fairly priced, neither as crazed as it was in 2005 nor as depressed as it was in 2011. Still, it's not terribly helpful to talk about the national market, because there's so much variation across the country.

For instance, according to the S&P/Case-Shiller real estate indexes, the Denver, Portland and San Francisco markets posted gains of 10 percent or more in the year through September 2015, while prices in Chicago, Cleveland, New York and Washington, DC, were up less than 3 percent.

How can you get a handle on the local property market? Ask a local real estate agent for details on recent sales, including how long it's taking properties to sell and how final selling prices compare to list prices. Visit real estate sites such as Realtor.com, Trulia.com and Zillow.com. Go to open houses in your neighborhood—even if you're looking to sell, not buy. That way, you can get a reality check on whether you are pricing your home properly.

If you are looking both to sell and buy within the same local market, you shouldn't be too bothered if the market is buoyant or depressed. Even if you're suffering on one side of the transaction, by receiving too little or paying too much, you presumably are benefiting on the other side.

Buying in a market that's overly exuberant? Think twice before getting into a bidding war. You could end up suffering from the so-called winner's curse. What's that? Winners of bidding wars often discover they paid too much, while those with cooler heads had a better handle on the home's value. Before you blithely boost your bid by $20,000, think about how many months you would have to work to save that sort of money.

72. REMODELING

When you sell your home, you might make back 60 to 80 percent of the money spent on remodeling projects. For proof, check out Remodeling magazine's annual survey at CostvsValue.com. The survey is based on selling your home within a year of making the improvements.

For example, according to the 2015 survey, a bathroom addition costs an average $39,578, but you might recoup just $22,875, or 57.8 percent, if you sell soon after. The longer you wait to sell, the less you are likely to recoup, because your improvements will no longer look spanking new.

In other words, as with homeownership in general, remodeling is part consumption and part investment. With that in mind, you should go ahead with remodeling projects only if they will give you pleasure commensurate with the dollars spent and not because you think they will boost your home's value. That said, if you're concerned about your home's resale value, you should probably avoid fixing up your home to the point where it is fancier than most others in the area. Instead, you are more likely to get a fair price if your house is comparable to others in the neighborhood.

In the market for a new home? Because remodeling projects tend to be money losers, you might look for a home that has been fixed up to your liking. That way, you may be able to buy the owner's home improvements at a discount.

73. RENTAL PROPERTIES

For many ordinary Americans, buying properties and renting them out has been a road to financial success. Typically, the strategy is to find places where the rental income can cover the mortgage payments and other ongoing costs. That way, the tenant effectively pays off your loan, plus you also benefit from any price appreciation. As you raise the rent over time, you can get to the point where you aren't merely covering costs, but pocketing a tidy sum each month.

Sound attractive? Keep three drawbacks in mind. First, your tenants won't treat the place the way you would. In shopping for rental properties, you might favor homes that are somewhat rundown. That way, it will matter less if the tenants are a little rough on the place.

Second, being a landlord is hard work. You will occasionally have to find new tenants and you will have yet another home to maintain. Even if you don't do the maintenance yourself, you'll need to find others to do the work—and that means not only extra costs, but also extra hassles. You could hire a property management firm to handle all these issues, though that might cost you 10 percent or more of your rental income.

Third, a rental property represents a big undiversified bet. Your tenants may fail to pay the rent, at which point you'll have no help when it comes to meeting the mortgage and paying other costs. Even if your tenants are well-behaved, they may not stick around for long. That means you may have short periods without any rental income.

74. TAXES WHEN SELLING A HOME

When you sell your primary residence, you can't claim a tax loss if you receive less than you paid. But you can avoid capital gains taxes on $250,000 of appreciation, or $500,000 if you're married filing jointly. To qualify for the $250,000 or $500,000 exclusion, you need to have lived in the house for at least 24 months during the prior five years.

What if your capital gain is more than these sums? You can add certain items to your home's cost basis, such as some of your closing costs and the amount spent on home improvements. That will trim your taxable gain.

Things are trickier if you sell a second home. In the past, you were able to move into a vacation property, live there for two years and get the full benefit of the $250,000 or $500,000 exclusion. That ploy no longer works. For instance, if you owned the place for five years but used it as your principal residence for just two years, only 40 percent of any gain is eligible for the exclusion—and you would owe capital gains taxes on the other 60 percent.

The new rules apply to 2009 onward. What if you owned a second home prior to 2009? You get some tax relief. To figure out what percentage of your gain isn't eligible for the exclusion, you take the amount of time the property wasn't your primary residence in the period since 2009 and divide it by the total number of years you owned the property—including the years prior to 2009.

PART IV

COLLEGE

IT'S A REAL EDUCATION, ESPECIALLY FOR PARENTS

F or parents and students facing college costs, the questions keep piling up. Is college worth the cost? What's the best way to prepare financially? Will our family receive financial aid? How much education debt is too much?

Earning a college degree may be an enriching experience that sets you up for a potentially more interesting career. But it's also a major investment, one that can pay off handsomely by making your human capital—your income-earning ability—more valuable. According to a June 2014 White House report, the median annual income in 2013 for those with at least a bachelor's degree was $62,300. That was $28,300 higher than the median earnings for those with only a high school diploma. These figures are for folks age 25 and older who are working fulltime. College graduates were also less likely to be unemployed, at 4 percent, versus 8 percent for those who only graduated high school.

The earnings for those with advanced degrees, especially lawyers and MBAs, are even higher. A 2012 Census Bureau study estimates that, relative to high school graduates, a bachelor's degree boosted lifetime earnings by 77 percent, a master's degree by 107 percent, a doctorate by 157 percent and a professional degree by 203 percent. Among those with a bachelor's, engineering majors were likely to have the highest lifetime earnings, while education majors should expect the lowest incomes. The big payoff from a college education is also most likely to be enjoyed by students who go to prestigious private colleges, while those who attend community colleges and technical schools fare less well.

Even if your child ends up with a bigger paycheck, it probably won't come cheap. If you have a newborn, you face four daunting financial tasks. First, you need to save for college over the next 18 years, while juggling other financial goals like retirement and buying a home. Second, as your teenager struggles with college applications, you get to struggle with the financial aid forms—and you'll both be on tenterhooks awaiting the outcome. Third, there's paying for the college years, which often involves a patchwork approach. You might dip into savings, receive some grant money, take out loans, get help from the grandparents and pay part of the cost out of your regular paycheck.

Finally, there's the aftermath, which may see your college graduate grappling with student loans, even as you work to pay off the money you borrowed. Figures from the Federal Reserve Bank of New York show education borrowing up 218 percent over the past 10 years—and some observers think this is the next debt crisis in the making.

75. TODAY'S COLLEGE COSTS

According to the College Board, it costs an average $19,548 in tuition, fees, room and board to send a child to an in-state university for the 2015–16 academic year. Even after subtracting out the inflation rate, that's 3.1 percent higher than the year before and up a cumulative 10 percent over the prior five years.

For a private college, the average tab for 2015–16 is $43,921, a 3.3 percent increase from a year earlier and up 10 percent over the preceding five years. Again, these are increases over and above inflation. Sound steep? At some elite private colleges, the cost is now more than $60,000.

Some have contended the real cost hasn't climbed nearly as fast as the sticker price, thanks to financial aid. Still, as published college costs have increased, so too have education loans. The College Board says 61 percent of recent four-year college graduates borrowed to pay their education costs, with their debts averaging $26,900.

It isn't just undergraduate borrowing that is increasing. A March 2014 report from the New America Foundation estimated that 40 percent of the roughly $1 trillion in outstanding student loans represented borrowing by students pursuing graduate and professional degrees.

What are families doing to prepare? A 2015 study by market researcher Ipsos Public Affairs and student-loan provider Sallie Mae found that 48 percent of parents with children under age 18 were currently saving for college, and the total amount socked away averaged $10,040.

76. DOS AND DON'TS FOR 2016

Got college-bound kids and want to get yourself on track financially? Here are some "to dos" for the year ahead:

• Fund a 529 college savings plan. Whatever you can put aside will come in handy once the college bills start rolling in.

• Use the EFC calculator available at CollegeBoard.org to figure out how much financial aid you might receive. In all likelihood, you will be unpleasantly surprised. EFC is an abbreviation for expected family contribution.

• See whether you qualify for any of the education tax credits and deductions, all of which have income thresholds. You'll find more details toward the end of this chapter.

• Check out the new CollegeScorecard.ed.gov, where you can get information about a college's annual cost, graduation rates and the salaries earned by graduates.

And here's what you shouldn't do:

• Don't stick college savings in a custodial account. It could mess up your tax return and derail your chances of getting financial aid.

• Don't withdraw money from retirement accounts to pay for college if you plan to apply for financial aid.

• Don't let your children dream of pricey private colleges that you simply can't afford—and caution them against taking on excessive student loans if their possible professions will make it a struggle to service these loans.

77. MANAGE EXPECTATIONS

We all want the best for our children. But what can you reasonably afford? If you're struggling to save enough for retirement, it may be unrealistic to think you can also help with college costs.

If that's the case, you should tell your children early on and preferably no later than the freshman year of high school. You don't want your kids to spend years imagining they will go to a college that you simply cannot afford and that, even with financial aid, is probably out of reach. Moreover, if you tell your children in time, it will give them the chance to work part-time jobs and perhaps save a little money toward college costs. Even if you can't offer financial help, you can offer advice. For instance, if your children plan to pursue careers that won't be especially lucrative, you should discourage them from attending a college that will necessitate taking on hefty student loans.

What if you can help financially? Let your children know how much assistance you can provide and where you'll draw the line. Many parents help with undergraduate costs, but tell their children that they're on their own when it comes to graduate school.

You should also talk to them about any other financial help you will—or won't—provide. If you can assist with a house down payment and a lavish wedding, that's wonderful. But if that sort of help isn't in the cards, you should say so. These financial conversations shouldn't just happen when your children are teenagers and they shouldn't be focused solely on the help you'll give them in their teens and 20s. Once they're adults, you might occasionally discuss your own retirement finances, how much they might inherit and what end-of-life decisions you would like made on your behalf.

78. SAVE SOMETHING

Take the figures from the College Board—the $19,548 average cost for a child at an in-state university for the 2015–16 academic year and the $43,921 for a private college. Multiply those sums by four years, throw in 3 percent annual inflation for 18 years, and you are looking at some $133,000 for an in-state university and $299,000 for a private college. That's how much it might cost to send today's toddlers to college.

To amass those sums, you would need to save roughly $300 a month for 18 years for the in-state university and $670 for the private college, assuming a 5 percent annual return and assuming you stepped up the sum saved each year with the 3 percent inflation rate. For most parents, that simply isn't doable, especially because they also need to save for their own retirement. In fact, retirement should take precedence: Your kids can take out loans to pay for college, but for retirement you'll need to start out with a heap of cash.

Still, save what you can. When it comes time to pay those college bills, you'll be grateful for any cash you have set aside. Where will the rest of the money come from? If you're like most parents, you will muddle through, paying college costs out of current income, perhaps getting some help from the grandparents, asking your children to take on loans and also borrowing money yourself.

If you put aside at least some savings, it may allow your children to graduate without crippling amounts of student debt. But that still leaves two questions: How should you invest your children's college savings—and what sort of account should you use?

79. INVESTMENT STRATEGY

You should probably be more conservative with your children's college savings than with your own retirement nest egg. Sound counterintuitive? Remember, your kids likely have no more than 18 years until they head off to college, while you may have decades until you quit the workforce—and you'll likely live a few decades beyond that.

The implication: While you might initially invest your children's college savings heavily in stocks, you should probably start moving toward bonds even before they enter high school. Let's assume you plan to put a quarter of your children's college fund toward each of the four years needed to earn an undergraduate degree.

With that in mind, you might look to have a quarter of your children's savings in certificates of deposit, short-term bonds or similar conservative investments when they're five years from their freshman college year. You might aim to have another quarter in conservative investments when they're five years from their sophomore year, and so on.

Why this caution? Over some five-year stretches, stocks have lost money. Another reason: While you might spend your retirement money over 20 or 30 years, the deadline is a lot harsher with your children's college savings, because the money is spent over a brief four-year period.

As you invest your children's college savings, also think about what sort of account to use, whether it's a 529 college savings plan, prepaid tuition plan, Coverdell education savings account or custodial account. As an alternative, some parents keep the money in their own name, perhaps stashing it in a regular taxable investment account, putting it in savings bonds or even using an individual retirement account.

80. SECTION 529 COLLEGE SAVINGS PLANS

While 529 college savings plans have drawbacks, they have emerged as perhaps the best choice for parents looking to sock away money for college.

These plans, named 529 after the relevant section of the federal tax code, allow you to save huge sums every year. Moreover, you can contribute no matter how high your income. Your savings grow tax-free as long as the money is used for qualified education expenses. Many states even offer state tax deductions or credits for contributing. For financial aid purposes, the plans are typically considered a parental asset, which means their impact on aid eligibility is far less than if they were deemed the student's asset. If you don't use all the money for one child's education, you can change beneficiaries and use the account to help another child. To learn more, go to SavingforCollege.com.

For well-heeled parents, 529 plans can be especially attractive. In 2016, you can't give another person more than $14,000 without worrying about the federal gift tax. But with a 529 plan, both parents could contribute five times that sum, or $70,000 each, and count it as their gift for the next five years. That gets the money growing tax-free more quickly, which potentially is a significant benefit. This might also be a smart strategy for wealthy grandparents.

What about the drawbacks? Some plans have high expenses, but you can sidestep that problem by favoring lower-cost plans. You can change your investment selection just twice a year, which means 529 plans aren't good for those inclined to trade. Finally, if you don't use the money for education and instead simply withdraw it, you'll face income taxes and tax penalties on the tax-deferred growth.

In January 2015, President Obama suggested eliminating the tax-free treatment for withdrawals from both 529 plans and Coverdell education savings accounts, even if the money was used for education expenses. After an outcry, the proposal was quickly scrapped. Still, it was a reminder that 529 investors could lose out if we get a rewriting of the tax code.

81. GRANDPARENTS AND 529s

If you have grandchildren, funding 529 plans is an intriguing option with three big benefits and one significant problem. First, as mentioned in the previous section, you can gift as much as $70,000 in 2016 and count it as your gift for the next five years. That can get a big chunk of money, as well as its future investment growth, out of your estate. If, however, you die before the five years are up, a pro-rated share of the gift will be added back to your estate.

Second, if you open the account rather than funding a 529 opened by the parents, you remain in control of the money. That means that, if your grandchildren's parents divorce, there's no risk the money will get divvied up and spent.

Third, unlike with other education accounts, your contributions to a 529 aren't irrevocable. In other words, if you later discover that your retirement portfolio is becoming depleted, you can reclaim the money in your grandchildren's 529s, though you'll owe income taxes and tax penalties on any investment growth.

What's the problem? If it turns out your grandchildren are eligible for financial aid, you'll want to time your 529 withdrawals carefully. When applying for financial aid, a grandparent-controlled 529 doesn't show up as an asset belonging to either the parents or the child, which is a plus. But when a grandparent makes a 529 withdrawal to pay college expenses, it counts as income for the student, which can badly hurt aid eligibility.

To get around this problem, you might use the 529 to pay college expenses starting in the second half of your grandchild's junior year. At that point, your grandchild should have made his or her final aid application, so the 529 withdrawal won't affect aid eligibility. Problem solved? Maybe not. If your grandchildren go to a private college that requires the CSS Profile financial aid form, they may be asked to disclose whether they are beneficiaries of a 529—including those funded by grandparents.

82. PREPAID TUITION PLANS

Prepaid tuition plans are a type of 529 plan. But unlike a 529 college savings plan, where you aim to earn healthy investment gains by picking from among a menu of mutual funds, a prepaid tuition plan is designed to let you lock in future tuition costs at today's price. In effect, your rate of return should equal the percentage by which tuition costs increase between now and when your kid heads off to college.

In practice, you may earn less than the rate of tuition inflation, because many prepaid plans charge a premium price for these future tuition credits. Moreover, the credits can only be used at certain colleges, so you should read the small print to see what happens if your child opts to go elsewhere.

Prepaid plans in some states have struggled financially and been closed at least temporarily to new investors. While state prepaid plans in states such as Florida, Massachusetts, Mississippi and Washington are backed by the full faith and credit of the state, other plans don't have that sort of backing, which means payouts could be scaled back if the plan doesn't earn a high enough return when investing participants' money.

As with a 529 college savings plan, parent-controlled prepaid tuition plans are treated as a parental asset for financial aid purposes and the gains are tax-free at the federal level as long as the money is used for qualified education expenses. You may also be eligible for special state tax breaks. To research plans, head to SavingforCollege.com.

83. COVERDELL EDUCATION SAVINGS ACCOUNTS

Like 529 college savings plans, a Coverdell education savings account can give you tax-free growth if the money is used for qualified education expenses. A Coverdell is also typically treated as a parental asset for financial aid purposes—another attractive feature.

But there the similarities end. While 529 college savings plans restrict you to the plan's menu of investment options, you have a much wider choice with a Coverdell, which means you could potentially slash your investment costs by, say, favoring index funds with rock-bottom annual costs. You can also use the Coverdell to pay for education expenses from kindergarten through college, while a 529 plan is restricted to college costs only.

But those advantages are offset by a few notable disadvantages. You can invest just $2,000 a year in a Coverdell. The amount you can contribute phases out if your modified adjusted gross income is between $190,000 and $220,000 and you're married filing jointly, or between $95,000 and $110,000 and you're filing as single or head of household. Above these income thresholds, contributions aren't allowed. These income eligibility thresholds do not rise each year with inflation.

You could sidestep the limits by having a family member with less income make the annual contribution. Indeed, you need to be aware of what others are doing, because the $2,000 annual limit is a total amount per child. Thanks to these various drawbacks, the Coverdell hasn't proven that popular, and some financial firms have stopped offering them, instead focusing their efforts on 529s.

Once the beneficiary of a Coverdell turns age 18, you can't make further contributions. The account needs to be emptied within 30 days of the beneficiary turning age 30. But if, as that deadline approaches, there happens to be money left in the account, you can keep the tax-free growth going by switching the account's beneficiary to another family member who is under age 30.

84. CUSTODIAL ACCOUNTS

If you open a regular investment account for your child, you need to set it up as a custodial account under your state's Uniform Transfers to Minors Act or Uniform Gifts to Minors Act. With an UTMA or UGMA account, you typically name yourself as custodian. That means you call the shots on how the account is invested. The money you put in the account is an irrevocable gift to your kid. To fund the account, you might take advantage of the annual gift-tax exclusion, which means you could contribute as much as $14,000 in 2016 without worrying about the gift tax.

There are three big drawbacks with custodial accounts. First, while investment earnings in the account of up to $2,100 in 2015 and 2016 would be taxed at a modest rate, gains above that level are taxed at the parents' rate, thanks to the so-called kiddie tax. That could mean a steep tax rate and, perhaps more important, some additional hassles at tax time.

Second, once your child reaches the age of majority, which is typically 18 to 21 depending on the state where you live, your kid can take control of the account—and the money could end up being spent on a fast car rather than a good education.

Third, in the financial aid formulas, a custodial account is considered a child's asset, rather than a parental asset, which means it could cost you dearly in financial aid.

JONATHAN'S TAKE: If you're saving for a child's college costs, a custodial account seems like a poor alternative to 529s and Coverdells, with their tax-free growth and favorable financial aid treatment. Got college money in a custodial account? You might move it to a 529, though that could trigger a big capital gains tax bill when you sell the custodial-account investments. What if you're confident your family won't qualify for financial aid and you want to invest for your child, so he or she will later have money for, say, a house down payment? In that scenario, a custodial account might make sense.

85. KIDDIE TAX

The kiddie tax is designed to prevent parents from transferring large sums to their children with the goal of saving on taxes. In 2015 and 2016, the first $1,050 of a child's investment gains are tax-free and the next $1,050 are taxed at the child's rate. Any investment gains above $2,100 in 2015 and 2016 are taxed at the parents' rate.

The kiddie tax typically applies to children under age 18 or, if they don't have much income from employment, under age 19. It also applies to young adults under age 24 who were fulltime students as of year-end. Instead of filing a separate tax return for a child, parents may be able to include the kid's investment gains on their own tax return. That way, you avoid filing an extra tax return, but arguably it isn't any simpler.

While the kiddie tax was a big issue in the 1990s, when many parents used custodial accounts to save for college, it shouldn't be as big an issue today. Why not? If you save for college, you now have two great college savings options available to you: 529 college savings plans and Coverdell education savings accounts. Neither account, with their potential tax-free growth, would trigger the kiddie tax.

What if you want to invest in a child's name with the goal of helping him or her save money for after college? You might invest in a way that's likely to generate less than $2,100 a year in annual investment gains. For instance, you could favor tax-efficient investment vehicles like stock index mutual funds or tax-managed stock funds.

86. SAVING IN THE PARENTS' NAMES

There's no law that says college savings have to be in a special education account. Yes, these offer tax advantages. Using a special account also appeals to our mental accounting: We like the idea that the money is segregated, and the separate account makes it less likely we'll spend the savings on something else.

Still, for many parents, keeping college savings in their own name often makes sense. You might stash the dollars in a regular taxable investment account, savings bonds, a retirement account or perhaps use it to pay down your mortgage. If your income is modest and there's a good chance your family will receive financial aid, you should probably focus your spare cash on other goals, such as buying a home and investing for retirement. If it turns out your income is higher than expected and hence your aid eligibility is less, you could always pay for college by, for instance, borrowing against your home's value or withdrawing your Roth IRA contributions.

Sticking college savings in a traditional IRA might also make sense, especially if you have children later in life. But if your kids qualify for financial aid, you should think carefully about when to make your traditional or Roth IRA withdrawals.

In addition, keeping college savings in your own name might be appealing if you favor flexibility. The fact is, you don't know whether your kids will go to college, whether you'll need the money for your own retirement, or what will happen to the tax code and financial aid formulas in the years ahead. Set against that is the tax-free growth offered by a 529 or a Coverdell. But given the relatively short time you have to invest for a child's college education, you might decide the tax savings won't be that significant.

87. RETIREMENT ACCOUNTS

If you're paying qualified education expenses, you can withdraw money from an IRA and avoid the usual 10 percent tax penalty levied on those under age 59½. Problem is, if you withdraw from a retirement account—and that includes taking tax-free withdrawals from a Roth IRA—you'll increase the income you have to report on your next financial aid application and potentially reduce aid eligibility.

One solution: You might borrow during the early college years and then withdraw from your IRA to repay the loans after your child has submitted his or her final financial aid application, which will likely be January of your kid's junior year. If you're over age 59½ at that juncture, you won't have to worry about the tax penalty.

What if you're under age 59½? If you're simply withdrawing contributions to a Roth IRA, the tax penalty won't be an issue. But if you are withdrawing from a traditional IRA or the investment earnings from a Roth IRA, you'll want to calculate how much in qualified education expenses you have for that year and then withdraw no more than that amount, so you avoid the 10 percent tax penalty.

Keep in mind that your qualified expenses will be less than the sum of tuition, fees, room and board if part of these costs was covered by other financial assistance, such as a Coverdell withdrawal or a Pell grant.

88. SAVINGS BONDS

At one time, it was popular to buy savings bonds to pay for a child's college costs. These days, you don't hear savings bonds discussed that often, partly because 529s and Coverdells seem like better alternatives and partly because yields on savings bond are now so modest. There's more about savings bonds in Part IX.

Still, for those who qualify, savings bonds can be a low-risk, tax-free way to save for college. You can cash in savings bonds and avoid income taxes on the accumulated interest if you use the money for tuition and fees at a qualified educational institution for yourself, your spouse or your child. In 2016, this tax break phases out if you are married filing jointly with modified adjusted gross income between $116,300 and $146,300. For other taxpayers, the phase-out range is $77,550 to $92,550.

To get the tax break, there are a few other conditions. The bonds need to be owned by one or both parents and you need to have been at least 24 years old when you bought the bonds. The bonds need to be either EE bonds issued after 1989 or Series I bonds. To qualify for the tax break, you also can't be married but filing separate tax returns.

89. FINANCIAL AID

College financial aid is a source of great hope, frequent confusion and often bitter disappointment. To get a handle on the topic, start by considering three points:

• While there are scholarships available for the academically and athletically gifted, much financial assistance consists of aid that is based on a family's financial need. This need is captured by a notion known as EFC, or expected family contribution.

• Financial aid can take the form of subsidized loans, unsubsidized loans, work study and grant money. If your children qualify for financial aid and they're desirable to colleges because of their academic brilliance, athletic abilities or some other quality, colleges may tweak an aid package to include more grant money. Indeed, if you are disappointed with the aid package that your child is offered, consider appealing to one of the college's financial aid officers. Such appeals are often successful if your child is the type of student the college is looking to recruit. In 2014–15, undergraduates received an average $14,210 in financial aid, $8,170 of which was grant money, according to the College Board.

• While folks often talk about the financial aid formula, there are actually two formulas. One is used by the federal government, which is the biggest source of financial aid and which assesses aid eligibility using information you provide in the FAFSA, or Free Application for Federal Student Aid, a daunting form with more than 100 questions. The other formula, known as the institutional methodology, is used by many private colleges when doling out their own money. These schools require that you also fill out the CSS Profile form, which includes additional details not included on the FAFSA. (CSS stands for College Scholarship Service.) While federal grants typically go to poorer families, private colleges use their endowments to distribute significant amounts of grant money to middle-class families.

You typically file for financial aid in the first two months of the year. If your child is a senior in high school, you should hear about financial aid when you hear whether your child has been accepted, which is usually around April 1 or shortly thereafter. To learn more about college financial aid, check out FinAid.org, an independent website, and also the U.S. Department of Education's StudentAid.gov.

90. EXPECTED FAMILY CONTRIBUTION

The amount you're expected to pay toward college costs is reflected in a number known as your EFC, or expected family contribution. Many parents are shocked by how much they're expected to cough up each year toward college costs. You can calculate your expected contribution under both the federal and institutional aid formulas using the EFC calculator available at CollegeBoard.org.

Let's say your EFC is $15,000 a year. If your teenager goes to a college that costs $20,000, you should receive $5,000 a year in financial aid. What if your kid goes to a $50,000-a-year college? You should receive $35,000 in aid.

That suggests you shouldn't dissuade your children from applying to colleges because they appear to be too expensive. Sure, if a college costs less than your expected family contribution, your out-of-pocket cost will be less. But if your teenager is choosing between two colleges, one that costs $2,000 more than your EFC and another college that costs $20,000 more, you should—in theory—be indifferent, because your out-of-pocket cost will be the same.

In practice, a lot will depend on the composition of the aid package. If the more expensive college offers an aid package that includes a substantial amount of student loans, you may want to favor the less costly college rather than send your children out into the world burdened by debt. In addition, not all colleges offer aid packages that fill the full gap between your EFC and the college's cost, and that could leave you scrambling to make up the shortfall.

91. AID ELIGIBILITY

The aid formulas take into account a host of factors, such as family size and whether you have more than one child in college at the same time. Still, much hinges on four key drivers of aid eligibility: the parents' income, the parents' assets, the child's income and the child's assets.

Under the formulas, parents are expected to contribute as much as 47 percent of income and as much as 5 to 5.6 percent of assets toward each year's college costs, though only higher-earning and wealthier parents will be assessed at such high rates. Students are expected to contribute as much as 50 percent of income and as much as 20 to 25 percent of assets.

For most families, the parents' income will be the biggest determinant of aid eligibility. While it doesn't make sense to ask your boss for a pay cut, you might take steps to hold down your income, including your investment income, during the four calendar years that will be used to gauge your aid eligibility. Aid eligibility is reassessed each year. The so-called base year—which covers the second half of your teenager's junior year in high school and the first half of the kid's senior year—is especially important.

You might also look carefully at the assets held by both parents and students, as well as what counts as an asset. In addition, if your child is applying to private colleges, you should pay attention to differences between the federal and institutional aid formulas.

92. FEDERAL VS. INSTITUTIONAL METHODOLOGY

The federal financial aid formula and the institutional formula used by many private colleges differ in notable ways, including how heavily they assess the income and assets of parents and students. But you should pay particular attention to two key differences.

First, while the federal formula ignores home equity, it's considered in the institutional methodology. You hear about parents who use their savings to buy an overly large home or undertake elaborate remodeling projects with an eye to increasing aid eligibility. That may help with the federal methodology, but it may not increase aid eligibility if your children plan to attend a private college.

Second, if a couple is divorced, the federal formula focuses solely on the finances of the custodial parent and, if remarried, the finances of his or her new spouse. The custodial parent is typically the parent with whom a child has spent the most nights over the past year or who provides the bulk of the child's financial support.

By contrast, with the institutional methodology, both parents may be considered, as well as the finances of any new spouses. One implication: If your child isn't likely to attend a college where the institutional formula is used, you should give careful thought to who should be listed as the custodial parent.

93. INCREASING AID ELIGIBILITY

Want to increase aid eligibility? Consider these strategies:

• Use taxable account savings to pay down debt. Consumer debts such as credit card balances and auto loans are ignored by the aid formulas, so they won't make you appear needier, while paying them off will reduce the money you have in regular taxable accounts, which is assessed. You might also use spare cash to pay down mortgage debt and make necessary purchases, such as buying a new car or replacing the roof.

• Stash college savings in the parents' names or in Coverdell and 529 plans. Don't use UGMA or UTMA accounts, which are considered the child's asset and assessed more heavily for financial aid purposes. If you have money in your child's name, consider spending it before applying for financial aid by using it to pay for items, such as summer camp, that are not considered part of the usual parental obligation. You could also liquidate the UGMA or UTMA account and use the proceeds to fund a 529 plan, though this may trigger a big capital gain, part of which could be taxed at the parents' rate because of the kiddie tax.

• Hold down your income during the years used to assess aid eligibility. Avoid realizing capital gains in your taxable accounts or, if you do, try to take offsetting capital losses. Also avoid tapping retirement accounts to pay college expenses. See if your employer will postpone paying your year-end bonus. These various steps are especially important in the base year for assessing financial aid eligibility, which is typically the calendar year that covers the second half of your student's junior year and the initial months of his or her senior year.

• Max out savings in retirement accounts. Tax-deductible contributions won't reduce your income for aid purposes, but it will help when it comes to assessing your assets. Money in retirement accounts is typically ignored in the aid formulas, while taxable account savings will reduce aid eligibility, so you might focus on fully funding 401(k) plans and IRAs in the years running up to college.

94. HELP FROM FAMILY

Family members, especially grandparents, often chip in to help with college costs. If your children are eligible for financial aid, you should discuss the best way to give this financial assistance.

For instance, while the annual gift-tax exclusion is $14,000 in 2016, there's no cap imposed on financial help with education costs, as long as the money is sent directly to the educational institution. Problem is, if the grandparents or others do this, it can result in a dollar-for-dollar reduction in financial aid.

Instead, family members might gift the money to the parents, who can then use it to pay college costs. Alternatively, family members might help with college costs after the final financial aid application is filed, which will typically be January of the student's junior year, or they could assist the student with paying off education loans after graduation.

Family members might also contribute to a 529 plan that the parents set up. This avoids the financial aid problems that can arise with 529s set up by grandparents and other family members, though it also means giving up control of the money.

95. EDUCATION BORROWING

According to the College Board, 61 percent of students graduating from four-year colleges during the 2013–14 academic year had borrowed to pay their education costs. The average amount borrowed was $26,900. Among the different types of financial aid given out to undergraduates during the 2014–2015 academic year, federal loans accounted for 34 percent, grants for 56 percent, and education tax breaks and work study for 9 percent.

The Federal Reserve Bank of New York calculates that, over the seven years through 2015's third quarter, student loans outstanding soared 97 percent, even as overall household debt declined. Research suggests that, among those who struggle to repay student loans, many had borrowed to attend a community or for-profit college, or failed to graduate.

The jump in education borrowing has been driven partly by rising college costs and partly by declining financial help from parents. Can't afford to help your children with college costs? Consider counseling them to avoid costly colleges that will leave them heavily in debt, especially if their planned career will pay them a modest income.

You might also suggest strategies that can hold down college costs, such as attending a community college for the first two years and then transferring to a more prestigious school, which they would then graduate from. Alternatively, you might suggest attending a nearby college and saving money by living at home initially. Room and board are a major college cost, accounting for an average 52 percent of total costs for in-state students at public universities, according to College Board figures.

While education loans are available from some banks, students should probably focus on federal loans. Some 90 percent of student loans are made by the federal government. Parents might also consider the federal loan program for parents, as well as a home equity line of credit or possibly a 401(k) loan.

96. STUDENT LOANS

To receive federal loans, you have to file the Free Application for Federal Student Aid, or FAFSA. There are three main federal student loan programs:

Subsidized Stafford loans. These loans, which are awarded based on financial need, don't incur interest while a student is in college. Repayment begins six months after graduation or, alternatively, if a student starts attending college less than halftime.

Unsubsidized Stafford loans. These loans, which aren't awarded based on need, incur interest while a student is in college, though the interest can be added to the loan balance if a student is still attending school.

Students often end up with a mix of subsidized and unsubsidized loans, both of which charge 4.29 percent interest if disbursed during the 12 months through June 30, 2016. The total amount that can be borrowed is capped each year. For instance, for a first-year undergraduate who is considered a dependent student, total subsidized Stafford loans are capped at $3,500, with the possibility of borrowing another $2,000 in unsubsidized loans.

What if a student isn't eligible for subsidized Stafford loans? He or she can always take out unsubsidized loans instead, potentially borrowing as much as $5,500 during the first year of college. In subsequent years, the annual amount that can be borrowed increases.

Perkins loans. These currently carry an interest rate of 5 percent. They are only awarded to students with exceptional financial need—and yet they now charge a higher rate than Stafford loans.

Student loans may also be available from the college itself. The interest rate charged may be less than on federal loans. In addition, some states have set up agencies or nonprofit organizations that provide loans to students who are residents or who go to in-state colleges, and loans are also available from private lenders. For more information, check out Edvisors.com, FinAid.org and StudentAid.gov.

97. PARENT LOANS

The federal government offers not just student loans, but also loans to parents through the PLUS program. PLUS loans incur interest immediately, but parents of undergraduates can defer all payments until six months after their child graduates. The interest rate is 6.84 percent for loans disbursed during the 12 months through June 30, 2016. You can borrow up to the cost of your child's college, minus any other financial aid received. To borrow through the PLUS program, parents are subject to a fairly lenient credit check, and you have to file the Free Application for Federal Student Aid.

Instead of a PLUS loan, you could borrow through a home equity line of credit, which may charge a lower interest rate. The interest on both PLUS and home equity loans is potentially tax-deductible. If you opt to borrow against your home, favor a home equity line of credit, which you can draw on as needed, rather than a home equity loan. The latter involves borrowing a lump sum, which will then show up as additional money in your regular taxable account—and possibly hurt you when you next apply for financial aid.

You might also borrow from your 401(k) plan. Such loans are typically limited to half your account balance, with the amount borrowed capped at $50,000. Some folks are attracted to 401(k) loans because the interest you pay ends up in your account, so you're effectively paying interest to yourself. Nonetheless, there is a real cost. The money borrowed is removed from your account, so the true price of these loans is the investment gains the money could have earned.

Finally, you might investigate taking out an education loan from a bank. If you have an excellent credit score, the interest rate may be below the 6.84 percent charged for PLUS loans. But if your credit score isn't so good, you would likely be better off with the federal PLUS program.

98. REPAYING EDUCATION LOANS

If you're struggling to pay your federal student loans or you're simply overwhelmed by the number of loans you have to pay each month, consider consolidating your federal loans through StudentLoans.gov. The interest rate on the consolidated loan will be based on the weighted average interest rate of your existing loans.

When consolidating, look into extending the term on the loan. Most federal loans are for 10 years, but you may be able to increase the repayment period to as long as 30 years, depending on the total sum involved. This will reduce your monthly payment, simply because you're extending the loan's repayment over more years. But thanks to that longer repayment period, you'll also end up paying more in total interest. Among the loans that can be consolidated are Stafford, Perkins and PLUS loans.

If you need further relief, investigate the federal government's various income-based repayment plans, which can lead to lower monthly payments, depending on your income and family size. For most borrowers, the top choice will be the Pay As You Earn Repayment Plan, which is being expanded so that it's open to anyone with federal direct student loans. Loan payments are limited to 10 percent of discretionary income. Discretionary income is defined as income in excess of 150 percent of the federal poverty level for your family size and state of residence.

You might also be able to get your student loans forgiven if you work for 10 years in the public or nonprofit sector. Others in the income-based repayment program may be eligible to have their undergraduate student loans cancelled after 20 years and their graduate school loans cancelled after 25 years. For more information, head to StudentAid.gov.

What about private loans? If you refinance, you may be able to lower your interest rate or at least extend the term of the loans, thereby reducing your monthly payment. To refinance, often you will need a good credit score and a cosigner on the loan, who is typically a parent, especially if you're applying to refinance soon after graduating. Currently, neither federal nor private student loans can be discharged through bankruptcy, except in rare circumstances, though there's talk in Washington of changing the rules.

99. EDUCATION LOAN INTEREST DEDUCTION

You can deduct the interest charged on your education loans, just like you can deduct the interest on a mortgage and on margin loans. But in the case of education loans, the tax break comes with limitations.

For starters, in 2015 and 2016, you can only deduct up to $2,500 in interest on qualified education loans. In addition, the ability to claim the deduction is subject to an income test. In 2015 and 2016, the deduction phases out if your income is between $130,000 and $160,000 and you're married filing jointly, or between $65,000 and $80,000 and you're single or you file as head of household. You can't claim the deduction if your tax-filing status is married filing separately.

Some good news: The deduction is claimed directly on your 1040, the main page of your federal tax return. That means you can get the tax savings even if you don't itemize your deductions on Schedule A.

100. AMERICAN OPPORTUNITY TAX CREDIT

The American Opportunity Tax Credit is a tax break available to help pay for up to four years of higher education for yourself or your dependents. For those eligible, it can be hugely valuable. Remember, a tax deduction shrinks your taxable income, so that a $1,000 tax deduction might save you $250 in taxes, assuming you're in the 25 percent federal income tax bracket. By contrast, American Opportunity is a tax credit, which means it gives you a dollar-for-dollar reduction in your total tax bill.

In 2015 and 2016, the American Opportunity credit could reduce your tax bill by up to $2,500 per student. The credit consists of 100 percent of the first $2,000 of qualified education expenses, including tuition, fees and course materials, and 25 percent of the next $2,000. What if your total tax bill is less than the total credit you're claiming? The American Opportunity credit is partly refundable.

You can't claim the American Opportunity Tax Credit at higher income levels. In 2015 and 2016, the credit phases out if you're married filing jointly and your income is between $160,000 and $180,000. If you're single or head of household, the phase-out range is $80,000 to $90,000. The credit can't be claimed if you're married filing separately.

You also can't claim the American Opportunity Tax Credit and the Lifetime Learning Credit, discussed next, for the same student in the same tax year. If you're eligible for both, you'll probably want to take the American Opportunity credit, which is more valuable. The Lifetime Learning Credit is more likely to be claimed by graduate students, who may have already used up their four years of the American Opportunity credit.

In addition, you can't claim the American Opportunity Tax Credit for expenses paid for with another tax break, such as a tax-free withdrawal from a 529 college savings plan or Coverdell education savings account. Faced with that choice, you would be better off taking the credit. Unless Congress acts, the American Opportunity Tax Credit will expire at year-end 2017, at which point it will be replaced by the less valuable Hope Scholarship Tax Credit.

101. LIFETIME LEARNING CREDIT

The American Opportunity Tax Credit is designed to help students pay for four years of undergraduate education. The Lifetime Learning Credit is geared toward those studying later in life: While it can be claimed for undergraduate expenses, it's more likely to be used for graduate school or professional degree courses. There's no limit on the number of years that you can claim the Lifetime Learning Credit.

The credit is worth up to $2,000 in 2015 and 2016. To hit the maximum, you would need $10,000 of qualified expenses, on which you can then claim a 20 percent tax credit, which is how you get to $2,000. Unlike the American Opportunity Tax Credit, the Lifetime Learning Credit is a per-tax-return credit, not per student, and it isn't refundable if it exceeds your tax liability.

The Lifetime Learning Credit isn't available to taxpayers with higher incomes. In 2015 and 2016, the credit phases out between $110,000 and $130,000 if you're married filing jointly, and between $55,000 and $65,000 if you're single or head of household. You can't claim the credit if you're married filing separately.

If you have exhausted your four years of the American Opportunity Tax Credit and your income is too high for the Lifetime Learning Credit, see whether you might be eligible for the Tuition and Fees Deduction, which could allow you to deduct up to $4,000 of qualified education expenses— assuming the deduction is revived by Congress. The Tuition and Fees Deduction, which will disappear for the 2015 tax year unless Congress acts, is available at somewhat higher income levels than the Lifetime Learning Credit. The deduction phases out between $130,000 and $160,000 if you're married filing jointly and between $65,000 and $80,000 if you're single or head of household.

PART V

FAMILY
PAYING THE PRICE
FOR PROTECTING LOVED ONES

L et's be honest: Nobody likes buying insurance, drawing up a will or thinking about replacing the roof.

There's a certain pleasure associated with saving for retirement, college or a house down payment. You get that enjoyable sense of progress as you watch your account balances balloon, plus the goals themselves are exciting. There is, alas, no such pleasure when rigging up your family's financial safety net. It's all about thinking through the bad stuff that might happen and then playing defense as best you can.

That brings us to a crucial notion many folks fail to grasp: When we talk about protecting loved ones, we're talking about fending off major financial threats to you and those who depend on you financially. For instance, the death of a child is a terrible thing. But unless your children are Hollywood stars, probably neither you nor anybody else depends on them financially. That means it doesn't make sense to buy insurance on your children's lives. Insurance salves financial wounds. It doesn't fix broken hearts.

Similarly, it would be bad if your television went kaput. But in all likelihood, you can afford to buy a new one, so you probably shouldn't buy the extended warranty. Insurance is about getting somebody else to shoulder risks you can't afford to shoulder yourself. A bum television doesn't fall into that category.

Your goal: Rig up a safety net that protects your family against major financial threats—and then stop there, knowing that money devoted to your safety net is a cost that will leave you with less for other goals. So what steps should you take to protect your family? Consider focusing on four areas: preparing for financial emergencies, getting the right insurance coverage, protecting against lawsuits and organizing your estate. The first three topics are tackled in this chapter. Estate planning is dealt with in Part XIII.

102. DOS AND DON'TS FOR 2016

Want to make sure your family is adequately protected against financial disaster? Here are some "to dos" for 2016:

• Compare your emergency fund to your monthly living expenses. Try to fatten up your emergency reserve if it's equal to less than three months' living expenses or if you fear you could lose your job.

• Look into cutting your insurance costs by raising the deductibles on your health, homeowner's and auto policies, and extending the elimination period on your disability and long-term-care insurance.

• If you have more than $1 million in investable assets, consider whether you have enough saved to handle life's financial disasters without help from life, disability and long-term-care insurance.

And here are some things not to do:

• Don't renew your health insurance through the federal or a state exchange without checking to see whether there's an alternative policy that offers better value.

• Don't buy cash-value life insurance solely because you think it'll be a good investment. The costs involved mean your cash value won't grow that fast—and you would likely be better off funneling the dollars into a regular retirement account.

• Don't roll over retirement savings from a 401(k) to an IRA if you fear you could be the target of a lawsuit.

103. EMERGENCY PLAN

Your plan for financial emergencies might have three components: a cash reserve, credit lines and low fixed living costs.

One rule of thumb says that, as an emergency reserve, you ought to keep six months' living expenses in conservative investments, such as a savings account or a money-market fund. This can be a heap of dough. For instance, if you make $75,000 a year, you might need to set aside $15,000 or $20,000 to cover your living expenses for half a year. Even if you're a diligent saver, it would likely take you at least a few years to accumulate that money. And once you have the money, it will probably languish in a savings account or a money-market fund earning precious little interest.

Could you make do with a smaller emergency reserve? You might hold less emergency money if you have easy access to borrowed money. We discuss credit lines and other ways to borrow in Part XII.

In addition, you might keep a smaller emergency reserve if you focus not on covering your family's total monthly living expenses, but on putting aside enough to cover just your family's fixed costs. The idea: If you lose your job or have some other type of financial emergency, you would slash discretionary spending and instead limit yourself to expenses that are absolutely necessary. The lower these fixed costs are, the less emergency money you would need. This notion is tackled in Part VI.

In the end, the size of your emergency fund will likely hinge on one question: How secure is your job?

104. HOW BIG AN EMERGENCY FUND?

Do you really need an emergency fund equal to six months' living expenses? Partly, that's a matter of personal preference and hence how much you need to set aside to feel financially secure. But you should also give some thought to your job situation.

While you might tap your emergency fund to pay for a major car or home repair, the No. 1 reason to have an emergency fund is to cover a prolonged period of unemployment. Indeed, if you're retired and don't rely on a regular paycheck, you arguably don't need a separate emergency reserve.

Still in the workforce? If your job is tenuous or you're self-employed, you may need the full six months of emergency money and perhaps more. But if your job is reasonably secure, you might keep just three months' living expenses in a savings account. Similarly, you might opt for a smaller emergency fund if your spouse also works, unless there's a risk you could both lose your jobs at the same time because you work for the same company or in the same industry.

JONATHAN'S TAKE: As you save for retirement and other goals, you may find yourself socking away money not just in 401(k) plans and individual retirement accounts, but also in a regular taxable account. You can tap that taxable account at any time without worrying about the 10 percent tax penalty that's typically levied on retirement account withdrawals before age 59½. As your taxable account grows, keeping a separate emergency fund may seem unnecessary. After all, if you lost your job, you could always dip into some of the retirement money you have in your regular taxable account.

105. INSURANCE

Insurance is a great way to cope with life's major financial risks—dangers such as getting sued, suffering a disability or dying prematurely and leaving your family in the lurch. Think of it as a way of pooling risk. You buy coverage from an insurance company, but what you're essentially doing is tossing dollars into a pot with other people. Those who suffer misfortune collect from the pot. Everybody else gets nothing back, which is usually what you want, because it's a sign that life is good.

While insurance is a great way to fend off life's major financial risks, it's far less appealing as a way of coping with lesser threats or when it's twinned with some sort of investment vehicle. We'll discuss this notion further in the pages ahead as we tackle the seven key types of insurance: health, life, disability, long-term care, auto, homeowner's and umbrella liability.

Any one of these policies might be affordable. But if you buy them all, you may find yourself blowing the family budget—unless you think carefully about how to tweak each policy. Those tweaks might include buying no more coverage than is really necessary, raising deductibles and opting for long elimination periods. The latter is the time you have to wait between making a claim and starting to receive benefits. The goal is to make sure you're covered for the major threats that could derail your financial future, while standing ready to pay smaller costs out of pocket.

One housekeeping tip: Make a point of keeping the latest copy of all insurance statements, and let family members know where they're located. Unless you have an outstanding claim or expect to make one, there's no need to keep old insurance policies.

106. HEALTH INSURANCE

The 2010 Patient Protection and Affordable Care Act, otherwise known as Obamacare, hogged the headlines again in 2015, especially leading up to June's Supreme Court ruling that insurance subsidies could be provided in states that didn't set up their own health care exchange. Yet most folks were largely unaffected by Obamacare because they receive health insurance through their employer or they're covered by Medicare. Still, however you get coverage, you are likely noticing two trends.

First, as health care costs rise, there's a push to get individuals to pick up more of the tab. This is showing up in higher premiums, deductibles and co-pays, plus certain medical costs are no longer getting covered. Partly, this is about employers, the government and insurance companies shifting more of the expense to individuals. But there's also an effort to get individuals to appreciate just how much health care costs, so they aren't quite so quick to seek medical help.

Second, individuals are being offered more health insurance choices, so they're compelled to consider how much coverage they want and whether they are willing to pay the associated price. Obamacare slots health plans into four categories, each with different levels of coverage and sometimes sharply different premiums. Those age 65 and up can choose from among ten Medigap plans that supplement the basic coverage offered by Medicare. Alternatively, seniors can skip original Medicare and a companion Medigap policy, and instead go for a Medicare Advantage plan.

Meanwhile, many larger employers now offer two or more health plans, so employees have to decide whether, say, they want to pay more so they can see any doctor they wish, or whether they prefer to save money by sticking with a limited group of physicians and seeking authorization for some medical services.

107. EMPLOYER HEALTH PLANS

At most employers, gone are the days when you paid little for health insurance and you could see pretty much any doctor you wanted. You may still be able to pick a plan that gives you ample flexibility, but you'll likely pay a steep price for the privilege.

Fortunately, this is an area where you can legally trade on inside information. Do you or other family members go to the doctor frequently? How much do you value the ability to see any doctor you want? How many, if any, regular prescriptions do you have? Do you expect to need a particular procedure in the year ahead?

If you have a choice in health plans, you can take all this family information and weigh which plan makes most sense, given the deductibles, co-payments for each doctor's visit, prescription drug benefit and network of doctors available to plan participants.

Your employer may also offer a flexible spending account, which you can fund out of pretax dollars and then use for medical costs not covered by the insurance company. When your employer's open enrollment period for benefits rolls around toward the end of the year, consider what health costs you might incur in the year ahead that won't be covered by the insurance company, and then use that to guide how much you contribute to the spending account.

Planning to change jobs? Until your new employer's coverage kicks in or until you purchase insurance through one of the health care exchanges, you may be able to continue your old employer's plan for a while, thanks to something called COBRA coverage.

108. HEALTH CARE ACCOUNTS

There are two types of tax-favored health care account, and they're sometimes confused. First, your employer may offer a flexible spending account, or FSA, which you can use to pay for health care expenses—such as deductibles and co-payments—that aren't covered by your employer's health plan. These accounts are funded out of pretax income, so you avoid income taxes on the money involved. Each year, employees commit to funding these accounts up to a dollar amount they choose, though that sum can't be greater than $2,550 in 2016.

Keep in mind that, with money in these accounts, it's "use it or lose it." The accounts typically need to be emptied by Dec. 31, though employers are allowed to offer a grace period that extends until mid-March. Alternatively, employers can stick with the Dec. 31 cutoff but allow employees to roll over as much as $500 from one year to the next.

What's the second type of account? If you have a high-deductible health insurance policy, you may get the chance to fund a health savings account, or HSA. Currently, to qualify, a plan must have a deductible of at least $1,300 if you're single and $2,600 if the coverage is for a family. If you have a qualifying plan, you can make tax-deductible contributions in 2016 of as much as $3,350 to an HSA if you're single and $6,750 if you have a family plan. You can contribute an additional $1,000 if you're age 55 and older.

Withdrawals used for qualifying medical expenses are tax-free. But every year, unlike an FSA, you don't need to empty the account largely or entirely. Instead, you can leave the money to grow and use it tax-free for future medical expenses, including medical expenses in retirement.

You can also use the money for other reasons, though you'll have to pay income taxes on your withdrawals and, if you are under age 65, a 20 percent tax penalty. Unlike with a traditional IRA or other retirement accounts, you aren't required to take minimum annual distributions starting at age 70½.

109. COBRA

If you leave your job and your employer has 20 or more employees, you will likely be able to continue your employer's coverage for up to 18 months at your own expense. You will be sent a so-called COBRA notice, named after the Consolidated Omnibus Budget Reconciliation Act, giving you 60 days to decide whether you want the coverage.

Your employer can charge you 102 percent of the premium it currently pays. That might turn out to be a large sum. Still, you will be able to continue coverage for a while, without worrying about immediately finding a new health plan.

The 60-day decision period opens the door to a small potential cost savings. During those 60 days, you will have coverage if you have a medical issue—at which point, if you see a doctor, you would need to pay for COBRA coverage. But if you don't use any medical services during those 60 days, you might decide not to continue coverage and instead buy insurance elsewhere to cover you after the 60 days are up. In effect, that would give you 60 days of free coverage.

If you aren't getting coverage through a new employer, where should you turn for health insurance? That's where the 2010 Affordable Care Act comes in. A policy bought through your state's health care exchange will likely be cheaper than COBRA coverage. Nonetheless, it may be worth paying to keep your old employer's coverage through the end of the year if you have already met the policy's deductibles or out-of-pocket maximums for the year, or you're getting close. If you buy a new policy, you'll have new deductibles and out-of-pocket maximums to meet.

110. OBAMACARE

Here are the basics of the 2010 Affordable Care Act:

• Most U.S. citizens and legal residents are required to have health insurance. Tax penalties are levied on those who don't.

• If you don't have health insurance through your employer and you aren't covered by Medicaid, you can typically receive a premium tax credit to help with insurance costs if your income is up to four times the federal poverty level. To see whether you qualify, try the subsidy calculator offered by the Kaiser Family Foundation at KFF.org.

• If your income is at or below 138 percent of the federal poverty level, you may qualify for Medicaid, which has been expanded in many—but not all—states.

• You cannot be denied coverage because of preexisting conditions.

• Families can purchase coverage either through state-based insurance exchanges or directly from insurers. But to receive the premium tax credit, you have to use an exchange.

• All plans are categorized as bronze, silver, gold or platinum, depending on the level of coverage offered.

• Children can remain on their parents' plan through age 26.

To get a quick overview of what Obamacare means for your family, head to AARP's HealthLawAnswers.org.

111. HEALTH CARE EXCHANGES

Roughly a third of states offer their own health care exchange. Residents of other states can use the exchange set up by the federal government at HealthCare.gov. If you shop for health insurance on your own, you don't have to buy through the exchanges. In almost all states, you can also purchase policies directly from insurance companies or through an insurance agent.

Sidestepping the exchanges probably won't save you money. Indeed, if you purchase policies outside the exchanges, you won't receive the tax credit that you might be eligible for. Still, shopping outside the exchanges could give you a wider choice. You can find policies, including those not offered through the exchanges, at sites such as eHealthInsurance.com and GoHealth.com. According to eHealthInsurance's eHealth Price Index, the average monthly premium in late November 2015 for policies meeting the Affordable Care Act criteria was $356 for individuals and $871 for families.

Policies bought both inside and outside the exchanges must include the same essential benefits, and all must be categorized as bronze, silver, gold or platinum. Moreover, the same key principle applies: It's illegal for an insurer to deny coverage because of preexisting conditions.

As you pick among policies, think carefully about the annual deductibles—which could be $2,000 or $3,000—and out-of-pocket maximums, and how you would meet that cost if you had a year with major medical expenses. For a health care policy to comply with the Affordable Care Act in 2016, the maximum out-of-pocket medical cost is $6,850 for individuals and $13,700 for families. This maximum, which doesn't include the monthly premiums paid to buy the policy, should help many folks avoid excessive medical debt—and it ought to be a factor when deciding how big an emergency fund you need.

112. MEDICARE

Are you approaching age 65, when you become eligible for Medicare? Spend some time perusing Medicare.gov, the federal government website. Here's what you'll discover:

• You typically aren't charged a premium for Medicare Part A, which helps cover hospital bills, a skilled nursing facility for a limited time, hospice care and some home health services.

• You are charged a premium for Part B, which covers doctor's visits, surgeries, lab tests and supplies such as walkers and wheelchairs. In 2016, most folks will pay a monthly premium of $104.90. Because of a technicality, roughly 30 percent of Medicare recipients—including those with high incomes, who are newly enrolled in Medicare or who aren't yet receiving Social Security—faced potentially steep premiums for 2016, but Congress capped the increase at 15 percent as part of the October 2015 budget deal. You also pay a monthly premium for Part D, the prescription drug program.

• In addition to the monthly premiums, you may rack up substantial out-of-pocket medical costs. To cover some of those costs, you can buy a Medigap policy, for which you'll pay an additional premium.

• Instead of so-called original Medicare, with its Parts A and B, you can opt for a Medicare Advantage plan. Also known as Part C, Medicare Advantage plans are privately run health plans for retirees. Many of these plans operate like a health maintenance organization, or HMO, which means you have less choice in the doctors you can see.

• Original Medicare doesn't cover dental care, eyeglasses, long-term care, over-the-counter medicines and hearing aids. Some Medicare Advantage plans cover items like vision and dental care. But like original Medicare, they don't cover all medical services—especially the biggest potential expense, which is a long stay in a nursing home.

Even with Medicare, retirees face substantial out-of-pocket medical costs. AARP figures that Medicare only covers half of beneficiaries' total health care costs. The Kaiser Family Foundation calculates that households on Medicare spend an average $4,722 on health care expenses each year. That's equal to 14 percent of their total spending, versus 5 percent for other households. Fidelity Investments estimated that a 65-year-old couple retiring in 2015 would spend an average $245,000, in today's dollars, on their retirement medical costs—not including the cost of long-term care.

113. MEDICARE PART A

Medicare Part A covers in-patient hospital care and the services you might need immediately after, whether at home, at a hospice or at a skilled nursing facility. For instance, Medicare might cover costs for a nursing facility while you are rehabilitating from an injury. It won't cover a nursing home if all you're receiving is custodial care, which involves help with daily living activities such as dressing, eating and bathing.

If you are already receiving Social Security retirement benefits, you will be automatically enrolled in Parts A and B at age 65. If not, you can sign up during a seven-month window that begins three months before you turn age 65. To enroll, visit your local Social Security office, apply online at SocialSecurity.gov or call 800-772-1213. To ensure that coverage for Parts A and B starts in the month you turn 65, you will want to sign up during the three months before your birthday.

Those who are eligible to receive any sort of monthly Social Security benefit, including spousal benefits, are also eligible to receive Part A for free, so there's usually no reason for Social Security recipients not to sign up. While you may not pay a premium for Part A, you will need to meet deductibles and make co-payments.

What if you are employed when you turn age 65? You can still sign up. If you don't, you can take advantage of a special eight-month enrollment period that typically starts when your employment ends. If you sign up during this period, you won't pay any penalty for signing up late. That penalty, in any case, is only an issue for those who aren't eligible to receive Part A for free.

114. MEDICARE PART B

While Part A covers in-patient hospital care and many expenses incurred during the aftermath, Part B covers outpatient care, including doctor's visits, diagnostic tests and medical equipment. A 20 percent co-insurance fee is charged for many services provided under Part B.

If you are receiving Social Security benefits, you will be contacted a few months before you turn age 65 with information about Medicare. You will then be automatically enrolled in Part B unless you opt out. Typically, you would want to opt out only if you're still working and covered by your employer's plan.

What if you aren't yet receiving Social Security? If you are retired, you should sign up for Medicare B by contacting Social Security during the seven-month initial enrollment period that starts three months before you turn 65. If you are retired and don't sign up during this initial enrollment period, your Medicare B premium may be permanently higher when you eventually enroll. That penalty is equal to 10 percent extra for every 12-month period that you could have been enrolled but weren't.

What if you are still employed? Signing up at age 65 and paying Part B's premium may not be necessary if you and—if married—your spouse are covered by your employer's plan. Instead, you can take advantage of a special eight-month enrollment period that typically starts when your employment ends. If you sign up during this period, you won't pay a penalty for enrolling late.

Your premium for Part B will be deducted from your Social Security check. What if you aren't yet receiving Social Security because you're delaying benefits to get a larger monthly benefit? Instead of writing a check for your Part B premium every month, you can arrange to have the premium automatically deducted from your checking or savings account.

115. MEDICARE ADVANTAGE

Original Medicare is a traditional fee-for-service program that allows seniors to get treatment from any hospital or doctor that accepts Medicare patients. But in recent years, an alternative has sprung up: Medicare Advantage plans.

These plans grew out of the Medicare law passed by Congress in 2003, which also authorized the Part D drug benefit. That law established new rules for private insurers that want to offer plans that compete with original Medicare, with its Part A and B. Today, roughly 30 percent of Medicare beneficiaries are in Medicare Advantage plans.

Many of the plans are some form of managed care. You might be covered only if you use the plan's network of doctors or, alternatively, you could be covered if you go to an out-of-network doctor, but you will pay more.

Medicare Advantage plans combine almost everything offered in original Medicare's Part A and B, plus the plans often include Part D prescription drug coverage. In addition, you don't need to buy a Medigap policy (and, in fact, insurers are barred from selling Medigap policies to those enrolled in Medicare Advantage). You pay a monthly premium for all of this, though your premium will often be lower than the combined premiums for original Medicare Part B and D, plus a Medigap policy.

Intrigued? You can find plans in your area using the Medicare Plan Finder at Medicare.gov. Before you sign up for a Medicare Advantage plan, check to see which of your doctors are in the plan's network. Unhappy with your Medicare Advantage plan? It's possible to return to original Medicare, though you may not be able to get the Medigap policy you want.

116. MEDICARE'S PRESCRIPTION DRUG BENEFIT

Part D drug plans are offered through insurance companies. While most seniors will want to enroll, it isn't mandatory. You will pay a premium, plus there's an annual deductible and a co-payment on each prescription that's filled. The plans don't cover all drugs. Rather, they are required to cover at least two drugs in each therapeutic category.

If you wait beyond age 65 to enroll in Part D, you may pay a penalty unless you were, in the intervening period, receiving a prescription drug benefit from elsewhere that was equally good. The penalty is equal to a permanent 1 percent increase in the base premium for every month you delay, so 10 months of procrastination will cost you a 10 percent higher premium for the rest of your retirement. Result: Even if you don't currently have any prescription drug needs, you will likely want to enroll at age 65.

As you shop for a plan, see whether the drugs you take are covered by the plan and at what cost. The list of covered drugs is known as the "formulary." Need help choosing a Medicare drug plan? Check out the Medicare Plan Finder at Medicare.gov.

117. MEDIGAP INSURANCE

Once you enroll in Medicare Part B, you have six months to choose the Medigap policy you want. During this six-month window, you can't be denied coverage or charged a higher premium because of past or current health issues. If you wait until later, insurers can use medical underwriting, which means policies could cost significantly more, depending on the state of your health, and you may not be able to get the policy you want.

Medigap insurance—sometimes called Medicare supplement insurance—comes in 10 standardized policies, except in Massachusetts, Minnesota and Wisconsin, which have a different set of policies. Depending on the Medigap policy you choose, you will receive help with various deductibles, co-payments and other gaps in Medicare's coverage.

For instance, a Medigap policy might cover your Part A deductible, the co-insurance for a skilled nursing facility or your Part B deductible. It might also cover you while you are traveling outside the U.S. Be sure to shop around: Premiums for the same Medigap policy can vary widely. To search for Medigap policies offered in your state, try the Medigap Policy Search tool at Medicare.gov.

It's possible to change Medigap policies, but tread carefully. Depending on the circumstances, there could be medical underwriting involved, you might pay significantly more and you may not be covered for preexisting conditions for up to six months. Don't cancel your old policy until you receive written notification that you've been accepted for the new policy.

While Medigap policies can plug many of the holes in Medicare, none of them plugs the biggest hole—coverage for custodial care at a nursing home. For that, folks will need to pay out of pocket, get long-term-care insurance or fall back on Medicaid, and sometimes a combination of all three.

118. MEDICAID

Medicaid is a means-tested program that provides hospital and medical coverage for those with low incomes and limited resources. It's funded by the federal and state governments, but the program is run by the states. Each state has its own rules about who is eligible and what is covered under Medicaid. The program provides comprehensive medical coverage—in some instances, more comprehensive than Medicare. Depending on the state, those who are eligible for Medicaid may be charged modest amounts for some services. A majority of Medicaid recipients are in managed-care programs run by private health plans.

While Medicaid is means-tested, income hasn't historically been the sole criteria for eligibility. You also needed to fall into certain categories, such as children in low-income families, the parents of these children, pregnant women, certain people with disabilities and low-income seniors.

Under the 2010 Affordable Care Act, Medicaid was greatly expanded so that states could offer coverage to those under age 65 with incomes at or below 138 percent of the federal poverty level. But fearful that the expansion would eventually be a burden on state budgets, almost half of all states have declined federal financing to expand Medicaid coverage.

In 2012, 22 percent of Medicaid recipients were seniors or those with disabilities, but they accounted for 64 percent of Medicaid spending, according to the Center on Budget and Policy Priorities. Indeed, Medicaid covers more than 60 percent of all nursing home residents. But qualifying for a Medicaid-paid nursing home involves meeting strict financial criteria—and will likely mean your heirs will receive little or nothing.

119. NURSING HOME COSTS

A majority of seniors will spend little or no time in a nursing home. Among those age 65 and older, 44 percent of men and 58 percent of women will need nursing home care, according to a November 2014 study by Boston College's Center for Retirement Research. But the average stay is less than 11 months for men and 15 months for women. In fact, 50 percent of nursing home stays for men and 39 percent for women last less than three months, which means Medicare—not Medicaid—likely paid the cost.

What if you stay longer? If you have few assets, Medicaid should pick up most of the tab. What if you have some savings? You could quickly deplete your nest egg: According to Genworth's 2015 Cost of Care Survey, the average annual cost of a semi-private nursing home room is $80,000. You might pay $281,000 in Alaska, $132,000 in New York, $89,000 in California and $88,000 in Florida, but just $51,000 in Texas. Nursing homes in big cities tend to be especially pricey.

Ideally, you will have enough saved by retirement so you can pay nursing home costs out of pocket and skip long-term-care insurance (or "self-insure," as financial experts sometimes call it). But that option is probably only open to those with seven-figure portfolios. What about everybody else? You might plan on applying for Medicaid to pay any nursing home costs. Problem is, to qualify, you will first have to spend down most of your assets.

That might not seem so terrible if you have little money. But if you have done a moderately good job of saving for retirement and have, say, a $400,000 or $500,000 portfolio, it is hardly an attractive prospect. What's the alternative? You might look into long-term-care insurance, including hybrid policies that combine life and long-term-care insurance.

While both men and women need to consider how they will pay for long-term care, it's a particularly pressing issue for women. Because they typically live longer than men, they will often find themselves looking after an ailing husband. But when they need care, they're on their own—and a nursing home may be the only option.

120. LONG-TERM-CARE INSURANCE

Long-term-care insurance has proven to be a problematic product. Many insurers have dropped out of the market. Others have jacked up premiums, making coverage unaffordable for both potential and current policyholders. A 2015 study by Boston College's Center for Retirement Research found that, among those who have long-term-care insurance at age 65, more than a third let their policies lapse, thus losing all benefits. One key reason: The premiums become too much of a financial burden.

Thinking of buying a policy? The younger you are when you buy a policy, the less likely you are to be rejected for health reasons and the lower the annual premium. But you'll pay those premiums for more years, plus there's more time for the insurance company to drop out of the market or tinker with the policy. One possible strategy: As you approach retirement, drop your disability and life insurance—and put those premiums toward long-term-care insurance instead.

Many folks purchase policies that will cover maybe three years of nursing home costs. Arguably, that's the wrong approach. Using savings, you might be able to afford a year or two in a nursing home. Instead, the big risk is spending five years or more in a nursing home. With that in mind, you might purchase a policy that will pay benefits for more years but hold down costs by opting for a long elimination period, such as six months or a year, which is the initial period when you have to cover costs before the insurance company starts paying.

You'll also need to decide what daily benefit you want, which is the maximum dollar amount the policy will pay each day you need care. To settle on the right number, think about how much you can afford out of pocket. For instance, between Social Security and portfolio income, you might be able to cover half the daily cost of a nursing home. You could then buy a policy that covers the rest. If married, consider a "shared benefit" rider that allows each spouse to use the other's benefit if one of you runs through the maximum benefit on your individual policy.

In addition, pay careful attention to the details. For a policy to start paying, what are the triggers? Usually, you have to display cognitive impairment or need help with at least two "activities of daily living," such as eating, bathing and getting dressed. See if the daily benefit rises each year with inflation. Find out what's covered if you opt for in-home care or if you're in an assisted living facility, rather than a traditional nursing home.

What if you buy a policy and the premiums rise so much that it becomes unaffordable? Rather than dropping the policy, talk to the insurer about whether you can keep the premium the same by reducing the size of the benefit. That isn't ideal—but at least you'll have some coverage after all those years of premium payments.

121. HYBRID INSURANCE POLICIES

Instead of purchasing pure long-term-care insurance, you could buy cash-value life insurance that offers long-term-care benefits. We discuss cash-value policies later in this chapter. If you need to pay for a nursing home, you could tap into the death benefit—and sometimes receive even more, depending on the policy—to cover long-term-care costs. If you don't end up in a nursing home, the policy's proceeds pass to your heirs.

A hybrid policy may appeal to folks who hate the idea of paying years of premiums for long-term-care insurance, but never getting anything back. It is, however, also a costly way to protect yourself. After all, you are buying life insurance at an advanced age, which is an expensive proposition, and yet you may not need life insurance at that juncture, because you don't have dependents who would suffer financially if you died suddenly.

You can also purchase tax-deferred fixed annuities that have a long-term-care rider. If you don't need long-term care, the money continues to collect interest. If care is needed, you can usually get access to a sum equal to some multiple of your original annuity investment. With the fixed annuity, you avoid buying life insurance you may not need—but you will likely be locking up a large sum that will then earn modest returns.

122. MEDICAID AND NURSING HOME COSTS

Medicaid eligibility rules vary from state to state. Still, before Medicaid starts paying your nursing home expenses, you will be expected to put much of your income and assets toward covering the cost, no matter which state you live in.

A major exception is your primary home. Depending on the state, between $552,000 and $828,000 in home equity may be protected in 2015. The house should also be exempt if your spouse, children under age 21, or a blind or disabled child of any age live there. If you are married, the at-home spouse can often keep all income that's solely in his or her name. The spouse who isn't in a nursing home may also be eligible to keep up to $119,220 of the couple's joint assets in 2015 and, depending on the financial circumstances, retain up to $2,981 of the institutionalized spouse's monthly income.

To qualify for Medicaid, you might be tempted to transfer assets to family members. But those transfers need to occur more than five years before you apply for Medicaid or you could be penalized. Let's say you recently transferred $70,000 to your children and the monthly cost for a local nursing home is $7,000, so you effectively gifted 10 months' worth of nursing home expenses. Even if you are eligible for Medicaid based on your current financial situation, Medicaid won't pay your nursing home costs for 10 months after you apply for assistance.

After you die or, if married, after your spouse dies, federal law requires that your state try to recover your Medicaid-paid nursing home costs from your estate. States also have the option to try to recover other Medicaid costs. Want more information? Head to Medicaid.gov.

123. LIFE INSURANCE

Wealthy families sometimes purchase life insurance to save on estate taxes. We discuss that in Part XIII. The chief reason to buy life insurance, however, is to provide for your family if you die prematurely.

With that goal in mind, think about who depends on you financially and how they would cope if you keeled over tomorrow. If you're single and don't support anybody, you probably don't need life insurance. Similarly, if you're married, the kids have left home, and you and your spouse are in good shape for retirement, you may not need coverage.

Instead, life insurance is crucial for those who have, say, young children, a stay-at-home spouse and few assets. If that describes you, you likely need a fair amount of life insurance—and yet 37 percent of Americans with children under age 18 don't have any, according to a 2015 Bankrate.com study. Among parents with life insurance, a third have $100,000 of coverage or less.

How much should you have? Experts sometimes advise buying enough insurance to cover your family's entire costs until the kids are through college, which is potentially a huge amount—and the insurance premiums may be unaffordable. Alternatively, one rule of thumb suggests you need coverage equal to five-to-seven times your income. That's more likely to fit within your family's budget, but it doesn't reflect your individual circumstances, including how old your children are, how much debt you have, the wealth you've accumulated and whether your spouse works.

What's the right answer? You might try the Life Wizard insurance planning tool offered by TIAA-CREF.org. More than anything, it's important to have at least some coverage. If you're the main breadwinner and you die, your family will likely have to make big changes. You want them to have money to carry them through this transition period. That might mean enough insurance to pay off the mortgage, fund college accounts and cover a few years of living expenses. If you have very young children and your spouse stays home to look after them, you may also want insurance on your spouse's life, because you would face added expenses if he or she died.

Once you decide how much life insurance to buy, next comes a big issue: Should you buy term or permanent life insurance?

124. TERM LIFE INSURANCE

Looking for a low-cost policy that will deliver a big payout to your family if you die prematurely? Term insurance, which provides a death benefit and nothing more, will likely be your best bet.

When you first buy, you typically need to take a medical exam. Many term policies are convertible into permanent life insurance. Most are one of two types: annual renewable term or level-premium term.

Level-term policies are priced so you pay the same premium every year for, say, 10, 15 or 20 years. You may be able to continue coverage beyond the end of the policy's term, but another medical exam might be required. If your health has deteriorated, that could create serious problems. To sidestep this issue, before you first purchase a policy, think carefully about how long you'll need coverage for. Don't skimp by buying insurance with a shorter term than you really need.

Meanwhile, with annual renewable term, the premium rises each year as you grow older. But these policies can give you more flexibility. They may be renewable up until age 95, with no further medical exam necessary.

Even if you can renew your term insurance late in life, you probably won't want to—because at that point the premiums can be exorbitant. But by then, you will likely no longer need coverage because your children will be out of the house, and you and your spouse should have enough socked away for retirement.

You might also hear about a third type of term policy: return-of-premium term life insurance. With these policies, if you live until the end of the term—which might be 20 or 30 years—some or all of your premiums are returned to you. That feature, however, means that the premiums on these policies are significantly higher than those on annual renewable term or level-premium term.

125. PERMANENT LIFE INSURANCE

While most folks don't continue term insurance into retirement, permanent insurance is designed to provide lifetime coverage. Also known as cash-value life insurance, a permanent policy involves far higher premiums, because part of each premium goes into an investment account. When you die, the investment account's cash value is used to pay the policy's stated death benefit. If the cash value is less than the death benefit, the difference is paid by the insurance company and represents pure insurance, just like a term policy.

In the early years of a cash-value policy, not much of your premium payment gets added to the cash value, partly because the salesperson's commission comes out of those early payments and partly because so much pure insurance needs to be bought. But as time goes on, more and more of each premium payment gets put toward the cash value. This is reminiscent of a mortgage with its shifting mix of principal and interest, which we discuss in Part XII.

Thanks to the buildup in cash value, you don't have to buy so much pure insurance when you're older and life insurance becomes so much more costly. Result: Cash-value life insurance can be affordable in old age, while term insurance isn't.

The proceeds from a life insurance policy are income-tax-free to your beneficiaries. What if you need to tap into a cash-value policy during your lifetime? You may be able to withdraw a sum equal to the amount you put into the policy, with no taxes owed. Alternatively, you could take out a policy loan, though the loan will likely charge an interest rate that's higher than the return your cash value is earning. Both withdrawals and any loans outstanding at your death will reduce the policy's death benefit.

126. THREE TYPES OF PERMANENT INSURANCE

Intrigued by cash-value life insurance? There are three varieties to choose from:

Whole life. This is the most conservative type of cash-value life insurance, with the insurer guaranteeing that your premiums will remain the same and that the policy's cash value will earn a minimum rate of interest. A whole-life policy can also earn additional dividends that help your cash value grow faster, though these additional dividends aren't guaranteed.

Lately, whole life has received a big push from advisors who advocate BYOB, or "be your own banker," which involves building up a whole-life policy and then using it as a source of borrowed money. But the benefits claimed are inflated, and some of the advice offered, such as reducing your 401(k) contributions so you can put more into a whole-life policy, is dubious at best.

Universal life. While a whole-life policy has a fixed interest rate, the interest paid by a universal life policy varies over time. With indexed universal life, which has recently surged in popularity, the interest you receive can be linked to the returns of a stock market index, often the S&P 500. Policyholders receive the S&P 500's gain, excluding dividends. The annual gain is capped, but you are also protected against losses. Universal life policies give holders some flexibility to vary premium payments and raise or reduce the death benefit.

Variable life. Instead of earning interest, a variable life policy allows you to invest the policy's cash value in a series of subaccounts, which are similar to stock and bond mutual funds. Many variable life policies are actually variable universal life, meaning they offer the flexibility to vary payments, like universal life. As stocks have rallied in recent years, sales of variable universal life have picked up.

If you aren't careful, cash-value life insurance's promise of lifetime coverage can break down. Suppose you take out a policy loan, cut back the premiums too much on a universal policy, make poor investment choices from among a variable policy's series of subaccounts or the interest rate drops sharply on a universal policy. In all of these situations, you may need to make big payments to keep the policy going—and without those big payments the policy could lapse or its death benefit could be sharply reduced.

127. INSURANCE COMPANIES

Insurance companies are either stock companies, meaning they are publicly traded and hence have outside shareholders, or they're mutual companies, which means they should be solely focused on helping policyholders. In practice, this oversimplifies the issue. Even a mutual company has multiple constituencies that it has to keep happy, notably its sales force and headquarter staff, including senior executives. Result: Just because you buy a cash-value policy from a mutual insurer doesn't mean that the salesperson isn't collecting a sizable commission or that the policy's ongoing costs will be low.

Still, it is worth keeping the distinction between stock and mutual insurers in mind if you're buying a whole-life insurance policy. Many such policies are so-called participating policies. That means they are eligible to receive dividends from the insurer. While stock companies also sell participating whole-life policies, a mutual insurer has the potential to make more generous dividend payments because it doesn't also need to compensate public shareholders. The largest mutual insurers include Guardian Life, Massachusetts Mutual, New York Life and Northwestern Mutual.

The distinction between stock and mutual companies is less important when purchasing other types of cash-value life insurance or buying term insurance. With these other policies, you should probably be more focused on the policy's cost and on the insurer's financial strength.

For instance, it's easy enough to get a bunch of term-insurance quotes with a quick online search. But before buying the policy with the lowest premium, check the insurer's rating for financial strength. Favor insurers that are rated A or better by A.M. Best, AA or better by Fitch, Aa2 or better by Moody's, and AA or better by Standard & Poor's. What if you're looking for cash-value life insurance? Comparing costs is harder. But you might check out Ameritas Life Insurance and TIAA-CREF. Both are rated highly for financial strength and have a reputation for selling lower-cost policies.

128. GREAT DEBATES: TERM OR CASH VALUE?

This is a debate between the confused and the self-interested. Ordinary consumers are typically confused by cash-value life insurance and leery of the steep premiums involved. Meanwhile, insurance salespeople are big proponents—but also biased, because cash-value policies pay them hefty commissions.

In pushing cash-value policies, salespeople tout the investment advantages, forced savings, chance to earn additional dividends and ability to borrow against the policy. But in the end, the case for life insurance rests on two unique advantages. First, it could salvage a family's financial future if the main breadwinner dies. Second, the proceeds are income-tax-free to the beneficiaries, and potentially also estate-tax-free. That's a key reason to buy a cash-value policy with the goal of having coverage at the end of your life, even if you die at a ripe old age.

Set against that tax advantage are three drawbacks. First, you probably don't need lifetime coverage. Instead, your need for life insurance will likely be over by your 50s or 60s because, by then, your kids will have left home and your spouse would have enough money if you died suddenly.

Second, because the premiums on a cash-value policy are so steep, you might skimp on the death benefit and leave your family in the financial lurch if you die prematurely. In fact, because the premiums are so steep, many policyholders drop their policies. The Society of Actuaries estimates that 39 percent of whole-life policies are terminated within the first 10 years. These folks would have incurred the steep upfront commissions charged by cash-value policies, but managed to accrue precious little cash value.

Third, if you're looking to invest, there are lower-cost options with better return potential than building up an insurance policy's cash value. For instance, you could fund a 401(k), with its initial tax deduction, tax-deferred growth and possible matching employer contribution.

What about that income-tax-free legacy for your heirs? If that's your goal, you could fund a Roth 401(k) or Roth IRA. The bottom line: Instead of paying the large premiums on cash-value life insurance, most folks would likely get better returns by buying low-cost term insurance and investing the money they save.

129. DISABILITY INSURANCE

Through their employer, many people have disability insurance, which provides them with income if they can't work. The term "disability" might suggest some sort of injury, but the vast majority of long-term work absences result from illnesses, such as heart disease or cancer. Don't have disability coverage through your employer? You might want to buy a policy on your own.

Think of it as protection for your human capital's income-earning ability. Disability insurance can be especially important for those who are single. While someone who is married can rely on the other spouse to keep bringing in a paycheck, you won't have that safety net if you're on your own.

Individual disability policies have elimination periods, such as 90 or 180 days, which is the time you have to wait for benefits to begin once you meet the policy's definition of being disabled. The longer the elimination period, the lower your premium will be. You can also hold down premiums by limiting the number of years that benefits are potentially paid and by reducing the monthly benefit amount. If you buy disability insurance on your own, using after-tax dollars, any benefits paid are tax-free. By contrast, if you have group coverage through your employer, any payout will be taxable.

Disability insurance is all about the details: You'll want to know whether the policy will pay you benefits if you can't do your current job or only if you can't do a similar job—or perhaps only if you can't work at all.

Disability benefits are also available from Social Security. But to receive them, your disability has to be sufficiently severe that it's expected to result in death or to prevent you from working for at least 12 months. Even then, once you're deemed eligible, you'll have to wait more than five months for payments to start.

130. AUTO INSURANCE

Many drivers view auto insurance as protection in case they wreck their car or the vehicle gets stolen. But the policies serve another, equally important purpose: They protect you in case you're sued. Here are the key elements of an auto policy:

Liability coverage. This tells you the maximum the policy will pay if you cause an accident in which somebody is hurt or which damages another vehicle or other property. Because of the risk of lawsuits, you may want to purchase an umbrella liability policy to provide additional protection. To qualify for umbrella coverage, the insurer may insist you raise the liability limits on your auto policy—which is probably a good idea.

Uninsured and underinsured driver coverage. This protects you if you're involved in an accident caused by another driver who either doesn't have insurance coverage or is underinsured. Even though you weren't responsible for the accident, your insurance company will often help pay your medical and auto repair bills if you have uninsured and underinsured driver coverage.

Collision and comprehensive. If you have an accident or your car is stolen, this covers the cost of repairing or replacing your own vehicle. Got a car that is only worth a few thousand dollars? You may want to drop collision and comprehensive coverage, because the financial loss would be modest if your car were totaled or stolen.

Deductibles. If you need collision and comprehensive coverage, consider raising the deductibles so you lower the premium. As always with insurance, the goal is to protect against big financial hits, not minor losses. You can also hold down your insurance costs by improving your credit score, maintaining a good driving record, claiming a low-mileage discount if you drive relatively little and favoring cars that are cheaper to insure. A sports car often comes with a large insurance bill, while minivans and SUVs are relatively inexpensive to insure.

131. HOMEOWNER'S INSURANCE

Homeowner's insurance protects your house and personal belongings against risks such as fire, falling trees, theft and water damage from burst pipes, while also providing coverage if someone has an accident at your home and sues you. But are you fully protected?

Take a look at the policy's coverage limits. Would you be able to rebuild your house for the sum specified—or should you call your insurer and ask that it be increased? Rebuilding could be far more costly than you imagine, in part because you would likely need to meet current building codes.

Homeowner's insurance typically caps how much it will pay out for specific items, such as jewelry, silverware, electronics, collectible coins, fine art and so on. If you have items that are especially valuable—meaning they're worth more than a few thousand dollars—you might talk to your insurance company about purchasing extra coverage.

Standard homeowner's insurance typically doesn't cover earthquakes or flooding caused by, say, an overflowing river or an ocean surge. Instead, you'll need a separate policy or a special rider to cover those risks. Damage caused by mudslides, sinkholes and riots also isn't covered, so you might obtain riders to cover these possibilities. If you operate a home business and have others regularly coming into your house, talk to your insurer about a special rider or a separate policy to cover the risks involved. In addition, in case you're sued, you may want umbrella liability coverage to supplement your homeowner's policy.

All this extra coverage will boost your premium payments. To offset that hit, you might look for ways to trim your premiums. For instance, you could raise the deductible on the policy from, say, $500 to $2,000. You might also qualify for a discount if you have smoke detectors, a sprinkler system, and a fire and burglary alarm system that alerts an outside service. In addition, you may get a discount if you buy a variety of policies, such as auto, home and umbrella liability coverage, from the same insurance company. Maintaining a good credit score can also help hold down your insurance costs.

132. RENTER'S INSURANCE

If you rent a house or apartment, your landlord's insurance policy might cover the building, but it typically won't cover your possessions. That is where renter's insurance can come in handy.

The policies cover personal possessions, including furniture, computers, televisions and jewelry. If these items are stolen or damaged by a fire or broken water pipes, you should be reimbursed either for the current cash value or for the replacement cost. A policy might provide $50,000 in total protection, with caps on certain categories, such as limiting jewelry coverage to $1,000 unless a special rider is purchased. Renter's insurance doesn't cover damage from floods caused by, say, heavy rains, and it may not cover hurricanes.

Many policies provide liability coverage in the event someone is injured at your home. This typically covers claims of up to $100,000, including the related legal costs. You may also receive living expenses if you're unable to live in the home for a period of time.

What if you figure your personal possessions aren't worth that much or replacing them won't cause that much of a financial burden? If that's the case, you may want to skip renter's insurance—unless your landlord insists you get a policy as a condition of renting the apartment.

133. ASSET PROTECTION

What does "asset protection" mean? It's about fending off creditors who have a legal claim on your assets. That claim might arise because you took on too much debt or because you ended up on the wrong end of a lawsuit. While these might seem like two quite different problems, in both cases you could end up filing for bankruptcy.

By the time bankruptcy or litigation is threatened, however, there isn't much you can do. It's probably too late to rearrange your finances by, say, gifting assets to your children. Such gifts could be deemed a fraudulent transfer. Instead, your best bet is to take steps now, before there's any hint of a financial claim against you. That's especially true if you're in an occupation that tends to attract legal claims, such as working as an accountant, doctor or lawyer. Lawsuits are also a risk if you work in real estate, including as an architect, builder or developer. What to do?

• Find out which assets enjoy creditor protection in your state and consider making the most of those assets. Your retirement accounts, and possibly your home, may be protected. A few minutes with an Internet search engine will likely turn up key details about the law in your state.

• Look into buying umbrella liability insurance to supplement whatever liability coverage you have through your auto, homeowner's or renter's policies.

• Think about whether your business life puts your investment accounts and other personal assets at risk and, if necessary, take steps to limit that risk.

• If you're wealthy, you might talk to an attorney about trust arrangements that can help protect your assets. Different trust arrangements are discussed in Part XIII.

What if you have already been slapped with a lawsuit or you're considering bankruptcy? You will need to hire a qualified attorney. Ask which assets enjoy creditor protection in your state. It might be ill-advised to move money into these assets now, but you also shouldn't pull money out. For instance, given the creditor protection enjoyed by retirement accounts, you don't want to use those accounts to pay legal bills and other expenses. If you fear a lawsuit, you should also immediately contact your insurance company to see if your various policies will provide liability coverage.

134. RETIREMENT ACCOUNTS

If you file for bankruptcy, the money in your retirement accounts should be protected from creditors. For employer-sponsored plans, such as 401(k) or 403(b) plans, the amount is unlimited. For IRAs, the protected sum is increased periodically and currently stands at $1,245,475. If you roll over money from an employer's plan into an IRA, this money should remain fully protected and not count toward the $1,245,475. But as a precaution, keep your rollover IRA in a separate account from your regular IRA.

What if somebody slips on your sidewalk and successfully sues you? Again, employer-sponsored plans should be protected. But solo 401(k) plans and IRAs, including rollover IRAs, are at risk under federal law. There's a good chance, however, that your state's law provides protection.

There are a few caveats to bear in mind. First, your retirement accounts aren't protected from the IRS if you owe federal taxes. Second, any money you withdraw from retirement accounts will no longer be protected, and creditors could seize it. Third, the Supreme Court ruled in 2014 that, if you file for bankruptcy, an inherited IRA isn't protected from creditors, unless you inherited the money from your spouse.

Retirement accounts aren't the only type of tax-sheltered account that's potentially off-limits to creditors. In some states, money in cash-value life insurance, annuities and 529 college plans also enjoys creditor protection.

135. HOMESTEAD EXEMPTION

The phrase "homestead exemption" occasionally refers to a break on property taxes that's available in some states. But at issue here is something quite different: In some states, you can't be forced to sell your home to satisfy the demands of creditors.

In states such as Alaska, California, Colorado and New Mexico, the amount of protection is capped at a relatively modest level. But in other states, such as Florida, Iowa, Kansas, South Dakota and Texas, the protection is quite broad.

A homestead exemption may help if you lose a lawsuit, have

nonmortgage debt or file for bankruptcy. But it only applies to your primary residence, not a second home. Moreover, it probably won't help you if you default on your mortgage or owe taxes.

Don't live in a state with a robust homestead exemption? You might see if you and your spouse can title your home and other assets as "tenancy by the entirety." This form of ownership is only available to married couples and only in some states. What's the advantage of tenancy by the entirety? You can't transfer your ownership stake without the consent of your spouse. That could prevent a forced sale of your home if one of you loses a lawsuit. It won't, however, help if you are both sued.

136. UMBRELLA LIABILITY INSURANCE

Got money in a regular taxable account? If you lose a lawsuit, the plaintiff won't have much trouble claiming that money—which is why you might want umbrella liability insurance, sometimes known as excess liability insurance.

With homeowner's and auto policies, a big chunk of your premium payment goes toward buying liability coverage. If somebody sues you because they're hurt at your home or because you cause an auto accident, your homeowner's and auto policies will cover your attorney's fees and any judgment against you. But the liability coverage may be capped at $250,000 or $300,000, and it could be significantly lower.

Plaintiffs might settle for that, rather than coming after your personal assets. But what if they demand more? That's where umbrella liability insurance comes in. It provides additional protection, perhaps $1 million or more, that's over and above what your homeowner's and auto policies provide. Umbrella liability insurance is typically purchased from the same insurer that covers your home and car.

In addition to providing protection if you're sued for damaging property or causing bodily injury, an umbrella policy can also cover other situations, such as if you're sued for slander or libel. Pay attention to the exclusions. For instance, the policies typically won't protect you if there's a legal claim resulting from your business or professional life, or if you deliberately damage somebody else's property.

Premiums seem to have increased a fair amount in recent years, but the policies remain relatively inexpensive compared to the potential payout. Got assets you're aiming to protect? It's worth looking into an umbrella policy.

137. BUSINESS LIABILITY

Just as you can purchase umbrella liability insurance to protect your personal life, there are policies that cover business liability. These might be part of a business owner's policy that also provides property coverage, or they can be bought separately.

General liability insurance typically covers bodily harm and property damage. But what about the risk that someone sues you for, say, behaving negligently or making a damaging mistake? For that, you might take out professional liability insurance such as the malpractice insurance purchased by doctors or the errors-and-omissions policies bought by lawyers, real estate brokers, consultants and others.

If you're self-employed or run a small business, you might also want to organize the business as a limited liability company or an S corporation, rather than operating it as a sole proprietorship. Why take that added step? If you run the business as a sole proprietorship, you could be personally liable if the business gets sued, while an LLC or S corporation can protect your personal finances from claims by creditors against the business. Typically, with an LLC or S corporation, you can't lose more than the money you put into the business.

While an LLC or S corporation can provide additional protection against creditors, it shouldn't make any difference from a tax point of view. If you operate a business as a sole proprietorship, you include the income and expenses of the business on your personal tax return, with the details listed on Schedule C. Similarly, both an LLC and S corporation are so-called pass-through entities, which means gains and losses pass directly through to the owners, who then include them on their personal tax returns.

Which is better, an LLC or S corporation? An LLC offers substantially more flexibility, involves less paperwork and may provide better protection if someone tries to seize your business stake to satisfy a personal debt. But if you envisage your business attracting venture capital funding and maybe even issuing shares to the public, you might use the S corporation structure because it's easier to turn an S corporation into a C corporation, the structure used by larger companies. Before making a decision, consider consulting a knowledgeable attorney, in part because there are differences in state law that could sway your decision.

PART VI

SPENDING

A WORD TO THE WISE
BEFORE YOU HEAD TO THE MALL

I f you come across a chapter on spending in a personal-finance book, you
should immediately be on high alert. There's a good chance the author is
about to berate you for spending too much and—horror of horrors—insist
that you create and follow a written budget.

So let's start with a basic truth: After exhaustive research, it's been
scientifically established that there are only three people in America who
draw up and follow detailed monthly budgets and, no, you wouldn't want to
go out for a drink with any of them.

What's the alternative? Consider a much simpler approach: Make sure
you save enough every month toward your various goals. If you do that,
there's no need to budget. Instead, you should feel free to spend your
remaining money on whatever takes your fancy. We'll tackle saving money
in Part VII.

That said, here are two suggestions: First, make sure you have some
sense for how much of your monthly spending goes toward fixed costs and
how much is discretionary. This can be crucial information if you find
yourself out of work, you get hit with large unexpected expenses or you're
figuring out how to generate enough retirement income. Second, think hard
about how you spend your money and what financial goals you pursue—
and make sure you're squeezing plenty of happiness from your hard-earned
dollars.

138. MAJOR EXPENSES

Some monthly expenses are pretty much unavoidable—and the two biggest are typically housing and transportation. On average, American families spend $18,000 a year on housing, according to the Bureau of Labor Statistics' Consumer Expenditure Survey that was released in September 2015. That's more than a third of the average American household's $53,500 in spending during 2014. Included in that figure are not just mortgage or rent, but also utilities, property taxes, furniture and appliances.

Don't forget that this is an average, one that's dragged down by those retirees who are living mortgage-free. For folks who just bought a house, often they'll be spending close to a third of their pretax income just on mortgage payments, homeowner's insurance and property taxes.

The BLS survey found that transportation eats up another $9,100 a year, or 17 percent of spending. This number takes into account vehicle purchases, gas, repairs and auto insurance, among other items. Add it up, and half our monthly spending is getting swallowed up by our cars and our homes.

We all need somewhere to live. Most of us need a car. The Federal Reserve's 2013 Survey of Consumer Finances found that 86.3 percent of families own a car or other vehicle. The question is, are you spending more on your home and transportation than is really sensible? You don't want to box yourself in financially by committing to fixed monthly costs that are too high. If you find yourself living paycheck to paycheck, take a close look at those fixed monthly expenses.

139. HOW OUR SPENDING HAS CHANGED

Over the past 50 years, we've seen two key changes in the way America spends, according to a June 2011 study by the Commerce Department's Bureau of Economic Analysis. First, we're devoting far less of our income to life's basics. Clothing, footwear, food and beverages accounted for just 11 percent of spending in 2009, down from 27.4 percent in 1959. This excludes restaurant meals, which have held fairly constant at around 6 percent of total expenditures.

Second, spending on health care, financial services and insurance has soared. For instance, health care rose from 5.9 percent of total spending in 1959 to an astonishing 19.7 percent in 2009. This includes hospital costs, doctor visits, prescription drugs and eyeglasses. Much of this cost wasn't paid directly by consumers, but rather by private insurers, Medicare and Medicaid.

Looking to spend less and save more? You should have plenty of leeway. Less of our income is needed to cover life's basics. Meanwhile, there are plenty of ways to cut your insurance costs, as you can learn in Part V, and also money-management costs, as you will discover in Part VIII. Health care is another area where you could potentially save money by exercising regularly, eating sensibly, not smoking, wearing a seat belt and taking other steps to look after your health.

140. SPENDING FOR FUN

How much do we spend on fun, broadly defined? Based on figures for 2014 from the Commerce Department's Bureau of Economic Analysis, it's a hefty sum.

U.S. households spent an average $4,100 on eating out and $1,300 on concerts, gym memberships, amusement parks, sports events, museums and movie theaters. We spent another $700 on cable and satellite television, $800 on tobacco, $1,000 on gambling, $1,000 on beer, wine and spirits, another $600 on alcohol when eating out, $700 on hotels and motels, and $1,100 on foreign travel.

Keep in mind that these are averages. For instance, the $800 average for tobacco lumps together both smokers and nonsmokers, so presumably the smokers are spending significantly more than $800 a year.

The Commerce Department looks at personal consumption using top-down economic data, while the Bureau of Labor Statistics' Consumer Expenditure Survey relies on individuals to report their own spending. How truthful are survey participants? It seems they aren't so truthful when it comes to spending on things like cigarettes and booze. According to the BLS survey for 2014, households reported spending $320 on tobacco and $460 on alcohol, far less than the Commerce Department's top-down data indicate.

It's important to spend money on things you enjoy—but it's also important to save enough for retirement and other goals. Saving enough? Keep spending as you are. Not saving enough? Maybe it's time to look closely not only at your fixed costs, but also at discretionary "fun money" spending.

141. DOS AND DON'TS FOR 2016

Want to get a handle on your monthly expenditures and whether all those dollars are being spent wisely? Here are some "to dos" for 2016:

• Calculate your monthly fixed living costs, including items like mortgage or rent, utilities, groceries and insurance premiums. How does this compare to your total income?

• Plan your next vacation months ahead of time. Research suggests that much of the pleasure from vacations comes from the anticipation.

• Count your blessings. You may be able to squeeze a little more happiness from your latest pay raise or last year's home remodeling if you pause for a moment and think how lucky you are.

And here are some things not to do:

• Don't make impulse purchases, especially if it's a major expenditure. We aren't very good at figuring out what will make us happy, so a cooling-off period before spending could come in handy.

• Don't take on a long commute without a lot of careful thought. Research tells us that commuting is terrible for happiness.

• Avoid living in a town where most of your neighbors will be richer. Bypass stores where you can barely afford to shop. Skip restaurants where you know the bill will be a nasty shock. If you put yourself in situations where you have less money than those around you, you'll likely feel unhappy.

142. FIXED VS. DISCRETIONARY EXPENSES

While it probably isn't necessary to track every dollar you spend, there is value in knowing one key number: How much of your monthly spending goes toward fixed costs.

We're talking here about the total monthly amount devoted to items such as mortgage or rent, property taxes, car payments, insurance premiums, student-loan payments, utilities, Internet access, phone and groceries. Given enough time, you could probably trim these fixed costs and, indeed, you might need to do that if you find you simply can't save enough for your various goals. Still, fixed costs are tough to reduce in the short term. By contrast, discretionary expenses—like vacations, entertainment and eating out—can be quickly eliminated if the need arises.

That need might arise if you find yourself out of work or you suddenly need to pay for, say, a major home or car repair. Until you find work or pay the repair bills, you might cut out discretionary expenses and instead limit your monthly spending to fixed costs. The amount of your fixed monthly costs might also help determine the size of your emergency fund, a topic we tackle in Part V.

In addition, knowing your monthly fixed costs is useful as you develop your retirement-income strategy. As discussed in Part II, you might endeavor to have enough regular monthly income from Social Security, any employer pensions, income annuities, dividends and interest to cover your fixed costs. That way, you can be reasonably confident you can pay the bills if there's a major slump in stock and bond prices.

143. KEEPING FIXED COSTS LOW

If you find it tough to save, the reason may not be lavish spending. Instead, there could be another explanation: Maybe your fixed monthly costs are too high, leaving you with little financial breathing room.

The biggest culprit is likely to be your mortgage or rent payment. For instance, if you live in a major city, it can be hard to find reasonably priced housing, even if you opt for a small place or a less desirable neighborhood. Alternatively, maybe you have boxed yourself in by committing to a slew of monthly payments, everything from car-lease payments to cell-phone plans to cable television.

Taken together, these fixed monthly costs can take a big chunk out of your income, especially if you're early in your career and not yet making decent money. What to do? You might aim to keep your fixed monthly costs at 50 percent or less of your gross (meaning pretax) income—and the lower, the better.

JONATHAN'S TAKE: I have come to believe that holding down fixed monthly living costs is perhaps the key contributor to financial success. If your fixed costs are low relative to your income, you will find it easier to save, you will be in better shape if you get laid off, you will need a smaller nest egg to retire in comfort and, if you become discontented with your current career, you'll have the financial flexibility to take a job that's less lucrative but perhaps more fulfilling.

144. RUNNING FAST ON THE HEDONIC TREADMILL

In 2014, 32.5 percent of Americans described themselves as very happy, versus a 42-year average of 33.3 percent, according to the General Social Survey. Over this 42-year stretch, inflation-adjusted per capita disposable income rose 110 percent. In other words, our standard of living more than doubled, but our reported level of happiness showed no improvement. Money, it seems, hasn't bought happiness.

You probably have experienced this phenomenon in your own life. Think about the major purchases you've made over the past five years. You might have bought a new house or car, purchased furniture for the living room or remodeled the kitchen.

In all likelihood, you eagerly anticipated these expenditures. You imagined how great it would be to take delivery of the new car or to have a spanking new kitchen. You thought about how these purchases would make your life so much better. And sure enough, you were happy at first. But within a few weeks or months, you likely found yourself barely noticing the new car and the new kitchen. Instead, you were increasingly preoccupied with and excited about something else—your next big expenditure and how that new purchase would somehow transform your life.

What's going on here? At issue is a psychological phenomenon known as the hedonic treadmill. We spend our lives lusting after the next promotion, the next pay raise or the next major purchase, only to find we quickly become dissatisfied and start hankering after something else.

This is another trait we can blame on our hunter-gatherer ancestors: They survived in a hostile world because they were never satisfied with what they had and strove constantly to get ahead—and we still carry those instincts within us. So how can we get more happiness out of our dollars? Academic research offers some intriguing insights, as you'll learn in the next section.

Our tendency to adapt to material improvements in our lives may thwart the pursuit of greater happiness. But adaptation can also save us from everlasting misery. Just as we grow accustomed to good things in our lives, we also adapt to terrible developments. Getting laid off, suffering a disability or a family member's death can all seem like events from which we will never recover. And yet we do.

145. GETTING MORE HAPPINESS FROM YOUR DOLLARS

How can we get off the hedonic treadmill—and squeeze more satisfaction out of our time and money? Here are some insights from the academic literature:

• Spend time with friends and family. Throw a party. Go out to dinner with friends. Fly across the country to see your children or grandchildren. Happiness research suggests a robust network of friends and family can be a huge source of happiness.

• Devote yourself to work and hobbies that you find challenging, you're passionate about, you think are important and you feel you're good at. While achieving our goals often isn't as satisfying as we imagine, making progress toward these goals can give us great satisfaction. Think about those moments when you're engaged in activities you love, you're completely absorbed and time just whizzes by. Those can be among our happiest times.

• Buy experiences, not possessions. The new car will likely go from a source of happiness to a source of unhappiness as it gets dinged up and breaks down. By contrast, a vacation can provide not just a wonderful week or two with family, but also many months of eager anticipation and many years of fond memories.

• Move closer to work. Research suggests a long commute can be terrible for happiness. We like to feel in control, and that's tough to do when you're dealing every day with traffic or public transportation.

• Don't move to a ritzier neighborhood than you can truly afford. Your wealthy neighbors will be a constant reminder that you aren't so fortunate.

• Give a little. Volunteering doesn't just help others. It can also make us feel good about ourselves. Ditto for buying gifts.

• Count your blessings. Okay, maybe the new car doesn't give you the same thrill it once did. But you might be able to squeeze a little more happiness from the vehicle if you pause for a moment, admire it and think how lucky you are.

146. MIDDLE-AGED AND MISERABLE

Yes, the midlife crisis is a real phenomenon. It seems happiness through life may be U-shaped. According to some—though not all—studies, most of us start our adult lives feeling pretty happy. But things deteriorate through our 30s, we often hit bottom in our 40s and then our happiness rebounds from there. In fact, our later years can be among the happiest times in our life.

What's going on here? It may be that our 40s are relatively unhappy because we're under substantial stress as we juggle children and work responsibilities, while perhaps also helping elderly parents. As we get into our 50s, the pressure starts to subside.

Alternatively, maybe our deteriorating happiness through our 30s and 40s reflects a realization that we won't fulfill our youthful ambitions, our accomplishments won't be all that notable and we won't make much of a mark on the world. We eventually come to terms with this, and that's when our happiness rebounds.

Whatever the reason for this phenomenon, it has practical implications. To make sure you don't reach your 40s feeling financially trapped, try to save diligently as soon as you enter the workforce. That will get you on track for retirement, because you'll enjoy decades of investment compounding, and you may be able to avoid some of the financial anxiety that consumes others throughout their adult lives.

By starting to save early, you might also give yourself options that can ease any midlife unhappiness, such as the financial flexibility to change careers. We are often happiest when we're engaged in activities that we're passionate about and that we think are important. If you save diligently, while also keeping your fixed living costs low, you may have the freedom later in life to work for a smaller paycheck but greater satisfaction.

147. GREAT DEBATES: DOES MONEY BUY HAPPINESS?

Ask folks the above question and they almost always answer with a robust "yes." And the research suggests that they are right—but maybe not to the degree they imagine.

If you lift people out of poverty, you can greatly improve their level of happiness. But from there, gains come more slowly, and it can take large sums of money to make someone measurably happier. A big reason is the hedonic treadmill: We quickly adapt to material improvements in our lives.

Still, those with higher incomes and greater wealth tend to report that they're happier. That suggests that happiness may hinge less on our absolute level of income and wealth, and more on how we stand relative to others. But there's another possible explanation. Perhaps what we're observing is a so-called focusing illusion: When you ask those who are better off about their level of happiness, they think about how fortunate they are and that prompts them to say that yes, of course they're happy.

But are they? It may depend on what we mean by happiness. A higher income, as well as a greater level of education, tends to lead folks to evaluate their lives more favorably. But these things don't necessarily help with day-to-day happiness. In fact, those earning higher incomes tend to report that they suffer more stress and anger during the day—hardly hallmarks of happiness.

Even if more money helps happiness, many other factors are also at work. We all have a happiness "set point"—a predisposition to be more or less happy—and research suggests this explains perhaps half of our reported level of happiness. By contrast, our life's circumstances, including the size of our paycheck, may only explain 10 percent of our happiness. What about the other 40 percent? That's the part we control. We can potentially boost our happiness by, say, spending more time with friends or finding a way to eliminate a long commute.

148. JONATHAN'S TAKE: MONEY AND HAPPINESS

I think money is sort of like health. It's only when you're sick that you realize how great it is to feel healthy. Similarly, it's only when you don't have enough money that you realize how great it is to be on a solid financial footing. More money may not make you happier—but not having money could make you extremely unhappy.

What does this mean for your personal finances? You want to get to the point where money isn't something you worry about. And the way you do that is to live beneath your means, save like crazy and try to accumulate a decent-size investment portfolio.

At first blush, this may not sound like a whole lot of fun. But the truth is, if you're like most people, the dollars you spend aren't buying you a whole lot of happiness. All those cars and houses and toys you want? They will likely bring you surprisingly little pleasure.

Instead, research suggests there are two keys to happiness. First, we need to spend our days striving after things we think are important. Second, we need to be surrounded by friends and family. We need fulfilling work—and we need community. If you manage your finances carefully and don't get sidetracked by excessive spending, you should be able to build a life where both are possible.

I have taken insights from the happiness research and used it to guide the way I arrange my life and spend my money. For instance, I sold the house in the suburbs and moved to the city, so I would have a shorter commute and avoid the hassles of homeownership. That freed up time to devote to two things I love—my family and writing. I'm not much of a spender. But I'm more than happy to spend money to bring together family members, whether it's for a vacation or a special dinner out.

PART VII

SAVING

NOT AN EXCITING WAY TO GET RICH, BUT ONE THAT WORKS

By definition, the money we don't spend is saved. So why bother with a separate chapter on saving? There are two reasons.

First, saving deserves its own chapter because there simply isn't enough of it going on. In 2015, the monthly savings rate ran at around 5 percent, far below the 9 to 13 percent we saw from 1950 through the mid-1980s. Yes, some people inherit fortunes or build successful small businesses. But for most of us, if we're to grow rich, we need to save diligently month after month.

Second, while saving money sounds simple, it doesn't come naturally to us. Like dieting and exercising regularly, it takes a lot of self-control to save money every month. Think about our hunter-gatherer ancestors. They didn't worry about stashing part of their paycheck in a 401(k) plan to pay for a retirement that might be decades away. Their focus was on surviving until tomorrow, and that meant consuming whenever they got the chance.

Today, we have constant chances to consume and, thanks to our ancient instincts, we're often tempted to seize those opportunities. But if we're to avoid a life of financial stress and eventually retire in comfort, we need to beat back our desires and save perhaps 12 to 15 percent of every paycheck for retirement, and even more if we have other goals. How can you get yourself on the right track? You might consider the many advantages of saving a healthy sum on a regular basis, and then nudge yourself to save by employing a host of tricks.

JONATHAN'S TAKE: For ordinary Americans, what's the secret to getting rich? It's no secret at all: You need to live beneath your means and save a healthy sum. Without that discipline, your chances of amassing significant wealth are slim. The good news: It doesn't take much to become a great saver. Suppose you're currently spending 95 cents out of every $1 you earn, while saving the other 5 cents. To increase your monthly savings rate by 100 percent, all you need to do is to trim your spending to 90 cents out of every $1 earned, a mere 5 percent decline.

149. AMERICA'S SAVINGS HABITS

In the 10 months through October 2015, Americans saved between 4.8 and 5.6 percent of their disposable personal income each month, calculates the Commerce Department's Bureau of Economic Analysis. This is savings as a percentage of after-tax income. Why is that important? The 10 percent-plus savings rates suggested by many financial experts are typically couched in terms of pretax income. Those suggested savings rates would be even higher if they were expressed as a percentage of after-tax income. In other words, the official savings rate is even more disappointing than it seems.

It wasn't always this way. During the 35 years through 1984, the annual savings rate averaged 11.1 percent and never fell below 9 percent, according to Commerce Department figures. Since then, the annual savings rate has never been as high as 9 percent. From 1985 to 1998, it averaged just 7.3 percent. From 1999 to 2014, it was even worse, averaging a meager 4.7 percent, despite a modest improvement since the Great Recession of 2008.

In short, what we've seen is a gradual collapse in our savings habits in the years since the Second World War. As memories of the Great Depression of the 1930s have faded and life in the U.S. has grown more comfortable and stable, it seems Americans have felt less urgency to save. By contrast, the savings rate in China is nearly triple that of the U.S., according to World Bank figures for 2013. Clearly, the Chinese aren't quite so confident about their financial future.

Increasing income inequality may also lie behind America's low savings rate, as well as our high household debt. As those lower down the income spectrum worry less about their financial future and more about keeping up with rising living standards, they have ended up spending more than is prudent.

In the late 1990s, some argued that America's collapsing savings rate shouldn't concern us, because it failed to take into account rising stock prices, which were more than compensating for our dismal savings habits. The same argument was made in the early 2000s about rising home values. Problem was, these exceptionally good stock and housing returns effectively borrowed from the future. Sure enough, the good times were followed by stretches of truly wretched performance—and those who hadn't saved were left shaking their heads at the sorry state of their finances.

150. DOS AND DON'TS FOR 2016

If you aren't a diligent saver, you are highly unlikely to amass a decent-size investment portfolio. Time to make amends? Here are some "to dos" for 2016:

• Set up an automatic investment plan with your favorite mutual fund, where money is plucked from your bank account every month and invested directly into the fund.

• As your portfolio balloons in value, look for ways to take advantage of your burgeoning wealth by scaling back your insurance coverage, sidestepping financial account fees and minimizing the amount you borrow.

• Talk to your children about your own financial struggles when you were younger. These stories will likely be more powerful than any lecture you could deliver on the importance of financial prudence.

And here are some things you shouldn't do:

• Don't despair if stock prices tumble. Instead, view it as an opportunity—and step up your savings rate to take advantage of the lower prices.

• Don't leave excess cash in your checking account. Instead, move it to a savings account, certificate of deposit or mutual fund. If you leave the money in your checking account, it'll earn little or no interest—and you may be tempted to spend it.

• Don't delay saving for retirement and don't let your adult children delay. Money may be tight when we're in our 20s or 30s, but time is in our favor and any money we manage to save could enjoy decades of investment compounding.

151. HOW MUCH SHOULD YOU SAVE?

One rule of thumb says that, if you're in the workforce, you should save 10 percent of your pretax income every year toward retirement.

But with both future investment returns and future employment uncertain, it's probably wiser to save 12 to 15 percent and to start socking away money as soon as you enter the workforce. By starting in your 20s, you will have a cushion if you later find yourself out of work, and you'll get greater potential benefit from investment growth.

What if you will receive a traditional employer pension or your employer matches part of your contribution to your 401(k) or similar plan? You might save somewhat less than 12 to 15 percent. On the other hand, if you don't start saving for retirement until your 30s or 40s, you will likely need to save far more. In addition, you probably have other goals, such as buying a home or putting the kids through college, and those goals will necessitate additional savings.

Add it all up and you might find you ought to save 20 percent of your income every year and possibly more. That, alas, is a target few people will hit. But even if your neighbors don't save that much, maybe you can. In all likelihood, you will never regret the sacrifice and you'll be thrilled with the results. As you will learn in the pages ahead, by saving regularly starting early in your adult life, you can enjoy a host of advantages—including getting time on your side, saving a bundle in taxes, avoiding all kinds of costs and sharply reducing the nest egg you need to support a similar spending level once retired.

152. THE EARLIER, THE BETTER

The sooner you start setting aside money for retirement and other goals, the easier it will be to amass the necessary sums, partly because you will have more months when you're saving and partly because you should benefit more from investment compounding.

Compounding is the process by which money grows over time. Imagine you started with $1,000 and earned 6 percent a year. During the first year, your $1,000 would earn $60, turning your $1,000 into $1,060. If that $1,060 again earns 6 percent during the second year, you'd be up to $1,124, as you notch gains not only on your original $1,000, but also on the $60 reinvested from the prior year. And so it goes on, with your $1,000 growing to $1,191 after three years, $1,338 after five years, $1,791 after 10 years, $3,207 after 20 years and $10,286 after 40 years.

The miraculous way that money compounds, which we discuss further in both Part VIII and Part X, is captured by the rule of 72. If you take your expected rate of return and divide it into 72, you can find out how long it will take to double your money. For instance, at 6 percent a year, it takes 12 years to double your money.

The numbers are even more impressive if you combine investment compounding with saving regularly. Suppose you earn 6 percent annually and also save $1,000 a year. At that rate, you would have $5,975 after five years, $13,972 after 10 years, $38,993 after 20 years and $164,048 after 40 years.

Problem is, the benefits of both compounding and saving regularly can seem meager in the early years. But if you keep at it for maybe a dozen or 15 years, you should reach a tipping point, where your annual investment gains start to surpass the annual amount you save. Suddenly, your portfolio will be hitting on both cylinders—and you may find your portfolio growing by leaps and bounds.

153. WHY SAVING IS A BARGAIN

There are all kinds of good reasons to save regularly. Here's another to add to the list: Saving is a bargain—and spending is mighty expensive.

How expensive? Let's say you earn an extra $1,000 and you are in the 25 percent federal income tax bracket. After deducting federal income taxes, Social Security and Medicare payroll taxes, and state income taxes, you might be left with $650 to spend. When you spend that $650, you might end up with barely $600 of merchandise, because in most places you will also need to pay sales taxes.

By contrast, if you put the $1,000 in your employer's 401(k) or similar retirement plan, you get to keep the entire $1,000. As an added bonus, if your employer matches your 401(k) contributions at 50 cents on the dollar, your $1,000 would become $1,500.

That's pretty enticing. Instead of $600 of spending, you might have $1,500 for retirement—and that $1,500 could double or triple in value, and perhaps more, by the time you quit the workforce. True, you'll need to pay income taxes when you withdraw the money in retirement. But all the intervening years of tax-deferred growth should go a long way toward offsetting that eventual financial pain.

154. HOW MONEY SAVES YOU MONEY

Life is cheaper when you have some savings. How so? Think of all the extra costs you incur when your finances are tight—and how you can sidestep those costs as you build up your retirement and taxable accounts.

For instance, as your savings grow, your need to borrow fades. Initially, that might mean never carrying a credit card balance and incurring finance charges. Later, you may have enough to pay cash when you buy a car. You might also put down 20 percent or more when you buy a home, thus avoiding the need for private mortgage insurance. Perhaps you'll even get to the point where you don't need a mortgage to purchase a house.

Your burgeoning wealth should also allow you to avoid fees for bouncing checks, having financial account balances below the required minimum, and paying bills late. Your lower debt and history of on-time payments should boost your credit score, which ought to trim your borrowing costs when you next need a loan.

Similarly, as your wealth increases, you may be comfortable raising the deductibles on your health, homeowner's and auto insurance and extending the elimination period on your disability and long-term-care insurance. You might even self-insure for nursing home costs, so you don't need a long-term-care policy. You might also decide your family would be fine financially if you died or suffered a disability, prompting you to drop your life and disability insurance.

All this can lead to a virtuous cycle. As your savings balloon, you can shave your cost of living further, giving you yet more money to save. There is, as they say, a reason the rich get richer.

155. DILIGENT SAVERS NEED LESS FOR RETIREMENT

One rule of thumb says that, for a comfortable retirement, you need to have enough savings and other sources of retirement income to replicate 80 percent of what you earned while you were in the workforce. But few retirees hit this lofty goal and, for those with good savings habits, it may not make sense to try.

To understand what's at issue, consider two examples. First, imagine that, while you were working, you saved around 10 percent of your income each year and you lost another 7.65 percent to Social Security and Medicare payroll taxes. Both those drains on your income would be gone once you retire, so aiming to have retirement income equal to 80 percent of your working income would likely give you a similar amount of disposable income.

Next, imagine that you were a great saver who socked away 25 percent of income, rather than 10 percent. Clearly, you're used to living on a relatively small portion of your paycheck. Result? To maintain your standard of living after quitting the workforce, you might need a nest egg and other sources of retirement income that together will give you not 80 percent of what you used to earn when working, but perhaps just 65 percent.

156. NUDGING YOURSELF TO SAVE MORE

How can you get yourself to sock away more money? Try these strategies:

• Automate your savings. Sign up for payroll deduction into your 401(k) plan. Also set up automatic investment plans, where money is plucked from your checking account every month and invested in a savings account or the mutual funds you choose. Once you have automated your regular savings, inertia kicks in and you're likely to stick with it. Got a pay raise? Make sure you save part of your increased income by upping the sum you save automatically every month.

• Save all windfalls. Think about the extra money you sometimes receive, such as overtime pay, income from a second job, tax refunds, a year-end bonus and the occasional inheritance. These sums aren't part of your regular paycheck, so you're probably used to living without this money and thus it can be a painless source of extra savings.

• Round up the mortgage check. Do you usually pay $1,422 every month? Instead, make out the check for $1,500. Extra principal payments can allow you to pay off your mortgage years earlier.

• Write down everything you spend. This can make you more careful about your spending. Also pay cash, rather than using a credit card. Spending seems more real when you have to hand over dollar bills.

• Stash savings in accounts you consider off-limits. While folks will let themselves spend money that's in their checking account, they are often reluctant to tap their savings and investment accounts. To take advantage of this mental accounting, get extra money out of your checking account and into an account you consider untouchable, like your brokerage account or your individual retirement account.

• Set a savings target for the months ahead—and then tell others about your goal. That may make you more tenacious. You might also think harder about why you're investing and try to visualize how great it will be to realize your financial dreams. That may give you additional motivation.

• Turn debt payments into savings. Just finished paying off a student or car loan? Let's say it was costing you $300 a month. Keep writing that check every month—but instead send it to your favorite mutual fund. You are used to living without the money, so this shouldn't be any great sacrifice.

157. WHERE TO STASH YOUR SAVINGS

You might take the savings opportunities available to you and array them from most to least attractive based on their tax advantages, investment costs and potential return.

For many of us, the most attractive place for our savings will be our employer's 401(k) or similar retirement plan, which can offer the investor's triple play: an initial tax deduction, tax-deferred growth and possibly a matching employer contribution. Depending on the size of that employer match and the vesting schedule for those contributions, you might effectively receive an immediate 50 or 100 percent return on your money.

Your next most attractive opportunity will likely be paying off high-cost debt, notably credit card debt. Don't have any? You might stash additional savings in a tax-deductible or Roth IRA, assuming you're eligible. You won't get an employer match, like you can with a 401(k), but the tax advantages are comparable.

After that, the decision is less clear-cut. If you aren't eligible for a tax-deductible or Roth IRA, you might fund a nondeductible IRA and possibly look to convert it to a Roth. Alternatively, if you're an aggressive investor, you could purchase stocks or stock funds in your regular taxable account and aim to invest in the most tax-smart way possible. What if you're more conservative? Look into paying down your mortgage and other debt.

Have yet more money to save? If you want additional tax-deferral, consider a tax-deferred fixed or variable annuity. But you should also carefully consider the drawbacks, notably the high expenses that are often charged. You can learn more about these various savings vehicles in Part XI, the chapter on taxes.

158. IMPROVING 401(K) PLANS

An employer's 401(k) or 403(b) is typically the best place to stash your savings, thanks to the initial tax deduction, tax-deferred growth and any matching employer contribution. Yet many employees fail to take full advantage of these plans, contributing little or no money. And those who do contribute either never make an investment choice or, if they do, never revisit it.

To improve employee decision-making, many employer-sponsored retirement plans have been revamped. New employees are often automatically enrolled in the plan and their annual contribution is automatically increased, unless they opt out.

To help employees make better investment decisions, many plans have reduced the number of investment options, so employees are less overwhelmed by the choice. More important, the default investment option has been changed. Before, if you didn't make a choice, your contributions would often end up in a low-risk, low-return investment, such as the plan's money-market fund or stable-value fund. The latter is typically invested in short-term bonds, with an insurance wrapper added, which allows the fund to maintain a stable share price.

Now, many plans have designated target-date retirement funds as their default investment option. These funds have broadly diversified portfolios of stocks and bonds that are geared to particular retirement dates. As that date approaches, the funds become more conservative.

159. PRAY FOR LOUSY RETURNS

In Part II, we discussed how sequence-of-return risk can derail a retirement. But what's bad news for retirees can be good news for retirement savers. While a stock market plunge can cause folks to freeze and stop adding fresh money to their retirement stash, this is the time when you should continue to sock away money regularly and even step up your savings rate.

Imagine your goal is to amass the maximum sum for retirement. What sequence of returns would you want? Sure, it's gratifying when a market rally bloats your portfolio's value. But what you really want are lousy returns throughout your working years, followed by a world-class rally right before you retire. That way, you would buy investments at rock-bottom prices and cash out at nosebleed valuations.

The importance of the sequence of returns, and how you react to good and rotten markets, is captured by the difference between time-weighted and dollar-weighted returns. Examples of time-weighted returns include the results you see published by mutual funds and exchange-traded index funds. They would accurately reflect your performance if you had invested, say, five years ago and never subsequently added or withdrew money.

But such time-weighted returns may be misleading if, for instance, the market had dropped sharply during the five years and then rebounded, and you continued to save regularly throughout this period, possibly using a strategy known as dollar-cost averaging. In that case, your personal performance would be higher than the time-weighted return, because some of your purchases would have occurred at the lower prices. To gauge your performance accurately, you would want to calculate a dollar-weighted return, which reflects when you bought and sold. Fortunately, some mutual fund companies do the calculation for their investors. This performance number is often labeled your "personal rate of return."

160. EASING INTO THE MARKET

While lousy stock market returns can be great for those saving for retirement, many investors don't see it that way. Their big fear: They'll invest in stocks, only to get hit with a devastating market decline that triggers both a hefty financial loss and also painful pangs of regret.

How can you overcome this fear? If you're young and just starting out, keep in mind that, while this month's investment may take place at lofty prices, you have decades of regular investments ahead of you, and those investments will occur at all kinds of different prices. It's easy to get caught up in the guessing game about the market's short-term direction, but today's market angst is a big distraction from the long-term story. Over the 40 years through September 2015, global stock markets returned an average of more than 9.6 percent a year, including dividends, enough to turn $1,000 into almost $40,000.

Things are trickier if you're older and have a large lump sum to invest. Perhaps you received an inheritance or a severance payment when you left your employer. Maybe you have been sitting in cash, worried about the stock market's short-term direction, but now realize that you're hurting your results.

What to do? History tells us that, on average, you would have earned the highest return by getting fully invested in stocks right away. Problem is, you won't get an "average" result. Instead, you have just one shot—and you probably can't afford the risk of dumping a huge sum into stocks and then seeing the market plunge 50 percent.

One possible strategy: Take the money you have earmarked for stocks, divide it into 24 or 36 equal sums, and then spoon the money into the market every month for the next two or three years. If the market drops 15 percent, double the size of your monthly investment. If it drops 25 percent, triple your monthly investment.

161. DOLLAR-COST AVERAGING

Suppose you contribute $400 each paycheck to your employer's 401(k) plan. Whether you know it or not, you're engaging in dollar-cost averaging. A good idea? Saving on a regular basis is a great habit to get into. But despite what some folks suggest, it's neither magical nor a sure way to make money in the markets.

To understand the purported magic, imagine your regular $400 investment goes into a stock mutual fund. Your first investment is at $10 a share, which means your $400 buys 40 shares. The market promptly plunges 20 percent, so your next $400 investment buys 50 shares at $8 apiece. You now own a total of 90 shares.

Over the weeks that follow, the market partially recovers, so your stock fund's share price rises to $9, halfway between your two purchase prices. But at $9 a share, your 90 shares—for which you paid $800—are now worth $810. There is, however, nothing magical about this. You ended up with a profit simply because you invested a constant dollar amount, so you bought more shares when the price went down.

Suppose, instead, that you focused on regularly buying 40 shares. You would have invested $400 when the share price was $10 and $320 when the price was $8, for a total of $720. What happens when the share price bounces back to $9? Your 80 shares would be worth $720, the same as the amount you paid.

In other words, dollar-cost averaging works because it's a slightly contrarian strategy, where you buy more shares when the market goes down. For the strategy to work, the investment needs to recover from any price decline. That is a reasonable bet with a diversified stock mutual fund, but it may never happen with an individual stock.

If a slightly contrarian strategy pays off, what if you were even more contrarian? That's the thinking behind value averaging.

162. VALUE AVERAGING

As an alternative to dollar-cost averaging, consider value averaging, a strategy developed by a former Harvard Business School professor, Michael Edleson, and described in his 1993 book, "Value Averaging."

The math involved is fairly complicated. But the idea is simple enough: You set a target growth rate for your stock portfolio and then vary your regular investment, depending on how your stocks perform. Let's say you want your portfolio to grow $500 a month. A month after you make your first $500 investment, your stock portfolio is worth $526. That means that, in the second month, you would need to invest $474 to hit your target portfolio value of $1,000. You might stash the other $26 in a money-market fund.

That cash in a money-market fund could come in handy if there's a spell when the market performs poorly and you need to invest substantially more than $500 each month. On the other hand, if the market enjoys a strong run, you could find yourself selling stocks to keep your stock portfolio on that $500-a-month growth path. That selling could trigger capital gains taxes and some messy tax accounting, but you can sidestep those problems by value averaging within your retirement accounts.

Like dollar-cost averaging, value averaging compels you to buy more shares when the market is depressed and fewer shares when it's buoyant. But with value averaging, the effect is even stronger. Indeed, value averaging can be seen as a cross between dollar-cost averaging and rebalancing, a concept we tackle in Part VIII.

163. TURNING YOUR CHILDREN INTO SAVERS

If there's one financial skill you should teach your children, it's the ability to delay gratification. This isn't just good for them. It's also good for you. After all, if your kids grow up to be financially irresponsible adults, there is a fair chance you will ride to the rescue. Want to teach younger children to be smart about money? Here are five strategies:

• Values are passed down through the generations in the stories that we tell. Talk about how you made ends meet when you first entered the workforce. Tell your kids how your parents or grandparents struggled financially.

• Encourage your children to save part of their allowance for larger purchases. You might have your children save a few dollars every week for a month or two, and then arrange a special trip to the mall so they can buy the toy of their dreams.

• Teaching your kids to delay gratification doesn't have to involve money. When you tell your children they can't have dessert until they eat their main course, or they can't play until they finish their homework, you are also teaching an important lesson about the need for self-discipline.

• Have your youngsters create a wish list of gifts they want for their birthday or the holidays, or items they want to save up for. Every month, go over the wish list with your children. Point out how much the list changes from month to month, so they start to see how quickly their desires pass.

• Your children may grow up spending your money, but you want them to feel like it's their own money that they're spending. To that end, push them to make financial choices. For instance, if they go on the school field trip, give them $5 for the museum gift shop. But tell them that, if they don't spend the money, they can keep it and spend it on something else. Similarly, when you go to restaurants, offer them a choice: They can order a soda—or they can drink tap water and have a dollar.

164. TEACHING TEENS AND ADULT CHILDREN ABOUT MONEY

As your children grow older, you will want to give them more financial responsibility, talk about money in depth and prod them to make smarter decisions. These strategies might help:

• As with younger children, you want your teenagers to feel like they are spending their own money, even if it's your money that they are spending. For instance, you might deposit their allowance in a bank account that comes with a cash-machine card. That way, when they want money, they'll no longer ask you. Instead, they will have to ask themselves and then head down to the ATM.

• You might give your teenagers a larger allowance but less often, such as once a month or once every three months. That will compel them to budget. You might also increase their allowance to include a clothing budget, so they have a growing sense of responsibility and they have to make more financial choices.

• Once your children are in the workforce, encourage them to save for retirement by, say, offering to give them 50 cents for every dollar they put into their 401(k) plan. Similarly, to encourage them to save for that first home, you might offer to contribute to a savings account intended to pay for a house down payment—but only if your children also contribute to the account.

• Set a good example. If you are obviously thoughtful and prudent in the way you handle money, your kids are more likely to follow your example. Consider showing them your account statements when they arrive in the mail. Discuss how you paid for their college education. Talk about what you have done to prepare for retirement. Any one of these discussions may have limited impact. But over time, your children will likely learn a lot.

165. ALLOWANCES

This is an issue that can prompt heated arguments among parents. Some insist that their children do chores in return for their allowance and that, once they're teenagers, they should earn their spending money by babysitting, cutting grass or getting a job at the local ice cream parlor. Others believe that pocket money shouldn't be tied to doing chores— because the latter is integral to being part of the family—and that forcing teenagers to take menial jobs gives them an uninspiring view of the work world and takes away from their far more important goal, which is getting good grades.

How should children use their allowance? Some parents apply the "spend, save, share" concept. With every week's pocket money, children are allowed to spend part of their allowance, but they are also expected to save toward a future purchase and give part to charity. Whatever rules you lay down, this is a great chance to talk to your children each week about money and help boost their financial savvy.

How much pocket money should you give? One rule of thumb says children should get a dollar a week for every birthday they've had, so a seven-year-old would receive $7 every week. Arguably, the dollar amount should be tied less to age and more to the financial responsibility that comes with it. For instance, if your teenagers are expected to buy their own clothes, you might need to give a 13-year-old more than $13 a week.

PART VIII

INVESTING
BEATING THE MARKET IS HARD, BEATING YOUR NEIGHBORS IS EASY

Investing is a toxic mix of fear and overconfidence that's colored by the recent past and driven by unfounded forecasts. Want to introduce a bracing dose of rationality? Start by thinking about what you can control— and what you can't.

Your investment performance has three components: There are the raw returns you earn, the risks you take to earn those returns and the costs you incur along the way. Most investors focus heavily on returns. Wall Street does everything possible to fan this interest, because investors' relentless pursuit of market-beating returns is a great moneymaker for brokers, fund companies and money managers. But the reality is, there's no surefire path to beating the market, and the harder you try, the worse your results are likely to be, because of all the investment costs you incur.

What's the alternative? You might focus less on returns and more on building a portfolio that avoids unnecessary risks and minimizes investment costs, including tax costs. Unlike returns, risk and costs are two aspects of investing over which you have a lot of control and where a little effort can pay big dividends.

To be sure, there are all kinds of strategies that will supposedly allow you to beat the market. For those who want to delve more deeply into the topic, some of those strategies are described in Part IX. Even this chapter, where we'll look at the basics of portfolio building, has the potential to befuddle the novice. But, as you'll discover in the pages ahead, you can keep yourself on track if you think of portfolio building as a simple four-step process.

166. FINANCIAL MARKETS 2015

As 2015 began, many investors were anxious about the year ahead. U.S. stocks were near their all-time high, but prices were swinging wildly. The dollar's value in the currency markets was soaring. Bond prices were also on the rise, driving the yield on the benchmark 10-year Treasury note back down toward 2 percent. Much of the handwringing was triggered by tumbling oil prices. While lower gas prices and heating bills promised to leave consumers with more money to spend on other items, it also threatened a slowdown in the energy sector, which had lately been an engine of economic growth.

Against this unsettled backdrop, market pundits—who are almost always bullish—seemed less exuberant than usual. Researcher Birinyi Associates said that 22 strategists that it tracked were estimating an average increase of 8.2 percent for the S&P 500-stock index in 2015, according to a *Wall Street Journal* report.

Despite all this, global stock markets fared reasonably well through 2015's first five months, with foreign stocks outshining U.S. shares. But then the Greek debt crisis rattled global financial markets. Investor nervousness was compounded by concerns over Puerto Rican municipal bonds and what might happen when the Federal Reserve finally raised short-term interest rates. The unease turned to panic in August, as all eyes focused on China's slowing economic growth. The S&P 500 quickly slumped more than 10 percent. On Wall Street, that counts as a "correction," as opposed to a "bear market," which is defined as a 20 percent decline.

Through the fall, stocks slowly recouped their summer losses, putting the S&P 500 up 1 percent in 2015 through Nov. 30. Developed foreign markets fared less well, slipping 1.9 percent, as measured by MSCI's Europe, Australasia and Far East index. Emerging stock markets got badly roughed up, with MSCI's emerging markets index down 14.8 percent.

As of Nov. 30, 2015, the stocks in the S&P 500 were yielding 2 percent and trading at 22 times trailing 12-month reported earning, making them expensive by historical standards. Since the market bottomed on March 9, 2009, the shares in the S&P 500 have climbed 207.5 percent, though they remain just 36.2 percent above their March 24, 2000, peak.

The benchmark 10-year Treasury note was yielding 2.21 percent as of Nov. 30, 2015, versus 2.17 percent at year-end 2014, once again defying expectations that interest rates were headed higher. Meanwhile, short-term interest rates remained miserably low, with money-market mutual funds yielding little or nothing, as the Federal Reserve continued to hold off raising rates.

Oil prices, which had plunged to $54 a barrel at year-end 2014, continued to slide in 2015, finishing November at $42. It was the same story with gold, which ended November at $1,064 an ounce, compared with $1,184 at year-end 2014. The dollar strengthened against major currencies, which trimmed the value of foreign investments held by U.S. investors. Many funds that invest in foreign bonds, including emerging market debt, were sporting losses as of late 2015.

This market performance came amid muted economic growth. Since the economic contraction of 2008 and 2009, real (after-inflation) gross domestic product has grown fairly steadily. But the pace of growth has been modest, averaging just 2.1 percent a year over the five years through 2014. Growth wasn't much different in the 12 months through September 2015, with the economy expanding at a 2.2 percent rate. The International Monetary Fund projects that the U.S. economy will grow 2.8 percent in 2016.

167. DOS AND DON'TS FOR 2016

Reviewing your investment strategy? Here are some "to dos" for 2016:

• Invest with humility. Even if you spot what seems like a compelling investment opportunity, there's always a chance you could be wrong—and your best defense is broad diversification.

• Take a hard look at the performance of any actively managed mutual funds and individual stocks you own. Are you sure you wouldn't be better off with market-tracking index funds?

• Consider increasing your allocation to foreign stocks. While investing abroad may seem risky, adding foreign shares can actually reduce a stock portfolio's overall volatility, so you might aim to have 30 to 40 percent of your stock portfolio invested overseas.

• Ask yourself whether you would be better off ditching all your mutual funds and individual stocks—and instead simplifying your life by purchasing a single target-date retirement fund.

And here are some things you shouldn't do:

• Don't invest based on somebody's short-term market forecast. Nobody can predict the direction of stock and bond prices, so you're better off focusing on things you can control, like how much you save and spend, the amount of risk you take and the investment costs you incur.

• Don't forget what happened to stocks in 2008. While a huge decline like that isn't likely, it's entirely possible we will see a drop of 20 percent or more, so you need to be mentally prepared.

• Don't be too quick to rebalance, especially if you are dealing with a beaten-down sector that's finally showing signs of life. While it feels good to take some profits, often the better strategy is to let your winners run for a year or two before you rebalance back to your target weights.

• Don't trade index funds. Two reasons to index are low costs and tax efficiency. If you frequently buy and sell index mutual funds and exchange-traded index funds, you throw away both those advantages.

168. BUILDING A SMARTER PORTFOLIO

As you make your way through this chapter, it's helpful to think of portfolio building as a four-step process. First, consider why you're investing. That will give you a sense for your time horizon and hence how much risk you can take. Keep in mind that some goals have a harsh deadline, such as the day you make the house down payment, while other goals involve spending your savings over time, as happens with retirement.

From there, proceed to the second step: settling on your asset allocation, which is your portfolio's basic mix of stocks, bonds and other investments. Stocks get all the media attention, but just over half of American families don't have any stock exposure, according to the Federal Reserve's 2013 Survey of Consumer Finances. Your asset allocation will be driven heavily by your time horizon, though you will also want to consider other factors, such as your job security and how comfortable you are taking risk.

After you have settled on your asset allocation, it's time for the third step: figuring out how you'll diversify your stock market money, your bond market money and so on. This means deciding what percentage of your portfolio you want in, say, U.S. smaller-company stocks, foreign-government bonds and U.S. high-yield junk bonds.

Now, you can proceed to the fourth and final task: selecting investments to build your desired portfolio. You will likely want to favor funds, especially those that will allow you to capture the market's performance at low cost.

Successful investing, however, isn't just about knowing the basics. It's also about attitude. To succeed as an investor, you need to avoid mental mistakes and approach the markets with the mindset of a seasoned investor.

169. MENTAL MISTAKES

Think back to late 2008 and early 2009, when the stock market offered investors one of the great buying opportunities. Did you take advantage—or did you simply sit tight or perhaps even panic and sell? We like to believe we're clearheaded and rational. But when it comes to managing money, we tend to be all too human. Here are three common mental mistakes:

Excessive self-confidence. We tend to attribute our investment winners to our own brilliance, while blaming our losers on others. In fact, during rising stock markets, our self-confidence can balloon, leading us to take more risk and trade excessively. But all that trading is costly, while the greater risk can come back to haunt us when the market next turns down.

Extrapolation. The stock market's daily performance may be unpredictable, but we often think we see patterns. For instance, we tend to extrapolate returns, prompting us to assume that a rising market will keep on rising—and that tumbling shares will continue to fall.

Loss aversion. Most of us are deeply reluctant to sell stocks at a loss, because it means admitting we made a mistake and giving up all chance of recouping the loss. The desire to "get even, then get out" can be a helpful trait during broad market declines, because it may stop us from selling at the worst possible time. But our reluctance to sell losers isn't so helpful with individual investments. If we own a badly run mutual fund or a stock that's in financial trouble, we might be better off selling, taking the tax loss and reinvesting the money elsewhere.

JONATHAN'S TAKE: I believe investing is sufficiently simple that most folks can learn the basics. But just because investing is simple doesn't mean it's easy. Saving for retirement, college and other goals is so important that you need to minimize self-inflicted investment wounds. Find it hard to keep your emotions in check? Can't think like a seasoned investor? That's a key reason to hire a financial advisor—though, as we'll discuss later in this chapter, that also can be risky.

170. THE SEASONED INVESTOR

How do you know you're a seasoned investor? Here are some signposts:

• You have mixed feelings about rising markets. Yes, it's great that your portfolio has grown fatter. But it also means future returns will be lower. By contrast, tumbling markets excite you, because you could get the chance to scoop up investments at bargain prices.

• You select stock and bond funds that you would be happy to hold for a decade or longer—and you do indeed hold them for that long.

• When you make investment decisions, you think not only about the potential return, but also about risk, investment costs, taxes, why you're investing and your broader financial picture.

• You can succinctly explain why you own the portfolio that you do, including the reasons behind each investment.

- When your investments lose value, you're never surprised, because you have a good handle on the likely risk and reward for every investment you own.

- You can coolly decide whether to buy or sell, without getting fixated on what's happened in the market recently or what price you paid for a particular investment.

- You're mentally prepared for parts of your stock portfolio to have wretched results over five and even 10 years, you have the patience and tenacity to stick with these sectors—and your financial goals wouldn't be at risk if stock returns were truly awful.

- You realize that markets are unpredictable and that it's extremely difficult to earn market-beating returns, so you always have some money in bonds and some money in stocks, and you avoid overly large bets on individual investments and narrow market sectors.

171. WHY WE INVEST

Often, we set ourselves up for trouble before we even buy our first investment—by failing to consider why we're investing. No, we shouldn't invest to earn the highest possible return, amass as much money as possible or prove how clever we are. Instead, we invest now so we can spend later on goals such as retirement, the kids' college or a house down payment.

As you pursue these goals, the amount of investment risk you take should hinge on three factors. The most important of the three: How far off do your goals lie? If you have five years or less to invest, the biggest risk is short-term market declines, so you should probably focus on cash investments and shorter-term high-quality bonds. Cash investments include savings accounts, money-market funds and short-term certificates of deposit, where returns are modest but you can be confident you won't lose money.

What if you have more than five years to invest? You're likely more concerned with making your money grow, especially after taking into account inflation and taxes. In pursuit of higher investment returns, you might buy riskier bonds, stocks and possibly alternative investments. Alternative investments include a grab-bag of stuff, including real estate, private-equity investments, timber, gold, commodities and hedge funds. Stocks, riskier bonds and alternative investments can suffer severe short-term losses. But if your time horizon is more than five years, you should have time to ride out any market dips.

Time horizon, however, shouldn't be the only driver of your asset allocation, which is your basic mix of stocks, bonds, cash investments and alternative investments. You also need to give some thought to two other factors: your human capital and your stomach for risk.

172. SHORT-TERM THREATS

If your time horizon is five years or less, the big threat can be summarized in two words: losing money.

To get a sense for the range of potentially rotten returns, consider the worst annual returns for some of Vanguard Group's mutual funds. In 2008, when the financial crisis hit with full fury, Vanguard's S&P 500-stock index fund declined 37 percent, its small-company index fund fell 36.1 percent and its total international-stock fund tumbled 44.1 percent. And these numbers don't fully reflect the punishment suffered: The market's slide started in late 2007 and continued into early 2009, before global stock markets bounced back beginning in March. The S&P 500's peak-to-trough price decline was a staggering 57 percent.

For bonds, 2013 was a rough year. How rough? Vanguard's long-term Treasury fund fell 13 percent that year, its inflation-indexed bond fund slumped 8.9 percent and its long-term corporate bond fund slid 5.9 percent. Vanguard's high-yield corporate bond fund, which invests in low-quality "junk" bonds, made money in 2013, returning 4.5 percent. Instead, its rough year was 2008, when it fell 21.3 percent, reflecting junk bonds' tendency to trade more like stocks than bonds.

Want to see how your funds performed? You might check the website for the fund company involved or head to Morningstar.com.

The bottom line: If you have money that you will need to spend in the next five years, you probably shouldn't own anything riskier than short-term bonds. The worst annual performance of Vanguard's short-term corporate bond fund was a 4.7 percent loss in 2008—and it easily recouped that loss the following year. Vanguard's short-term Treasury fund has given shareholders an even smoother ride, including notching a 6.7 percent gain in 2008's turbulent market.

For greater safety, you might go for money-market mutual funds, which strive to maintain a stable $1 share price, or even an FDIC-insured savings account or certificate of deposit. One tip: You may find you can come out ahead by buying longer-term CDs, with their higher yields, even if you have to cash out before maturity and pay an early-withdrawal penalty.

173. LONG-TERM THREATS

If you're a long-term investor, the biggest risk isn't short-term market declines—unless you panic and sell during those declines. Instead, the big risk is failing to beat back the twin threats of inflation and taxes.

Suppose that, after investment costs, you earn 4 percent a year. If you lose 25 percent of that gain to taxes, you'll be left with 3 percent. But if annual inflation is also 3 percent, you are—in financial terms—just running in place. How can you earn returns that outpace taxes and inflation? Smart tax management, especially the use of retirement accounts, can greatly reduce the threat from taxes. We tackle that topic in Part XI.

Even with smart tax management, you'll find it tough to fend off inflation with Treasury bills, money-market funds, savings accounts and other cash investments. With these, the best you can hope for are returns that approach the inflation rate—and you may earn substantially less, as investors have in recent years, thanks to the artificially low short-term yields engineered by the Federal Reserve and other central banks around the world.

Instead, to outpace inflation, you'll need to look to bonds and especially stocks. With bonds, you might earn 0 to 2 percentage points a year more than inflation, depending on how much risk you take. The potential return from stocks is greater, though so too is the risk. Over the long run, U.S. stocks have delivered close to 7 percentage points a year more than inflation. But given today's rich valuations and relatively sluggish economic growth, you probably shouldn't expect long-run returns on a globally diversified portfolio that are more than 4 percentage points a year above inflation.

174. YOUR HUMAN CAPITAL

If you are still in the workforce, give some thought to your paycheck as you design your portfolio. Let's say you are a university professor with a steady income and a traditional pension awaiting you upon retirement. Both your paycheck and your future pension are akin to collecting interest from a huge position in bonds. You may want to diversify that big bond position by investing heavily in stocks.

By contrast, if you're a contract worker or a commission salesperson whose income can vary sharply from month to month, your human capital looks more like a stock than a bond. To compensate, you may want to tilt your portfolio toward bonds.

As you settle on an investment mix, also think about the industry where you work. Often, realtors own rental real estate, Silicon Valley employees dabble in technology stocks and doctors buy medical shares. These folks may think they have an edge because of their intimate knowledge of their own business. But from a risk perspective, they're effectively doubling down, betting both their paycheck and their portfolio on the same sector of the economy.

The most egregious example: Employees will often invest heavily in their own employer's stock. But if the company gets into financial trouble, they could end up both out of work and also holding a fistful of worthless shares.

175. PERSONAL RISK TOLERANCE

Your time horizon and human capital may suggest that you ought to invest heavily in stocks. These aren't the only factors to consider, however. Suppose you're a unionized government worker with 25 years to retirement. At first blush, it seems like you ought to invest heavily in stocks.

But before you dive into the market, give some thought to how much risk you need to take to reach your goals—and how much risk you can stomach. Even if your job situation suggests you can take a lot of investment risk, you might hold a more conservative portfolio if you're already well on track to meet your various goals. More important, you shouldn't take a lot of risk if you are uncomfortable with wild fluctuations in your portfolio's value. The danger: Stocks dive, you sell in a panic and you end up locking in your losses at the worst possible time.

Personal risk tolerance is tricky to assess because it changes over time. When markets rise, we often grow more bullish as we extrapolate those gains into the future and we attribute our fattened portfolio to our own brilliance. We may also feel we can take extra risk because financially we're ahead of where we expected to be. But when markets dive, these good feelings can evaporate, and we often grow less risk tolerant. To get a sense for how risk tolerant you really are, try to recall how you felt and how you behaved in late 2008 and early 2009. Did you sell stocks, sit tight or buy more? To refresh your memory, you might pull out your account statements from those years and look at the trades you made.

Even if you have been a nervous investor in the past, you may discover you grow more comfortable as you become accustomed to the market's craziness. While 20-year-olds should supposedly have a healthy appetite for risk because they won't need income from their portfolio for many decades, often the investors who are bravely buying at market bottoms are wizened market veterans in their 50s and 60s.

176. ASSET ALLOCATION

Your asset allocation is the key driver of your portfolio's risk and return. The more you have in stocks, the higher your potential long-run return, but the rougher the ride will be. You're fine with a rough ride? In theory, buying a 100 percent stock portfolio will give you the highest return.

Still, there are good reasons to hold other assets. Stocks aren't guaranteed to win, even over long holding periods. During the 10 years through year-end 2008, the S&P 500-stock index lost 1.4 percent a year, including reinvested dividends, while the broad bond market returned 6.2 percent. Moreover, a portfolio that includes some combination of the four major assets—stocks, bonds, cash investments and alternative investments—offers three benefits that you can't get by owning just one of these four assets.

First, by holding multiple assets, you can get the same reward with less dramatic day-to-day and month-to-month swings in your portfolio's value, thanks to the lack of correlation among these assets. This is the magic of smart portfolio building, and it can make investing far more pleasant.

Second, by owning assets that aren't perfectly correlated with one another, you can reduce the chance that you'll suffer big losses. Those losses can wreak havoc with your portfolio's long-run return, while steadier performance can help your nest egg compound at a faster rate.

Finally, you can turn this lack of correlation into additional portfolio gains—by engaging in regular rebalancing.

177. CORRELATIONS

Stocks fluctuate more in value than bonds, so you can calm down a stock portfolio by adding a small position in bonds. The calming effect may be greater than you imagine. Bonds don't just bounce around less than stocks. They could climb in value when stock prices are tumbling, especially if you own government bonds.

At issue here is the crucial concept of correlation. Most parts of the global stock market are highly correlated. In other words, when U.S. large-company stocks are slumping, there's a good chance U.S. small-company shares, developed foreign markets and emerging markets are also getting hammered.

By contrast, stocks and bonds aren't closely correlated. It's quite possible that bonds will tread water and perhaps post gains when stocks fall in value, thus helping to offset your stock market losses and prop up your overall portfolio's value. Similarly, you can be pretty confident that your cash investments (which are, in effect, just very short-term bonds) won't fall in value, so they too can stem your portfolio's loss.

This is also the promise held out by alternative investments. The hope is that, when stocks are getting trounced, perhaps your gold shares, real estate investment trusts or market-neutral mutual fund will head in the other direction.

But noncorrelated assets, whether you own bonds, cash, alternative investments or all three, aren't just a potential source of solace during turbulent stock markets. By helping you avoid large short-term losses, they could also boost your long-run return.

178. COMPOUNDING AND VOLATILITY

Owning a mix of stocks, bonds, cash and alternative investments can reduce the chances of a huge short-term decline in your portfolio's value. That's crucially important, because the math of investment losses is brutal. If you lose 10 percent, you need to make 11 percent to get back to even. If you're down 20 percent, you need a 25 percent gain to recover the money lost. What if you lose 50 percent? Now, it'll take a 100 percent gain to make you whole.

Imagine two portfolios. Over the next five years, the first portfolio notches annual returns of 15 percent, -10 percent, 25 percent, -15 percent and 10 percent. The second portfolio has annual returns of 5 percent, 10 percent, 5 percent, -5 percent and 10 percent. If you add up the annual returns for each portfolio and divide by 5, you get a simple average of 5 for both portfolios. Yet the cumulative gain for the second portfolio was 27 percent, while the first portfolio earned just 21 percent. What explains the difference? The first portfolio had a couple of bad down years, which it struggled to recover from.

To reflect this, mutual funds report their performance using compound average annual returns. This annualized gain is the return the funds would need to earn each year to produce the cumulative amount made for shareholders over, say, the past five or 10 years. For instance, our first portfolio had a five-year compound annual return of 3.9 percent, while our second portfolio had an annualized gain of 4.9 percent.

Clearly, avoiding big portfolio declines can help your portfolio's performance. But to get the full benefit, you need to layer on an additional strategy: rebalancing.

179. REBALANCING

Once you settle on target portfolio percentages for stocks, bonds, cash investments and alternative investments, you'll want to check where you stand at least once a year and also after major market moves. Why? You may find you have drifted far from your target percentages.

Let's say you earmarked 50 percent of your money for stocks and 50 percent for bonds. Stocks then plunge 20 percent, while bonds climb 10 percent. Result? Your 50-50 mix would now be 42 percent stocks and 58 percent bonds. To get back on target, you should rebalance. If you're dealing with a tax-sheltered retirement account, you might sell some bonds and purchase stocks. But with a taxable account, any selling could trigger capital gains taxes, messy tax accounting and possibly trading costs. Instead, you might try to rebalance within your taxable account by directing new savings, as well as any dividend and interest payments, to the stock side of your portfolio.

This rebalancing will keep your portfolio's risk level in line with your targets. If stocks have declined, it can also set you up nicely for any market rebound by ensuring you have a full position in stocks.

But much of the time, you will probably find yourself cutting back on stocks. This will ensure you aren't hurt excessively by the next market downturn, but it will likely also crimp your long-run return, because you are selling what should be your best-performing investment. That said, rebalancing has the potential to enhance returns—especially if you're rebalancing among stock market sectors or among bond market sectors. We'll discuss this later in the chapter.

180. HOW OFTEN SHOULD YOU REBALANCE?

Investors take all kinds of approaches toward rebalancing: Some rebalance every quarter, some every year and some only after major market moves. What's the right strategy? Rebalancing every year has the virtue of simplicity and it introduces a healthy dose of self-discipline. But there are five reasons to be a little more flexible.

First, you should pay attention to the investment costs involved. This shouldn't be an issue if, say, you own no-commission mutual funds bought directly from the fund companies involved. If there's any sort of trading cost involved, however, you should factor that into your decision.

Second, you need to consider the tax consequences. That isn't a worry if you are rebalancing within a retirement account. But if you are handling a taxable account, any selling could trigger capital gains taxes. That may prompt you to rebalance less often.

Third, a sharp rise or fall in the stock market may push you far off your target percentages. Your portfolio might suddenly be substantially more aggressive or conservative than you intended, and you might want to rebalance right away.

Fourth, because stocks tend to fare better over time, there's a decent chance you will earn better long-run returns if you rebalance, say, every two years. The reason: You will give your stocks longer to earn returns before you cut them back. This, of course, means you will have more in stocks, on average, and thus it's a riskier strategy.

Finally, in the stock market, there is evidence of momentum, the tendency for shares to continue performing well if they've recently had strong returns. That also might lead you to rebalance less often, especially if stocks are recovering from a bear market and are in the early stages of a rebound. There's a chance that the upward share-price momentum from the initial recovery will carry over into the year ahead.

181. JONATHAN'S TAKE: ASSET ALLOCATION GUIDELINES

Your mix of stocks, bonds, cash and alternative investments will be driven by your goals and individual circumstances. Still, it's helpful to have some guidelines. For retirement savings, one rule of thumb says you should take 100 and subtract your age. Whatever the result, that's the percentage of your investment portfolio that you should put in stocks. For instance, the rule suggests a 30-year-old should have 70 percent in stocks.

As rules of thumb go, it isn't bad. But I would tweak it. I think those in their 20s and 30s could have as much as 90 percent in stocks, though I wouldn't go any higher. I believe everybody should keep a minimum 10 percent in bonds, because it notably reduces risk without putting much of a dent in returns. Among retirees, I would peg stocks at a minimum 30 percent. If you have less than that, you leave yourself vulnerable to long-run inflation. Indeed, with the right portfolio design, I think a 50 percent stock allocation may make more sense for retirees.

What about alternative investments? I don't think they're a necessary part of a portfolio. But if you want a position in a mix of, say, gold stocks and real estate investment trusts, I would probably cap that position at 10 percent of your portfolio, no matter what your age.

Finally, cash investments make sense for money you plan to spend in the near future, such as savings earmarked for a house down payment or spending money for the next five years of your retirement. But I don't see cash as a necessary part of a long-term investment portfolio. If you are inclined to hold cash for the long haul, consider instead a high-quality short-term bond fund or your 401(k) plan's stable-value fund. Both should offer somewhat higher yields than a savings account or a money-market mutual fund.

Settled on your portfolio's target asset allocation? It's time for the next step: deciding how you will diversify within these asset classes.

182. DIVERSIFICATION

The key driver of your portfolio's risk and return is your asset allocation between stocks and more conservative investments. The more you invest in stocks, the greater the swings in your portfolio's value—but the higher your potential return.

How can you improve the odds of getting that richer reward? What can you do to lessen those wild price swings? That's where diversification comes in. Put simply, diversification involves buying lots and lots of individual securities from all over the globe.

For instance, you can damp down your portfolio's volatility if you diversify across U.S. stocks and foreign shares, including emerging markets. As mentioned earlier, different stock market sectors tend to be highly correlated. Still, when U.S. stocks tumble, maybe foreign markets won't fall as much and perhaps a declining dollar might boost the value of foreign stocks for U.S. holders, thus helping to trim your portfolio's overall loss.

Diversification also increases the chances you'll be rewarded for the risk you are taking. If you purchase just a handful of stocks, it's entirely possible you could earn wretched returns in a year when the overall stock market generates dazzling performance. In fact, if a company you own gets into financial trouble, you could lose everything you invested in that stock.

As you increase the number of stocks you hold, the potential damage done by a few troubled companies becomes less and less. You also reduce your portfolio's "tracking error." In other words, it becomes more likely that your returns will approximate those of the broad market averages— and thus there is a greater likelihood you'll get rewarded for the risk you are taking.

183. DIVERSIFYING STOCKS

As you consider how to diversify your stock portfolio, you might look at the world of stocks through three prisms:

By geography. You will likely want exposure to U.S. shares, developed foreign stock markets such as Germany, Japan and the U.K., and also emerging markets like Brazil, China and India. Based on the allocations in the FTSE Global All Cap Index, roughly 50 percent of the world's stock market value is accounted for by U.S. shares, 40 percent by developed foreign markets and 10 percent by emerging markets.

By company size. Stocks are often categorized as small, midsize and large (or "blue chip") based on their total stock market value (otherwise known as their "capitalization" or "cap"). You will likely want exposure to all three categories, whether you're buying U.S. stocks or investing in developed foreign markets.

By whether a company is considered a growth or value stock. Growth stocks are typically more expensive based on market yardsticks like dividend yield and price-earnings ratios, but they offer the prospect of rapidly growing revenues and profits. Value stocks aren't growing so quickly, but they have the advantage of being less richly priced.

You should probably have exposure to all the different stock market segments described above. Fortunately, you can get that exposure with a relatively modest number of investments—thanks to mutual funds and exchange-traded index funds.

184. GREAT DEBATES: HOW MUCH ABROAD?

Over the decades, the recommended allocation to foreign stocks has crept ever higher. In the 1980s, stashing 10 or 20 percent of a stock portfolio in international markets was considered enough. In the model portfolios offered in the pages ahead, a third of the stock market money is in foreign stocks. But some experts recommend an even larger allocation. Their contention: Investors should weight markets according to their stock market capitalization, which would mean having roughly 50 percent of your stock market money in foreign shares.

Sensible? It's important to have some allocation to foreign stocks, because that helps reduce a portfolio's overall volatility. But you get most of this risk reduction with the first 20 percent allocated to foreign stocks. Moving additional money overseas can further reduce risk, but at a diminishing rate. The implication: Those who think U.S. shares will outperform foreign stocks over the long haul, or who are uncomfortable investing overseas, might stop at a 20 percent allocation. Only time will tell whether that helps or hurts performance—but it shouldn't make too much difference to your portfolio's overall volatility.

As you ponder how much to invest in foreign stocks, also think about how your investment assets match up with your future liabilities. What liabilities? That's a fancy Wall Street term for your investment goals. If you plan to retire in the U.S. and send your children to U.S. colleges, the bulk of your future spending will be in U.S. dollars. That suggests you should be leery of taking too much currency risk, especially as you approach the time when you'll start drawing down your portfolio.

How much currency risk are you taking? Don't just consider your stocks. Instead, think about your overall portfolio, including how it might change as you approach retirement. Over the 20 years before you quit the workforce, you might move from 80 percent stocks to more like 50 percent, with the balance going into bonds—typically U.S. bonds.

Factor in those U.S. bonds, and suddenly your assets may be closely aligned with your spending, even if your stock portfolio is heavily invested in foreign stocks. Let's say you own 50 percent stocks and 50 percent bonds, with the bonds entirely in U.S. securities but with the stocks invested 40 percent abroad. Overall, your portfolio would be 80 percent in U.S. dollar-denominated investments and 20 percent in foreign investments. Given that the bulk of our retirement money will be spent on U.S. goods and services, you probably wouldn't want more than 20 percent invested abroad—and more conservative retirees might aim for somewhat less.

185. DIVERSIFYING BONDS

How should you diversify your bond portfolio? You can slice up the world of bonds in six ways:

By geography. As with stocks, you can divide the world of bonds between U.S., developed foreign and emerging markets. But the case for buying foreign bonds isn't as compelling. The investment costs can be high, and you could be introducing the wild card of currency swings into what's supposedly the conservative part of your portfolio.

By maturity. Bonds have maturities of up to 30 years and occasionally longer. But the longer the maturity, the more a bond will fluctuate in price in response to interest-rate changes. Historically, you have earned much of the yield of longer-term bonds by purchasing securities with five years or less to maturity.

By how interest payments are calculated. While most bonds make fixed interest payments, some offer interest payments that "float" with the overall change in interest rates or increase along with inflation.

By whether the interest is taxed. Interest from corporate bonds is fully taxable. Interest from Treasury and some government agency bonds isn't taxable at the state level. Municipal bonds are exempt from federal taxes and, if you own bonds from your own state, possibly also state and local taxes.

By whether the issuer is part of the public or private sector. Corporate bonds are riskier than government bonds, but offer higher yields.

By the quality of the issuer. While bond investors can usually expect to get both the promised interest payments and their principal back at maturity, that isn't a sure thing with so-called junk bonds, which are issued by companies with shaky finances. To compensate investors for the greater risk of default, junk bonds offer higher yields.

Sound overwhelming? It'll seem less baffling if we look at some sample portfolios.

186. SAMPLE PORTFOLIO: ONE FUND

Suppose you have settled on a basic mix of 60 percent stocks and 40 percent bonds. This 60-40 mix is often referred to as a balanced portfolio. How should you go about building your desired portfolio?

You can find mutual funds that offer this combination in a single fund, thus giving you one-stop investment shopping. For instance, you could buy a traditional balanced fund, though you might find the stock portion is invested largely or entirely in U.S. shares, with no foreign exposure.

Alternatively, you could purchase a target-date retirement fund that has a 60-40 mix. Target-date funds often have more diverse portfolios than traditional balanced funds, including more invested abroad. You'll also find that these funds become more conservative as they approach their target date. Target-date funds, which are found in many 401(k) plans, are geared to folks retiring in the year specified in the fund's name or within a few years of that date.

Financial advisors and other experts often criticize target-date funds as cookie-cutter solutions that aren't customized to reflect each individual's particular financial needs. But this criticism is self-serving: Target-date funds are a threat to financial advisors, because they provide investors with well-diversified portfolios—without the need to hire a financial advisor.

Most of the major fund companies now offer target-date funds, including Fidelity Investments, T. Rowe Price Group and Vanguard Group. Target-date funds—and also balanced funds—might be appealing if you're looking for simplicity. They are also a good choice if you find investing nerve-racking, because all you see is a single share price, which will move relatively sedately compared to the shares of more narrowly focused funds.

187. SAMPLE PORTFOLIO: THREE FUNDS

Target-date retirement funds are a great solution for many folks. But what if you want to build your own balanced portfolio? You could do it with as few as three mutual funds:

- U.S. stocks: 40 percent
- Foreign stocks: 20 percent
- U.S. bonds: 40 percent

Because you're buying one fund for each of these three key market sectors, you should avoid funds that are too specialized in their focus. For instance, for your lone U.S. stock fund, you might look for a fund that buys large and small companies and doesn't tilt strongly toward growth or value stocks. That's the sort of mix you get with a total stock market index fund, which seeks to replicate the performance of a broad market index, such as the Wilshire 5000. Examples include Fidelity Spartan Total Market Index Fund, Schwab Total Stock Market Index Fund and Vanguard Total Stock Market Index Fund.

Like U.S. total stock market index funds, you can find total international stock index funds. The latter invest in both developed foreign markets and emerging markets. Examples include Fidelity Spartan Global ex US Index Fund, iShares Core MSCI Total International Stock ETF, Vanguard FTSE All-World ex-US Index Fund and Vanguard Total International Stock Index Fund.

What should you do for bond exposure? You might purchase a bond fund that focuses on higher-quality bonds with short or intermediate maturities. A popular strategy: Play it safe with bonds, by sticking exclusively with short-term securities, and compensate for the lost yield by investing somewhat more heavily in stocks.

188. SAMPLE PORTFOLIO: EIGHT FUNDS

As your wealth grows, you might venture beyond a one-fund or three-fund portfolio and get a little more sophisticated. Here's what an eight-fund balanced portfolio might look like:

- U.S. large-cap stocks: 27 percent
- U.S. small-cap stocks: 9 percent
- Real estate investment trusts: 3 percent
- Developed foreign stock markets: 14 percent
- Emerging stock markets: 5 percent
- Gold stocks: 2 percent
- Short-term corporate bonds: 25 percent
- Inflation-indexed Treasury bonds: 15 percent

What do these extra funds get you? You gain greater control over your diversification, with dedicated exposure to, say, emerging markets and U.S. small-cap (or "capitalization") stocks. You add alternative investments through real estate investment trusts and gold stocks.

You also improve the diversification of your bond allocation with the addition of inflation-indexed Treasury bonds, an intriguing diversifier thanks to the guaranteed inflation protection, though less intriguing at today's modest yields. On top of all this, you introduce the chance to goose returns by rebalancing within asset classes.

189. SAMPLE PORTFOLIO: 12 FUNDS

Consider yourself an investment junkie? Here's what a balanced portfolio might look like if you were willing to buy a dozen funds:

- U.S. large-cap value stocks: 13 percent
- U.S. large-cap growth stocks: 13 percent
- U.S. small-cap value stocks: 5 percent
- U.S. small-cap growth stocks: 5 percent
- Real estate investment trusts: 3 percent
- Developed foreign markets large-cap stocks: 10 percent
- Developed foreign markets small-cap stocks: 4 percent
- Emerging stock markets: 5 percent
- Gold stocks: 2 percent
- Short-term corporate bonds: 23 percent
- Inflation-indexed Treasury bonds: 14 percent
- High-yield junk bonds: 3 percent

This portfolio is probably most notable for what it doesn't include. There are no bonds from developed foreign markets. This avoids inserting currency risk into the conservative portion of a portfolio. Similarly, there's no emerging-market debt, which is now mostly denominated in local currencies, not U.S. dollars. In addition, there's no dedicated U.S. mid-cap exposure, in large part to hold down the number of funds.

Academic research suggests you can boost performance by tilting a portfolio toward value and small stocks. We'll discuss that further in Part IX. You could easily adapt the above portfolio to that strategy by upping the allocation to U.S. large- and small-cap value funds, while shrinking the stake in the two growth funds. Alternatively, you could anchor your U.S. stock portfolio with a total market index fund, which would give you broad U.S. stock market exposure, and then add U.S. large- and small-cap value funds to provide the tilt. The latter strategy may involve lower investment costs, and somewhat smaller tax bills, than buying the two growth funds and two value funds, plus you'll own fewer funds.

Beyond the chance to tilt toward value or growth, what's the advantage of this more complicated portfolio? As with the moderately complicated portfolio, you gain greater control over your diversification and get the opportunity to bolster returns through rebalancing, but to an even greater degree.

190. REBALANCING WITHIN ASSET CLASSES

Earlier, we discussed rebalancing between stocks, bonds and other asset classes. This might boost returns over the short run by forcing you to buy stocks during a market decline, which then sets you up nicely for the market rebound. But over the long run, this rebalancing will likely crimp your returns because you'll often be cutting back on stocks. Instead, the main reason to rebalance between asset classes is to control risk by keeping your portfolio's asset allocation in line with your target portfolio percentages.

By contrast, rebalancing within asset classes has the potential to boost returns. Suppose you own the moderately complicated portfolio described earlier, which includes 27 percent in U.S. large-cap stocks, 9 percent in U.S. small-cap shares, 14 percent in developed foreign stock markets and 5 percent in emerging stock markets. Let's also assume that these different parts of the global stock market generate similar long-run returns.

As long as these various investments don't notch the same return every year, you should bolster your long-run returns if you follow a strategy of regularly rebalancing back to your target percentages. Let's say U.S. large-cap stocks outperform U.S. small-cap shares this year, but next year U.S. small-cap stocks make up the ground lost. If you rebalanced at the end of this year, you should boost returns next year by making sure you have a healthy weighting when small-cap stocks outperform. Over long periods, rebalancing among stock market sectors might add around half a percentage point a year to your return.

This comes with a few caveats. You need to make sure that any performance advantage isn't eroded by investment costs and taxes. In addition, while rebalancing sounds simple, it can be tough in practice. It means bucking the crowd and buying into parts of the market that others currently loathe—not an easy thing to do.

191. GREAT DEBATES: CAN THE MARKET BE BEATEN?

Over the short term, there's no doubt that the market can be beaten. Every year, whether through luck or skill, there are plenty of stock funds that outperform the market averages. But what about the long term? As the time frame gets stretched, the number of winners shrinks.

This is no great surprise. Before costs, investors collectively earn the market's return, because together we are the market. After costs, we must—as a group—lag behind. As the years pass and the investment costs mount, the chances of outperforming the averages grow slimmer and slimmer.

To be sure, there are investment heroes who beat the odds and come out on top. Berkshire Hathaway Chairman Warren Buffett, with his 50-year record of beating the market, is probably everybody's favorite example. But in many ways, this is the power of anecdotal evidence: We remember big lottery-ticket winners, because they make the evening news. We forget about the million of losers, because they're never mentioned.

As you will learn in the next chapter, there are strategies—such as overweighting value stocks or putting more in smaller-company stocks— that have generated market-beating returns over long periods. But the academics who have documented these results typically note that the extra reward comes with extra risk. In addition, if you aren't careful, any performance edge could be devoured by investment costs. Still, if you pursued these strategies by buying and holding low-cost index funds for many decades, there's at least a moderate chance you could earn returns that are better than the broad market averages.

But this is hardly the sort of strategy that appeals to most folks who are looking to beat the market. Instead, they envisage buying funds run by hotshot managers, dabbling in initial public stock offerings and actively trading individual shares. These strategies are no doubt entertaining, they appear like an easy road to riches and they generate enough occasional winners to keep investors coming back. But they're unlikely to succeed over the long haul, in part because of the high investment costs involved.

192. SELECTING INVESTMENTS

Once you've settled on your target mix of stocks, bonds, cash investments and alternative investments, and then decided how you'll diversify within these categories, you have your portfolio's framework. This will drive your portfolio's risk level and its potential return. The next step: Decide which investments you'll buy for each slot in your portfolio, such as the 15 percent you plan to invest in large-cap value stocks, the 5 percent you have earmarked for emerging stock markets or the 10 percent for short-term bonds.

For the vast majority of investors, the right choice will be funds, whether it's actively managed mutual funds, index mutual funds or exchange-traded index funds. If you're investing through your employer's 401(k) or similar retirement plan, mutual funds may be your only choice.

What about buying individual stocks and bonds? Unless you have a multi-million-dollar portfolio, it's hard to purchase enough individual investments to get broad diversification. One rule of thumb suggests you need at least 20 individual stocks to be diversified. While that might be enough to reduce the risk that you will be seriously hurt by a single rotten stock, you still run the risk that your stock portfolio's performance will lag far behind the market averages. To eliminate that risk, you will probably need to buy funds.

Moreover, when investing in foreign securities, funds are the only practical choice for the typical investor. An additional reason to favor funds: You'll likely find it less nerve-racking than owning individual securities, because the diversification offered by funds should make for a smoother ride.

Any exceptions? You might avoid fund expenses by purchasing individual Treasury bonds, where there's scant risk of default and hence diversification isn't that important. That's discussed in Part IX. If you have the speculative urge, you might also set aside 3 to 5 percent of your portfolio for a "fun money" account and use that to purchase individual securities.

193. MUTUAL FUNDS

Looking to buy funds to build your desired portfolio? You'll be immediately confronted with a crucial choice: Should you buy actively managed funds, market-tracking index funds or some combination of the two?

Most funds are actively managed, meaning they try to pick securities that will outpace some market index. This has proven tough to do, with the vast majority of active funds generating market-lagging results.

For proof, check out the regularly updated study from S&P Dow Jones Indices, part of McGraw Hill Financial. The so-called SPIVA study (short for Standard & Poor's Indices Versus Active), which can be found at spindices.com, compares the performance of actively managed stock and bond funds to appropriate benchmark indexes. The results are not encouraging for active funds, with most funds trailing behind the market.

Why have actively managed funds struggled? You can blame it on two issues: The cost of active management and the efficiency of the markets. We take a closer look at investment costs in the sections that follow, including the cost of using a financial advisor. Later in the chapter, we turn to the issue of market efficiency.

The poor performance of actively managed funds has driven many investors to dump active funds and instead buy index funds, which simply seek to replicate the performance of a benchmark index. According to the Investment Company Institute, stock index mutual funds accounted for 20.2 percent of stock mutual fund assets at year-end 2014, up from 11.6 percent a decade earlier.

Moreover, mutual funds aren't the only way to index. If you go the indexing route, you'll need to choose between index mutual funds and exchange-traded index funds. Over the past decade, ETFs have exploded in popularity, and their total assets now rival those of index mutual funds.

194. WHY COSTS MATTER

When the stock market can soar 30 percent in a year and individual stocks can quickly double, investment costs might seem like a minor issue. But the market doesn't soar 30 percent every year, and most of your stocks, if they double in value, will likely take many years to do so.

Indeed, in a lower-returning market, costs can loom large. Suppose the stock market notches 6 percent a year. If you lose 1.5 percentage points to mutual fund expenses and other costs, you would be left with 4.5 percent. Trade frequently? You could surrender 25 percent of your annual gain to taxes, which means your 4.5 percent would become less than 3.4 percent. That might not seem so bad—unless inflation is running at 3 percent, in which case you're making almost nothing.

You can't do anything about inflation. But you can do your best to hold down investment costs and minimize taxes. Let's say you bought a mutual fund that charges 0.5 percent in annual expenses and held it inside a Roth IRA. Even if the fund's manager picks stocks that perform no better than the market, you would earn a 5.5 percent annual return, leaving you comfortably ahead of the 3 percent inflation rate.

Investors are increasingly aware of the damage done by high investment costs. A 2015 study by Chicago investment researcher Morningstar found that, over the prior decade, 95 percent of new investor dollars had flowed into mutual funds and exchange-traded funds with annual expenses that are among the lowest 20 percent.

So which costs should you watch out for? Try to keep a close eye on trading costs, fund annual expenses and the amount you pay for financial advice.

195. TRADING COSTS

You're highly unlikely to earn market-beating returns either by picking individual securities on your own or hiring a fund manager to do so on your behalf. That doesn't mean your stocks and bonds won't enjoy occasional market-beating years. But long term, even if your investment picks are better than average, any edge will likely be more than offset by the trading costs you incur:

Brokerage commissions. These get all the advertising attention, but don't let those $5 trades fool you. Brokerage commissions are often the least important cost when buying and selling stocks.

Bid-ask spreads. Every stock has two prices, the price at which you can buy (the ask) and the lower price at which you can sell (the bid). Result: If you bought and immediately resold a stock, you would lose money, perhaps as much as 5 percent with a thinly traded small-cap stock.

Markups. If you buy a bond that has been issued and is now trading in the secondary market, the brokerage firm involved will take the current asking price and add a markup. The markup on bonds sold to individual investors might be 2 or 3 percent of the price.

Sound grim? The good news is, if you invest through mutual funds, you should enjoy lower trading costs because funds can use their buying power to demand tiny commissions, markups and bid-ask spreads.

There are, alas, also two pieces of bad news for mutual fund investors. First, funds suffer market-impact costs. Their own buying can drive up the price of a security, making it more expensive to accumulate a position, and their selling can drive down a security's price, so they end up with less money when they sell. Second, if you invest in mutual funds, you have to pay all the fees charged by the funds themselves.

196. MUTUAL FUND COSTS

As a fund investor, you incur the fund's trading costs—but you also have the costs associated with buying, owning and selling the fund itself.

Mutual fund commissions. Broker-sold funds, sometimes referred to as load funds, might charge a commission when you buy, an ongoing commission that's levied every year (known as a 12b-1 fee) and a commission when you sell.

Investing on your own? You can buy no-load funds, which don't charge any sort of commission. What if, instead of buying your no-load funds directly from the mutual fund company involved, you invest through one of the fund marketplaces operated by discount brokerage firms? You may pay a transaction fee when you buy or you could find that the funds levy somewhat higher annual expenses.

Annual fund expenses. All funds charge annual expenses to cover the cost of managing the fund and handling administrative tasks. In addition, the annual expenses may include a 12b-1 fee to cover marketing and distribution. This fee is often used to compensate brokers. A fund's trading costs aren't included in its published annual expenses.

Fund expenses are expressed as a percentage of fund assets, so a fund with a 1.5 percent expense ratio is charging you $1.50 a year for every $100 you have invested. You can also think of this as the breakeven hurdle rate. If a fund charges 1.5 percent a year, it has to pick securities that beat the market by 1.5 percentage points just to match the performance of the fund's benchmark index.

Account maintenance fees. You might be charged an annual fee if you hold your funds in a brokerage account or in an IRA.

On top of all this, there's the biggest investment cost of all: taxes. We tackle that topic in Part XI.

197. LOAD FUNDS

Many load mutual funds have a bewildering array of share classes, each typically designated by a letter. Working with a financial advisor who is compensated through commissions? The broker will likely suggest one of three share classes:

A shares. These charge a significant upfront commission, often 5.75 percent for stock funds, and a modest ongoing 12b-1 fee, typically 0.25 percent per year. Despite the upfront cost, A shares are often the best choice for longer-term investors and those with large sums to invest. If you invest a significant sum with one mutual fund company, or once your account has grown large enough, the upfront purchase commission can be sharply reduced. Ask your broker about so-called rights of accumulation.

B shares. These funds charge a hefty annual 12b-1 fee, usually 1 percent, and a back-end commission if you sell in the first five or six years. That so-called contingent deferred sales charge might scale down from 5 to 1 percent as you hold the fund for longer. If you have a modest sum to invest and, say, an eight-year time horizon, these can occasionally be the best share class to buy. But most of the time, you would fare better with another share class, given the sizable 12b-1 fee on B shares and the fact that the back-end commission isn't reduced if you invest large sums.

To curb abuses, fund companies sometimes cap the amount that can be invested in B shares at $100,000. Dishonest brokers may try to sidestep this restriction and earn larger commissions by spreading an investor's money across multiple fund companies. Dishonest brokers may also pitch B shares as having "no initial commission," while neglecting to mention the back-end charge.

C shares. These shares might charge a 1 percent commission if you sell in the first year. After that, there's no back-end commission. You will, however, incur a large annual 12b-1 fee that's often 1 percent, similar to B shares. But while B shares can convert to A shares after perhaps seven years, at which point the 1 percent 12b-1 often drops to 0.25, this never happens with C shares. The upshot: C shares make most sense for those who are investing for only a few years.

198. FEE-BASED ACCOUNTS

Historically, brokers have been paid through the commissions they charge every time you buy and sell. But spurred by the example of fee-only financial planners, even the major brokerage firms are now looking to reduce the emphasis on commissions and instead charge a percentage fee based on an account's size. For instance, a financial advisor might charge 1 percent annually on a $1 million account, equal to $10,000 a year.

This eliminates many of the conflicts-of-interest that come with paying commissions. Still, fee-based arrangements can be expensive—and perhaps so expensive that good investment performance is unlikely.

For a $250,000 or $500,000 account, the advisor's fee might be 1.5 percent. Add that to the annual expenses of the mutual funds that are bought, which could be 1 percent, and clients might find themselves paying 2.5 percent a year. It is extremely unlikely that the funds involved will perform well enough to compensate for those costs and keep up with the market averages over the long haul. What if you have less than $250,000 to invest? You'll struggle to find a traditional advisor who will manage your account on a fee basis. Instead, check out the burgeoning group of online advisors.

JONATHAN'S TAKE: Despite the drawbacks, paying fees is preferable to paying commissions. But here are three pieces of advice: First, try to limit the fee to 1 percent—and even less if you have a seven-figure portfolio. Make sure the same percentage is charged on all accounts you have with the advisor, even if it's, say, a small Roth IRA. Also make sure the fee is lowered if you add significant money to the account.

Second, push your advisor to find you funds with low annual expenses, preferably below 0.5 percent, on average. Third, make sure that, in return for your annual fee, you get more than just management of the money you have with the advisor. Your advisor should meet with you regularly, help you develop a financial plan, provide guidance on your workplace retirement plan, and offer advice beyond investments, including suggestions on estate planning, insurance, and handling debt and real estate.

199. CONFLICTS OF INTEREST

A good advisor could prove to be your financial salvation. But it doesn't always work out that way. The risk: Your advisor is either incompetent or puts his or her interests ahead of yours.

With any luck, after reading this guide, you will know what prudent investment advice looks like, so you can tell if an advisor is pushing some dubious strategy. But you also need to be alert to the potential conflicts of interest that come with the four different methods of compensating an advisor:

Commissions. If advisors are paid through commissions, they have an incentive to get you to trade more frequently and to buy higher-commission products.

Percent of assets. If an advisor is compensated by charging, say, 1 percent of the assets that you have invested, that helps to align your advisor's interests with yours because you both benefit if the account grows in value. Nonetheless, it does create subtle conflicts. For instance, advisors might dissuade clients from taking money from their investment account to pay down debt because the shrunken account would generate less in fees. Advisors might also push clients to claim Social Security early, so the investment account shrinks more slowly in the early years of retirement and hence generates larger fees. Looking for an advisor who charges fees, not commissions? You might try the National Association of Personal Financial Advisors, located at NAPFA.org.

Hourly fee. Only a small number of advisors work on an hourly basis. There is a risk they will drag out the work, costing clients more than is necessary. But the potential financial loss would be relatively modest. Many hourly advisors are part of the Garrett Planning Network. You can search for members at GarrettPlanningNetwork.com.

Flat monthly or annual fee. Again, only a small number of advisors charge flat monthly or annual fees, though this includes some of the fast-growing online advisors. The risk is that, even if you get a lot of value in the initial months, your need for help diminishes over time and yet you keep paying that regular fee. But as with the hourly arrangement, the risk seems modest and is more than offset by knowing precisely what you're paying.

The method of compensation and the total cost are crucial. But price isn't the only consideration. You also need to ask tough questions, so you're confident an advisor is likely to provide good advice.

200. INTERVIEWING ADVISORS

If you need a financial advisor, by all means ask colleagues and neighbors for recommendations. But keep in mind that a lot of folks are good friends with their advisors. What they pay in fees, and the quality of the advisor's recommendations, are secondary considerations. Want to hire a top-notch advisor? Forget friendship—and focus on asking the right questions:

• How are you compensated and what's the total cost I can expect to pay each year? Ask for a dollar amount, not just percentages. What other expenses will I incur, such as fund expenses and account fees?

• Are you held to a suitability or a fiduciary standard? An advisor who is held to a fiduciary standard must act in your best interest. Those held to a suitability standard, which is what happens when a broker is paid commissions, must merely recommend investments that are suitable.

• What credentials do you hold? There's a maddening array of credentials held by advisors, some of them meaningless. You should be comforted if an advisor is a Chartered Financial Analyst (CFA), Certified Financial Planner (CFP) or Chartered Financial Consultant (ChFC). If they have a business, accounting or law degree, that's all the better. While brokers will trumpet that they've passed, say, the Series 7 or the Series 6, those are technically licenses that allow them to do business, not credentials that prove they're knowledgeable about the finer details of personal finance.

• Where have you worked and how long have you been in the investment business? While everybody needs to start somewhere, there's no need to let an advisor learn the ropes with your money.

• How would you describe your investment philosophy? Here, you're looking for an intelligent summary of how they navigate the financial markets, not a series of clichés or hollow boasts about beating the market.

• What complaints have been lodged against you by customers? While there might have been legal claims, most formal complaints result in arbitration proceedings. If advisors are licensed with FINRA, you can see whether there are any "disclosure events" by going to FINRA.org and using the site's BrokerCheck database.

• Beyond putting together a portfolio, what other aspects of my financial life will you help with? Some advisors assist with tax returns, estate planning, insurance and when to claim Social Security. Will they charge extra for these services—and do they outsource them to another firm?

201. ONLINE ADVISORS

Looking for a low-cost advisory service? It may be no farther away than your computer keyboard.

In recent years, there's been a proliferation of online advisors, including firms such as Betterment.com, FutureAdvisor.com, Jemstep.com, LearnVest.com, MotifInvesting.com, PersonalCapital.com, Rebalance-IRA.com, SigFig.com, Wealthfront.com and WiseBanyan.com. These firms typically either charge a percentage fee, based on the assets you invest, or they levy a monthly charge. Either way, you'll likely pay far less than the 1 percent of assets or more charged by many traditional advisors. Many of the online advisors further trim your costs by recommending low-cost exchange-traded index funds.

Bigger financial firms are also muscling into the low-cost advice business. Vanguard Group's Personal Advisor Services costs just 0.3 percent a year. Charles Schwab has a free advisory service that uses its own and other firms' exchange-traded index funds. For a fee, discount broker TradeKing will also build a portfolio of ETFs for you. Fidelity Investments is expected to launch an online advisory service in 2016.

The downside is that you typically lose the face-to-face contact you enjoy with a traditional advisor. The advice you receive is usually focused solely on your portfolio, while many traditional advisors will help with your broader financial life. Still, these computer-driven services can offer a more rigorous investment approach than you get with many traditional advisors, who may be basing decisions more on gut instinct and an occasional review of your portfolio. In addition, if you have less than $250,000 to invest, it's hard to find an advisor who will manage your account on a fee basis and give your finances the attention they deserve, so an online advisor may be your best bet for low-cost, high-quality advice.

202. GREAT DEBATES: SHOULD YOU HIRE A FINANCIAL ADVISOR?

There are two great reasons to hire a financial advisor—and two great reasons not to.

An advisor can potentially provide you with both financial expertise and a steadying hand that keeps you on the right financial track. Traditionally, it's been the expertise that was emphasized: Brokers would pride themselves on picking good stocks for clients and offering insights into the market's direction. But increasingly, advisors are less a source of expertise and more a conduit for it. They draw on insights from their firm's research department, invest clients' assets with professional money managers and get investors' questions answered by turning to a network of accountants, estate-planning lawyers and insurance experts.

That means many advisors are doing less advising and more coaching. They might push clients to save more, get their estate plan updated and stick with their stocks during market declines. This sort of coaching can be enormously valuable, given the self-inflicted financial wounds investors often suffer when left to their own devices.

Set against these two advantages are two notable disadvantages. First, and most obvious, is the cost involved. Paying 1 or 1.5 percent of assets every year to an advisor might sound reasonable—but, when converted into dollars, it often turns out to be a huge sum.

Second, many advisors are not especially insightful and some are downright crooked. This creates a quandary for investors: They need an advisor because they don't feel qualified to manage their own money—but that means they probably also aren't qualified to judge whether an advisor is any good. Still, hiring a moderately good advisor is probably better than leaving your cash languishing in a savings account. But before you hand over your life's savings, you ought to thoroughly investigate at least three advisors, ask the tough questions and don't hire anyone unless you're confident you have the right person.

203. MARKET EFFICIENCY

You come across a company with a great product that's growing like a weed, you buy the stock—and the shares go nowhere. The Commerce Department announces robust economic growth for the latest quarter—and stocks tumble.

What's going on here? Stock and bond prices reflect both currently available information and also investors' collective expectations about future developments. When that new information becomes available, investors quickly buy and sell securities based on whether the news was better or worse than expected. Suppose a company reports a 25 percent increase in earnings. Impressive? If analysts were forecasting 29 percent growth, the stock could get pummeled.

This puts ordinary investors in a tough spot. No matter how much research you do, you're highly unlikely to know something that other investors don't know (unless you are trading on insider information, which is not advised). True, you could prove better at interpreting this information by, say, predicting correctly that a company's new product will be more successful than other investors imagine. But how likely is this, especially when you're competing against professional investors with business degrees, great analytical tools and access to the latest market research?

Alternatively, you could hire some of these professionals to pick investments for you, which is what you do when you purchase actively managed mutual funds. But history tells us most active funds lag behind the market. It isn't that these managers are dummies. The problem is that they and other professional investors are super-smart. If there are investment bargains to be had, they don't stay that way for long.

The markets aren't perfectly efficient. But they are efficient enough that, once you figure in investment costs, it's unlikely you will earn market-beating returns, whether you invest on your own or hire a professional money manager. The upshot: More and more investors are opting to index.

204. INDEXING

The math of investing is brutally simple: Before costs, investors collectively earn the market's performance. After costs, they must earn less. In fact, investors collectively trail the market averages by an amount equal to the investment costs they incur. Some folks may get lucky and beat the averages. But the vast majority won't.

What to do? You might focus on capturing the market's return at the lowest possible cost—by purchasing market-tracking index funds. Index funds buy many or all of the securities that make up a market index in an effort to match that index's performance. The funds almost always fall short of their goal, because they charge annual expenses and incur trading costs. Result: If a market index is up 8 percent in a year, the corresponding index funds might earn 7.8 or 7.9.

That might not sound great. But it's a lot better than most actively managed funds, which might earn just 6.5 or 7 percent, on average, because of their higher costs. Admittedly, by purchasing index funds, you give up all chance of beating the market. But you also eliminate the risk that you will fall far behind. As an added bonus, index funds tend to be highly tax-efficient, because they don't actively trade their portfolio and thus they are slow to realize capital gains. That means they can be an especially good choice if you are investing taxable account money, as we'll discuss in Part XI.

Convinced? You still have a key choice: Should you buy index mutual funds or purchase exchange-traded index funds?

JONATHAN'S TAKE: I'm a huge fan of indexing, whether with index mutual funds or ETFs. Extraordinarily few investors manage to beat the market over the long term, so why try? With index funds, you may not beat the market—but you'll beat most other investors.

205. INDEX MUTUAL FUNDS VS. ETFs

Index funds come in two flavors. The pioneers were of the mutual fund variety. With a mutual fund, you can buy and sell just once a day, with the share price established as of the 4 pm ET market close. If you purchase no-load index funds, typically your only cost is the fund's annual expenses.

The upstart competitors are exchange-traded index funds, or ETFs, which are listed on the stock market. You can trade them throughout the day, just like any other stock. ETFs have exploded in popularity over the past decade. They usually have lower annual expenses than comparable index mutual funds—but they ought to, because they don't have the administrative costs associated with shareholders' buying and redeeming shares. Instead, those costs are borne directly by the shareholders themselves. If you want in or out of an ETF, you have to go through a brokerage firm and trade the exchange-listed shares. That will mean paying the bid-ask spread, typically a brokerage commission and maybe also an annual brokerage-account maintenance fee.

Which are better, index mutual funds or ETFs? Many folks end up with ETFs because they're looking to trade frequently in and out of the market, a costly strategy that can quickly wipe out indexing's low-cost advantage. ETFs also come in more varieties, so they may be your only choice if you want a more specialized index fund, and you can buy them no matter which brokerage firm you use. In addition, ETFs have the potential to be more tax-efficient than index mutual funds, thanks to a peculiarity related to the way ETF shares are created.

ETFs will often be the better choice if you plan to invest a large sum and leave it there for many years. But that doesn't describe the behavior of many ordinary investors, who might invest a modest sum initially and then add to their holdings frequently thereafter. If that describes you, you will likely find that index mutual funds make more sense, because you'll avoid the trading costs involved with frequent ETF purchases.

206. PICKING ACTIVE FUNDS

You've heard all the arguments in favor of indexing—but you still want to try your hand at picking actively managed funds. What should you look for as you seek market-beating funds for each slot in your target portfolio?

• You want fund managers with great performance over five years and preferably longer. If a mutual fund has notched market-beating returns but the manager responsible has since moved on, the record is meaningless.

• You want managers with strong records relative to an appropriate benchmark index. If we've had a period when small-company growth stocks have sparkled, small-company growth-stock managers will have good absolute performance. But how do these managers compare to an index of small-company growth stocks?

• You want to see consistency. If a manager has a great five-year record but it's built on one spectacular year, you may be looking at a fluke performance.

• You want annual expenses of less than 1 percent, and the lower, the better. An actively managed fund will charge more than an index fund. Still, if the expenses are too high, the manager will find it awfully tough to beat the market.

• You should lean toward funds with lower portfolio turnover, preferably 40 percent or below. Like high expenses, high turnover means high costs—and it'll be that much harder for the manager to beat the market. High turnover also usually means big annual taxable distributions.

• You should favor smaller funds. If a fund's dazzling record has attracted billions of new dollars from investors, the manager could struggle to invest the money involved and may be forced to buy less attractive investment ideas.

As you search for actively managed funds, be sure to spend some time on Morningstar.com, where you can find the data you need to analyze funds.

207. CORE AND EXPLORE

Actively managed funds or index funds? Many investors opt for "all of the above." They build a core position in index funds, thus ensuring that part of their money captures the market's return, and then enhance it with actively managed funds in hopes of goosing performance.

For instance, once you've settled on your target investment mix, you might build two parallel portfolios, one entirely of index funds and the other with active funds. Alternatively, you might use, say, 80 percent of your savings to build your target portfolio using index funds and then invest the other 20 percent in actively managed funds that seem promising, without worrying too much about which market sectors these managers focus on.

Some investors take a third approach: They view the market for blue-chip U.S. stocks as highly efficient, so they index that portion of their portfolio using, say, an S&P 500-index fund. A third of all money in stock and bond index mutual funds is in S&P 500 funds. Meanwhile, these investors figure smaller U.S. stocks and foreign markets are less efficiently priced, so an active manager has a better shot at generating market-beating returns.

The latter argument is a little dubious: The reason small stocks and foreign markets may be less efficiently priced is because it's more expensive to trade these shares—and thus trying to exploit the inefficiencies may not be worth the trading costs involved. Moreover, actively managed funds that focus on smaller U.S. shares and foreign markets tend to charge higher annual expenses. Those high expenses also make it harder to earn market-beating returns.

208. INDEX MUTUAL FUND MANAGERS

Led by founder John C. Bogle, Vanguard Group introduced the first index mutual fund for ordinary investors in 1976. The fund, which tracks the S&P 500-stock index, was slow to attract investors. But as it took hold through the 1980s and 1990s, Vanguard introduced additional index funds that tracked other parts of the market. By the late 1980s, other major fund companies were also trying to get into the market.

Still, for ordinary investors, Vanguard remains the leading provider of index mutual funds, in part because of its unusual ownership structure. Vanguard is effectively owned by the shareholders of its mutual funds, who are rewarded for their ownership through lower annual expenses. This allows Vanguard to offer index funds with rock-bottom annual expenses.

Other lower-cost providers of index funds include Fidelity Investments and Charles Schwab. Schwab's index funds have a minimum initial investment of just $100, making them an intriguing choice for investors with limited means. To keep up with the world of indexing, visit Bogleheads.org and check out the latest conversations.

While Vanguard dominates the market for index mutual funds geared to ordinary investors, Dimensional Fund Advisors has carved out a niche among financial advisors, who are drawn to DFA's unique collection of index funds. The strategies employed by DFA funds are heavily influenced by academic research.

209. EXCHANGE-TRADED FUND MANAGERS

State Street Global Advisors launched the first exchange-traded index fund in 1993 with the introduction of SPDR S&P 500 ETF. As of late 2015, the fund had some $180 billion in assets and was easily the largest ETF.

Still, if anything, State Street's SPDR family of ETFs has been playing catch-up in recent years. In 2000, the iShares group of ETFs, then owned by Barclays Global Investors and now part of BlackRock, was launched. Thanks to an aggressive marketing campaign that saw a slew of new funds introduced, iShares quickly grabbed significant market share and today ranks as the largest manager of ETFs.

Reluctantly, Vanguard followed suit in 2001 with its own lineup of ETFs, which were based on the firm's existing collection of index mutual funds. BlackRock's iShares, State Street's SPDR ETFs and Vanguard are now the three largest managers of ETFs, though a host of smaller players have also entered the market. WisdomTree has a broad selection of funds that weight stocks by their earnings and dividends. PowerShares offers a slew of ETFs focused on narrow industry sectors. Charles Schwab has a relatively small collection of stock and bond funds, most of which have very low annual expenses.

210. ACTIVE FUND MANAGERS

Want to put together a portfolio of actively managed mutual funds? Your first hurdle: the overwhelming number of funds to choose from.

You could narrow your focus by sticking with one of the big three no-load mutual fund companies—Fidelity Investments, T. Rowe Price Group and Vanguard Group—and then picking among their funds. But you may be shortchanging yourself.

Other fund families worth checking out include American Century Investments, Artisan Funds, Baron Funds, Charles Schwab, Dodge & Cox, Janus, Loomis Sayles, Nicholas Funds, Pimco Funds, Oakmark Funds, TIAA-CREF and William Blair Funds. Also spend some time investigating fund companies that have a distinctive investment approach, like Conestoga Small Cap Fund, Fairholme Fund, FPA Funds, Longleaf Partners Funds, Mairs & Power, Royce Funds, Selected American Shares, Sound Shore Fund and Tweedy, Browne. These funds all specialize in a single part of the market or are renowned for a particular stock-picking style. Perhaps that focused effort will pay off.

It can be a paperwork nightmare if you buy funds directly from a host of fund companies. An alternative: Use one of the mutual fund marketplaces that are operated by many brokerage firms, including the brokerage arms of major fund companies like Fidelity and Vanguard. If you use one of the marketplaces, you may have to pay a transaction fee when you trade funds or the funds might charge slightly higher annual expenses. Still, that might seem like a small price to pay, given the convenience of holding all your funds in one place.

To find actively managed funds that hold promise, you'll need to play detective. Head to the library and leaf through back copies of *Forbes*, *Kiplinger's Personal Finance* and *Money* magazines. Check out *The Wall Street Journal*'s regular section devoted to mutual funds. Spend some time on Morningstar.com. Soon enough, you will have a list of funds that have decent returns for the past three or five years. But will that market-beating performance continue? That's the big question with actively managed funds—and, much of the time, the gamble doesn't pay off.

PART IX

FINANCIAL MARKETS
*TAKING RISK,
HOPING DESPERATELY FOR REWARD*

Y ou should consider this chapter, and the one that follows, as optional. After reading Part VIII, those who find investing laborious or befuddling should have all the information they need to build a sensible investment portfolio. Instead, the next two parts are for investment junkies, those who want a deeper understanding of the debates and concepts that consume finance professionals.

In this chapter, we'll talk about what drives stock and bond returns, including the connection to economic growth and the importance of valuations. This is the basic return you should capture if you buy index mutual funds or exchanged-traded index funds.

We will also discuss various ways investors try to improve upon this return. They might do so by guessing the overall market's direction, overweighting particular sectors or picking investments that perform better than average. In particular, we'll discuss factors associated with superior stock market returns. We'll look at various bond market categories, everything from Treasury notes to junk bonds to emerging-market debt. We'll wrap up the chapter with a quick look at cash investments and an overview of different alternative investments.

Inevitably, this survey will be less than comprehensive. In their hunger for higher returns, investors employ an astonishing array of strategies—and only a smattering are covered here. This chapter's goal: Offer some thoughts that might make you a better judge of markets and asset classes, and perhaps allow you to earn somewhat better returns.

This chapter's survey is also a little skewed. How so? We spend more time on stocks than bonds, because stocks are both more complicated and more interesting. Yet, for most investors, bonds are the bigger part of their portfolio. The Federal Reserve puts the value of all U.S. bonds at $38.5 trillion, compared to $36.2 trillion for stocks. What if you look at both U.S. and foreign markets combined? The global bond market is valued at $85.9 trillion, versus $63.5 trillion for the global stock market.

211. WHAT'S HOT

Overall, it was a tepid year for stock and bonds. But for investment junkies inclined to dig into the numbers, there were some fascinating developments. After five years of lackluster returns, foreign stock markets finally showed some life in 2015, with the performance of developed foreign stock markets rivaling U.S. shares. Emerging markets also looked like they might be big winners in 2015, but the markets crumbled after surging early in the year.

Meanwhile, within the U.S. market, large-company stocks outpaced smaller-company shares and growth stocks beat out value shares. That made it a disappointing year for those who take their cues from academic research. In particular, academic studies suggest that value stocks will outperform growth stocks—and yet just the opposite happened not only in 2015, but also over the past five and 10 years.

The enthusiasm for indexing remains unabated, with money continuing to pour into exchange-traded index funds. But it's unclear how much of this money is coming from long-term investors who believe the way to win the investment game is to humbly accept the performance of the market averages—and how much is coming from traders who are using ETFs to dart in and out of the market.

The enthusiasm for yield also remains unabated, with money chasing preferred stock and lower-quality bonds. But many buyers seem to be oblivious to the risks they are assuming. Remember, if an investment offers the prospect of a high return, there must be high risk involved—even if the risk isn't immediately apparent. Puerto Rican municipal bonds provided a reminder of that risk, as investors who snapped up the bonds for their high yield instead ended up watching the island commonwealth default on some bond payments and threaten default on others. It was the same story with master limited partnerships, which lured investors with juicy yields but then sank along with falling oil production.

As memories of the 2007–09 stock market collapse continue to fade, the passion for alternative investments has also apparently died down. There's far less chatter about hedge funds, long-short funds, managed futures funds and market neutral funds, in part because results have been mostly unexceptional. Gold also had weak results in 2015, and bitcoins were rarely headline news.

212. DOS AND DON'TS FOR 2016

This chapter is designed to get you to think—but not necessarily to act. Still, here are some "to dos" for 2016:

• Consider what low stock and bond returns would mean for your financial future, and whether you ought to compensate by spending less and saving more.

• Avoid fund expenses by buying Treasury bonds directly from the federal government through TreasuryDirect.gov.

• Historically, money-market funds have been one of the best options for cash investments. But today, you'll likely fare better with an online savings account or by purchasing certificates of deposit and, if necessary, selling your CDs before maturity and paying the early withdrawal penalty.

• If you want to add alternative investments to your portfolio, don't overlook gold stocks. They are far below their 2011 highs, they have a long history of low correlation with the stock market, and they don't involve the hefty investment costs of either hedge funds or "liquid alt" mutual funds and exchange-traded funds.

And here are some things you shouldn't do:

• Don't adopt thoroughly discredited investment strategies. In particular, market timing and technical analysis remain surprisingly popular with ordinary investors—and yet academics and professional investors are in broad agreement that these strategies don't work.

• Don't overweight growth stocks. Academic research says value stocks outperform. The value effect could weaken, now that it's received so much publicity. But it seems unlikely that growth stocks, despite their relatively strong performance in 2015, will suddenly emerge as long-run winners.

• Don't chase yield, whether it's with bank loan funds, junk bonds, emerging-market debt or elsewhere. Collecting lots of interest may be comforting—but often you end up with risk that approaches that of the stock market.

213. WHY STOCKS SHOULD BEAT BONDS

Stocks were a great investment over the past century, but miserable performers between early 2000 and early 2009. That wretched period still looms large in the minds of some investors. What can we expect in future? Nobody knows. But for stock investors, there's reason for both optimism and caution.

The broad U.S. stock and bond markets have generated roughly similar returns over the past 16 years. But that shouldn't persist. Stocks are riskier than bonds, so they should be priced to deliver higher returns. When you buy a stock, you become an owner, with the prospect of endless gains if things go well and the possibility of losing everything if they don't. Meanwhile, as a bond investor, you are merely a lender, with limited upside—represented by the yield—but also less risk. If a company gets into difficulty, its bondholders will be paid off before stock investors receive anything. The bottom line: If stocks didn't hold out the prospect of higher returns, people would be crazy to buy them (which, in retrospect, was true in early 2000).

But it isn't just that investors demand a higher return when they buy a risky asset like stocks. Corporations should also supply it. As the economy grows, corporate earnings ought to climb, and shareholders may also collect dividends. By contrast, with bonds, overall yields shouldn't be greater than the growth rate of nominal gross domestic product—and right now they're below the GDP growth rate. That suggests bond investors will earn modest returns, and they could see bond prices tumble if interest rates rise.

While the long-term outlook may be brighter for stocks than for bonds, there's one caveat and one wildcard. The caveat: The full benefit of economic growth doesn't necessarily flow through to shareholders. Earnings per share likely won't match the economic growth rate, which means share price gains will probably lag behind GDP. And then there's the wildcard: What value will investors put on corporate earnings and dividends? The fact is, as of late 2015, U.S. stocks aren't cheap.

214. INFLATION

When we discuss investment performance, we typically talk about nominal returns. But as an investor looking to increase your wealth, what you should care about are real returns, which are your results over and above inflation.

Over the past 50 years, inflation—as measured by CPI-U, the most widely used measure—has climbed 4.1 percent a year. But there's been a notable deceleration in recent decades. Average annual inflation ran at 7.4 percent in the 1970s, 5.1 percent in the 1980s, 2.9 percent in the 1990s and 2.3 percent in the 15 calendar years since year-end 1999.

Some observers worry that the Federal Reserve's loose monetary policy will reignite inflation. But so far, there's been scant evidence, with inflation climbing just 0.2 percent over the 12 months through October 2015.

Decelerating inflation has been good news for bond investors, who are especially vulnerable to inflation. Most bonds pay a fixed rate of interest, so inflation represents an unrecoverable subtraction from a bond investor's real return—unless that inflation subsequently turns to deflation.

By contrast, stocks can fare okay if inflation is high. Initially, accelerating inflation may depress share prices. But corporations can typically adjust to higher inflation, by raising the price they charge for their goods and services, thus compensating for any increase in wages and materials costs. That means corporate earnings can continue to grow faster than inflation. Assuming share prices rise along with those higher corporate earnings, stock investors will enjoy inflation-beating gains.

215. HISTORICAL ECONOMIC GROWTH

Over the 12 months through September 2015, nominal gross domestic product grew 3.1 percent and real GDP—meaning growth above the inflation rate—was up 2.2 percent.

This is below the average 2.9 percent real rate for the 50 years through year-end 2014. Still, it's been an encouraging stretch, given how rocky economic growth has been since 2000. Between 1997 and 2000, we had four consecutive years with GDP growth above 4 percent. Since then, we've had only two years—2004 and 2005—when growth reached 3 percent. Real GDP growth was dragged down by the Great Recession, with the economy shrinking 0.3 percent in 2008 and another 2.8 percent in 2009. But even before the Great Recession, economic growth was tepid. Real GDP has grown just 1.7 percent a year in the 14 full calendar years since year-end 2000, compared with a 3.4 percent annualized rate for the 10 years prior to that.

A big question: Are there structural impediments that are restraining economic growth, and do those impediments mean we won't return to the historical average of roughly 3 percent a year?

Experts have suggested economic growth may be slower because of the continued drag from the borrowing binge of the early 2000s, which is limiting the ability of some consumers to spend freely. Others have argued that income inequality is crimping economic growth. Low-income earners tend to save less of their income and spend more, so slow wage growth could mean slow economic growth. Yet others wonder whether the economy is being hurt by the aging population and the workforce's slower growth.

All this should concern stock investors. The reason: Slow economic growth would mean slower growth in corporate profits—and that would be bad news for share prices.

216. WHAT DRIVES ECONOMIC GROWTH

Real economic growth is driven by increasing the number of workers and by raising their productivity. The latter is the reason innovation is so important. If productivity rises, we increase GDP per capita, which means the standard of living for the average American ought to rise.

As both the number of workers and their productivity rises, GDP should grow. Over the past 50 years, the U.S. has enjoyed 2.9 percent annual growth in real GDP, with roughly half coming from productivity gains and half from increases in the working population.

That real GDP growth should, in turn, propel corporate earnings higher. As corporate profits rise, share prices will also tend to climb. The two, however, don't move in lockstep, and there's a decent chance that, in future, shares will lag behind economic growth.

Still, if you're a stock market investor and hence hoping for higher corporate earnings, you might cheer for greater immigration, while also being concerned about the aging population and the falling birth rate. Greater immigration should mean more workers and hence faster economic growth. But fewer babies and lots of workers reaching retirement age isn't so good, because that means fewer workers and potentially higher taxes to pay for retirees' Medicare and Social Security benefits.

Over the 10 years through 2022, the Bureau of Labor Statistics projects that the civilian workforce will grow at just 0.5 percent a year, versus 1.2 percent for 1992–2002 and 0.7 percent for 2002–12. That slowing growth is one reason some observers argue that we'll see disappointing GDP growth in the years ahead—and possibly modest stock returns.

JONATHAN'S TAKE: While the U.S. and other developed nations could grow more slowly as their populations age, this isn't yet an issue for emerging markets like India, Malaysia and Mexico. The implication: You may want to include a healthy exposure to emerging markets in your portfolio.

217. STOCK RETURNS AND ECONOMIC GROWTH

Day to day, stock prices are driven by the latest news—government data, corporate announcements, political developments, you name it—which is why it's so hard to forecast short-term performance. But in theory, over the long term, the key driver of stock returns should be economic growth.

That certainly appears to have been the case over the 50 years through year-end 2014. During that stretch, nominal U.S. economic growth (which includes inflation) averaged 6.7 percent a year, per-share profits for the companies in the S&P 500-stock index rose 6.4 percent and, lo and behold, the S&P 500-index climbed 6.6 percent. Meanwhile, annual inflation ran at 4.1 percent.

In other words, the growing economy drove up corporate profits and that, in turn, propelled share prices higher. On top of that, investors also collected dividends. Fifty years ago, the S&P 500 companies collectively generated a yield of 3 percent. As of year-end 2014, the yield was 1.9 percent. The stock market's share price-to-earnings multiple was 18 at the beginning of the 50 years and the P/E was 20 at the end.

Problem is, the past 50 years are a little misleading, as you'll learn in the next section. Yes, there may be a long-run relationship between economic growth and stock returns. But stock investors likely won't reap the full benefits of economic growth.

Moreover, economic growth and stock returns seem barely related in the short term. Why not? Investors don't care whether the economy is booming or suffering right now. Instead, they're focused on what might happen next year or the year after that. This is the reason savvy investors will often buy stocks in the midst of a recession, anticipating that the economy will soon recover.

218. FALLING TAXES AND RISING MARGINS

Based on the U.S. experience of the past 50 years, there appears to be a tight connection between economic growth and stock returns. But the story is messier than it seems. While economic growth and per-share profits for the S&P 500 companies grew at a similar pace over the past 50 years, earnings per share were only able to keep up with economic growth because of falling corporate tax rates and rising corporate profitability.

The top corporate tax rate has dropped from 52 percent in the early 1960s to 35 percent today. Thanks to complicated tax maneuvering, many companies manage to pay substantially less than 35 percent. Result: The corporate income tax as a percentage of GDP has plummeted over the past 50 years. As corporate income taxes have fallen and profit margins have widened, after-tax corporate profits have grown from 6.3 percent of GDP in 1964 to 10.5 percent in 2014.

Trouble is, falling corporate taxes and widening profit margins are onetime gains. Stock investors can't benefit again from after-tax corporate profits rising from 6.3 percent of GDP to 10.5 percent—unless there were a sharp contraction first. That doesn't mean tax rates couldn't fall further and profit margins couldn't widen further. But there are limits to both. Corporate taxes can't get any lower than zero. Meanwhile, the share of GDP that goes to corporate profits, which comes at the expense of salaries and wages, can't keep growing and growing, and it could reverse.

That would be grim news for stock market investors. Over the past 50 years, the combination of falling taxes and rising profitability has helped offset one of the most insidious threats to stock market investors: dilution.

219. DILUTION

As corporations issue more shares and as new companies emerge, existing shareholders see their claim on the economy's profits diluted. Indeed, the economy's fastest growth often occurs among privately held companies. Ordinary stock market investors can't buy into these private companies until they have grown large enough to be taken public in an IPO, or initial public offering.

The historical dilution suffered by existing shareholders has been estimated at around two percentage points a year by money managers Robert Arnott and William Bernstein in a September/October 2003 article for the *Financial Analysts Journal*. In other words, if the economy grows at a nominal 5 percent a year, earnings per share might grow at 3 percent. If earnings per share trail the economy's growth rate, share-price appreciation is also likely to lag, unless there's an offsetting rise in the stock market's price-earnings ratio.

Could you compensate by investing in faster-growing companies? For instance, would it make sense to invest in IPOs? Even though companies sold through IPOs are often growing fast, they typically prove to be disappointing investments. Why? Fast growth alone doesn't make for a good investment. It also matters what price you pay for that growth.

That brings us to one of investing's most counterintuitive notions: Often, slower-growing companies and slower-growing countries turn out to be better stock market investments—because they can be bought at more reasonable valuations.

220. PRICE-EARNINGS RATIOS

How much you make as a stock market investor depends on how fast earnings per share grow at the companies you own and on how much you collect in dividends. But it also depends on the price you pay. How can you gauge how expensive stocks are? Probably the most popular measure is the price-earnings ratio, which is a company's stock price divided by its earnings per share. Suppose you have a $34 stock with earnings per share of $2 for the past 12 months. The stock would have a P/E of 17.

P/E ratios can be tricky to analyze. For starters, make sure you understand what earnings are being used. Some P/Es are calculated using the last 12 months' reported earnings. Based on that measure, the U.S. market's average P/E multiple was 16.1 over the past 100 years and 18.9 over the past 50 years. As of late November 2015, it stood at 22, above the 50-year average.

Some investors prefer instead to use expected operating earnings for the next 12 months. This has the benefit of looking to the future, which is what investors care about. It also ignores the onetime writedown of assets, which can distort reported earnings, and instead focuses on underlying corporate profitability.

Using expected operating earnings has its own problems, however. You are relying on analysts' forecasts, which are notoriously rosy. Moreover, while writedowns may be onetime, they do reflect an admission of management error (yes, money was lost) and those onetime writedowns seem to occur all too often.

Whether you are looking at trailing or expected earnings, those numbers are captive to the business cycle. During economic booms, robust earnings can make the market's P/E ratio appear more reasonable than it is—which could be the case right now. Conversely, during recessions, companies may lose money, driving up the market's P/E ratio and scaring off investors, when in truth it may be a great time to buy. To address this issue, some investors have turned to cyclically adjusted P/E ratios or they look at other popular measures of the market's value, such as dividend yields and price-to-book value.

221. CYCLICALLY ADJUSTED PRICE-EARNINGS RATIOS

Because standard price-earnings ratios can be misleading, some investors rely on cyclically adjusted price-earnings ratios, or CAPE, a measure developed by Yale University professor Robert Shiller and fellow economist John Y. Campbell. CAPE is often referred to as the Shiller P/E.

The Shiller P/E is based on an average of reported earnings for the past 10 years, with earnings from earlier years adjusted upward to reflect inflation. This averaging has the benefit of smoothing out earnings, which can fluctuate widely from year to year. The average Shiller P/E was 19.7 over the past 50 years and 16.7 over the past 100 years. But the average since year-end 1989 has been 25.3, suggesting that the CAPE multiple may have moved into a permanently higher range. As of late November 2015, it was at 26.4.

If the Shiller P/E has moved permanently higher, that's both good news and bad news. The good news is, we may not see a reversion back to the

50-year average P/E of 19.7, which would knock 25 percent off current share prices. The bad news is, with valuations so elevated, returns are likely to be modest because we probably won't see valuations climb much higher. Those rising valuations have helped to contribute to the stock market's impressive long-run return.

If you want to dig deeper into the data on U.S. market valuations, do an Internet search for Robert Shiller's home page and then click on the Online Data tab. Meanwhile, at StarCapital.de/research/StockMarketValuation, you can find the Shiller P/E for foreign markets, as well as other valuation measures. You can also find thought-provoking commentary on P/Es at CrestmontResearch.com.

222. EARNINGS YIELDS

Stock investors often grow more enthused as share prices climb, which isn't rational. After all, shoppers don't rush enthusiastically to the department store the day after the sale ends and prices go back up.

One possible solution: Think like a bond investor. If bond yields drop from 6 to 5 percent, bond buyers immediately grasp that their nominal return will be lower. Similarly, stock investors might feel less cheery about rising share prices if they focus on earnings yields, which are the amount of corporate earnings they buy with every dollar invested. Earnings yields are the reciprocal of price-earnings ratios: Instead of dividing a company's share price by its earnings per share, you divide the earnings by the price.

Those earnings might be paid out as dividends, used to buy back stock or reinvested in the business with a view to boosting future earnings growth. For buyers in late 2015, the earnings yield on the S&P 500 was 4.5 percent, down from 7 percent at year-end 2011. That means that, compared with four years ago, every dollar invested buys you a claim on 36 percent less in earnings. A bond investor wouldn't be happy to receive 36 percent less in interest. Shouldn't stock investors feel the same way?

Earnings yields figure prominently in the so-called Fed model, which was popular in the late 1990s. The Fed model compares the S&P 500's earnings yield, using forecasted earnings for the next 12 months, with the yield on the 10-year Treasury note. If the S&P 500's earnings yield is above the 10-year Treasury yield, the model suggests stocks are more attractive than bonds.

While the Fed model retains a following among investors, its popularity has waned, in part because it doesn't appear to have predictive power. The model also has a fundamental flaw: It isn't clear why you should compare corporate earnings, which rise over time, with the fixed steam of interest from government bonds.

223. DIVIDEND YIELDS

Many companies don't pay dividends, so looking at dividend yields won't necessarily tell you whether one stock is better value than another. But it can be useful in gauging how expensive the overall market is. As of late November 2015, the S&P 500 companies were yielding 2 percent. That's an improvement over the 1.2 percent at year-end 1999, but well below the level of earlier decades. Yields stood at 3.5 percent at year-end 1969, 5.2 percent at year-end 1979 and 3.2 percent at year-end 1989, and have averaged 3 percent over the past 50 years and 4.1 percent over the past 100 years.

The market's dividend yield has trended down partly because stocks have become more expensive over time and partly because companies have instead used their spare cash to buy back their own shares. Historically, total shares outstanding have grown almost every year, as employees exercise stock options and companies issue new shares to raise cash or finance acquisitions. But that's changed over the past decade: Corporations have been big buyers of their own stock, and these share buybacks have roughly offset new issuance.

Buybacks are seen as a more tax-efficient way of returning money to shareholders, because the money is used to cash out investors who want to depart without saddling the remaining shareholders with taxable dividends. Buybacks may also reflect the past decade's slow-growth economy. With fewer chances for profitable expansion, some companies have decided instead to use spare cash to repurchase shares.

Trouble is, companies appear to be terrible market timers. They aggressively bought back their own shares ahead of the 2007 stock market peak, slashed their buying during the market slump that followed and now, with stock prices up sharply over the past seven years, they're once again aggressively buying back shares. One explanation: Buybacks are driven less by companies' belief that their shares are undervalued and more by a desire to offset the dilution caused by employees exercising stock options. The latter is more likely to happen during buoyant markets, as the options gain value along with rising share prices.

Will the buyback craze continue? It's hard to know. Buyback programs are often quietly abandoned, while dividends seem like a surer thing, because companies are loath to cut their dividend. Over the 50 years through year-end 2014, there were 12 years when the share price of the S&P 500 companies declined—but just five years when dividends dropped. Knowing they have to pay a regular dividend can be a healthy discipline for management, forcing them to be more careful in handling the company's cash. Meanwhile, for investors, dividend-paying stocks can provide a fairly reliable and growing stream of income. Over the 50 years through 2014, the dividends paid by the S&P 500 companies grew at an average 5.7 percent a year, comfortably ahead of the 4.1 percent annual inflation rate.

224. PRICE-TO-BOOK VALUE

If you open a company's annual report and turn to the page showing its balance sheet, you'll see something called stockholder's equity, which is the value of the company's assets minus its liabilities. Stockholder's equity reflects the amount investors have put into the company through stock offerings and reinvested earnings—and how much they might receive if the company were liquidated and all liabilities paid off.

Investors will sometimes take stockholder's equity, figure out this "book value" on a per-share basis, and then compare it to the current stock price. A stock might be considered undervalued if it trades below book value and overvalued if it trades well above.

But this can be overly simplistic. For instance, if a company has to write down the value of some of its assets, that can take a big chunk out of book value—and make its shares seem overvalued based on price-to-book value. Similarly, if a company has intangible assets such as brand names and patents, these may not be listed at full value on the asset side of the ledger, and thus they won't be fully reflected in stockholder's equity. Based on price-to-book value, certain companies—such as banks and insurers—look consistently cheap, while technology companies often appear expensive.

Despite its flaws, price-to-book value remains a popular yardstick, especially among value investors. While price-earnings ratios based on recent or expected earnings can sometimes be misleading, book value often provides a steadier gauge of a company's value.

225. HISTORICAL VALUATIONS

If you had bought U.S. stocks a century ago, at year-end 1915, you would have paid 11 times trailing 12-month reported earnings and earned an initial dividend yield of 4.5 percent.

In the years that followed, the market and valuations fluctuated widely, with shares posting healthy gains in the 1920s, suffering mightily in the 1930s, bouncing back in the 1940s, roaring in the 1950s, losing steam in the 1960s and struggling through the 1970s.

By July 1982, after more than 16 years of often wretched stock returns, investors had scant appetite for stocks. Shares traded at less than eight times earnings and had a dividend yield of 6.2 percent. A spectacular two-decade bull market followed, interrupted only briefly by the 1987 market crash and the 1990 market decline. By early 2000, U.S. stocks were trading at a flabbergasting 29 times earnings and yielded just 1.2 percent.

There followed not one but two huge bear markets, both of which saw the value of U.S. stocks roughly cut in half. By the end of the second bear market, in early 2009, stocks were at a statistically meaningless 110 times earnings. That price-earnings multiple resulted from severely depressed corporate profits at many corporations and huge losses at a few companies.

A truer gauge of stocks' value was the dividend yield, which stood at 3.6 percent, though even that was a little misleading because many companies were slashing their dividends at the time. Still, by the 2009 stock market bottom, stocks were yielding more than 10-year Treasury notes. That had been typical up until 1958, but many market participants never thought they'd see it again.

Since the 2009 market bottom, shares have tripled in price. After that long rally, U.S. stocks were at 22 times trailing earnings as of late November 2015, with a dividend yield of 2 percent. That's not cheap by historical standards, which raises a key question: What return can investors expect from here?

226. WHITHER STOCKS?

Predicting short-term stock market returns is impossible. Even forecasting long-run returns is tough to do with any precision. Still, it's important to have some sense for what you might earn over the next 10 years, so you don't save too little or spend too much.

Where to begin? Don't simply extrapolate recent returns or rely on long-run historical averages. Instead, consider stock market returns in terms of three components: the dividend yield, earnings growth and the price put on those earnings, in the form of the price-earnings ratio.

If you buy the stocks in the S&P 500 today, you will get a dividend yield of 2 percent. You might assume that the economy—and hence corporate profits—will grow at a nominal 4 percent a year, comprised of perhaps 2 percent inflation and 2 percent real economic growth. Combining the 2 percent dividend yield and 4 percent nominal growth would give you a 6 percent return.

But what about the market's P/E? It's higher than the long-run historical average based on cyclically adjusted 10-year earnings, so the odds suggest P/Es are more likely to fall over the next 10 years than climb. But that's not a certainty. A 2012 study by Vanguard Group looked at a variety of financial metrics, and found that both cyclically adjusted P/E ratios and P/Es based on trailing 12-month reported earnings were the best predictors of stock returns over the next 10 years. Even so, they explained just 40 percent of returns.

In addition to falling P/Es, stock investors face three other risks. First, profit margins may shrink. Second, earnings per share may lag behind economic growth because of share dilution. Third, economic growth may be sluggish. All this suggests there's a risk of disappointment. Result? Over the next 10 years, stocks might have a total return—share-price gain plus dividends—of less than 6 percent a year, while inflation runs at 2 percent. This sub–6 percent return doesn't reflect the hit from investment costs and taxes. The outlook for foreign stocks appears brighter, thanks to lower valuations, and thus a globally diversified portfolio might return somewhat more than 6 percent a year, before costs and taxes.

What if the stars align, the bad stuff doesn't happen and the U.S. market's P/E climbs from current levels? While that might seem like a happy prospect, don't be too quick to cheer: You may discover that you're effectively borrowing from the future.

227. BORROWING FROM THE FUTURE

Stock prices should rise with per-share earnings growth. What if we do better than that in the year ahead, thanks to rising P/E multiples? Given that the stock market has rebounded nicely from the 2007–09 bear market, we wouldn't be playing catch-up after a period of depressed valuations. Instead, we would likely be borrowing from the future.

As our portfolios grow fatter, that might not seem so bad. But remember, richer valuations mean future returns will likely be lower, and any new dollars invested will buy shares at those higher valuations. In fact, as discussed in Part VII, those still saving for retirement should probably pray for lousy returns.

This same phenomenon occurs with other investments. Remember the housing boom during the initial years of this century? Annual price increases raced far ahead of inflation. But those gains effectively borrowed from the future, resulting in wretched returns from mid-2006 onward.

Similarly, bond investors notched handsome returns as the 10-year Treasury yield plunged to record lows in 2012. But from there, returns have been relatively weak, and any new dollars invested have bought bonds at extremely modest yields.

228. MARKET TIMING

When you look at charts of long-run stock returns, the road to wealth seems obvious: You want to own shares during bull markets and sidestep those nasty market declines. Yet that has proven extraordinarily difficult to do. Stock market gains and losses tend to occur in short bursts, so it's all too easy for market timers to be caught flat-footed. While market-timing was popular decades ago, today money managers typically stay fully invested in the market, and instead try to add value through stock-picking.

But doesn't it make sense to steer clear of stocks when they are well above their historical valuations? Problem is, stocks can stay overvalued for many years and may never revert to the low valuations we've seen in the past. Shares have, by historical standards, been expensive for much of the past 25 years. Those who took that as a sell signal would have missed the 2000–02 and 2007–09 bear markets—but they would also have missed the huge gains of the 1990s, when U.S. stocks returned more than 400 percent, including dividends.

Instead of focusing on valuations, some investors try to divine the market's direction by studying stock-price movements and searching for patterns. This search drives so-called technical analysis, which is the study of past security-price movements in order to predict what will happen next.

For instance, among market timers, a popular strategy is to track the stock market's 200-day moving average. If the stock market moves above the average closing price for the past 200 trading days, this is taken as a buy signal, while falling below is seen as a signal to sell.

Does this work? For a February 2013 article for MarketWatch.com, Mark Hulbert, founder of the newsletter Hulbert Financial Digest, looked at how you would have fared historically if you had used the 200-day moving average to time the market. He found that, since 1990, your annualized return would have been just 3.8 percent, compared with 7.3 percent if you had simply bought and held stocks.

229. FAT TAILS

Extreme events happen more frequently than we imagine. Think back over the past two decades in the financial world. We had the stunning stock market rally of the late 1990s and the subsequent stunning decline, especially among technology stocks. We had the housing mania that peaked in mid-2006 and the grueling bust that followed. We had the financial crisis of 2008, with reverberations still felt today. In his 2007 book *The Black Swan*, Nassim Nicholas Taleb highlighted how the supposedly improbable occurs with surprising frequency—and yet folks are shocked every time.

Such extreme events suggest that, instead of market returns being normally distributed, with most years seeing middling performance, the tails of this humped-back distribution curve tend to be fat because of the surprising number of extreme events, hence the term "fat tails." This can be seen as evidence of market inefficiency: Far from being rational, investors tend to be a little manic, becoming both overly exuberant and excessively pessimistic in response to economic and political developments. For those looking to time the market, this might make their venture seem more promising.

But fat-tail events might also be viewed as another reason for humility. Few people forecasted the extreme events that we have seen in recent decades. Given that these extreme events seem to be relatively commonplace, we should probably avoid making overly large bets on any one investment, so we don't miss out on the next surprising market surge or run the risk of seeing our portfolio hurt by the next unforeseen disaster.

230. STOCK PICKING

While market timing has fallen from favor, many investors still have an enduring belief in good old-fashioned stock-picking. The hope: If they invest with a collection of skilled mutual fund managers who each have a laser-like focus on one part of the market, they can earn above-average returns.

This approach has led to "style box" investing. Investors might buy a selection of U.S. stock funds that focus on large-capitalization, mid-cap and small-cap stocks. Within these three size ranges, they might purchase a top-rated growth fund, value fund and blended-style fund. That means they end up with nine different U.S. stock funds. Similarly, they might then purchase a collection of mutual funds that give them exposure to foreign stocks and to the bond market.

A recipe for success? It seems not. S&P Dow Jones Indices, part of McGraw Hill Financial, puts out a regularly updated study comparing actively managed funds to appropriate market indices. Over the 10 years through midyear 2015, the vast majority of funds in the nine U.S. style boxes underperformed their benchmark index. The failure rate ranged from 91 percent for mid-cap blend funds to 61 percent for large-cap value funds. Meanwhile, among international funds, the failure rate varied from 92 percent for emerging-market funds to 57 percent for international small-cap funds. Results for bond funds were equally dismal. The full report can be found at spindices.com.

This market-lagging performance should be no great surprise. It isn't easy to find market-beating stocks and bonds. Every trading day, investors pore over the market, hunting for bargains. If a stock is undervalued, it's unlikely to stay that way for long. But while the search for winning stocks is often fruitless, it isn't cheap. Many stock funds charge 1 percent or so in annual expenses and might incur another 0.5 percent in transaction costs, for a total of 1.5 percent. Sure enough, that's the sort of shortfall you typically see each year when you compare funds to their benchmark index.

231. HIGHER RETURNS THROUGH HIGHER RISK?

The efficient market hypothesis suggests that investments are properly priced most of the time, so you're unlikely to earn superior long-run returns by trying to identify market-beating stocks. This insight, coupled with ample evidence that most professional money managers don't beat the market, has led many investors to give up on actively managed funds. Instead, these investors have sought to capture the market's return at the lowest possible cost by buying market-tracking index funds.

What if you want to earn more than the market is delivering? The capital asset pricing model, which assumes efficient markets and which was developed during the 1960s, offered its answer: You need to take greater risk. We're talking here not about crazy risk, such as betting everything on one stock, but rather risk that can't be eliminated through broad diversification.

How do you measure this risk? Initially, it was assumed to be captured by a single factor, volatility, which was measured using something called beta. The overall stock market has a beta of 1, but you could potentially raise your portfolio's beta to, say, 1.1 by favoring more volatile stocks or using leverage.

Problem is, beta proved to be a poor predictor of returns. Research found that low-volatility stock portfolios generated higher risk-adjusted returns than high-volatility portfolios. In fact, in recent years, there's been a surge of interest in low-volatility portfolios, prompting the launch of exchange-traded index funds such as iShares MSCI USA Minimum Volatility ETF and PowerShares S&P 500 Low Volatility Portfolio, as well as mutual funds like Vanguard Global Minimum Volatility Fund.

With beta failing as a predictor of stock returns, academics started casting around for other factors that might explain why some groups of stocks perform better than others. Over the past three decades, a slew of research has been conducted on the topic, which has turned up four factors that appear to be associated with superior returns—and, no surprise here, Wall Street has been quick to capitalize.

232. ENHANCED INDEXING

In recent years, Wall Street has been abuzz with terms like smart beta, factor investing and fundamental indexing. What's this all about? Think about the money-management business from Wall Street's perspective.

Actively managing portfolios is lucrative for financial firms. But many investors have wised up to their poor performance, prompting them to buy index funds instead. Problem is, index funds aren't nearly as profitable for Wall Street. What to do? Wall Street's answer: Find a way to make more money off indexing by offering index-like funds that hold out the promise of market-beating returns.

Welcome to the world of enhanced indexing, where the goal is to capture the performance of those parts of the market that tend to outperform. Enhanced indexing has two strands.

The first strand focuses on factor investing, which involves overweighting stocks with certain attributes. Academics have long contended that, if you want higher returns, you need to take greater risk. That greater risk comes partly from favoring stocks over more conservative investments. But even within the stock market, academic research suggests you can enhance returns by taking the risk of overweighting four types of stocks: smaller companies, value stocks, those displaying price momentum and those with greater gross profitability.

The second strand involves a push to adopt alternative systems for weighting the stocks held within an index fund. Known as fundamental indexing, the idea is to own companies based on their economic importance, rather than their value as judged by the market. That economic importance is assessed using measures such as a company's total earnings, dividends or sales.

You can now buy mutual funds and exchange-traded index funds that seek to take advantage of factor investing and fundamental indexing. ETFs, in particular, have been launched thick and fast, as Wall Street firms vie to get their slice of the market for enhanced indexing.

JONATHAN'S TAKE: With my own portfolio, I tilt toward value stocks and small-company stocks. But I am not entirely convinced that these two sectors will continue to outperform, which is why I make sure my portfolio also includes funds that give me exposure to the broad stock market, both in the U.S. and overseas.

233. SMALL-STOCK EFFECT

Historically, small-company stocks have outperformed shares of larger corporations. For academics, this outperformance wasn't, by itself, surprising. Small stocks are more volatile than large stocks, so theory suggests they ought to compensate investors with higher returns. Instead, academics were intrigued because this outperformance was greater than could be explained by small stocks' higher volatility, as measured by beta.

The small-cap effect was detailed in a 1981 academic paper by Rolf Banz, then at Northwestern University. If greater volatility didn't fully explain small stocks' outperformance, what else was going on? It seems small-stock investors were getting rewarded for taking a risk that wasn't reflected in volatility.

This extra reward might be compensation for the higher trading costs involved with small-company stocks or the greater risk that these companies will end up in bankruptcy, because small stocks aren't as financially strong as large-cap stocks. Alternatively, it might be explained by the relative dearth of information available on smaller companies, in part because they aren't widely followed by analysts.

Why does it matter whether the small-stock effect, as well as other market anomalies, can be attributed to greater risk? If there is greater risk involved, such as the chance that you'll lose far more than the broad stock market during the next market slump and perhaps even see some of your holdings go bankrupt, the superior performance will likely continue. But if the extra return isn't a reward for taking extra risk, there's a good chance it will disappear as investors flock to take advantage of this "free lunch."

The discovery of the small-stock effect spurred the 1981 launch of an index fund devoted to U.S. microcap stocks. It was the first mutual fund offered by Dimensional Fund Advisors, which sells its funds through independent financial advisors. Since then, DFA has been at the forefront in creating funds based on the latest academic research. Many other fund companies now also offer small-cap index funds.

234. VALUE EFFECT

Like small-company stocks, value stocks have outperformed historically. Value investing is often associated with legendary investor Benjamin Graham, co-author of *Security Analysis*, the classic investment tome first published in 1934. But the value effect received its most famous academic endorsement in a 1992 paper by finance professors Eugene Fama and Kenneth French, who defined value stocks as those whose shares trade at a low price relative to their book value.

The following year, the two professors proposed their three-factor model. That model argued that a portfolio's return could be largely explained by its exposure to the overall stock market, to small-cap stocks and to value stocks.

Value's outperformance, which has occurred historically in both the U.S. and foreign markets, has been attributed to the greater risk involved. The companies involved often have shaky finances. That means there's a danger they could get into serious difficulty, especially during an economic downturn, and shareholders might lose everything.

Still, not everybody has been convinced by the risk argument. Before academics documented value's outperformance and attributed it to risk, these stocks were typically viewed as less risky than growth stocks, because their share prices were less volatile. An alternative explanation: It could be that the value effect is a behavioral phenomenon. Perhaps investors become overly enamored of growth companies and pay too much for their shares, while mistakenly shunning value companies, where growth prospects often appear grim. If that's the case, it could be that the value effect will disappear as investors adjust their behavior.

Intrigued by the value effect? There are plenty of index funds available that allow you to tap into U.S. large-cap and small-cap value stocks. Vanguard Group offers four value-tilted index mutual funds that are available directly to investors, while Dimensional Fund Advisors offer a variety of value funds through its network of independent advisors. There are also many ETFs available, including those from BlackRock's iShares unit, State Street's SPDR ETFs and Vanguard.

In addition, you might tilt your foreign stocks toward value. A new option: In December 2015, Vanguard Group plans to launch the Vanguard International High Dividend Yield Index Fund as both a mutual fund and an ETF.

235. MOMENTUM EFFECT

What goes up, it seems, keeps going up. Numerous academic papers have documented momentum in stock prices, notably the 1993 paper by Narasimham Jegadeesh and Sheridan Titman. Many quantitatively driven money managers follow a value strategy, but also look for upward price momentum, with a view to buying beaten-down value stocks that are starting to revive.

Researchers have found that stocks with strong short-term performance, typically over 12 months or less, often continue to perform well during the 12 months that followed. What's behind this share-price momentum? It seems difficult to explain the rewards of momentum investing in terms of increased risk (though that argument has been made).

Instead, it could be that, when good news emerges about a company, investors bid up the share price. But the initial share-price increase doesn't fully reflect the good news, perhaps because some potential buyers are concerned the improvement may be a flash-in-the-pan. Gradually, investors shed their concerns and purchase the stock, causing the shares to continue climbing.

PowerShares offers a series of ETFs that use momentum strategies, including funds focused on U.S. stocks, international shares and industry sectors. Other offerings include iShares MSCI USA Momentum Factor ETF and SPDR S&P 1500 Momentum Tilt ETF.

236. PROFITABILITY EFFECT

The latest contribution to factor investing comes from Robert Novy-Marx, a finance professor at the University of Rochester. He examined the stock market performance of companies based on their profitability, as measured by the ratio of gross profits to assets. Gross profits are a company's revenues minus what it cost the company to make the goods that were sold.

Don't confuse gross profits with net income, which is the earnings number that investors typically look at. Novy-Marx notes that net income isn't necessarily a good indicator of profitability because it can be depressed by, say, spending on research and development or an aggressive advertising campaign. That spending can mean greater profits down the road, yet it takes a short-term toll on reported earnings and thus can make companies look less profitable than they really are.

Novy-Marx found that buying companies with high gross profits, which is a form of growth investing, generates higher stock market returns. He also found that the strategy is especially effective if you buy more profitable companies, but focus on those with lower share prices relative to book value. In other words, by combining Novy-Marx's profitability criteria with French and Fama's value criteria, you should be able to identify stocks that are profitable but undervalued.

It would be hard to argue that buying more profitable companies is a riskier strategy, so there's a greater danger that the premium offered by the profitability effect will disappear relatively quickly. Both Dimensional Fund Advisors and AQR Capital Management have introduced funds designed to take advantage of the profitability effect. As they and others seek to exploit Novy-Marx's insight, the stocks involved could see their prices bid up—and future returns will be lower.

237. FUNDAMENTAL INDEXING

Historically, index funds have weighted stocks based on their total stock market value. But critics claim this overweights expensive stocks, because a stock's importance in an index climbs as its share price climbs. One solution: Change the way you weight stocks.

That's the idea behind fundamental indexing, which was developed by

Research Affiliates, a Newport Beach, Calif., money manager headed by Robert Arnott. In 2005, the firm launched its Research Affiliates Fundamental Index, or RAFI, which weights companies by fundamental measures of size, rather than by each company's market value.

Those fundamental measures of size include sales, cash flow, dividends and book value. By weighting stocks in an index fund using these measures of a company's fundamental value, the hope is to underweight stocks that are currently overvalued, while overweighting those stocks that are undervalued. This results in portfolios that look similar to those created by fans of factor investing, with tilts toward value stocks and small-cap shares.

Both PowerShares and WisdomTree offer a huge array of stock ETFs that are fundamentally weighted, while Charles Schwab offers six mutual funds and six ETFs that use fundamental weightings. Fundamental weighting is also employed by some bond funds, including PowerShares Fundamental High Yield Corporate Bond Portfolio and PowerShares Fundamental Investment Grade Corporate Bond Portfolio, both exchange-traded funds.

Arguably, the criticism of weighting securities by total market value is more telling when it comes to bonds. How so? If a stock has a high market value, that represents the collective enthusiasm of investors and could be viewed as a positive sign. But if a government or corporation has a substantial amount of debt outstanding, that represents a hefty need for borrowed money. That isn't a positive sign—and yet these are the issuers with the biggest representation in index funds that weight according to market capitalization.

238. WHAT DETERMINES BOND RETURNS?

On Sept. 30, 1981, the yield on the benchmark 10-year Treasury note hit a high of 15.84 percent. More than three decades later, on July 25, 2012, the yield touched bottom at a slim 1.43 percent. And that, in many ways, was the big financial story of the past three decades. As interest rates fell, bond prices rose. That enriched existing bondholders, while also boosting enthusiasm for stocks, which appeared more attractive as bond yields declined. The fall in interest rates made it cheaper for almost everybody to borrow, including corporations, governments and homebuyers.

But the big decline in interest rates is over. With the 10-year Treasury note finishing November 2015 at a yield of 2.21 percent, there's precious little room for interest rates to fall further—and ample room for them to rise. That means that, from here, all bond investors can reasonably expect to earn is the yield on the bonds they buy. Just purchased a 10-year Treasury yielding 2.21 percent? You shouldn't expect to collect anything more than that.

That 2.21 percent is barely above the 1.9 percent core inflation rate (which excludes food and energy) for the 12 months through October 2015. Moreover, the ride in the years ahead could be rough. In recent years, the Federal Reserve has artificially depressed interest rates in an effort to spur the economy's growth. But as the Fed retreats from its loose monetary policy, interest rates could climb, driving down the price of existing bonds. Remember, interest rates and bond prices move in opposite directions, so rising rates mean lower prices for existing bonds.

How high could rates climb? Historically, bond yields have closely tracked nominal economic growth. For instance, if GDP grows at 4 percent (including inflation) over the next few years, the yield on the 10-year Treasury note could rise toward that level. What to do? You might start by looking at your bond portfolio, considering the risks you're exposed to—and asking how you would react if the worst came to pass.

JONATHAN'S TAKE: While a globally diversified stock portfolio might return 6 percent a year over the next decade, bond investors probably shouldn't expect to earn much above 3 percent—and that assumes you lean toward corporate bonds and hence take a moderate amount of credit risk. That 3 percent or so may barely outpace the inflation rate.

239. RISK AND BOND RETURNS

Bond investors face a number of risks, such as inflation eroding the spending power of their interest payments and the possibility that the issuer of their bonds might default. But with interest rates so low, the big concern today is that rates will rise sharply. That will drive down the price of existing bonds, which will appear less attractive compared to newer bonds with their higher interest payments.

For an individual bond or bond fund, this risk is captured by a measure known as duration. For instance, if a bond has a duration of seven years, its price will likely climb 7 percent if interest rates fall by one percentage point and lose 7 percent if rates rise by a full point. If interest rates climb by one percentage point, bond investors today could easily lose more to price losses than they'll collect in interest over the course of a year. And it's entirely conceivable that rates could climb by more than one point.

On their websites, many mutual fund companies report the average duration of the bonds in their funds. You can also find duration information for funds at Morningstar.com. Looking at big potential losses on your intermediate or long-term bonds? If you swap into short-term bonds or cash investments, you will reduce the chance of a large loss, but you will pay a price in the form of reduced income.

What if you stay put and interest rates do indeed increase? You might focus on the silver lining: Rising rates will ultimately help your bond portfolio, as you invest new savings—and reinvest interest payments and the proceeds from maturing bonds—at the higher yields. One rule of thumb: If you're reinvesting your interest payments, you will benefit over the long haul if interest rates rise, provided your investment time horizon is longer than the duration of your bonds or bond funds.

By contrast, in that scenario—where your time horizon is longer than your bonds' duration—falling interest rates will work against you. Yes, the price of your bonds will get a short-term boost from an interest-rate decline. But your long-run return will be hurt because you will be reinvesting interest payments at the lower yield.

What if you would rather not see your bond portfolio roughed up by rising rates? Instead of a portfolio with, say, 60 percent stocks and 40 percent bonds, you might opt for 75 percent stocks and 25 percent cash investments—or, alternatively, close-to-cash investments, in the guise of short-term bonds and certificates of deposit. The expected long-run return of those two portfolios should be similar. Indeed, historically, shorter-term bonds have delivered much of the yield of longer-term bonds, but with significantly less risk.

240. COSTS AND BOND RETURNS

In today's low-yield world, it's more crucial than ever to hold down investment costs. Suppose a bond fund charges 1 percent in annual expenses. If the fund owns bonds yielding 10 percent, the after-cost yield collected by the fund's investors would be 9 percent. That means investors are losing a tenth of their investment income to expenses. But if the fund's bonds are yielding 3 percent and the fund charges 1 percent, investors will collect just 2 percent, as expenses snag a third of their potential yield.

Moreover, what counts is your return after inflation and taxes. You can fend off taxes by holding your bonds in a retirement account or buying municipal bonds. But inflation is harder to combat—and high expenses, whether they're charged by a fund or you incur them trading individual bonds, could leave you earning a yield that's below the inflation rate.

None of this would matter if bond-fund managers or individual investors were skilled enough to earn back their expenses and post market-beating results. But there's scant evidence of that. Instead, over five-year periods, the top performers in any particular bond-fund category will usually be those funds with the lowest annual expenses.

There's also a danger that higher-cost funds will prove riskier than their low-cost competitors. Managers of higher-cost funds may be especially aggressive as they strive to overcome their costs and thereby keep up with lower-expense funds. That extra risk could come back to haunt these fund managers—and their shareholders.

Costs can also be a big issue when buying and selling individual bonds, thanks to the large markups that retail investors often pay. Check out the Market Data page offered by FINRA.org, where you can get details on individual bond issues. If you plan to buy or sell an individual bond in the secondary market, it's helpful to review recent trade data to see whether you're being offered a fair price. Better still, if you want to buy individual bonds, consider purchasing new issues and then holding the bonds to maturity.

241. GREAT DEBATES: BONDS OR BOND FUNDS?

Investors will often tout the benefits of individual bonds, while disparaging bond funds. Why? Owners of individual bonds not only avoid fund expenses, but also enjoy a comforting degree of certainty. If you buy a seven-year bond, you know how much interest you will receive each year and what sum you'll get back when the bond matures in seven years. By contrast, if you own a fund that focuses on bonds with an average maturity of seven years, you can't be sure how much interest you'll collect each year or what your fund shares will be worth seven years from now.

But the greater certainty of individual bonds is something of an illusion. If interest rates rise, both individual bonds and bond funds will fall in value, and holders of both could potentially lose money if they're forced to sell. On top of that, the performance difference between the individual bond and the fund likely won't be that great—and the individual bond comes with greater risk. If you purchase an individual bond, you're making a big bet on a single issuer, while a fund offers broader diversification. That big bet could come back to haunt you, as holders of Puerto Rican municipal bonds learned to their regret in 2015.

Moreover, when ordinary investors buy individual bonds, they're often charged huge markups, though you can sidestep this problem by purchasing new issues. A bond fund, meanwhile, should benefit from institutional pricing. Funds are also easier to buy and sell, plus you can reinvest your fund distributions in additional fund shares, no matter how small those distributions are.

That ability to reinvest is a key advantage, especially when interest rates climb. Yes, rising interest rates will depress the price of both individual bonds and bond funds. But with a fund, you can easily take advantage of those higher rates by reinvesting your distributions in additional fund shares.

242. NEW BOND ISSUES

The case for low-cost funds, including index funds, is especially compelling when it comes to bonds. But you might do even better—by buying newly issued Treasury, municipal and corporate bonds, and then holding them to maturity.

That way, there's typically no commission involved, you pay the same offering price as everybody else, including institutional investors, and you don't have to worry that the dealer has marked up a bond's price excessively. In the secondary market, where already issued bonds are traded, individuals often pay 2 or 3 percent more for bonds than institutional investors, and the markup (or markdown if you're selling) could be as much as 5 percent. The secondary market can be an especially rough place for retail investors in municipal bonds.

To purchase new Treasury bond issues, check out TreasuryDirect.gov. Most new municipal bond issues have a so-called retail order period, which allows individuals to place orders ahead of institutional investors. One problem: Your brokerage firm may not have access to the muni issues you're interested in. Similarly, it can be difficult to get your hands on new corporate bond issues. It may pay to work with a broker or brokerage firm that specializes in these bonds.

The biggest drawback with purchasing individual bonds is the lack of diversification. This isn't an issue with Treasurys, where a default is highly unlikely (though it may not seem that way amid all the political wrangling in Washington). But with munis and corporates, the risk of default is real. Unless you have huge sums to invest, you may not be able to buy enough issues to protect yourself against the financial impact of one or two rotten bonds.

243. TEN-YEAR TREASURYS

The total value of all U.S. bonds was $39.5 trillion as of June 30, 2015, according to the Securities Industry and Financial Markets Association. Treasury bonds were the biggest component, accounting for 32.2 percent, followed by mortgage bonds at 22.1 percent, corporate bonds at 20.6 percent and municipals at 9.4 percent.

But the Treasury market isn't important simply because of its size. It also provides investors with a crucial number: the yield on the 10-year Treasury note. This benchmark rate is used for all kinds of purposes, including figuring out a fair price for corporate bonds, valuing stocks, forecasting inflation and pricing mortgages.

Why is the 10-year Treasury so important? Many investors view it as the risk-free rate. In other words, if no other investment seems compelling, you could always buy 10-year Treasurys and collect the stated interest rate for the next decade, confident that there's little risk that you won't get your regular interest payments and that you won't get your principal back upon maturity.

Even though your nominal return is pretty much guaranteed, there remains a big risk: inflation. That explains the appeal of inflation-indexed Treasury bonds.

Not so worried about inflation and happy to buy regular Treasury bonds? While there are mutual funds that invest in Treasurys, you may want to avoid fund expenses and instead purchase individual Treasury bonds directly from the government. That does, however, come with drawbacks. A fund allows you to reinvest your regular interest payments, no matter how small, in additional fund shares. But to reinvest in individual Treasury bonds, you'll have to wait until you have accumulated $100 in interest and until the next auction occurs. It's also more of a hassle to sell individual Treasury bonds.

As of mid-2015, there was more than $14 trillion in Treasury and government agency securities outstanding. Individuals were modest players—at least in relative terms: They owned $1 trillion of individual bonds and mutual funds held another $1.1 trillion. The biggest holders were foreign institutions and individuals at $6.2 trillion.

244. INFLATION-INDEXED TREASURYS

Inflation-indexed Treasury bonds, formally known as Treasury Inflation Protected Securities, or TIPS, were first sold in January 1997, with the 10-year note initially yielding 3.45 percentage points more than inflation. Unfortunately, yields have been trending lower ever since. They did briefly spike above 3 percent in late 2008. But that rich yield didn't last long, and 10-year TIPS were yielding just 0.7 percent more than inflation as of Nov. 30, 2015.

While the yield on regular 10-year Treasury notes is often depicted as the risk-free rate, arguably that distinction belongs to 10-year TIPS. Not only are you protected against defaults, but also you're protected against inflation. The principal value of an inflation-indexed Treasury bond is stepped up along with the inflation rate. The semiannual interest payment is then calculated by applying the bond's rate to this increased principal value. For instance, if inflation runs at 3 percent and you buy bonds yielding 1 percent, your annual total return would be 4 percent. One warning: If you own TIPS in a regular taxable account, you will owe federal income taxes each year on both the interest payments and the step-up in principal value.

Want to get a handle on expected inflation for the next 10 years? Take the yield on regular 10-year Treasurys, which was 2.21 percent as of Nov. 30, 2015, and subtract the 0.7 percent offered by 10-year TIPS. The 1.5 percent difference is the annual inflation rate expected by investors over the next 10 years.

TIPS can be purchased directly from the government. But you might also check out low-cost mutual funds, such as Fidelity Spartan Inflation-Protected Bond Index Fund and Vanguard Inflation-Protected Securities Fund. There are also low-expense ETFs available, including iShares TIPS Bond ETF and SPDR Barclays TIPS ETF.

245. FLOATING RATE TREASURY NOTES

In January 2014, the U.S. Treasury began selling floating rate notes. The notes have a two-year maturity, with interest paid quarterly. Their yield changes based on the interest rate for 13-week Treasury bills. Through TreasuryDirect, the minimum purchase amount is $100. As with other Treasury bonds and many government agency bonds, the interest is taxable at the federal level, but exempt from state and local taxes.

With short-term interest rates currently so low, the yields on floating rate Treasurys are tiny. But the risk is also modest. Many bond investors fear rising interest rates, because it drives down the price of existing bonds. Yet owners of floating rate notes will benefit from a rise in short-term rates, because it will push up their yield. You can learn more at TreasuryDirect.gov.

246. SAVINGS BONDS

Savings bonds come in two flavors: EE and I. Series EE bonds pay a fixed interest rate for up to 30 years. For bonds purchased in the six months starting Nov. 1, 2015, that rate is a meager 0.1 percent a year. Meanwhile, I bonds increase in value along with inflation, plus holders can earn a small additional sum. For I bonds bought in the six months starting Nov. 1, 2015, the additional sum is 0.1 percent, over and above inflation.

Given that I and EE bonds both pay the same rate, but I bonds also offer inflation protection, I bonds are guaranteed to be the better deal—unless you plan to hold for 20 years or more. The unusual wrinkle: The Treasury Department guarantees that the value of EE bonds will double in value over 20 years. That means that, while the interest rate is just 0.1 percent a year for those with shorter holding periods, you're guaranteed 3.5 percent a year if you keep your EE bonds for 20 years. What if you sell any earlier? You're stuck with the 0.1 percent.

With both EE and I bonds, you can defer paying taxes until you sell or the bond matures, at which point the accumulated interest is subject to federal income taxes, but not state and local taxes. You may, however, be able to avoid that tax bill if the proceeds are used for college costs. You can learn more in Part IV.

Savings bonds can be purchased in amounts as small as $25. An individual could potentially buy $25,000 of savings bonds in a year, with the maximum set at $10,000 for EE bonds, $10,000 for I bonds and $5,000 for I bonds bought with a federal tax refund. You can sell a savings bond after holding it for one year. But if you sell within the first five years, you lose the last three months of interest. For more information, go to TreasuryDirect.gov.

247. MUNICIPAL BONDS

Municipal bonds can pay interest that's exempt from federal taxes and, if you own bonds from your own state, maybe state and local taxes as well. Sound appealing? Before buying, you should calculate whether munis make sense given your tax bracket. We tackle that topic in Part X.

If munis will give you a higher tax-equivalent yield, you might be tempted to purchase a muni fund that focuses on bonds from your state, so the interest is exempt from state as well as federal taxes. But these funds come with added risk. It isn't simply that you're focusing on bonds from a single state. Also, single-state muni funds often own relatively long-term bonds, so they could get hit hard by rising interest rates.

Many munis are issued with 20- or 30-year maturities. The issuer can often call the issue after 10 years. That means investors get their money back early, but they could be giving up a bond with an attractive yield. Bond calls are less likely to occur if interest rates head higher from here, because municipalities will find it tough to replace the called bonds with lower-interest debt.

Don't want to take so much interest-rate risk? Some national municipal bonds funds—those that buy bonds from around the country—focus on short-term or intermediate-term bonds. This may be a safer option, though you'll pay a price in lower yields and less tax savings.

Vanguard Group has an impressive array of municipal bond mutual funds with low annual expenses, while both BlackRock's iShares and State Street's SPDR ETFs have a fistful of municipal bond ETFs. Prefer a state-specific muni fund? You may have to cast a wider net to find a fund that focuses on your state's bonds, including checking out closed-end funds, which are discussed later in this chapter.

What about individual bonds? Those can be a decent bet if you buy and hold new issues, though you need to pay careful attention to credit quality. While municipal bonds were once viewed as almost risk-free, their reputation is now less sterling, thanks to recent defaults by Puerto Rico, Detroit and others. As of mid-2015, there was $3.7 trillion in municipal securities outstanding. Individuals were easily the biggest holders, owning $1.6 trillion of individual bonds, with another $1 trillion held by mutual funds.

To keep track of your portfolio, consider making use of BondView.com. What if you're buying or selling existing individual bonds in the so-called secondary market? Unscrupulous brokers may charge huge markups when you buy and hit you with large markdowns when you sell. To arm yourself with information before trading, check out recent activity using the Municipal Securities Rulemaking Board's EMMA (Electronic Municipal Market Access) system at MSRB.org. If the issue hasn't traded recently, try EMMA's price discovery tool, which allows you to see trading activity for bonds with similar characteristics.

248. MORTGAGE BONDS

New mortgages are often securitized, meaning they're packaged into bonds and sold to investors. An attractive investment? Mortgage bonds should yield more than comparable government bonds, in part to compensate investors for so-called prepayment risk.

That's the risk that homeowners will pay off their mortgages early, perhaps because they move or refinance or because they make extra principal payments. That early payment on a mortgage is more likely to happen if rates fall. Homeowners with older, higher-interest mortgages realize they could do better, so they refinance or pay ahead on their loan.

That creates an asymmetry in how mortgage bonds perform. When rates rise, mortgage bonds are likely to fall, just like other bonds. But if rates fall, mortgage bonds may not perform as well as other bonds, because of those prepayments. If you own mortgage bonds, what you really want is for interest rates to stay relatively constant.

Looking for a low-cost mortgage-bond fund? Check out mutual funds such as Fidelity GNMA Fund, Vanguard GNMA Fund and Vanguard Mortgage-Backed Securities Index Fund, and ETFs like iShares MBS ETF, SPDR Barclays Mortgage Backed Bond ETF and Vanguard Mortgage-Backed Securities ETF.

249. CORPORATE BONDS

As of late November 2015, top-quality corporate bonds were yielding 4.01 percent, while medium-grade bonds were yielding 5.44 percent, according to the Federal Reserve. That's more than you can earn on comparable Treasury bonds—with good reason.

When you buy both corporate and Treasury bonds, you take interest-rate risk, meaning your bonds could fall in price if interest rates rise. But corporate-bond investors take an additional risk that government bondholders don't have to worry about: There's a chance the companies involved could default on their interest payments.

In addition, corporate bonds are often callable before maturity, meaning an issuer can pay off its bonds early. This can be bad news for investors, who may have to surrender a bond with a relatively attractive yield. That's another risk Treasury investors don't have to worry about.

To compensate for these risks, holders of higher-quality corporate bonds might collect an extra one to two percentage points in annual yield compared to Treasurys. That extra yield should provide a partial buffer against rising interest rates. Given the risk of rising interest rates, you might reduce your interest-rate risk by favoring shorter-term bonds, but stick with corporate rather than government bonds, so you don't give up too much yield. There is, however, a price to be paid: When stocks next nosedive, corporate bonds will likely provide less protection than government bonds.

Vanguard Group has a variety of low-cost corporate-bond mutual funds, both actively managed and indexed, that target securities with different maturities. A host of exchange-traded corporate-bond funds are available from iShares, SPDR ETFs and Vanguard.

250. PREFERRED STOCK

Preferred shares have a devoted following among a segment of investors, who are attracted by the relatively generous yields, typically 4 percent and above. Despite their name, preferred shares are more like bonds than regular (or "common") stock. Forget price appreciation. Over the long haul, almost all of your return will likely come from a preferred's regular dividend payments.

Preferred shares might climb in price if interest rates decline. But unlike common stock, preferred shares don't benefit from rising corporate earnings. Those higher earnings may make the preferred's dividend more secure, but they won't result in the dividend being increased, because that is typically fixed.

Preferreds usually have a 30-year maturity, though they can often be called after five years. Keep that in mind when analyzing an individual issue. For instance, a preferred might have a high nominal yield, which is simply the annual dividend payment divided by the current share price. But the issue might be callable at a price that's below the current trading price. If the company retires the issue before the maturity date, current buyers would suffer a price loss. This potential loss is reflected in the yield-to-call, which will be below the nominal yield.

If a company files for bankruptcy, preferred shareholders only receive money after bondholders are paid off. Does that mean preferreds are risky? That's rather like asking, are bonds safe? There's a big difference between Treasurys and junk bonds. Similarly, preferreds come in all kinds of flavors—and the best guide to risk is probably the yield. If you see an unusually high yield, it could mean the company's finances are shaky.

If you own preferreds in a regular taxable account, some will qualify for the federal government's special dividend tax rate, which is 20 percent or less, while others are taxed at the income tax rate, which can be as high as 39.6 percent. Want to keep things simple? Instead of purchasing individual issues, check out exchange-traded index funds such as iShares U.S. Preferred Stock Index and SPDR Wells Fargo Preferred ETF.

251. JUNK BONDS

High-yield junk bonds can offer impressive interest payments. The question is, how big a price will you pay in defaults? Junk bonds are rated below investment grade by credit-rating services such as Fitch Ratings, Moody's Investors Service and Standard & Poor's, meaning there is a serious risk you won't get your money back. Historically, some 5 percent of junk bonds have defaulted each year, though defaults in recent years have been running at more like 2 or 3 percent.

To compensate for the risk of defaults, junk bonds have, on average, yielded some 6 percentage points more than comparable Treasury bonds. But the spread over Treasurys has fluctuated widely. In June 2007, it was at an all-time low of 2.4 percentage points. Less than a year and a half later, in November 2008, the spread widened to almost 20 percentage points during the panic selling of the financial crisis.

During 2015's first 11 months, the spread over Treasurys increased from 4.9 to 6.3 percentage points, close to the historical average, as concerns over credit quality caused bond prices to fall. The spread would have been even tighter if Treasury yields weren't so low. That means junk-bond investors have a relatively modest margin for error, should the default rate pick up. Junk bonds also tend to trade more like stocks than bonds, so a tumbling stock market could drag down junk-bond prices.

While there are some ETFs that focus on junk bonds, most junk-bond funds are actively managed mutual funds. As you pick among them, pay attention not only to fund costs, but also to the credit quality of the portfolio. You can get the necessary information at Morningstar.com. A fund that focuses on lower-quality junk bonds will often sport a higher yield. But that higher yield may prove to be scant compensation if there's a flurry of defaults.

JONATHAN'S TAKE: While I have a small stake in junk bonds, I'm hardly a fan. The time to buy junk is during economic downturns, when concerns about defaults drive up yields. Problem is, that's also the time when you want to buy stocks—and stocks are likely to deliver better returns as markets rebound in anticipation of an economic recovery.

252. FLOATING RATE LOANS

As investors have sought both higher yields and protection against rising interest rates, some have turned to floating rate funds, also known as bank-loan or leveraged-loan funds. Examples include ETFs such as Highland/iBoxx Senior Loan ETF, PowerShares Senior Loan Portfolio ETF and SPDR Blackstone/GSO Senior Loan ETF, and mutual funds like Fidelity Floating Rate High Income Fund and Pimco Senior Floating Rate Fund. There are also closed-end funds that focus on bank loans, many of which use leverage to goose their yield.

The loans held by these funds have their rates pegged to short-term interest rates. That means you aren't locked in at current yields, which is the danger faced by those owning regular fixed-rate bonds. But while bank-loan funds may be a good defense against rising interest rates, you could suffer if the economy turns down.

The reason: The loans involved are typically made to companies that are rated below investment grade. Because they're less financially strong, the risk of default is higher. In the event of a bankruptcy, bank loans typically have seniority over other debt, so holders are more likely to get their money back. Still, buyers of bank-loan funds should be prepared for a rough ride. How rough? In 2008, the funds lost almost 30 percent, according to Morningstar.

253. DEVELOPED MARKET BONDS

You should think of international bond funds not as a standalone investment, but as a further way to diversify a portfolio. Consider the T. Rowe Price International Bond Fund, which was launched in 1986. In the

28 full calendar years since then, the fund has lost money in 10 years, or more than a third of the time, and it looks like 2015 will also be a losing year. That's hardly the sort of performance that would endear it to conservative investors.

On the other hand, the fund occasionally delivered strong returns at just the right time. During that 28-year stretch, the S&P 500-stock index lost money in five years—1990, 2000, 2001, 2002 and 2008—and the T. Rowe Price Group fund posted gains in three of those five years, thus helping to bolster a diversified portfolio's performance at a time when its stock market investments were suffering.

An international bond fund can potentially post handsome gains either because foreign interest rates decline, pushing up the price of existing bonds, or because the dollar declines in value. The T. Rowe Price fund doesn't hedge its currency exposure. But some international bond funds do hedge, either occasionally or all the time. This will make the funds less volatile, which might appeal to conservative investors.

Among providers of ETFs, iShares and SPDR ETFs have an extensive array of international bond funds. In addition to the T. Rowe Price fund, you can purchase international or global bond mutual funds from companies such as American Century Investments, Fidelity Investments and Vanguard Group. International funds invest exclusively abroad, while global funds own a mix of U.S. and foreign securities.

254. EMERGING-MARKET DEBT

Emerging-market bonds have posted impressive returns over the past few decades, as emerging-market economies have grown more robust. That, in turn, has bolstered the credit quality of emerging-market debt, resulting in a narrowing of the spread between the yield on emerging-market debt and that available on U.S. Treasury bonds.

From here, however, returns are likely to be more muted. As of year-end 2015, emerging-market debt was offering relatively low yields. Moreover, the historical tightening of the spread between emerging-market debt and Treasury bonds was a onetime gain. The spread may tighten further, but the big gains have already been had. Also keep in mind that, in a crisis, emerging-market debt funds can suffer steep losses, such as 2008's 18 percent drubbing.

Two decades ago, emerging-market debt was often denominated in U.S. dollars, so investors didn't have to worry about currency risk. Today, emerging-market governments—which are easily the biggest issuers of emerging-market debt—are more likely to sell bonds denominated in their own currencies. These local currency bonds will be more volatile, but could prove to be a better diversifier for a portfolio that's mostly devoted to U.S. stocks and bonds.

Intrigued? Check out funds such as Fidelity New Markets Income Fund and Vanguard Emerging Markets Government Bond Index Fund. Before buying an emerging-market bond fund, find out whether the fund focuses on dollar-denominated bonds, local currency bonds or some combination of the two, so you know how much currency risk you're taking.

255. CLOSED-END FUNDS

Exchange-traded index funds have exploded in popularity since the first U.S. fund was launched in 1993. But ETFs weren't the first investment funds to be listed on the stock market. That distinction belongs to closed-end funds, which have traded in the U.S. since 1893. Today, there are more than 600 closed-end funds, which collectively manage almost $300 billion in assets. For more information, check out the Closed-End Fund Center at CEFA.com.

Every closed-end fund has two prices. There's the price of the publicly traded shares—and then there's the value of the fund's assets expressed on a per-share basis, otherwise known as its net asset value. Closed-end fund shares are initially sold at a premium to net asset value, with the premium representing the money earned by the brokerage firms concerned. Often, funds quickly fall to a discount, at which point you might be able to buy a dollar of assets for just 90 cents.

A majority of closed-end funds focus on bonds, both taxable and tax-free. Indeed, the world of closed-end funds includes a vast array of single-state, tax-free municipal bond funds.

Be warned: Many closed-end bond funds use leverage to boost returns. The funds issue short-term debt at relatively low interest rates and then use the proceeds to buy longer-term bonds offering higher yields. The interest rate differential helps pad the yield paid to shareholders. But those higher yields come at a price: When bond prices fall, owners of leveraged closed-end funds will suffer steeper losses than those in unleveraged funds.

256. COVERED CALLS

In search of extra income, investors sometimes skip bonds—and instead sell call options against their stock portfolio. The buyers of these call options get the right to call away the underlying stock at a specified "strike" price either when the option expires or at any time up until the option's expiration date. In return for that right, the buyers pay a premium to the sellers.

Selling call options has two key drawbacks. First, trading options is a zero-sum game: For every winner, there's a loser. In fact, it's less than a zero-sum game once you factor in the trading costs involved. As a seller of call options, you're the winner if the underlying stock goes nowhere, because you make a little extra dough by pocketing the call premium. But you could end up as the loser if the stock climbs above the strike price. You might miss out on big investment gains—and the call premium you received may not come close to compensating.

That brings us to the second drawback. If you sell covered calls, you may see all of your good stocks called away and you might be left holding a bunch of duds. This could be more painful than you might imagine. How so? Most years, the market's performance is driven by a minority of stocks with strong performance, a phenomenon known as skewness. This shouldn't be surprising: The most a stock can lose is 100 percent of its value, but the potential gain is unlimited. In many years, there will be a small number of stocks that score gains of 200 percent, 300 percent or more. If you write covered calls, your stocks that get called away could be among the market's big winners.

Want more income from your portfolio? You'll likely achieve your goal at a lower investment cost, and with fewer hassles, by simply keeping a little less in stocks and a little more in bonds.

257. CASH INVESTMENTS

Cash investments include things like Treasury bills, savings accounts, money-market deposit accounts, money-market mutual funds and certificates of deposit, where there's little chance you will lose money and which can typically be sold at short notice (though, in the case of CDs, there will usually be an early-withdrawal penalty).

Historically, cash investments like Treasury bills and money-market mutual funds have paid a yield that roughly approximates the inflation rate. That means they can help preserve the spending power of your money before taxes, but you'll likely find you are losing money, once the taxman gets his share. In recent years, however, it's been far worse, as the Federal Reserve has kept short-term interest rates close to zero in an effort to stimulate the U.S. economy.

In addition to the long-run threat from inflation and taxes, holders of cash investments have also suffered the occasional short-term scare. During the 2008–09 financial crisis, accountholders at failed banks had uneasy moments, even if they were eventually made whole, thanks to FDIC insurance. Over the past four decades, a few money-market mutual funds have "broken the buck," with their share price falling below the standard $1 net asset value. Perhaps the most notable failure was the Reserve Primary Fund, which slipped to 97 cents in September 2008.

Still, cash investments are far safer than stocks or bonds. Got money you expect to spend within the next year or two? Cash investments are typically the only prudent choice, given the chance of short-term losses with anything riskier. To find higher-yielding CDs and savings accounts, head to Bankrate.com.

What if you plan to hold cash investments as part of your longer-term portfolio? If you have a 401(k) plan at work that includes a stable-value fund, you might keep your cash allocation in the fund, which may offer a somewhat higher yield than, say, a money-market mutual fund. You could also keep longer-term cash holdings in short-term bonds, which will give you a higher yield, though there is a risk you'll have a year with modest losses. Alternatively, you might purchase longer-term CDs to get a higher yield, figuring that higher yield will compensate for any early-withdrawal penalty, should you need to cash out before maturity.

258. FDIC INSURANCE

The Federal Deposit Insurance Corporation provides protection for bank accounts, including checking accounts, saving accounts, money-market deposit accounts and certificates of deposit. In the event of a bank failure, you're insured for up to $250,000 per insured bank, with the insurance applying to each ownership category. Among the ownership categories are accounts solely in your name, accounts held jointly with someone else and bank products held in an IRA.

Suppose you have $250,000 in a savings account in your name and your spouse has a similar sum. You also both have IRAs that hold CDs worth $250,000. In addition, you have a joint account that holds $500,000. The FDIC would ascribe half the joint account to you and half to your spouse, and insure it for the full $500,000. Add it all up and you would together be covered for $1.5 million—and that's just at one bank. You could do the same all over again at a different bank. To increase FDIC coverage, some financial firms will help you set up a so-called sweep account, where your money is spread across a variety of banks to increase your FDIC coverage.

Keep two caveats in mind. First, FDIC deposit insurance only applies to bank products. FDIC insurance would cover a money-market deposit account, but not a money-market mutual fund. Second, before purchasing a certificate of deposit through a broker, ask whether it's covered by FDIC insurance. To learn more, go to FDIC.gov/deposit. In particular, check out the brochure entitled "Your Insured Deposits."

259. ALTERNATIVE INVESTMENTS

What counts as an alternative investment? Opinions differ. But the list might include gold, silver, stocks of mining companies that focus on these two metals, hedge funds, mutual funds that endeavor to act like hedge funds, timber, farmland, residential and commercial rental properties, real estate investment trusts, commodity funds that buy everything from agriculture to energy futures contracts, venture capital funds that invest in privately held companies, stocks of energy and natural-resource companies, and even bitcoins.

These various investments have one thing in common: They hold out the promise of performing well when stocks are getting crushed. Or, to use Wall Street lingo, these are potentially uncorrelated assets. That's a valuable quality. If you own something that rises in value when stocks fall, not only will you find investing less nerve-racking, but also you could turn this lack of correlation into additional investment gains through regular rebalancing.

Keep five caveats in mind. First, past correlations can be a lousy guide to future correlations. Take commodity futures. These are now widely owned by investors. As a result, not only are long-run returns from commodity-futures funds likely to be lower than history suggests, but also they are more likely to rise and fall with the same overall investor sentiment that drives stock returns.

Second, in some cases, the diversification benefit may be an illusion. For instance, timber is seen by some institutional investors as a great way to diversify financial assets like stocks and bonds. But the apparent lack of correlation may simply reflect the absence of daily price information on your 1,000 acres of timber.

Third, many of these alternative investments come with steep investment costs. Hedge funds are the most notable culprit, though mutual funds that employ hedge-fund-like strategies are also far from cheap.

Fourth, some alternative investments can't be quickly sold, including rental properties, hedge funds and venture capital funds. That lack of liquidity makes rebalancing difficult.

Finally, never forget that low correlation is a double-edged sword. It may help when stocks are falling, but you could find yourself disappointed by your alternative investments as they tumble in value while stocks roar ahead.

260. GOLD

Many alternative investments can be slotted into one of two categories: They are either hard-asset plays, like commodities and real estate, or they are financially engineered to perform unlike conventional stocks and bonds, which is what you get with many hedge funds and hedge-fund-like mutual funds.

Among hard assets, the classic investment is gold, which is widely seen as a hedge against inflation and political turmoil, and viewed as a good diversifier for financial assets like stocks and bonds. Gold soared in the 1970s, collapsed in the 1980s and came roaring back over the decade beginning 2001, eventually peaking at $1,921 per ounce in September 2011. Since then, the price has slumped, finishing November 2015 at $1,064 per ounce, down from $1,184 at year-end 2014.

As gold soared over the decade through 2011, so too did the assets of SPDR Gold Shares, an exchange-traded fund backed by gold bullion. The fund, which was launched in 2004, became a popular alternative to owning gold itself, because it saved investors the hassles that come with storing, transporting and insuring their holdings of gold coins or bars.

While gold may provide offsetting gains when stocks and bonds are losing value, you may be disappointed with your long-run performance. Over time, price gains on gold should roughly match the inflation rate, which means all you're doing is preserving the spending power of your money—and maybe not even that if you buy at the wrong time and once you figure in taxes.

As an alternative, some investors focus instead on the stocks of gold-mining companies, which have the potential to outpace inflation over the long run. Gold stocks are more volatile than gold bullion, but this added volatility means they can be a better diversifier for financial assets. Many mutual fund companies offer funds that invest in mining stocks, including American Century Investments, Fidelity Investments and Vanguard Group. Also check out Market Vectors Gold Miners ETF.

JONATHAN'S TAKE: Gold stocks can be a great way to diversify a stock portfolio. But to turn this uncorrelated performance into greater wealth, you need to set a target portfolio percentage for your gold stocks and then regularly rebalance back to your target. All this takes a fair amount of investment courage: Many folks will find themselves unnerved by gold stocks' volatility—and frozen in place when they ought to be rebalancing.

261. BITCOINS

Bitcoins may be intended as a new currency, but they also have similarities to an alternative investment—and perhaps the closest parallel is gold. Neither bitcoins nor physical gold have any intrinsic value: They don't pay interest like a bond and they don't generate earnings and dividends like a stock. Instead, the value ascribed to both bitcoins and gold is born mostly of faith and trust.

True, gold has some limited use—mostly for jewelry—and historically it has been recognized as a store of value by some governments, while bitcoins can make neither claim. Still, like gold, bitcoins have a value largely because owners trust that the supply is limited and because they have faith that others will also view them as valuable.

In some ways, bitcoins are superior to gold. While both are recognized as a medium of exchange not controlled by any national government, bitcoins are a lot cheaper to buy, hold and sell. You don't have all the costs associated with trading and storing gold.

In recent years, bitcoins have been subject to large speculative swings in value. But assuming the market for bitcoins isn't discredited or replaced by some other virtual currency, all you can expect from bitcoins over the long run is a return equal to the global inflation rate—which is exactly what you can expect from gold. As such, while you might be able to make a short-term speculative gain, it's unlikely to be a great long-run investment. What if you do make large gains? There's good news: The IRS has said that profits earned by bitcoin owners will be subject to capital gains taxes, not income taxes.

The regulations governing bitcoins remain in flux, but things are becoming clearer. In January 2015, Coinbase.com opened the first U.S.-based bitcoin exchange. In May, itBit.com launched a bank trust company subject to supervision by the New York State Department of Financial Services, and Gemini.com followed in October.

262. REAL ESTATE INVESTMENT TRUSTS

Real estate investment trusts come in two basic flavors. Mortgage REITs earn interest by providing financing to real estate owners and operators. Equity REITs purchase and operate properties such as apartment buildings, shopping centers, warehouses and office buildings. They collect rent and other income, which is then passed along to shareholders, and also occasionally make money by selling properties at a profit. Equity REITs account for 90 percent of REIT assets.

In the 1990s, equity REITs were laggards compared to the broad U.S. stock market. Since then, they have generated strong performance despite a few rough years, notably 2007 and 2008. Investors should expect more rough years ahead. Equity REITs, which were yielding almost 9 percent at year-end 1999, were paying out just 3.7 percent as of Oct. 31, 2015.

REITs must distribute at least 90 percent of their taxable income to shareholders each year. Those dividends can be deducted against a REIT's taxable income, so most REITs pay no corporate income taxes. Because of this favorable tax treatment at the corporate level, the dividends paid to REIT shareholders don't qualify to be taxed at the long-term capital gains rate. Instead, they're taxed as ordinary income. Because of that tax treatment and because REITs kick off so much income each year, you should probably hold your REITs in a retirement account.

Most major mutual fund companies, as well as the big ETF providers, now offer funds that invest in REITs. There are also many closed-end funds focused on real estate. For more on REITs, check out the website REIT.com/investing.

263. HEDGE FUNDS

For years, hedge funds were the status symbol of the investment world, promising superior returns to the lucky few who could afford the price of admission. But more often than not, the superior returns haven't materialized—and lately hedge funds have lost some of their luster.

These lightly regulated investment funds use a broader array of strategies than the typical mutual fund. For instance, a hedge fund might try to boost returns by borrowing money and then using that money to purchase additional investments. It might also buy some investments, hoping they'll rise in value, while also selling short other investments, in a bet they'll fall in value.

While hedge funds have a reputation for delivering outsized returns, that isn't always the objective. Yes, some funds gun for big gains, making large, leveraged bets. But others are focused on "absolute returns," meaning they aim to generate healthy returns year after year, no matter what's happening in the financial markets.

To invest in a hedge fund, you need at least a $1 million net worth, excluding your primary residence, or to have earned $200,000 in each of the past two years (or $300,000 together with your spouse). Many hedge funds, however, set the bar even higher, demanding huge initial investments that are only affordable by institutional investors and the extremely wealthy.

Hedge-fund ownership may be an exclusive club—but the membership fees are, alas, equally rich. Hedge funds typically charge 1 or 2 percent of assets each year, while also taking 20 percent of any gains. What if you buy a fund of funds, which is a hedge fund that invests in other hedge funds? You will have to deal with a second layer of fees, which might take an additional 1.5 percent of assets and 10 percent of gains. Weighed down by fees with like that, it's hardly surprising that most hedge funds turn out to be poor investments.

264. HEDGE-FUND-LIKE MUTUAL FUNDS AND ETFs

A hedge fund might allow you to cash out just once every three months. By contrast, mutual funds provide daily liquidity, meaning you can get out at the end of any day that the market is open, while ETFs can be bought and sold throughout the trading day. For that reason, mutual funds and ETFs that pursue hedge-fund-like strategies are sometimes referred to as liquid alternatives or simply "liquid alts." What sorts of funds are available? Here is a sampler:

• Long-short funds, such as Schwab Hedged Equity Fund, which go long some stocks in the hope they will rise, while shorting others in a bet they'll fall. Long-short funds typically have more invested in long positions than in their short positions, while market neutral funds maintain equal-size long and short bets.

• Global macro funds, like William Blair Macro Allocation Fund and IQ Hedge Macro Tracker ETF. The latter seeks to mimic the performance of a hedge fund index. The index, in turn, tracks the results of hedge funds that have the freedom to invest anywhere.

• Managed futures funds such as WisdomTree Managed Futures Strategy Fund, an ETF that aims to generate positive returns that are uncorrelated to the financial markets. The ETF buys a mix of currency, commodity and Treasury bond derivatives.

• Merger arbitrage funds, like Arbitrage Fund and Merger Fund, which aim to make money by betting that mergers and acquisitions will be successfully completed.

Keep three caveats in mind. First, some liquid alt funds have steep annual expenses. Second, the strategies involved can generate big annual tax bills, so the funds are best held in a retirement account. Third, these funds all represent a bet on active management—a bet that historically hasn't panned out.

JONATHAN'S TAKE: You should never buy a fund unless you fully understand its strategy. If you don't, there's a risk you'll suffer an unpleasant surprise—and end up selling out, possibly at the worst possible time. That's why I think most investors should stick with easy-to-understand alternative investments, such as funds that focus on gold stocks and real estate investment trusts.

265. MY STORY: HOW I POSITION MY PORTFOLIO

Currently, I have roughly 70 percent of my portfolio in stocks and 30 percent in bonds, savings accounts and other interest-generating investments. This seems like a reasonable amount of risk for a 52-year-old to take, though I would likely boost the stocks to 75 percent if we saw a market decline of 25 percent or more.

The bulk of my bond portfolio is in short-term corporate bond funds, because I suspect interest rates will head higher from today's modest levels and, as a rule, I would rather play it safe with bonds and take risk with my stocks. I have a small position in emerging-market debt and a tiny stake in a junk bond fund. In calculating my allocation to bonds, I also include the private mortgage I wrote for my daughter. You can learn more about that in Part XII.

What about stocks? I have almost everything in index funds. My written portfolio targets call for 63 percent in U.S. stocks and 37 percent in foreign stocks. The U.S. portion is split evenly between a total stock market index fund, which gives me broad market exposure, and index funds that focus on large-company and small-company value stocks. In addition, I own an index fund that buys U.S. real estate investment trusts, though I currently own less than my target weighting, because I consider U.S. REITs to be overvalued.

Meanwhile, for foreign exposure, I own index funds focused on developed foreign markets, international small-company stocks and emerging markets. I also have smaller positions in funds that own foreign REITs and gold stocks.

Foreign stocks strike me as better value than U.S. shares, so I'm currently modestly overweighted in foreign stocks and modestly underweighted in U.S. shares, relative to my written portfolio targets. I am even toying with revising those written targets, raising my foreign allocation to a permanent 40 percent of my stock portfolio.

PART X

INVESTMENT MATH
A NUMERICAL DIGRESSION
FOR NERDY READERS

In recent decades, professional money management has become less about intuition and best guesses, and more about using tremendous computer power to dig into the numbers and tease out insights. The ranks of Wall Street investment managers and traders are increasingly dominated by those who are most mathematically adept.

This mathematical firepower revealed the superior returns available from investing in value stocks, shares with price momentum and companies with higher gross profitability. Money managers now use these insights as they screen vast amounts of data, hunting for a collection of stocks that will deliver market-beating returns.

Mathematical muscle is also used to simulate how investors' portfolios might fare over time. In particular, there's been a big focus on Monte Carlo analysis, which allows you to analyze how a portfolio might perform in hundreds of different market scenarios. This can be especially valuable for retirees as they try to figure out how much they can safely withdraw each year from their savings.

Fear not: To succeed as an ordinary investor, you don't need to turn yourself into a "quant," which is Wall Street lingo for a quantitative investor. But it is helpful to have a grasp of basic investment math. That might sound daunting. The notions involved, however, are quite simple. Often, you don't even have to do the calculations yourself, because there are plenty of online calculators that'll do the work for you. Instead, what's important is having a rough understanding of how the math plays out.

266. HOW MONEY COMPOUNDS

Suppose you earn 10 percent this year and 10 percent next year. Your cumulative gain would be 21 percent. Why? Imagine you invested $100. The first year's 10 percent gain would turn your $100 into $110. Because you start the second year with $110, the next year's 10 percent gain boosts your portfolio's value by $11, not $10. That brings your total to $121, for a two-year cumulative gain of 21 percent.

Got a series of annual returns and you'd like to find out the cumulative gain? Divide each return by 100 and add 1, and then multiply the numbers together. For instance, a 10 percent return would become 1.1. Again, let's assume you earned 10 percent in two consecutive years. Here's the calculation:

1.1 x 1.1 = 1.21

To turn the 1.21 back into a percentage, you would reverse the earlier calculation, first subtracting 1 and then multiplying by 100, which in this case would give you 21 percent.

What if you lost money during one year and you want to calculate your cumulative return? Once again, divide by 100 and add 1. In the case of a negative return, it becomes something less than 1. For instance, if you lost 10 percent in a year, that loss would be represented by 0.9. Here's how the math would look if you lost 10 percent in the first year and then gained 10 percent the following year:

0.9 x 1.1 = 0.99

To turn this back into a percentage, you would follow the usual process—subtract 1 and then multiply by 100—which would give you a cumulative return over the two years of -1 percent.

267. ANNUALIZED VS. CUMULATIVE RETURNS

Above, the cumulative gain in our first example was 21 percent. The annualized gain, however, was 10 percent. This is known as a geometric average: It's the amount you would have to earn each year to achieve the cumulative result. Note that this is different from simply dividing the cumulative gain by the number of years—the so-called arithmetic average. The latter wouldn't give you the annualized return, because simple averaging doesn't take into account the effects of compounding.

Suppose that, over the next five years, you earned annual returns of 10 percent, -10, 5, 0 and 15. Your cumulative gain would be 19.5 percent, which you can find by performing this calculation:

1.1 x 0.9 x 1.05 x 1 x 1.15 = 1.195

To turn this into an annualized (or geometric) return, you would need the help of a financial calculator or a spreadsheet. If you had that handy, you'd discover that the annualized return over the five years is 3.6 percent.

By contrast, the arithmetic average—which you find by simply adding up the performance each year and dividing by the number of years—would be 4. Unless you earn the same return every year, the geometric average will always be less than the arithmetic average. In fact, if there's a wide gap between the geometric and arithmetic average, that's a sign that a portfolio is highly volatile. This volatility isn't good for efficient investment compounding.

268. RULE OF 72

How long will it take to double your money, given a particular rate of return? You can get a rough answer by dividing 72 by the annual return. For instance, if you expect to earn 7 percent a year, it would take just over 10 years to double your money. But at a 3 percent annual return, the compounding process is much slower, with your money doubling every 24 years.

Obviously, the higher the return you earn, the easier it will be to achieve your financial goals. But keep three caveats in mind. First, don't make the mistake of assuming a high return to make your financial plan work. If anything, you should assume low returns and hope to be pleasantly surprised.

Second, historical returns are a dubious guide to the future, especially given today's rich stock market valuations and tiny bond yields. Finally, you have to take high risk to earn high returns—which means the ride could be rough and the risk may not be rewarded.

269. LOSSES HURT MORE THAN GAINS HELP

Imagine your portfolio lost 25 percent last year. To recoup that loss, you would need to earn not 25 percent, but just over 33 percent. You can show this mathematically as:

0.75 x 1.3333 = 1

This is the reason that volatility is so damaging to investment compounding. While the occasional losing year is almost inevitable if you invest in the stock market, you should be leery of pursuing a strategy   like buying stocks with margin debt or purchasing leveraged exchange-traded index funds—that can result in large losses, because you need huge gains to recover from such losses.

270. TAXED VS. TAX-DEFERRED COMPOUNDING

By using retirement accounts, or by pursuing tax-efficient strategies in a taxable account, you can get tax-deferred growth. How valuable is this growth? Imagine a husband and wife. Both invest $1,000 for 40 years and earn 6 percent a year before taxes.

The husband pays 25 percent in taxes every year on his entire 6 percent investment gain, so his $1,000 grows annually at an after-tax 4.5 percent. If you earn 4.5 percent a year for 30 years, your cumulative gain would be 481.6 percent. (On your financial calculator, this would show up as 5.816 before you subtract 1 and multiply by 100.) That means the husband's $1,000 grows to $5,816.

Meanwhile, the wife puts her $1,000 into a nondeductible retirement account, where her money grows tax-deferred at 6 percent annually. After 40 years, she cashes out the account and pays 25 percent in taxes on her four decades of investment gains.

Before taxes, her $1,000 would grow to $10,286. What's her after-tax gain? Remember, her contribution to the retirement account was nondeductible, meaning she didn't get an initial tax deduction for her $1,000 contribution and hence she doesn't have to pay tax on that $1,000 when she withdraws it. Instead, only the $9,286 in gains is taxable. Knock off 25 percent from that sum for taxes, add back the $1,000 nondeductible contribution and the wife would be left with $7,964, compared with $5,816 for her husband.

271. TAXABLE VS. MUNICIPAL BONDS

Taxable bonds—such as those issued by corporations—typically have relatively high yields, but you have to pay tax each year on the interest you earn, assuming you hold the bonds in a taxable account. Municipal bonds offer yields that are usually lower, but the interest should be tax-free. So which should you buy?

Imagine you are in the 25 percent marginal federal income tax bracket and a 5 percent state income tax bracket, for a combined marginal rate of 30 percent. You're considering buying a municipal bond that yields 4 percent, and that yield will be tax-free for you at both the federal and state level. How much would a taxable bond have to pay to give you the same after-tax yield?

First, you have to convert your marginal tax bracket into a decimal by dividing it by 100. That turns your 30 percent to 0.3.

Next, you subtract this 0.3 from 1, giving you 0.7.

Finally, you divide the municipal bond's 4 percent yield by 0.7, giving you 5.71 percent. This 5.71 percent is the yield that a taxable bond would have to offer to give you the same after-tax yield as the 4 percent municipal bond.

What if you're considering buying munis from an out-of-state issuer, so they would be tax-free at the federal level, but not the state level? In the above example, instead of adjusting for a 30 percent marginal rate, you would use 25 percent. Result: To find the tax-equivalent yield, you would divide the municipal bond's yield by 0.75.

What if you're starting with a taxable bond—and trying to figure out how much a municipal bond would need to pay to be competitive? Instead of dividing the taxable bond's yield by 0.7 or 0.75, you would multiply it by these figures. Suppose you are looking at a taxable bond that's yielding 5 percent. If you multiply this 5 percent by 0.7, you would get 3.5 percent, which would be your after-tax yield from the taxable bond—and which is the amount that an in-state municipal bond would have to pay to give you the same yield.

Even if municipals deliver a higher after-tax yield than taxable bonds, they aren't necessarily your best bet, as we discuss in Part XI.

272. COMPOUNDING WITH REGULAR INVESTMENTS

Investment compounding over long periods can produce impressive results—but the results are even more impressive when you combine that compounding with regular savings. For instance, if you invest $100 initially and left it to grow at 5 percent a year, you would have $339 after 25 years, thanks to the 239 percent cumulative gain. But if you invested $100 at the start of each of the 25 years, for a total of $2,500, you would have $5,011 after 25 years.

You can do this calculation with Excel or with a financial calculator, such as Texas Instruments Business Analyst II Plus (TI-BA II Plus). Alternatively, you could use an online savings calculator, such as the Savings Calculator at Dinkytown.net.

One warning: Pay attention to when additional savings are credited. You end up with a lower accumulated value if additional savings are credited at the end of each year, rather than at the beginning, because that means those savings miss out on a year of investment gains.

273. COMPOUNDING AND TIME

Imagine a brother and sister, who are twins. The sister saves $5,000 a year for 10 years, from age 25 to age 35, earning 6 percent a year. At age 35, she would have $69,858. She doesn't add any more money to the account. Instead, she leaves the $69,858 to grow at 6 percent a year for another 30 years, until age 65. If you compound at 6 percent a year for 30 years, your cumulative gain would be 474 percent, equal to 5.74 when expressed as a decimal. To find out how much the sister would have at age 65, you would perform this calculation:

$69,858 x 5.74 = $400,985

Meanwhile, her twin brother gets off to a slower start. He doesn't start saving until age 35, which is when his sister stops. To have roughly the same sum at age 65 as his sister, the brother would have to save $4,785 every year for 30 years, from age 35 to age 65. That isn't significantly less than the $5,000 that his sister had to save every year for a mere 10 years to accumulate the same sum, thus illustrating the power of starting early.

As you might gather from the various examples above, you can accumulate greater wealth if you start with a larger initial investment, save more on a regular basis, start earlier (and hence save and invest for longer), earn higher returns, reduce unnecessary volatility and defer taxes.

274. FUTURE VALUE VS. PRESENT VALUE

When you estimate how much a dollar today will be worth in the future, or how much a series of regular deposits will be worth in the future, you're calculating a future value. But sometimes, you'll want to reverse engineer this calculation.

Suppose you figure you'll need $40,000 in four years to make a house down payment. To have that sum, how much would you need to set aside today—or how much would you need to save every month? This is a present value calculation. To do the calculation, you need to estimate your likely rate of return. Let's say you can earn 3 percent a year.

To have $40,000 in four years, you would need to invest $35,539 today, assuming a 3 percent annual return. Alternatively, to have $40,000 in four years, you would need to save $783 every month, again assuming a 3 percent annual return. You can do these calculations with a financial calculator or by playing around with the Present Value Goal Calculator at Dinkytown.net.

On occasion, you might hear experts refer to the "time value of money." The notion: $1 today is worth more than $1 a year from now, because you could earn interest or investment returns during the intervening 12 months. In the above example, you can see that, to have $40,000 in four years, you need less than $40,000 today—illustrating the time value of money.

275. COMPOUNDING WITH REGULAR WITHDRAWALS

When saving for retirement, the combination of investment gains and regular savings can produce impressive results. But once you retire, this winning combo turns into a tug-of-war. Instead of adding savings to your portfolio, you're making withdrawals—and your annual withdrawals will often be greater than your portfolio's annual investment gains. The big question: How long can you sustain this losing fight before running out of money?

You can run a simple scenario at Dinkytown.net using the calculator labeled "How long will my retirement savings last?" Keep in mind that this calculator assumes you earn the same return every year. What if results vary? The big danger: You get hit with a vicious bear market early in retirement. To see how things might play out, try the calculator at FIRECalc.com.

276. INFLATION

This is a somewhat nerdy point, but the loss from inflation is slightly different from an investment loss. To understand why, suppose you have $1,000 and your favorite candy bar increases in price by 5 percent, from $1 to $1.05.

Previously, your $1,000 would have bought 1,000 candy bars at $1 each. If the price increases by 5 percent to $1.05, you might imagine that you have suffered a 5 percent loss of purchasing power, and thus your $1,000 would buy just 950 candy bars. But in fact, at $1.05 each, your $1,000 would buy 952 bars, plus you would get 40 cents in change.

How does this look mathematically? If you had a 5 percent investment loss, you would multiply your $1,000 by 0.95. But to gauge the impact of 5 percent inflation, this would be the calculation:

$1/1.05 = 0.952$

The implication: 5 percent inflation (0.952) isn't quite as damaging as a 5 percent investment loss (0.95).

What if inflation ran at 5 percent a year for 10 years? You would multiply 0.952 by itself nine times, which is easy to do with a financial calculator. Result: Over 10 years, the purchasing power of your money would shrink by 38.6 percent—or, to put it another way, $1 in 10 years would have the spending power of 61 cents today.

277. NOMINAL VS. REAL RETURNS

Even if we clock investment gains, we may not be making any financial progress if our investment gains aren't outpacing the twin threats of inflation and taxes. For instance, if we earn 3 percent this year but inflation is running at 5 percent, we're losing money—and the loss would be even greater once we factor in taxes.

In the previous section, we saw that a 5 percent investment loss was more damaging than 5 percent inflation. Earlier, we also saw that the punishment from a 25 percent investment loss was greater than the benefit from a 25 percent investment gain.

That leaves one last comparison: How does the damage from inflation compare to the benefit of an investment gain? If we gain 5 percent in a year, we multiply our portfolio's value by 1.05. Meanwhile, if we want to know the loss of purchasing power from 5 percent inflation, we would multiply our portfolio's value by 0.952 (the product of 1/1.05). So what if we have a year with both a 5 percent investment gain and 5 percent inflation? We could do this calculation:

$1.05 \times (1/1.05) = 1$

In other words, the damage from 5 percent inflation is equal to the benefit from a 5 percent investment gain. For rough calculation purposes, investors sometimes subtract the inflation rate from their nominal (before inflation) gain to get their real (after inflation) gain. This produces an accurate result when both are the same—but not otherwise.

Let's say you have a 10 percent nominal gain and inflation is running at 4 percent. If you simply subtract the 4 percent inflation from your 10 percent nominal return, you get a 6 percent real return. But to get a more accurate answer, you would need to do this calculation:

$1.1 \times (1/1.04) = 1.0577$

Thus, the real return is 5.8 percent.

278. TOTAL RETURNS

An investment's performance often has two components: the capital gain or loss and the income generated. For instance, one of your stocks might gain in price, while also paying you a quarterly dividend. Similarly, mutual fund owners need to consider not only share price changes, but also the income and capital gains distributions that they receive throughout the year.

By combining an investment's price change and the income it generated, you can calculate the investment's total return. Often, investors will make rough-and-ready calculations. An example: If the S&P 500-stock index gains 7 percent during the year and also pays a 2 percent dividend, you might estimate the total return at 9 percent. While this is accurate enough for most purposes, it won't be the precise result. For that, you would need to know when dividends were paid and at what price investors were able to reinvest this money.

Fortunately, many financial firms provide this data. For instance, you can find total returns for mutual funds both from individual fund company websites and from Morningstar.com.

A caveat: When comparing the five-year total returns on, say, two mutual funds, make sure that you're looking at the same five-year period for both funds. A fund's five-year record through June 30 can differ radically from its results through March 31 if, for instance, there was a big bear market five years ago and that loss disappears from the record when you look at the more recent five-year period.

279. GORDON EQUATION

Want to know the expected return for an investment? You might take your cues from the Gordon Equation, named after the late Myron Gordon, a finance professor at the University of Toronto. The equation suggests you can calculate an investment's expected return by combining two numbers: the income generated by the investment and the expected growth rate in that income.

Let's say you have a bond that yields 3 percent. You can't expect that 3 percent yield to grow, so 3 percent would also be your expected return. What if you buy a stock that's yielding 3 percent? If you figure corporate earnings will grow 3 percent a year and the company will increase its dividend at the same rate, you're looking at a 6 percent expected return.

This 6 percent expected return assumes that the company's share price keeps pace with the rise in the dividend payment. That's a reasonable long-run expectation, though short-term results will likely be all over the map. But assuming share prices do indeed climb with dividends, the Gordon Equation is another way to bring together income and capital gains—and thereby calculate total return, the topic discussed in the previous section.

280. HOW INTEREST IS CALCULATED

You can think of the interest charged on a loan as the mirror opposite of the investment gains on your savings. If you borrow $1,000 and the interest rate is 12 percent a year, you can calculate the simple interest cost in the same way you would calculate investment gains:

$1,000 x 0.12 = $120 in interest expense

That means that your loan balance after one year would be:

$1,000 x 1.12 = $1,120

Just as investment gains compound over time, so too can interest costs. Suppose you borrowed $1,000 for five years, and you didn't pay any of the interest or repay any of the sum originally borrowed. Your loan balance after five years would be:

$1,000 x 1.12 x 1.12 x 1.12 x 1.12 x 1.12 = $1,762

To make it easier for borrowers to compare loans, lenders are required to disclose the annual percentage rate, or APR, that they charge. This standardized loan rate takes into account both the interest charged and any fees involved.

281. AMORTIZING LOANS

In the above example, we assumed you didn't pay the interest or repay any of the sum originally borrowed. Instead, the amount owed was allowed to balloon in value. This is unrealistic. Most loans are amortizing, meaning that each month you pay not only the interest charged, but also repay part of the sum originally borrowed.

A classic example is a 30-year fixed-rate mortgage. The payment each month stays the same. That payment is set so that not only do you pay the interest incurred each month, but also you gradually reduce the loan's principal balance, with the goal of repaying the entire sum borrowed after 30 years.

While the monthly payment stays the same over the 30 years, the amount that goes to interest and principal changes each month. In the initial years, most of the monthly payment goes toward interest. But as the loan balance shrinks, less interest is owed each month and more money gets directed toward paying down principal.

To see what this sort of amortization schedule looks like, try the Mortgage Calculator at Bankrate.com. Let's say you take out a $200,000 30-year fixed-rate mortgage with a 6 percent annual interest rate, equal to 0.5 percent per month. The mortgage payment would be $1,199.10 per month.

In the first month of the loan, when the loan outstanding is $200,000, you would pay 0.5 percent of that sum in interest, or $1,000. That leaves $199.10 that can be put toward principal.

In the second month, the loan outstanding has shrunk to $199,800.90, thanks to the prior month's principal payment. The 0.5 percent interest cost on that amount comes to $999. That means a slightly larger sum— $200.10—can be put toward principal. And so it goes for another 358 payments, or 29 years and 10 months.

PART XI

TAXES
WHERE WE TRY TO MAKE SENSE OF SOMETHING THAT DOESN'T

Hunting for investment winners is fun. Managing taxes is tedious. Yet a few hours each year devoted to minimizing your portfolio's tax bill will likely yield a far bigger financial return.

Imagine you invest $10,000 for 30 years and earn 8 percent a year. If you lost 25 percent of your gain to taxes every year, you would have $57,435 after 30 years, which is fairly impressive. Now, instead, suppose you could defer all taxes for 30 years, at which point you got dinged at 25 percent on your 30 years of tax-deferred growth. Result: You would walk away with $77,970, or 36 percent more.

There are two golden rules when managing taxes. First, it's usually better to pay taxes later. If you have a choice between paying taxes this year and paying in 10 years, you should take the second option. During the extra 10 years that you hang onto money earmarked for Uncle Sam, you can use that money to earn additional gains for yourself. This tax deferral is one of the compelling advantages offered by retirement accounts. It's also the reason people will realize investment losses and bulk up on tax deductions during the current tax year, while putting off income and capital gains until later.

Second, when you pay taxes, you want to pay at the lowest rate possible. That means favoring investments that are taxed less onerously. This should be a key factor when investing your taxable account. But it also means seizing the opportunity offered by years when you have little taxable income, which may include your early retirement years or a year when you're out of work. Indeed, while paying taxes later is rule No. 1, sometimes rule No. 2 means breaking rule No. 1.

Ready to get started? This chapter begins with an overview of the federal tax code and then offers a host of strategies for managing your investment tax bill.

282. AMERICA'S TAX SYSTEM 2015

No major federal tax legislation was passed in 2015. But numerous tax proposals have been making the rounds—and there's a growing chance we will see a rewriting of the tax code in the years ahead.

The last big rewrite was in 1986, resulting in significant simplification. But in the three decades since, the tax code has grown increasingly cluttered with new taxes, deductions, credits and special savings accounts. While there isn't bipartisan agreement on the solution, both Democrats and Republicans seem to agree that the tax code has become too unwieldy and needs simplifying.

In January 2015's State of the Union Address, President Obama proposed a number of changes, including revamping the tax breaks for education and raising the top capital gains rate to 28 percent. He also proposed getting rid of the step-up in cost basis that occurs if you own investments in a taxable account when you die. Currently, the step-up in basis eliminates the capital gains tax bill that would otherwise be owed, so nixing this benefit would be a big loss for wealthier families.

The following month, in the White House's 2016 budget, retirement accounts were targeted. President Obama proposed eliminating the "net unrealized appreciation" tax break, preventing nondeductible retirement-account contributions from being converted to a Roth and forcing most beneficiaries of a retirement account to empty the account within five years of the original owner's death. Spouses, together with those in certain special situations, would be exempt from the latter provision. The budget also proposed requiring minimum annual distributions not only for regular retirement accounts, but also for all Roth accounts. Right now, minimum distributions aren't required for Roth IRAs, assuming you're the original owner.

While none of these proposals became law, investors should take the flurry of proposals from the White House, presidential candidates and others as a warning sign: Political risk is rising—and the tax code may get changed in ways that derail our carefully constructed financial plans.

283. DOS AND DON'TS FOR 2016

Want to boost your after-tax wealth? Here are some "to dos" for 2016:

• Check whether it still makes sense to own municipal bonds, given your marginal tax rate.

• Consider selling tax-inefficient investments in your taxable account and repurchasing them in a retirement account. At issue here are investments such as taxable bonds, real estate investment trusts and actively managed stock funds.

• If you have a year with relatively little taxable income, look into converting part of your traditional IRA to a Roth IRA.

• If you have taxable account investments that are underwater, consider taking tax losses.

And here are some things you shouldn't do:

• Don't sell winning taxable account investments until you have held them for more than a year, so the gain will be taxed at the lower long-term capital gains rate.

• Don't wait until the year after you turn age 70½ to take your first required minimum distribution from your retirement accounts. You'll have to take a second distribution before year-end and that could push you into a higher tax bracket.

• Don't do a 60-day rollover from a former employer's retirement plan to an IRA. This can create a nasty tax trap, as you'll learn later in this chapter.

• Don't put any money in a tax-deferred annuity until you have maxed out your employer's retirement plan and your IRA, and also considered whether it makes more sense to pursue a tax-efficient stock strategy in your taxable account. And never, ever buy a tax-deferred annuity within an IRA.

284. INCOME TAX BASICS

The federal tax code can be utterly baffling, which helps explain why 56 percent of individual tax returns are completed by a tax preparer and many of the rest use tax software. Still, while every nuance of the tax code won't be explained here, it's important to understand the basics so you can better manage your annual tax bill.

How is your federal tax bill calculated? You start by adding up your gross income. That means toting up the money you received over the past calendar year from your job, investments, rental properties and elsewhere.

Next, you figure out how much of this income is taxable by knocking off your personal exemptions, standard or itemized deductions, and any other deductions you have, including those for retirement account contributions. You will likely discover there's a large amount of income each year on which you pay no income taxes, though you may pay Social Security and Medicare payroll taxes on this money.

After that, you calculate how much you owe Uncle Sam on your taxable income. That isn't as straightforward as it seems, thanks to the multitude of different tax rates, including seven federal income tax brackets, capital gains taxes, the alternative minimum tax and the Medicare surtax.

Finally, once you have figured out your total tax bill, you may be able to trim it by claiming various tax credits, such as the child tax credit and the credit for daycare costs. There are also various education tax breaks, which are discussed in Part IV. All done? Unfortunately not. Many Americans then get to do it all over again, thanks to state income taxes.

If you want to learn more about the federal tax code, check out the interactive tax forms at TaxPolicyCenter.org. The Tax Policy Center is a joint venture of the Urban Institute and Brookings Institution. The interactive forms explain each line on the tax return, including how many people are affected.

285. TAXABLE INCOME

In this chapter and elsewhere in the *Money Guide*, you will see references to your "income" or your "taxable income." But these are messy notions.

As a rule, you can think of your taxable income as your income after deducting personal exemptions, your standard or itemized deduction, and any other deductions you are eligible for. But not everything hinges on your taxable income. For instance, various taxes and tax breaks hinge on your "adjusted gross income," "modified adjusted gross income" and "combined income."

Consider some examples. At the bottom of the first page of Form 1040, you will find your adjusted gross income, or AGI. Depending on how high your AGI is, the value of your itemized deductions and your personal exemptions may be reduced, and you might find your eligibility for various tax credits is affected, such as the credit for daycare expenses.

Your modified adjusted gross income, or MAGI, is your AGI with certain adjustments added back. Among other things, MAGI is used to determine whether your traditional IRA contributions are tax-deductible and whether you can make regular annual contributions to a Roth IRA.

Finally, combined income is a concept used to determine whether your Social Security benefits are taxable. Combined income is your AGI, plus interest from municipal bonds and half of your Social Security benefit.

286. FIVE FEDERAL TAXES

You might hear companies complain about the corporate income tax, and the wealthy berate the estate tax. But in fact, just 11.6 percent of the federal government's revenue comes from the corporate income tax and just 0.6 percent from the federal estate and gift tax, according to a March 2015 report by Congress's Joint Committee on Taxation. These figures pale next to the 79.7 percent that comes from taxes on individual incomes, such as income taxes and Social Security payroll taxes (though, to be fair, a portion of these payroll taxes are paid by employers).

In fact, your income could be subject to as many as five different federal tax systems. First, if you have a job, and hence you have what's called earned income, you pay Social Security and Medicare payroll taxes. For many folks, this is the biggest tax they pay.

Second, there's the federal income tax, which is why we spend the early months of each year sweating over Form 1040. Why is the form so complicated? One reason: In addition to payroll and income taxes, you may owe three other taxes, especially if you have a hefty income or you have so-called unearned income, which is income from investments.

That brings us to our third tax: If you have qualified dividends or you sell investments that you held for more than a year, you may pay taxes at the long-term capital gains rate, rather than at the higher income tax rate. The dividend and long-term capital gains rate is 0 or 15 percent for everyone except those in the top 39.6 percent tax bracket, who pay 20 percent. This potential tax advantage should heavily influence how you invest your taxable account.

Fourth, you may be subject to the Medicare surtax, which took effect in 2013 and was introduced to help pay for Obamacare. Unlike the standard Social Security and Medicare payroll tax, the Medicare surtax can ding not only your salary, but also your investment gains. In effect, it's two taxes—an additional payroll tax and an extra investment tax on high-income earners.

Fifth, there's the alternative minimum tax, or AMT. Initially introduced to ensure those with high incomes paid at least a minimum amount of federal income taxes, the AMT now hits many middle-class families, especially those with a large number of dependents or sizable state and local tax deductions.

287. PAYROLL TAXES

Unless you're self-employed, it is easy to forget about the Social Security and Medicare payroll tax. Your employer takes the payroll tax from your paycheck before it does almost anything else, including deduct those 401(k) contributions. Those contributions may reduce your income for purposes of calculating income taxes, but they don't shrink the income that's subject to the payroll tax. Moreover, unless you have self-employment income, you won't even be reminded that you're paying the payroll tax when you fill out your federal tax return.

Yet, for many folks, the payroll tax takes a bigger bite out of their income than the federal income tax. Let's say you are the sole breadwinner in a family of four, you earn 2014's U.S. median household income of $53,657, your only income comes from your job and you claim the standard deduction. In 2016, you would lose $2,801.05 to federal income taxes and $4,104.76 to the payroll tax—and this assumes your employer pays half the payroll tax.

Surprised? There may be seven federal income tax brackets ranging from 10 to 39.6 percent. But for many families, only the 10 and 15 percent brackets come into play, plus they can take advantage of exemptions, deductions and credits. That means their marginal tax rate is fairly low, and their average tax rate is even lower. By contrast, in 2016, the payroll tax for most folks is a flat 15.3 percent, with 7.65 percent paid by employees and 7.65 percent by employers. That 7.65 percent is further divided, so that 6.2 percent goes to Social Security and 1.45 percent to Medicare.

High-income employees get some relief from the payroll tax once their salary for 2016 crosses the $118,500 mark. At that juncture, they no longer have to pay any more Social Security tax, though they have to pay the 1.45 percent Medicare tax on every dollar of income they earn. If their total income—including investment income—is high enough, however, they may get hit with a nasty surprise: the Medicare surtax.

288. MARGINAL VS. AVERAGE TAX RATES

Imagine you're single, you claim the standard deduction and you have income of $50,000 in 2016. You would be in the 25 percent federal income tax bracket, but that isn't how much of your income you lose to taxes.

On the first $10,350 of income, you wouldn't owe any federal income taxes, thanks to your $6,300 standard deduction and your $4,050 personal exemption. The next $9,275 would be taxed at 10 percent and the subsequent $28,375 would be taxed at 15 percent. That gets you up to $48,000 in total income. It's only at that point that your income starts getting taxed at 25 percent. In other words, while you're in the 25 percent marginal federal income tax bracket, just $2,000 of your $50,000 income would be taxed at that rate. Your total federal income tax bill would be $5,683.75, putting your average tax rate at 11.4 percent for your $50,000 in gross income and 14.3 percent for your $39,650 in taxable income.

For high-income earners, their true marginal tax rate may differ from the rate for the top tax bracket that they're in, because each additional dollar of income also causes lost tax benefits, such as a reduction in the amount they can claim in itemized deductions and personal exemptions.

Your marginal tax rate is crucial for figuring out whether you should buy taxable or tax-free bonds, how much all that mortgage interest is costing you, and whether it makes sense to convert your traditional IRA to a Roth IRA. Most taxpayers pay federal taxes at a 15 percent marginal rate or lower. But your marginal rate isn't a good indicator of what your total bill will be for the year. For that, you'd want to know your average rate. For all taxpayers, the average federal tax rate in 2013 was 13.4 percent of total income.

289. STANDARD VS. ITEMIZED DEDUCTIONS

For 2015, the standard deduction is $12,600 if your tax-filing status is married filing jointly, $9,250 for heads of household and $6,300 for single individuals. For 2016, the standard deduction remains the same for those married filing jointly and for single individuals, but for heads of household it rises to $9,300. The standard deduction is slightly higher if you are elderly or blind. You take the standard deduction if it's greater than the sum of your various itemized deductions. In 2013, the standard deduction was claimed on 69 percent of individual tax returns.

Why is the standard deduction so important? Besides representing a sum you can earn each year without getting taxed, it also should guide your financial behavior. For instance, if you take the standard deduction, you aren't getting any tax benefit from the mortgage interest you pay, so it may make sense to pay off your mortgage more quickly. You only benefit from the mortgage-interest tax deduction if you itemize your deductions using Schedule A.

A subtle point: Imagine you're single and your itemized deduction is $8,000, mostly because of mortgage interest. All that interest might seem like a valuable tax deduction. But arguably, it's only valuable to the extent that it exceeds 2016's $6,300 standard deduction—and thus your mortgage interest isn't generating huge tax savings.

On Schedule A, you also list other deductions, including property taxes, medical and dental expenses, charitable contributions, and state and local income taxes. Instead of deducting state and local income taxes, you may be able to deduct state and local sales taxes—a useful deduction for those who live in states with low or no income tax. As of late 2015, we didn't know whether this tax break would be available for the 2015 tax year.

Even if you itemize, you may not get the full tax benefit from all the items listed on Schedule A. In 2015, your itemized deductions are reduced if your adjusted gross income is above $309,900 and you're married filing jointly, above $284,050 and you're head of household, and above $258,250 and you're single. In 2016, the reduction will affect you if your income is above $311,300 and you are married filing jointly, above $285,350 if head of household and above $259,400 if single.

At these income levels, the value of your personal exemptions also phases out. The full value of each personal exemption is $4,000 in 2015 and $4,050 in 2016. You can typically claim a personal exemption for yourself, your spouse and all dependents.

290. MEDICARE SURTAX

The standard Medicare payroll tax is 2.9 percent, half of which may be paid by your employer, leaving your share at 1.45 percent. Add that to the 6.2 percent Social Security tax and you get the total 7.65 percent payroll tax. If you have a high income, you will notice that the Social Security tax stops getting collected once you hit that year's threshold, which for 2016 would be $118,500. But there's no cap on the Medicare tax, which is collected on every dollar you earn.

Sound rough? Starting in 2013, it got rougher. Once your taxable income gets above $200,000 if you're single or head of household and above $250,000 if you're married filing jointly, the Medicare tax jumps by 0.9 percentage point to 3.8 percent (though, again, 1.45 percent may be paid by your employer). Moreover, once you're at this income level, the 3.8 percent Medicare surtax doesn't just apply to earned income. Your net investment income is also taxed at these rates.

Net investment income includes your realized capital gains, dividends and interest, though not interest from municipal bonds. Let's say you realize a long-term capital gain that would otherwise be taxed at 15 percent. Now, you will also pay an additional 3.8 percent, bringing the total tax on the gain to 18.8 percent. Here's more salt for the wound: The income thresholds aren't indexed for inflation. That means that, in the years ahead, more folks will find themselves paying the 3.8 percent Medicare tax.

291. ALTERNATIVE MINIMUM TAX

The alternative minimum tax, or AMT, is a parallel tax system that forces you to calculate how much you owe in federal income taxes using a completely different set of rules. The Urban-Brookings Tax Policy Center forecasts that 4.8 percent of taxpayers will pay the AMT in 2016. An estimated 66 percent of those paying the tax earn between $200,000 and $500,000. The AMT tends to hit folks who live in states with high state income taxes and include those taxes among their itemized deductions. It often also snags those who realize large capital gains or who have three or more children. If the amount owed under the AMT is greater than under the usual income tax calculation, you have to pay the difference.

For individuals, the AMT consists of just two tax rates, 26 and 28 percent. When calculating how much you owe under the AMT, you can't claim personal exemptions or the standard deduction. You can claim itemized deductions, though what counts is severely curtailed. For instance, no deduction is allowed for state, local or property taxes. You can still deduct charitable gifts and most mortgage interest. Deductible retirement plan contributions, which aren't reported as an itemized deduction, also reduce your income for AMT purposes.

While you can't claim personal exemptions when calculating how much you owe under the AMT, you do get the benefit of the much larger AMT exemption. That exemption is adjusted each year for inflation. For unmarried individuals, the exemption is worth $53,600 in 2015 and $53,900 in 2016. For married couples filing jointly, the exemption is $83,400 in 2015 and $83,800 in 2016. The AMT exemption phases out at higher income levels, so the effective marginal AMT tax rate is often higher than the notional 26 and 28 percent rates.

292. MANAGING YOUR EARNINGS

If you're like most employees, you don't have any control over when you receive your wages. Instead, as you seek to limit your annual tax bill, the key financial levers at your disposal include increasing your tax-deductible retirement account contributions, carefully managing your taxable investment accounts and making sure you take full advantage of the available tax deductions and credits.

What if you're a senior executive or a business owner who can influence the company's payroll policy? You might have more room for maneuver. For instance, if you know federal or state taxes are likely to rise next year, you might arrange for year-end bonuses to be paid this year.

If you're self-employed or own a small business, there's even more you might do. Got a lot of income in 2016 but suspect 2017 will be thinner? You might hold off billing clients so you get paid in 2017. Think 2017 will be a good year? You might wait until next year to buy new computer equipment or plan on maxing out your SEP IRA or solo 401(k) contributions.

293. MANAGING YOUR INVESTMENT TAXES

As a regular employee, you may find it tough to shift earnings from one year to the next. But there's plenty you can do to manage the tax bill generated by your investments. The rest of this chapter is devoted to three strategies you ought to focus on.

First, make the most of the tax-sheltered retirement accounts available to you. That will mean not only stashing as much money as possible in these accounts, but also carefully weighing whether to fund traditional or Roth retirement accounts.

Second, ponder which investments to hold in your retirement accounts and which in your regular taxable account. In all likelihood, you'll want to use your retirement accounts to hold investments that would otherwise generate big annual tax bills, while keeping more tax-efficient investments in your taxable account.

Third, seize the opportunity offered by years when your income is relatively low. Those low-income years may allow you to generate additional taxable income, while still paying taxes at a relatively low rate. To that end, you might sell stocks with large unrealized capital gains that you no longer want to hold or perhaps convert part of your traditional IRA to a Roth IRA.

JONATHAN'S TAKE: Investors spend hours picking investments, while paying scant attention to taxes and investment costs. But the fact is, when you buy an investment, you never know whether you have yourself a winner. By contrast, managing your tax bill and holding down investment costs are two surefire ways to improve your portfolio's performance.

294. RETIREMENT ACCOUNTS

Retirement accounts come in a bewildering array of flavors. Employer-sponsored plans include 401(k), 403(b), 457 and profit-sharing plans, as well as the SIMPLE IRA and SEP IRA. On top of that, there are individual plans such as traditional and Roth IRAs, and also tax-deferred fixed and variable annuities.

How can you make sense of that mess? All of these accounts offer tax-deferred growth. That means you don't have to pay taxes on any investment earnings until you draw down these accounts, typically in retirement. At that point, withdrawals are usually taxed as ordinary income, which could trigger a federal income tax rate as high as 39.6 percent. Sometimes, however, retirement accounts offer three additional benefits, as well as one big drawback.

First benefit: Some accounts offer an initial tax deduction. That's the case with a tax-deductible IRA. Contributions to employer plans are often also effectively tax-deductible, because your contributions are taken out of pretax dollars.

Second, accounts such as the Roth 401(k) and Roth IRA won't give you an immediate tax deduction, but they offer the chance not just for tax-deferred growth, but tax-free growth. You may even have a choice between, say, a tax-deductible 401(k) and Roth 401(k) or between a tax-deductible IRA and Roth IRA. You can, alas, never get both a tax deduction and tax-free growth.

Third, your employer's retirement plan may include the chance to earn a matching contribution. Not contributing enough to your employer's plan to earn the full match? That ranks as one of the most foolish financial mistakes.

Finally, there's the big drawback: Some retirement accounts are inordinately expensive. That's an issue with some employer-sponsored plans. But the biggest culprits are many, but not all, tax-deferred annuities.

295. EMPLOYER PLANS

If you work for a larger employer, you might be offered a 401(k), 403(b) or 457 plan. In general, private companies offer 401(k) plans, nonprofit and educational institutions offer 403(b) plans, and government organizations offer 457 plans. All operate under roughly similar rules.

The 2016 contribution limit for these plans is typically $18,000. Those age 50 and up can make an additional catch-up contribution of $6,000, for a total of $24,000. Any matching employer contribution doesn't count toward these annual limits. Some companies also offer profit-sharing plans, which are funded solely by the employer, with no money expected from you.

If you work for a small employer, you might have access to a SIMPLE IRA. (SIMPLE is an acronym for Savings Incentive Match Plan for Employees.) The 2016 contribution limit is $12,500, with those 50 and up able to contribute an additional $3,000, for a total of $15,500. Employers are required to either contribute 2 percent of an employee's pay to a SIMPLE IRA or, alternatively, match 100 percent of each employee's contribution, up to 3 percent of pay.

If you're self-employed, you could fund a SEP IRA. (SEP stands for Simplified Employee Pension.) You can contribute as much as 20 percent of your net self-employment income, up to $53,000 in 2016. You can make this contribution even if you are covered by, say, a 401(k) at another job. Alternatively, if you're self-employed, you might consider a solo 401(k), where the 2016 total contribution that you can make, as both employer and employee, is also capped at $53,000. On top of that, those 50 and older can make a $6,000 catch-up contribution, for a total of $59,000.

For most folks, funding their employer's plan should be their top financial priority each year, not least because of the potential matching employer contribution. Failing to contribute isn't the only danger, however. You should also watch out for high costs and pay heed to vesting provisions if you're considering a new job. In addition, think twice before taking out retirement plan loans.

296. MATCHING CONTRIBUTIONS

It's hard to overemphasize the importance of putting at least enough in your employer's 401(k) or 403(b) plan to earn the full matching employer contribution. But to drive home the point, consider an extreme example.

Suppose your company is likely to have layoffs. Meanwhile, the local employment market is sufficiently depressed that you fear it will take many months to find a new job. Your instinct is to hoard every dollar possible for what could be a lengthy period of unemployment. Nonetheless, if your employer offers a retirement plan with a matching contribution, you would likely be better off funding the plan, even if you fully intend to cash out your savings if you're laid off.

Let's say you are in the 15 percent federal income tax bracket and you put $2,000 in the plan. Your out-of-pocket cost would be $1,700, thanks to the initial tax savings. At the same time, your employer matches your contribution at 50 cents on the dollar, with the matching contribution vested immediately. Result: Your $2,000 investment gets you a $1,000 match, bringing your account balance to $3,000.

If you are then laid off and you cash out your retirement account balance, you might lose 15 percent to federal income taxes, plus another 10 percent to the tax penalty for making a retirement account withdrawal before age 59½. That combined 25 percent hit still leaves you with $2,250, well above your $1,700 out-of-pocket cost. Moreover, if you are unemployed for a long period, you may have little taxable income in the year you cash out your retirement account balance, so your income tax bracket could be below 15 percent.

297. LEAVING YOUR EMPLOYER

If you're changing jobs, take two steps to protect your retirement. First, if you have an outstanding loan from your 401(k) or 403(b) plan, get it paid off. If you don't and you leave your job, the loan will be considered a distribution, triggering income taxes and probably tax penalties. There's more on 401(k) loans in Part XII. Second, if there's a vesting schedule for your employer's contribution to the retirement plan, see when the next vesting occurs and, if it's soon, consider delaying your departure so you collect the extra money.

Once you leave your employer, you'll have a choice: You may be able to leave your retirement plan balance in your old employer's plan, move it to your new employer's plan or transfer it to an IRA. What's the right choice?

You'll probably want to move the money if your old employer's plan offers a limited selection of high-cost investment options. This, unfortunately, is often the case with small-business plans. You may also want to consolidate your retirement money in an IRA if simplifying your finances is a priority. Make sure you move the money using a trustee-to-trustee transfer or you could find yourself caught in a nasty tax trap. In addition, if you own your employer's stock in the plan, investigate the "net unrealized appreciation" strategy, which we discuss later in this chapter.

While consolidating in an IRA sometimes makes sense, there are three reasons to keep your retirement money where it is or move it to your new employer's plan. First, it could mean a smaller tax bill if you have an IRA with nondeductible contributions that you plan to convert to a Roth IRA. Second, you might keep money in a 401(k) or similar employer plan—and out of an IRA—if you're worried about lawsuits, a topic we discuss in Part V. While both IRAs and 401(k) plans enjoy some creditor protection, the protection is greater for 401(k) and similar plans.

Third, some employer plans are particularly well-designed—and you could find it tough to do better with an IRA. A good plan may include a small but diverse list of institutional funds with rock-bottom annual expenses, making it relatively easy for employees to build sensible portfolios. For instance, Vanguard Emerging Markets Stock Index Fund charges 0.33 percent a year if you invest $3,000, but the biggest retirement plans can get access to a share class that costs just 0.1 percent. In addition, an employer's plan may include a stable-value fund that offers a combination of fixed share price and moderate yield that's hard to find outside a 401(k).

298. TRUSTEE-TO-TRUSTEE TRANSFERS

If you move money from one retirement account to another, try to arrange a trustee-to-trustee transfer, also known as a direct rollover. That involves asking your brokerage firm, mutual fund company, bank or former employer's 401(k) administrator to send a check that's made out to your new retirement plan custodian. For instance, the check might be payable to "First Fiduciary Trust Company FBO [for benefit of] Jane Smith." The check may be sent directly to your new retirement account provider or it could be mailed to you, and you then have to forward it.

Instead of a trustee-to-trustee transfer, some folks opt for a check made out to them personally, sometimes known as a 60-day rollover or indirect rollover. Problem is, if you do a 60-day rollover from a former employer's retirement plan, you will typically receive a check for just 80 percent of the account balance, with the other 20 percent dispatched to the IRS. You can reclaim the other 20 percent on your next tax return—but only if you manage to roll over 100 percent of the account balance within 60 days. That won't be an issue if you have wads of cash sitting around.

But for most people, getting the money together will be a struggle. What if they fail? The 20 percent not rolled over will be considered a retirement account distribution, which means they will likely get hit with both income taxes and a 10 percent tax penalty. The bottom line: Don't let your old employer send you a check made out to you personally. Instead, go for the trustee-to-trustee transfer.

299. NET UNREALIZED APPRECIATION

Got company stock in your 401(k) plan? If you leave your employer, consider taking advantage of the net unrealized appreciation, or NUA, strategy. The idea is to transfer everything in your 401(k) to an IRA— except your employer's stock. These shares, instead, get deposited into a regular taxable brokerage account.

This triggers an immediate income tax bill on the stock's cost basis, which is the amount you paid for the stock or the amount it was worth when you received it as a matching employer contribution. If you are under age 59½, you will likely also have to pay a 10 percent tax penalty on the stock's cost basis. But in return for paying that tax bill, you get a tax break: All of the appreciation in the stock's value is potentially taxable at the long-term capital gains rate. This can be a significant advantage, because retirement account withdrawals are usually taxed at the higher income tax rate.

While the stock's appreciation within the 401(k) will be taxed at the long-term capital gains rate, the subsequent appreciation—after you pull the stock out of the 401(k)—will only be taxed at the capital gains rate if you wait a year before selling.

The NUA strategy makes most sense if the stock has greatly appreciated in value. What if the shares haven't climbed that much? You may want to avoid the immediate income tax bill and possible tax penalty by transferring everything, including the stock, to an IRA.

300. INDIVIDUAL RETIREMENT ACCOUNTS

IRAs come in two flavors: traditional and Roth. With a traditional IRA, you may get an initial tax deduction, but withdrawals are taxed as ordinary income. With a Roth, there's no upfront tax deduction, but all withdrawals in retirement can be tax-free.

For 2015 and 2016, you can contribute up to $5,500 to all IRAs combined, provided you have at least that much in earned income. (Investment income doesn't count.) If you're age 50 or older, you can make an additional catch-up contribution of $1,000, for a total of $6,500. You have until April 15, 2016, to make your 2015 contribution.

If you stash those dollars in a traditional IRA, you can always deduct your contribution if you aren't covered by an employer's retirement plan. What if you or your spouse has a retirement plan at work? You'll need to check the income limits for 2015 and 2016.

To fund a Roth, it doesn't matter whether you're covered by a workplace retirement plan. Instead, all that matters is whether you meet the income thresholds for that tax year.

If you're lucky enough to qualify for both a traditional and Roth IRA, you should weigh the choice carefully. What if you qualify for neither? You can always fund a nondeductible IRA. That may sound like a drab consolation prize—but it could open the door to a Roth conversion.

Finally, don't forget about your spouse. Even if your husband or wife has no earned income, he or she may still qualify for a so-called spousal IRA.

301. DEDUCTING IRA CONTRIBUTIONS

Suppose you aren't covered by an employer's retirement plan and—if married—your spouse isn't, either. In that scenario, you can take a tax deduction for your contribution to a traditional IRA, no matter how high your income.

But if you have a retirement plan at work, income thresholds come into play. If your tax-filing status is single or head of household, your ability to take a tax deduction for your IRA contribution phases out if your 2015 modified adjusted gross income is between $61,000 and $71,000. Above $71,000, you can't take a deduction, though you can still make nondeductible contributions. For 2016, the phase-out range is the same— $61,000 to $71,000.

Meanwhile, if you are married filing jointly and you're covered by a retirement plan at work, your ability to deduct your IRA contributions phases out if your combined income is $98,000 to $118,000 in 2015. For

2016, the range again remains the same—$98,000 to $118,000.

What if you aren't covered by an employer's plan, but your spouse is? In that situation, the deductibility of your IRA contribution phases out between $183,000 and $193,000 in 2015 and between $184,000 and $194,000 in 2016.

What if one spouse doesn't work? As long as the other spouse has enough earned income—remember, you can only make the full $5,500 or $6,500 IRA contribution if you have that much in earned income—the couple can fund an IRA on behalf of the nonworking spouse. If the spouse who works is covered by an employer's retirement plan, the deductibility of the nonworking spouse's IRA contribution phases out between $183,000 and $193,000 in 2015 and between $184,000 and $194,000 in 2016.

302. QUALIFYING FOR A ROTH IRA

To claim a tax deduction for your traditional IRA contribution, much hinges on whether you are covered by a retirement plan at work. That doesn't come into play with a Roth IRA. Instead, all that matters is your income.

If you are single or head of household and you have enough earned income, you can fully fund a Roth IRA in 2015 if your modified adjusted gross income is less than $116,000. The amount you can contribute is phased out if your income is between $116,000 and $131,000. Above $131,000, no contribution is allowed. For 2016, the phase-out range is $117,000 to $132,000.

If you are married filing jointly, your ability to fund a Roth phases out if your combined income is between $183,000 and $193,000 in 2015 and between $184,000 and $194,000 in 2016.

What if you're eligible to make only a partial Roth contribution of, say, $3,000 out of a possible $5,500? You can put the remaining $2,500 in a traditional IRA, though your contribution won't necessarily be tax-deductible.

303. TAX-DEDUCTIBLE VS. ROTH ACCOUNTS

You may qualify to fund both a tax-deductible and Roth IRA. Alternatively, perhaps your employer offers the chance to fund either a tax-deductible or Roth 401(k). Which should you go for?

A key factor is whether you think your tax bracket in retirement will be higher or lower than it is today. If you expect your tax rate in retirement to be the same or higher, you should favor the Roth, giving up today's tax deduction in return for tax-free growth.

Conversely, if you think you'll be in a lower bracket, you should opt for the traditional IRA, taking a tax deduction at your high tax rate today while knowing you'll pull those dollars out of your IRA at a lower tax rate once you're retired. Many folks will be in this camp. The reason: You can deduct today's retirement account contributions at your marginal tax rate, which could be 25 percent or higher, but in retirement your withdrawals might be your only income—and thus you'll probably pay taxes at an average rate that's well below 25 percent.

What if you're unsure what your retirement tax rate will be? You might hedge your bets, dividing your money between traditional and Roth accounts.

While tax considerations often favor traditional IRAs, the Roth IRA might still be appealing, thanks to some unique advantages. Unlike with a traditional IRA, you can withdraw your regular annual contributions from a Roth IRA at any time for any reason. Just put $5,500 in a Roth? You can pull that money out tomorrow with no taxes or penalties owed.

Under current law, you also don't have to take required minimum distributions from a Roth IRA once you turn age 70½. That means you can leave the account to continue growing tax-free, and you might even bequeath the account to your children or other beneficiaries. A Roth IRA can make a wonderful inheritance, giving your beneficiaries years of tax-free income using a strategy known as the "stretch IRA." We discuss the stretch IRA further in Part XIII, including the risk that Congress might nix the strategy.

Like the idea of sidestepping required minimum distributions with a Roth IRA? If you fund a Roth 401(k), be sure to transfer it to a Roth IRA before you reach your 70s, because minimum distributions are required from a Roth 401(k). Avoiding required minimum distributions is also a reason to convert a traditional IRA to a Roth IRA.

304. HOW TO THINK ABOUT THAT TAX DEDUCTION

Assuming you follow the rules, a Roth IRA or Roth 401(k) will give you tax-free growth—and it doesn't get much better than that. But what about traditional 401(k) plans and IRAs, where you can get an initial tax deduction, but everything withdrawn in retirement is taxable as ordinary income?

Occasionally, you'll hear so-called experts—who often have some other investment they're promoting—criticize tax-deductible retirement accounts, arguing that people are setting themselves up for huge tax bills in retirement. That may be the case. But if you run the numbers, you find the initial tax savings frequently end up paying for the final tax bill. Indeed, a tax-deductible account can give you tax-free growth, just like a Roth (though, as you'll discover in the next section, there's a subtle difference that nerdy types might consider).

Imagine you saved $8,000 in your employer's 401(k) plan and you're in the 25 percent federal income tax bracket. Thanks to the $2,000 in initial tax savings, your out-of-pocket cost is $6,000. Over the next 30 years, your $8,000 grows fivefold—or 400 percent—to $40,000. At that point, you cash it out, paying 25 percent in taxes, equal to $10,000.

That $10,000 represents 400 percent growth on your initial $2,000 in tax savings. In effect, the tax deduction paid the final tax bill, leaving you with tax-free growth on your $6,000 out-of-pocket cost. What if your tax bracket is lower in retirement, which is often the case? In that scenario, you'll have made out at Uncle Sam's expense.

Still, if you fund tax-deductible retirement accounts, it's worth keeping those embedded tax bills in mind as you approach retirement, so you have a better handle on the post-tax value of your retirement savings. The fact is, $10,000 in a tax-deductible retirement account will buy fewer groceries than $10,000 in a Roth.

305. FURTHER NERDY THOUGHTS ABOUT THAT TAX DEDUCTION

Okay, so you read the previous section and you see how a tax-deductible retirement account can give you tax-free growth, just like a Roth. In fact, if your tax bracket is lower in retirement, a tax-deductible retirement account can let you come out ahead at the taxman's expense. Meanwhile, if your tax bracket in retirement is higher, you'll be happy you funded a Roth.

But what if your tax bracket stays the same? All even? It depends. Go back and look at the previous section, where we assumed you were in the 25 percent tax bracket both when you funded the account and when you're retired. Instead of putting $8,000 in your employer's traditional 401(k), suppose you put $6,000 in the Roth 401(k). Your initial out-of-pocket cost would be the same in both instances and you would have the same after-tax sum in retirement. So, yes, it would be all even.

Now, imagine instead that you plan to max out your IRA. You have a choice: Put $5,500 in a tax-deductible IRA or $5,500 in a Roth. Either way, the account doubles in value between now and retirement, growing to $11,000. With the Roth, that will mean $11,000 in spending money.

With the tax-deductible IRA, you will owe taxes when you tap the account. If you're in the 25 percent tax bracket, you would be looking at a

$2,750 tax bill. Fortunately, you also had the initial tax deduction, which would have been worth $1,375 if you had been in the 25 percent tax bracket when you funded the account. In an effort to cover the eventual tax bill on your IRA, you decide to invest the $1,375 tax savings in the same investments that you own in your IRA, so the $1,375 also doubles in value. That way, it would grow to $2,750 and cover the final tax bill, right?

Wrong. The problem: The $1,375 would have to be invested in a regular taxable account, where its growth would be taxed and hence it wouldn't grow to $2,750. That's why, if you suspect your tax bracket will be the same in retirement as it is now, you should favor Roth accounts over traditional retirement accounts.

306. ROTH CONVERSIONS

Why convert a traditional IRA to a Roth IRA? The rationale is similar to the reasons you might funnel your regular annual contributions into a Roth rather than a traditional IRA. There are, however, three additional considerations.

First, you might convert to a Roth if you have a year with low taxable income, so you pay tax on the conversion at a relatively modest rate. Remember, when you convert, you have to pay income taxes on the taxable sum converted.

That brings us to the second reason you might convert: Suppose that, in the past, you made nondeductible contributions to your traditional IRA. When you convert, you don't have to pay taxes on those nondeductible contributions. Be warned: For tax purposes, you can't pick which IRA to convert. Instead, you have to assume that the money comes proportionally from all your IRAs combined—which might mean a larger tax bill than you had hoped.

Third, you should convert only if you have money in a regular taxable account to pay the tax bill triggered by the conversion. Using this taxable account money to pay the conversion tax should, thereafter, lower your annual tax bill. How so? Not only will your IRA withdrawals no longer be taxable, but also you'll shrink the size of your taxable account, so that account no longer generates as big a tax bill. Think of it this way: By converting to a Roth and paying the tax bill with taxable account money, you effectively move money from your taxable account—where it's getting taxed each year—to a Roth, where it can grow tax-free.

A frequent question asked by those age 70½ and older: Can you convert a traditional IRA to a Roth—and count the conversion toward that year's required minimum distribution? The answer, alas, is no. We discuss required minimum distributions in more detail later in this chapter.

JONATHAN'S TAKE: I'm a huge fan of Roth accounts. If you have a year with relatively little taxable income, consider converting a portion of your traditional IRA to a Roth. In retirement, you might tap your Roth if you have a year with high expenses and you don't want to pull money from traditional retirement accounts, which could nudge you into a higher tax bracket. Better still, try not to spend your Roth—and instead bequeath it to your favorite relative.

307. CONVERTING NONDEDUCTIBLE IRAS TO A ROTH

When you convert a traditional IRA to a Roth IRA, you don't have to pay taxes on your nondeductible contributions. Let's say that, over the years, you have made $20,000 in nondeductible contributions to an IRA that is now worth $30,000. When you convert, you don't have to pay taxes on the $20,000 in nondeductible contributions. Thus, the conversion would potentially add just $10,000 to your taxable income, while giving you a $30,000 Roth that will grow tax-free thereafter.

Sound appealing? Here's the hitch: Suppose that, in addition to your $30,000 nondeductible IRA, you also have a $170,000 rollover IRA from your old employer's 401(k). When you convert your $30,000, you have to assume that the money comes pro-rated from all your IRAs combined. That means it's coming out of the $200,000 total IRA. Result: Instead of just $10,000—or 33 percent of the sum converted—being taxable, you would find that $27,000, or 90 percent, would be taxed. The reason: The $20,000 in nondeductible contributions represents just 10 percent of your IRA's $200,000 total value.

What to do? If you have made nondeductible contributions and you're considering a Roth conversion, you might hold off rolling your former employer's 401(k) into an IRA. Alternatively, if you have that money already sitting in a rollover IRA, you may be able to move it into your new employer's retirement plan. That might leave you with just a single IRA, containing nondeductible contributions. You could then convert that account and pay a relatively modest tax bill.

308. MY STORY: ROTH IRA

For years, my income was too high to deduct a traditional IRA contribution or fund a Roth IRA, so I was left making nondeductible contributions to a traditional IRA. Meanwhile, before 2010, I couldn't convert my traditional IRA to a Roth, because my income was above the

$100,000 cutoff. But in 2010, the law changed, so that anybody could convert.

I jumped at the opportunity, converting my $111,249 traditional IRA to a Roth. The sweetener: I only had to pay taxes on $62,674 of additional income. Why not more? By then, my traditional IRA contained $48,575 of nondeductible contributions. Those contributions represented dollars that had previously been taxed, so the IRS didn't expect me to pay income taxes on them again. Result: I now had $111,249 growing tax-free—but, to get that tax-free growth, I only had to make a onetime tax payment of around $20,000.

In subsequent years, I would make my $5,000 annual nondeductible IRA contribution (the maximum is now $5,500, plus an additional $1,000 if you're 50 or older) and then later convert it to a Roth. That, along with market gains, further fattened my Roth.

For tax purposes, you can't convert just your nondeductible IRA. As I explained in the previous section, you have to assume that any conversion comes pro-rated from all your IRAs combined. Aware of this rule, I held off rolling my old 401(k) into an IRA, so all I had was a nondeductible IRA.

Now that I have a fairly substantial Roth IRA, my hope is to leave it untouched and bequeath it to my children. Under current law, I'm not obligated to take required minimum distributions from my Roth—and, assuming my kids inherit the account, they would be able to draw it down slowly using the "stretch IRA" strategy. Unfortunately, it increasingly looks like the politicians will kill the stretch strategy and insist that nonspouse beneficiaries empty all IRAs within five years. Even if that happens, my children will receive a pool of income–tax free money, which should make for a handsome inheritance.

309. ROTH'S FIVE-YEAR RULE

If you make regular annual contributions to a Roth IRA, you can withdraw those contributions at any time with no taxes or penalties owed. It's a different story, however, with the account's investment gains.

Those gains will be subject to both income taxes and tax penalties if you withdraw them within the first five years and if you are under age 59½ (or, to put it another way, you need to wait five years and until after age 59½ for the account's growth to be totally tax-free). The five-year clock starts on Jan. 1 of the tax year for which you made your first regular annual contribution—and it doesn't reset with each subsequent annual contribution or if you open a Roth at another financial firm.

What if you are over age 59½? From then on, if you made a withdrawal, you wouldn't owe a tax penalty if your first annual contribution had been made less than five years earlier. You could owe income taxes, but it's unlikely. How come? When you withdraw, the IRS lets you assume that any withdrawals initially consist of your original annual contributions. If you are drawing down the account relatively slowly, you probably wouldn't start pulling out the account's investment earnings until after you crossed the five-year mark.

Now, consider a different scenario: What if you convert a traditional IRA to a Roth? In that situation, a slightly different five-year rule comes into play. This time, the rule applies not only to the account's investment earnings, but also to the sum converted. In other words, if you withdraw the sum converted within the first five years, you would owe a tax penalty if you were under age 59½. You wouldn't, however, have to pay income taxes, because you already paid income taxes on the money involved when you did the original conversion. Unlike with regular annual contributions, a new five-year waiting period applies to each conversion.

What if you made a conversion more than five years ago and you're under age 59½? Because you have met the five-year rule, you can withdraw the sum converted with no penalty or income taxes owed. It's only if you touch the account's investment gains that taxes and penalties come into play—though you may be able to avoid the penalty if you meet one of the allowable IRS exceptions.

310. EARLY-WITHDRAWAL PENALTIES

If you withdraw money from a retirement account before age 59½, you typically have to pay both income taxes and a 10 percent tax penalty. But there are some situations where the penalty wouldn't apply:

- Distributions made after your death.
- Distributions made after you become permanently disabled.
- Withdrawals from an IRA to pay higher-education expenses. These withdrawals can hurt financial aid eligibility, a topic discussed in Part IV.
- Withdrawals of up to $10,000 from an IRA to buy a home. The $10,000 is a lifetime limit, and the provision can be used only by those who haven't owned a house within the past two years. Are you married? Together, you could withdraw $20,000.
- Distributions made as part of a series of substantially equal periodic payments over your life expectancy. If these distributions are from an employer's plan, you need to have left your job. Be warned: Calculating your annual withdrawal can be complicated.
- Distributions to pay deductible medical expenses that exceed 10 percent of your adjusted gross income.

• Withdrawals from an IRA to pay health insurance premiums while unemployed.

• Distributions from an employer's retirement plan made after you left your job at age 55 or older.

These exceptions to the penalty apply to both traditional and Roth accounts. But with the Roth, you may also avoid income taxes if you're under age 59½, though only in a few carefully defined scenarios, such as when withdrawing your regular annual contributions or when withdrawing the sum converted to a Roth after meeting the five-year rule.

311. MYRA

MyRA is a new retirement savings vehicle geared to those who don't currently have a retirement plan offered through their employer. Like a Roth IRA, there's no initial tax deduction, but all growth is tax-free. Indeed, to fund a myRA, you have to meet the same income thresholds as a Roth IRA.

Accounts are opened online. Subsequent investments are made in any amount, either through payroll deduction or by electronic transfer from a bank account. The account is invested in a single investment whose earnings are driven by government bond yields. An account's balance is capped at $15,000, at which point it stops earning interest.

The hope is that a myRA account will allow workers to get started with modest regular contributions—something that's difficult to do at most financial firms, which often insist on steep minimum initial investments. Once the account has grown to a decent size, investors might roll over the account to a Roth IRA at, say, a mutual fund firm and then continue their regular savings program at the fund company. You can learn more about myRA at myRA.Treasury.gov.

312. TAX-DEFERRED FIXED ANNUITIES

Tax-deferred annuities come in two types: fixed and variable. Historically, fixed annuities have been pretty straightforward. You get a specified yield for the term of the annuity. Thus, it's a simple matter of deciding whether the yield seems attractive compared to the alternatives, whether the issuing insurance company appears to be financially strong and whether you're willing to lock up your money in the annuity structure until age 59½.

But picking among fixed annuities has grown more complicated, for two reasons. First, many annuities offer first-year teaser rates or other come-ons, which make it harder to compare one annuity with another.

Second, some insurers have been pushing a relatively new breed of fixed annuity known as an indexed annuity. These annuities offer returns that are pegged to a market index, such as the S&P 500-stock index, while offering downside protection.

Problem is, investors never get the index's full annual total return. Instead, returns are based on the index with dividends excluded, plus the amount you can earn in any given year is often capped. On top of that, you typically face steep surrender charges if you cash out in the first 10 years or so. Those surrender charges are necessary because indexed annuities pay huge commissions to the salespeople involved, and the annuity needs to recoup that money from investors.

313. TAX-DEFERRED VARIABLE ANNUITIES

From a tax perspective, you can think of a tax-deferred variable annuity as similar to a nondeductible IRA. You won't get an initial tax deduction, but you do get tax-deferred growth.

Problem is, unlike a nondeductible IRA, you can't convert a variable annuity to a Roth IRA. On top of that, a variable annuity gives you much less investment choice and you'll face much higher expenses. Within an annuity, you get to choose from among a series of subaccounts that are similar to mutual funds. Each subaccount has its own investment expenses.

Layered on top of that is the expense of the variable annuity itself. This expense charge might be used to cover the annuity's administrative costs, compensate brokers who sell the annuity and pay for various guarantees, such as a guarantee that the annuity will have some minimum value when you die. It's debatable how valuable these guarantees are. But the net result is that variable annuities typically have total annual expenses that approach 3 percent of assets per year, which makes it tough to earn healthy long-run returns.

Some unscrupulous brokers encourage clients to buy tax-deferred annuities within their IRA. That means the clients are putting a tax-deferred account within a tax-deferred account, which doesn't make a whole lot of sense—and the advice is usually driven not by the best interest of clients, but by the broker's desire to collect the hefty commission from selling a variable annuity. That commission is typically greater than the commission that a broker can earn by selling a mutual fund.

JONATHAN'S TAKE: Not all annuities are a terrible investment. For instance, Fidelity Investments and Vanguard Group offer relatively low-cost variable annuities, and these might appeal to high-income earners who have maxed out their retirement accounts and are looking for additional ways to get tax-deferred growth. In particular, the tax deferral from a low-cost variable annuity may be attractive if you're inclined to buy taxable bonds, real estate investment trusts or actively managed stock funds, all of which tend to be relatively tax-inefficient.

314. TAXABLE ACCOUNTS

With a retirement account, your investments grow tax-deferred, so you don't have to worry about tax bills until retirement. But with a taxable account, trading too much or buying investments that pay a lot of immediately taxable interest can mean a heap of pain at tax time.

To avoid that pain, consider four strategies, which are discussed in the sections that follow. First, focus on generating long-term capital gains by hanging onto your individual stocks or stock funds for more than a year—preferably much more. The maximum long-term federal capital gains rate in 2015 and 2016 is 20 percent, well below the 39.6 percent maximum income tax rate. What if you hold your winning stocks or stock funds for a year or less? The higher income tax rate applies.

Second, periodically sell losing investments. The resulting tax losses can be used to offset realized capital gains and up to $3,000 in ordinary income each year. When taking tax losses, watch out for the wash-sale rule.

Third, when buying stocks and stock funds in a taxable account, favor those that pay qualified dividends. These dividends are taxed at the same rate as long-term capital gains.

Fourth, if you're in a high tax bracket and your taste runs to conservative investments, you might buy tax-free municipal bonds rather than taxable bonds. Munis pay interest that is typically exempt from federal taxes and, if you own bonds from your own state, potentially state and local taxes as well.

What does all this mean for your overall portfolio? That's where the crucial issue of asset location comes in—deciding which investments to hold in your retirement accounts and which in your taxable account.

315. INCOME VS. CAPITAL GAINS

The tax code is designed to encourage folks to save and invest. That's one reason for the wide array of retirement accounts. But it also explains the preferential tax treatment given to stocks and other longer-term investments held in regular taxable accounts. That preferential tax treatment shows up in two ways.

First, if you buy, say, a stock that appreciates in value and you hold that stock for more than a year, it's taxed as a long-term capital gain. In 2015, long-term capital gains are taxed at 20 percent if your taxable income is above $464,850 and you're married filing jointly, above $439,000 and you file as head of household, or above $413,200 and you're single. In 2016, the 20 percent rate applies at $466,950 if married filing jointly, $441,000 if head of household and $415,050 if single. For everybody else, the long-term capital gains rate will be 0 or 15 percent. That 0 percent rate on long-term capital gains is a handsome tax break enjoyed by those whose total taxable income falls within the 10 and 15 percent federal income tax brackets.

Whatever rate you pay, it should be well below the tax rate on your ordinary income. Moreover, that capital gains tax bill only comes due when you sell and realize your gain. Hanging onto winning investments in your taxable account effectively gives you tax-deferred growth, just like a retirement account.

Second, Uncle Sam rewards taxable-account investors for owning stocks that pay qualified dividends. Those dividends are taxed at the same rate as long-term capital gains. Most large U.S. companies pay dividends that are qualified, as do some foreign corporations. Real estate investment trusts typically don't pay qualified dividends, so you'll have to pay income taxes instead. Even if a corporation pays a dividend that's qualified, you also need to hold the shares for more than 60 days to get the favorable tax treatment.

In addition to these taxes, you may also be dinged for the 3.8 percent Medicare surtax. This surtax applies to income, including investment income, of couples filing jointly with modified adjusted gross incomes above $250,000. If you file as a single individual or head of household, the surtax kicks in once your income exceeds $200,000. Thanks to the 3.8 percent surtax, the top federal capital gains rate is effectively 23.8 percent, not 20 percent.

316. DEFERRING CAPITAL GAINS

Taxable-account investors are encouraged to hold winning investments for more than a year, so that the appreciation is taxed at the long-term capital gains rate, rather than at the higher income tax rate. But arguably, you should set your sights not on 12 months, but on 20 years and preferably longer.

Why? By holding onto a winning investment, you defer the capital gains tax bill. But to milk the most out of this tax-deferred growth, you need extraordinarily low portfolio turnover. This was the key insight in a 1993 *Journal of Portfolio Management* article written by Robert Arnott and Robert Jeffrey, and titled "Is Your Alpha Big Enough to Cover Its Taxes?"

Let's say you own a stock mutual fund with 100 percent turnover, which means it typically holds its investments for 12 months. Even if you swap into a fund with 50 percent turnover, the typical holding period would only be 24 months. That means the fund is deferring taxes for just two years, which isn't a great benefit.

Instead, if you want to get tax deferral in a taxable account that's financially meaningful, you need a portfolio turnover rate of just 10 percent, which implies a 10-year average holding period, or even 5 percent, which would mean a 20-year holding period. You could achieve that sort of tax deferral by buying and holding individual stocks or by purchasing broadly diversified stock index funds, most of which have modest turnover.

This is a lesson some investors learn too late: They buy actively managed stock funds in their taxable account, which then make large taxable distributions each year. These investors find themselves in a quandary. If they sell and swap to index funds, they would suffer a big onetime tax hit, as they realize capital gains on the funds they currently own. To avoid this dilemma, think carefully about the investments you buy for your taxable account—and favor those that you would happily hold for many decades and that should generate modest tax bills.

317. MUTUAL FUND TAXATION

Got mutual funds in your regular taxable account? You can potentially get taxed either because of what the fund does or because of what you do.

Let's start with the former. Each year, a mutual fund is required by law to distribute virtually all of the interest and dividends that it earns, as well as any realized capital gains. Those are bundled together into periodic income and capital gains distributions. When these distributions are made, a fund's share price drops by a comparable amount, so investors are no better off in terms of their pretax wealth. Nonetheless, taxable shareholders have to pay taxes on these distributions.

Bond and money-market funds typically pay income distributions every month, while stock funds might hold off until the end of year and then make a single set of distributions. If you own a fund when those distributions are made, you have to pay taxes on the sums involved, even if you only just bought the fund shares and even if you opt to reinvest the distributions back into the fund. For that reason, taxable account investors are often cautioned against making big stock mutual fund investments right before year-end.

Want to hold down the tax bill that your funds generate? In your taxable account, you might favor stock funds that pursue a buy-and-hold strategy, such as index mutual funds, exchange-traded index funds and tax-managed funds. These funds are typically slow to realize their capital gains—and, when they do, the gains are usually taxable at the long-term capital gains rate. By contrast, many actively managed stock funds have portfolio turnover of around 60 or 70 percent, which means they're typically holding shares for roughly 18 months.

While buying tax-efficient funds can help, you also need to temper your own behavior. In other words, even if your funds don't make big taxable distributions, you can end up with big tax bills if you're too quick to sell your funds. A silver lining: When you sell a fund, your cost basis for tax purposes includes not only the amount you invested, but also any distributions you reinvested in additional fund shares.

318. WASH-SALE RULE

If you own a stock in a taxable account that falls in value, you can take some of the sting out of that loss by selling your shares, realizing a capital loss and then using that loss to reduce your annual tax bill. A good idea? Problem is, selling means giving up any chance of making back the loss.

Many folks aren't keen to do that, so they often look to buy back the shares. But if they do that too quickly, they can invalidate the tax loss. At issue here is the wash-sale rule. If you buy the same or a substantially identical security within 30 days before or after you sold the losing stock, you aren't allowed to claim the tax loss. The rules for what is allowable and what isn't are a matter of debate. Still, let's say you sell a stock and soon after buy options that give you exposure to the same shares. That would count as a wash sale and invalidate the loss.

That doesn't mean the loss can't ever be used. Instead, the earlier invalidated loss is added to the cost basis of the new security you bought. To make use of that loss, you will have to wait until you sell the new security, assuming you do so without running afoul of the wash-sale rule.

319. MUNICIPAL VS. TAXABLE BONDS

To figure out whether it makes sense to buy tax-free municipal bonds or taxable bonds, you first need to find out your marginal federal and state income tax brackets. Let's say you are in the 33 percent federal income tax bracket and a 7 percent state tax bracket. Meanwhile, suppose you are choosing between a muni bond from your own state that yields 3.05 percent and a corporate bond that pays 5.05 percent. Both have similar credit quality and duration.

Which is the best bet, given your tax situation? You would need to calculate the tax-equivalent yield for the muni bond. To that end, you would take your tax brackets (33 and 7 percent), convert them to decimals (0.33 and 0.07), add them together (0.4) and then subtract that figure from 1. You would then divide the resulting number into the muni's yield.

That would mean dividing the muni's 3.05 percent yield by 0.6. That gives you a tax-equivalent yield of 5.08 percent, which is more than the 5.05 percent yield on the corporate bond. Result: The municipal bond is the better deal. Or maybe not. You might also consider an alternative strategy: buying taxable bonds in a retirement account, which we discuss next.

If you need help calculating tax-equivalent yields, try an online calculator, such as those offered by Bankrate.com and Fidelity.com. These calculators can generate slightly different results, depending on each calculator's embedded assumptions. You can also learn more about the math involved in Part X.

Bear in mind that your tax bracket can change from year to year. Even if munis make financial sense today, they may not make sense when you retire. At that juncture, you might pocket more income by buying taxable bonds, even after paying the resulting tax bill.

320. MUNICIPALS VS. TAXABLE BONDS IN A RETIREMENT ACCOUNT

If you're in a high income tax bracket, buying tax-free municipal bonds in your taxable account might seem like a no-brainer. But there's a strategy that could give you a better return: Use your taxable account to pursue a tax-efficient stock strategy, while buying taxable bonds within your retirement account.

The taxable bonds should have a higher yield than tax-free munis and, because you're buying them in a retirement account, you don't have to worry about paying tax each year on the interest generated. Meanwhile, in your taxable account, you might favor stock investments that will be taxed at the preferential long-term capital gains rate, including any qualified dividends you receive.

This strategy doesn't sit well with some people, who prefer to have bonds in their taxable account, where they can be easily sold if these folks suddenly need cash. But you can effectively do the same thing, even if you have stocks in your taxable account and bonds in your retirement account. How? Suppose you suddenly need $20,000.

To generate the cash, you could sell $20,000 of the stocks you have in your taxable account. If we're in the midst of a bear market, the timing wouldn't be ideal. But in this case, it wouldn't matter because you would simultaneously move $20,000 from bonds to stocks within your retirement account. Result: Your stock exposure remains the same, you have sold $20,000 in bonds—and you have the cash you need.

321. ASSET LOCATION

After reading Part VIII and Part IX, you know what sort of portfolio you want. But once you've settled on your asset allocation, you need to consider your so-called asset location: Which investments should you hold in your retirement accounts and which in your taxable account? The goal is to minimize your investment tax bill by keeping investments that generate a lot of immediately taxable income in your retirement accounts, while favoring relatively tax-efficient investments in your taxable account.

For your retirement accounts, that might mean holding taxable bonds, real estate investment trusts, actively managed stock funds and individual stocks you plan to trade actively. These investments will tend to generate a lot of ordinary income or short-term capital gains, so they would usually be taxed at income tax rates, rather than at the lower long-term capital gains rate. By keeping these investments in a retirement account, you defer that tax bill, plus you avoid the hassle of reporting all this activity on your tax return.

Meanwhile, in your taxable account, you might favor tax-efficient investments that you intend to hang onto for the long haul, such as stock index mutual funds, exchange-traded stock index funds, tax-managed stock funds and long-term individual stock holdings. These investments will tend to generate modest annual tax bills and, when there are taxes to be paid, they will typically be paid at the long-term capital gains rate.

What about index funds that invest in foreign stocks? If you hold these in a taxable account, some of the dividends received by the fund may not be qualified, and hence you'll have to pay taxes at the income-tax rate. On the other hand, by holding international stock index funds in your taxable account, you benefit from the fund's credit for foreign taxes paid—a benefit that's lost if you hold the fund in a retirement account.

For your taxable account, you might also favor tax-free municipal bonds, especially if you are a conservative investor and you're in a high tax bracket. But also consider whether you would be better off sticking with long-term stock holdings in your taxable account, while buying taxable bonds in your retirement account.

JONATHAN'S TAKE: Don't let your mix of retirement and taxable money drive your asset allocation. Yes, it makes sense to hold tax-inefficient investments in your retirement accounts and tax-efficient investments in your taxable account. But if, say, you are young and inclined to put much of your money in stock index funds, you'll likely end up holding these tax-efficient funds in your retirement accounts.

322. LOW-INCOME YEARS

If you ever find yourself with a year when you pay no income tax, don't celebrate. Instead, rue the wasted opportunity.

Imagine it's December, you have been out of work all year and you have almost no taxable income. Or let's say you just retired, you haven't yet claimed Social Security and you are looking at a year with no money owed to Uncle Sam. To take advantage of these low-income years, you might convert part of your traditional IRA to a Roth IRA, knowing the tax bill will be relatively modest. Alternatively, if you have a stock in your taxable account that you've been reluctant to sell because you have a large unrealized capital gain, you might seize the opportunity to unload the position.

How much should you sell? Suppose you expect to be taxed at a 25 percent marginal rate once you find a job or once you turn age 70½ and start taking required minimum distributions from your retirement accounts. To head off big tax bills later, you might generate enough taxable income now to get to the top of the 15 percent tax bracket. In 2016, that would mean total income of $96,000 if you're married filing jointly, which would trigger a federal tax bill of $10,367.50. If you are single, it would take $48,000 in total income to get to the top of the 15 percent bracket, resulting in a $5,183.75 tax bill. These figures assume you take the standard deduction and personal exemptions, you have no children, and all tax is paid at ordinary income tax rates.

One caveat: If you're in your mid-60s or older, a large Roth conversion or hefty realized capital gains may boost your income sufficiently that you end up not only paying a big tax bill, but also getting charged higher premiums for Medicare. For others, it could reduce Medicaid eligibility or trim the tax credit they receive toward the cost of insurance purchased through a health care exchange.

323. TAXES IN RETIREMENT

When drawing down a portfolio in retirement, the standard advice is to start with your taxable account, next turn to traditional retirement accounts and, finally, tap any Roth accounts. That way, you let traditional retirement accounts grow tax-deferred for longer and allow your Roth accounts to grow tax-free for longer still.

While that's generally good advice, you may want to tweak it. Retirement can prove surprisingly taxing, especially once you turn age 70½ and start taking required minimum distributions from your retirement accounts. All withdrawals from 401(k) plans, IRAs and their ilk are typically taxed as ordinary income. Moreover, those withdrawals could, in turn, drive up your taxable income so that up to 85 percent of your Social Security benefit is subject to taxes. This is sometimes referred to as the "tax torpedo."

How can you avoid the torpedo? Two strategies may help. First, endeavor to pay off your mortgage by retirement. That way, you'll avoid the need to draw down your retirement accounts to make mortgage payments. Those retirement account withdrawals could generate enough taxable income to trigger taxes on your Social Security benefit.

Second, you might use your early retirement years to trim the size of your retirement accounts by either drawing down those accounts or converting a portion to a Roth IRA. For instance, if you expect to be in the 25 percent federal tax bracket once you start required minimum distributions in your 70s, you might aim to generate enough income in your 60s to get to the top of the 15 percent bracket. To give yourself more room for maneuver, you could delay claiming Social Security until later in retirement—which, in any case, can be a smart thing to do. Strategies for claiming Social Security are discussed in Part II.

You might also look to take extra-large retirement account withdrawals if you have a year with sizable itemized deductions, perhaps because of medical expenses. These itemized deductions could be offset against your taxable income, perhaps allowing you to tap your IRA at a relatively low tax cost.

324. SOCIAL SECURITY TAXATION

If your income is high enough, between 50 and 85 percent of your Social Security retirement benefit may be taxable. Don't be confused: There isn't an 85 percent tax rate on Social Security. Rather, we're talking about 85 percent of your benefit being subject to federal income taxes.

Will you get hit with this tax? Start by calculating your combined income, which is your adjusted gross income, plus any municipal bond interest and half your Social Security benefit. Your adjusted gross income would include distributions from a traditional IRA, but not from a Roth.

If you file as a single individual or head of household, and your combined income is between $25,000 and $34,000, up to 50 percent of your benefit may be taxable. If your combined income is above $34,000, up to 85 percent of your benefit may be subject to tax.

If you are married filing jointly, up to 50 percent of your benefit may be taxable if your combined income falls between $32,000 and $44,000, and up to 85 percent may be taxable if your combined income is above $44,000.

A majority of Social Security recipients don't pay tax on their benefit. But eventually, that's likely to change—because the various thresholds aren't indexed for inflation, so more and more folks will likely find themselves paying the tax.

325. REQUIRED MINIMUM DISTRIBUTIONS

Once you reach age 70½, you have to start taking required minimum distributions, or RMDs, from your retirement accounts. There are three exceptions. First, if you're still working at age 70½, you don't have to take distributions from your employer's 401(k) or similar plan until you retire, unless you own 5 percent or more of the company, in which case distributions must begin at age 70½. Second, you aren't required to take RMDs from so-called nonqualified variable annuities. These are annuities bought with after-tax dollars, as opposed to annuities bought through an employer's plan or in an IRA. Third, you never have to take distributions from a Roth IRA, though your beneficiaries—other than your spouse—will need to take RMDs. Be warned: RMDs must be taken from a Roth 401(k), which is a reason to roll over your Roth 401(k) to a Roth IRA.

If none of these three exceptions applies, you have to take distributions starting in the year you turn age 70½. You can put off taking your first distribution until April 1 of the following year. That, however, might not be a smart move: You'll have to take your second distribution before the end of the year, and the two distributions combined will likely be taxed more heavily than if you had taken them in separate years.

To calculate your RMD for the current year, you divide your retirement account balance as of the prior Dec. 31 by a life expectancy factor. You use one of three different IRS life expectancy tables, depending on your financial situation. For instance, if your account balance was $500,000 as of year-end and you are age 75, the distribution period is 22.9 years if you're using the Uniform Lifetime Table. To figure out how much you need to withdraw, you would divide $500,000 by 22.9, giving you a minimum distribution of $21,834. You can withdraw more than this amount—but you should be careful not to withdraw less. The penalty for not taking a distribution is an amount equal to 50 percent of the sum that should have been withdrawn, but wasn't. Often, mutual fund companies and brokerage firms will calculate your RMD for you. There are also online calculators available, such as those offered at Fidelity.com and TRowePrice.com.

In December 2014, Congress voted to allow so-called qualified charitable distributions for the 2014 tax year. Many are hoping for a similar last-minute reprieve for the 2015 tax year. This provision lets those age 70½ and older contribute up to $100,000 directly from their IRA to a qualified charity and count the contribution toward their RMD. The charitable gift isn't tax-deductible—but the IRA distribution also isn't included in your taxable income. You can learn more about qualified charitable distributions toward the end of Part XIII.

326. RECORDKEEPING

What tax information should you hang on to? Here are three pointers:

• Keep seven years of tax returns, including supporting materials. The IRS has three years to audit your tax return or six years if it suspects substantial underreporting of income. What if you have been playing fast and loose with your taxes? You probably shouldn't throw anything away.

• Keep cost-basis information for assets held in your taxable account. This should include how much you paid for your house, plus the cost of any subsequent home improvements. You may be able to add those improvements to your home's cost basis when you sell and thereby reduce any taxable gain. You should probably also keep records of how much you paid for individual investments, unless your financial firms provide it. Mutual funds are now required to provide cost-basis information for funds bought in 2012 or later, and many firms provide information for funds purchased prior to that year.

• Keep a record of all nondeductible IRA contributions—and make sure your heirs know where to find the details. If you bequeath your IRA, your beneficiaries won't have to pay taxes when they withdraw those nondeductible contributions.

PART XII

BORROWING
GOING INTO DEBT
WITHOUT GETTING INTO TROUBLE

Debt is sometimes depicted as evil. That's silly: Without borrowed money, many of us would struggle to pay for college, we'd find it tough to buy our first car and—if we were compelled to pay cash—we probably couldn't afford to own a home until we were in our 40s or 50s.

Debt allows us to purchase items we can't currently afford, thus smoothing out consumption over our lifetime. Indeed, borrowing in our early adult years should be viewed as a rational strategy. With decades of paychecks ahead of us, we should have plenty of time to pay off any loans before we quit the workforce, so we can retire debt-free.

That, at least, is the theory. In practice, many folks end up borrowing too much. The vast majority of American households have some form of debt. While overall household debt is below the 2008 peak, many observers have recently sounded the alarm about student loans. It's crucial to avoid borrowing more than you can comfortably handle.

It's also crucial to hold down your borrowing costs. You can do that by regularly checking your credit reports for errors, maintaining good credit scores, favoring secured loans, considering taxes, refinancing when the opportunity arises and paying down debt when it makes sense. You might view your debts as "negative bonds" and pay them off ahead of schedule if that offers a higher post-tax return than the investment alternatives. Ridding yourself of all debt by retirement can make a ton of sense, both because it eliminates a major expense and because it can help you avoid the "tax torpedo," a nasty retirement tax trap described in Part XI. Got too much debt? We offer some strategies at the end of this chapter.

An organizational note: This chapter discusses all kinds of borrowing—except education loans. Because education loans are an integral part of college financial aid packages, it made more sense to include them in Part IV, the chapter on paying for college. There, you'll also find some tips on how to trim your monthly loan payments if you have already graduated.

327. AMERICA'S DEBTS 2015

Almost 75 percent of American families are in debt, according to the Federal Reserve's 2013 Survey of Consumer Finances. The most common types of borrowing are mortgage debt, installment loans like car and student loans, and credit card balances.

Every three months, the Federal Reserve Bank of New York puts out a report on household debt. As of September 2015, the overall picture was heartening. Over the five years through September 2008, the amount of debt carried by American families soared 68 percent. That was a key cause of the financial crisis that hit with full fury in late 2008.

In the years that followed, Americans shed debt, as they both paid back the money they borrowed and also defaulted on loans. As of September 2015, Americans were carrying 5 percent less debt than in September 2008, despite an uptick in borrowing since mid-2013. According to the New York Fed, the typical American family has $46,150 of loans outstanding, including mortgage debt, home equity loans, car loans, credit card debt and student loans. That might seem modest given the large mortgages often needed to buy homes in major East and West Coast cities. But remember, homes are substantially cheaper in many parts of the country, plus the median is influenced by retirees with little or no debt and by the third of American households that don't own a home and hence have no mortgage.

While most types of debt have been shrinking over the past seven years, student loans have soared 97 percent. The money borrowed should help make the U.S. economy more productive and help the students involved earn higher lifetime incomes. Still, this burgeoning debt speaks to the financial sloppiness of the baby boomers, who are providing notably little financial help to their college-bound teenagers, thus compelling their children to borrow more. Today's fear: The recent crop of college graduates won't be able to handle the debts they've taken on, triggering a new financial crisis.

In March 2015, President Obama directed federal officials to investigate whether borrowers should be able to discharge federal student loans in bankruptcy. While borrowers can get help with credit card debt, auto loans and mortgages by filing for bankruptcy, federal and private student loans can't be discharged, except in rare circumstances.

Where do the most financially responsible Americans live? According to Experian, one of the three major credit bureaus, the 10 cities with the highest average credit scores are all in the Midwest, including Minnesota, Wisconsin, South Dakota, North Dakota and Iowa. Meanwhile, three Mississippi cities made the list of 10 cities with the lowest credit scores.

328. DOS AND DON'TS FOR 2016

Not sure you're handling your debts properly? Here are some "to dos" for 2016:

• Get the basics right: Pay all bills on time and never carry a credit card balance.

• Make sure you use a credit card that gives you cash back, frequent-flier points or other rewards.

• Get free copies of your credit reports from the three major credit bureaus by heading to AnnualCreditReport.com.

• Make extra principal payments on your mortgage. Even if you have a home loan with a rock-bottom interest rate and even with the tax deduction, the interest you save by paying down your mortgage is likely greater than the interest you could earn by buying bonds.

• Set up a home equity line of credit. The fees involved are modest and it could come in handy if you have a financial emergency.

And here are some things not to do:

• Don't get into the habit of leasing cars unless you really want to drive a new car every three years—and you're confident you can afford such an expensive habit.

• Don't take out a 401(k) loan if you think you will be changing jobs. If you fail to get the loan paid off before you leave your employer, it'll be considered a retirement account distribution, triggering income taxes and possibly tax penalties.

• Don't use a for-profit credit counseling agency or debt-settlement firm if you find yourself in financial trouble. Instead, look for a nonprofit credit counseling agency.

329. DEBTS, INTEREST RATES AND INFLATION

The interest rate you're charged on a loan will likely bear some relationship to the current inflation rate. Prevailing interest rates are typically above inflation, so that lenders make money, even after the corrosive impact of inflation is factored in. In the case of mortgages and car loans, the premium over inflation may be relatively modest. In the case of credit cards, it can be huge.

That might make high inflation seem like a major enemy, just as it is for investors. But it depends on the type of loan. Rising inflation and rising interest rates can be bad news for borrowers if they have loans with floating interest rates, such as credit card debt and adjustable-rate mortgages. It's a different story, however, with fixed-rate loans.

Imagine that you took out a 30-year fixed-rate mortgage at 4 percent, at a time when inflation was 2 percent. If inflation then accelerated to 5 percent, your mortgage payments would stay the same, but your salary would likely increase with the inflation rate. Even though your income is worth no more in inflation-adjusted terms, you would be better off because a major expense—your mortgage—hasn't increased along with consumer prices.

We saw this scenario in the high inflation 1970s. Homeowners with mortgages were major beneficiaries, while those who lent to them suffered, because the loans were repaid with depreciated dollars. If inflation picks up from today's modest level, we could see the same phenomenon again. What if, instead, inflation and interest rates fall from today's already low levels? As we discuss later in this chapter, this might be a reason to refinance fixed-rate loans or pay down debts faster than scheduled.

330. CREDIT REPORTS

Every year, you are entitled to a free copy of your credit report from each of the three major credit bureaus: Equifax, Experian and TransUnion. Your all-important credit score is based on the information in these reports. To view your three reports, go to AnnualCreditReport.com. It's a good idea to check your credit reports every year, especially if you plan to borrow a large sum to buy, say, a house or car. You might even rotate through the three credit bureaus, reviewing one report from one bureau every four months.

What should you look for? See if there are any accounts you don't recognize. That could be an indication that you're a victim of identity theft.

Also check your credit reports for inaccuracies, such as incorrect information about debt payments, past employers or places where you have lived. Look for any debts that are listed more than once. Filed for bankruptcy more than 10 years ago? That should no longer appear in your credit reports.

If you spot erroneous information in any of your three reports, contact either the credit bureau itself or the company that supplied the incorrect information. Through their websites, Equifax.com, Experian.com and TransUnion.com, all three credit bureaus allow you to submit an online request to have inaccuracies fixed.

331. CREDIT SCORES

Credit scores are a source of shame for some, pride for others and confusion for pretty much everybody. Whatever the case, it's worth understanding how they are calculated, because your credit scores don't just affect whether you get accepted for a loan or a credit card and what interest rate you'll pay. They are also looked at by insurance companies and by landlords when vetting tenants. In addition, while potential employers can't see your credit score, they can request a version of your credit report.

There are multiple credit-scoring systems, though the FICO score is easily the most widely used. FICO scores come in different flavors: The score looked at by a credit card issuer may differ from that looked at by an auto lender. Even when using the same scoring system, the three credit bureaus can come up with different results if they have different information in the credit report they maintain for you.

FICO scores range from 300 to 850. The typical score is around 690 and a score above 720 indicates you're considered a very good risk. How can you improve your credit score? Whether you pay your bills on time is the biggest factor affecting your FICO score. Lenders, in particular, are quick to report late payments to the credit bureaus.

How much you owe is also important. For instance, it's best to use 10 percent or less of the available borrowing limit on your credit cards, and that's true even if you pay off the balance in full every month. In fact, canceling a credit card can hurt your credit score because you will likely end up using a higher percentage of your remaining available credit, and that will make you appear financially stressed. One strategy: Pay off your credit cards before the statement closing date. That way, your card company will have little or no balance to report to the credit bureaus, which should help your credit score. It's also helpful to have a long credit history and to use different types of credit, including both credit cards and installment loans like mortgages and auto loans. In addition, avoid applying for credit too often.

In 2015, Fair Isaac—the company behind the FICO score—introduced a new scoring system that analyzes consumers' payment history with utility, cable and cell phone bills, among other items. The hope is to provide a new way to assess the creditworthiness of those who have little or no history of taking on debt or who have had past problems with debt, such as bankruptcy or foreclosure.

Typically, you have to pay to learn your credit score. Even websites that promise to reveal your credit score for free often come with some catch. That, however, isn't the case with educational sites such as Credit.com, CreditKarma.com, CreditSesame.com and Quizzle.com. You can also learn your credit score for free if you use certain financial institutions, such as carrying a credit card from Citigroup or Discover Financial Services.

332. WHAT WON'T HURT YOUR CREDIT SCORES

Your credit reports and credit scores are, more than anything, a reflection of how responsible you are in handling your debts. Lenders are quick to report late payments and other issues to the credit bureaus.

What about other aspects of your financial life? When it comes to your credit scores, the items that don't matter are quite surprising:

• Your income and net worth don't directly influence your credit scores or appear in your credit reports. Your credit reports, however, may list current and former employers.

• Overdrawing your bank account won't affect your credit scores unless your bank brings in a collection agency to collect the debt.

• Late payments on bills from your insurance company, cell phone provider or local utility typically won't ding your credit scores, unless you're being assessed under the new scoring system introduced by Fair Isaac in 2015 and described in the section above. Ditto for paying the rent late. If, however, you're really late on a bill and it ends up with a collection agency, your credit scores could take a hit.

333. IDENTITY THEFT

Identity theft occurs when someone uses your name, address, Social Security number and other personal information to borrow money, open a credit card account or commit fraud in some other way.

To guard against identity theft, review financial statements carefully for any charges you don't recognize. Regularly check your credit reports for accounts you didn't open. Become concerned if you receive a bill from a company you don't recognize. That may mean someone has opened an account in your name. Also be concerned if you receive a letter saying a loan application has been rejected. That could indicate someone is trying to use your identity to borrow money.

What if you believe you are the victim of identity theft? Contact the companies where accounts have been opened and ask that they be closed. File a report with the Federal Trade Commission at

FTCcomplaintAssistant.gov and call the local police to report the crime. Place a fraud alert on your file at the three major credit bureaus. To find out how, go to Equifax.com, Experian.com and TransUnion.com. If you place a fraud alert in your file at one credit bureau, that bureau should notify the other two bureaus. You might even consider freezing your credit.

To learn more about identity theft, check out the Federal Trade Commission's site at Consumer.gov/idtheft.

334. FREEZING YOUR CREDIT

If you fear your identity has been stolen or you're very concerned about the risk, one option is to freeze your credit. Once your credit is frozen, the credit bureaus can't release information from your credit reports without your permission, effectively stopping someone from borrowing money using your identify.

To freeze your credit—also known as a security freeze—you have to contact the three major credit bureaus. You can get details at each of their websites, Equifax.com, Experian.com and TransUnion.com.

The cost to freeze your credit varies by state. Often, it's free for victims of identity theft and sometimes also for seniors. Even if there's a fee, the three bureaus typically charge just $5 to $10 to freeze your credit and a similar fee to unfreeze it. The latter will become necessary if, say, you apply for a mortgage or a new credit card. Keep in mind that it isn't just lenders who look at your credit reports. A credit freeze could also interfere with a job application or renting an apartment.

335. DEBT RATIOS

How much can you prudently borrow? You might check on yourself the way a banker would. If you apply for a mortgage, lenders will often assess your borrowing ability using two key measures: your housing and debt ratios. The housing ratio looks at your expected or current monthly mortgage payment, including principal, interest, property taxes and homeowner's insurance. As a rule, this shouldn't be more than 28 percent of your pretax monthly income. For instance, if you earn $60,000 a year or $5,000 a month, your total mortgage payment shouldn't be above $1,400.

The debt ratio looks at all your debt payments, including mortgage, auto loans, student loans and minimum credit card payments. If you are divorced, the debt ratio will also include any child support and alimony you pay. Typically, these various obligations shouldn't be above 36 percent of your gross monthly income, which would equal $1,800 if you earn $5,000 pretax every month. What if you apply for a mortgage and you don't have any other debts? A lender may be willing to lend you more, so your monthly mortgage payments are above 28 percent of your gross income.

Even if you aren't applying for a mortgage, keep these ratios in mind. For instance, the difference between the housing ratio's 28 percent and the debt ratio's 36 percent is 8 percentage points. The implication: Lenders don't want borrowers devoting more than 8 percent of their gross income to nonmortgage debt. Let's say you are taking out an auto loan. You might calculate whether the auto loan will push your nonmortgage debt payments above 8 percent of income. Alternatively, imagine you're advising your children on college borrowing. You might calculate whether your children's eventual student-loan payments will be more than 8 percent of their likely income.

336. SECURED VS. UNSECURED DEBT

It's helpful to think about your debts in two buckets: secured and unsecured. What's the difference? Secured debt is backed up by an asset you own. For instance, your mortgage is secured by your home, your brokerage-account margin loan by your portfolio and, in most cases, your auto loan by your car. Because lenders have an asset they can seize if you fail to make your debt payments, the interest rate tends to be relatively low.

Personal bank loans and credit card debt are unsecured, hence the relatively high interest rates charged. Those high rates are needed to compensate lenders for the money lost to defaults. What about education loans? Those might also appear to be unsecured. But with federal education loans, the government has ways of reclaiming its money—including asking your employer to garnish your wages, taking your federal and state tax refunds, and even garnishing your Social Security retirement benefit.

If possible, avoid unsecured debt and instead favor debts that are secured by an asset, so you pay a lower interest rate. That, however, isn't the only consideration: You'll also want to consider taxes.

337. TAX-DEDUCTIBLE INTEREST

You can potentially deduct the interest on the three types of loans: education loans, mortgages and margin debt. Education loans are discussed in Part IV.

Suppose you take out a loan costing 6 percent and you're in the 25 percent federal income tax bracket. If the interest is tax-deductible, your after-tax cost is just 4.5 percent. Keep that tax-deductibility in mind as you consider how best to borrow. Tax deductibility also comes into play as you weigh which debts to pay down first or whether, instead, you should invest your spare cash.

You can deduct the interest on up to $1 million borrowed to buy, build or improve a first or second home. You can also deduct the interest on an additional $100,000 of home equity borrowing used for any other purpose, unless you're subject to the alternative minimum tax. For AMT purposes, you can only deduct mortgage interest if the loan was used to buy, build or improve a home.

You can also deduct the interest on loans used to buy taxable investments. In other words, you can take out a margin loan against your portfolio's value and deduct the interest if you buy stocks—but you can't deduct the interest if you use the money to buy municipal bonds or a new car. An important detail: You need to offset deductible investment interest against net investment income. The latter includes taxable interest that you earned, and perhaps also dividends and realized capital gains.

338. MORTGAGES

The Federal Reserve's 2013 Survey of Consumer Finances found that 65.9 percent of homeowners had a mortgage or other debt that was secured by their home. That isn't surprising, given how much homes cost. It also isn't especially alarming: A mortgage is typically the cheapest way for most folks to borrow. Because your home is collateral for the loan, the interest rate will usually be low—and it's even lower once you figure in the tax deduction.

Could you trim your cost further? The larger your house down payment, the lower your rate will potentially be. A larger down payment may also either reduce the cost of private mortgage insurance or, if you put down 20 percent or more, allow you to avoid it all together. In addition, in the months leading up to your mortgage application, you might check your credit report for errors and work to raise your credit score, so you qualify for a preferential rate.

It's possible to lower the rate on a new mortgage by paying points. Each point is equal to one percent of the loan's value, so paying one point on a $200,000 loan would cost you $2,000. A smart move? Paying points might look like a big money saver if you keep the loan for 15 or 30 years. But there's a good chance you will refinance or move long before then, so paying points may not make financial sense. According to a 2015 survey by the National Association of Realtors, recent home sellers had typically owned their property for nine years—and presumably many had refinanced once or more during the time they owned their homes.

You could also cut your initial mortgage rate by skipping a fixed-rate mortgage and instead opting for an adjustable-rate loan. But that comes with extra risk.

339. FIXED VS. ADJUSTABLE

Most folks instinctively opt for a fixed-rate mortgage, where your principal-and-interest payment stays the same every month. But in all likelihood, an adjustable-rate mortgage, or ARM, will be cheaper. ARMs are priced off short-term interest rates, while fixed-rate mortgages are priced off intermediate-term rates—and short-term rates are generally lower than intermediate-term rates.

With an ARM, there's a risk that the interest rate you're charged will increase at the next adjustment date. ARMs often have both periodic and lifetime caps that limit how much the rate can increase. Let's say an ARM has a two-percentage-point periodic cap, a six-point lifetime cap and a one-year adjustment period. Every year, the rate you're charged could climb two percentage points, though it can never climb more than six points above your initial rate.

Not sure you want to take that much risk? Instead of a pure ARM, many homebuyers take out a 3/1, 5/1, 7/1 or 10/1 hybrid ARM. With these loans, your rate is fixed for the first three, five, seven or 10 years, and then the rate adjusts every year thereafter. At that point, the rate could climb sharply. But there's also a good chance you might move or refinance within the first five or six years, so you may never feel the bite from the mortgage's adjustable rate.

As you ponder what mortgage to get, give some thought to your job situation. If you have a secure job with a steady paycheck, you might take the risk of an ARM and, fingers crossed, get rewarded with a lower average rate over the course of the mortgage. But if your income fluctuates, you should probably look for predictability in the rest of your financial life, including favoring fixed-rate mortgages.

340. CONFORMING VS. NONCONFORMING

A conforming loan is one that meets the standards used by Freddie Mac and Fannie Mae, making them eligible to be purchased by either institution. Result: A conforming loan often charges a somewhat lower interest rate, perhaps 0.25 percentage point less than a comparable nonconforming loan.

To qualify as a conforming loan, a mortgage has to meet a number of conditions, the most notable of which is size. According to the Federal

Housing Finance Agency, for 2016, a conforming loan for a single-family home typically has to be $417,000 or less. In more expensive parts of the country, however, a single-family home loan can be as large as $625,500 and still qualify as conforming. In Hawaii, the conforming loan limit goes as high as $721,050.

What if a loan is larger? It's considered a jumbo loan. Such loans are more difficult for lenders to securitize, by packaging them into mortgage bonds and then selling these bonds to investors. Instead, lenders will often keep a jumbo mortgage on their own books, hence the higher cost and stricter scrutiny of borrowers.

341. CLOSING COSTS

As you struggle to save enough for a house down payment, it's easy to forget that the down payment is just the beginning. To close the deal, you will face a slew of other costs, including legal fees, mortgage-application costs, title insurance and a home inspection. Together, these costs might add up to $3,000 to $6,000, though they can be substantially more. One rule of thumb puts closing costs at 2 to 5 percent of a home's purchase price.

How can you trim that cost? Try shopping around for title insurance, which many experts view as overpriced. Additional competition has emerged from a new breed of online title insurers, notably EntitleDirect.com, which operates in 40 states and Washington, DC. There are also regional firms such as TitleForward.com, which handles transactions in Florida, Georgia, Maryland, Pennsylvania, Virginia and Washington, DC, and OneTitle.com, which does business in New York.

Your real estate broker may happily offer the names of a local home inspector and mortgage banker. But you will likely fare better if you do your own search. In fact, it's probably a bad idea to use a home inspector who lives in the town where you're buying. The inspector is no doubt anxious to win referrals from local real estate agents and may be reluctant to issue a tough assessment. Meanwhile, there's a good chance you can get a cheaper mortgage by skipping both local banks and well-known national banks. Instead, look for lenders offering competitive rates by checking websites such as Bankrate.com and HSH.com.

As you budget for a home purchase, keep in mind that you may face additional costs, including moving costs and the expense of some initial redecorating. In addition, there will often be at least a few immediate home repairs, because of problems the seller neglected to mention and the home inspector failed to spot.

342. MY STORY: A PRIVATE MORTGAGE FOR HANNAH

In 2015, my biggest financial transaction involved my daughter, Hannah, who was age 26 at the time. I lent her $381,000 at 3.97 percent to buy her first home, with the loan structured as a 30-year fixed-rate mortgage. Because I've written articles about family loans, I know many readers think they're a recipe for family tension and financial disaster. But I believe much depends on who's doing the borrowing. Hannah has a secure job and impeccable financial habits, so I consider the loan a fairly safe bet.

The paperwork was handled by National Family Mortgage in Belmont, Mass., which specializes in private mortgages. It also recorded the mortgage with the appropriate local authority, thus ensuring that Hannah could deduct the interest she pays me. National Family Mortgage charges a setup fee of $725 to $2,100, depending on the loan's size, and a minimum $15 a month if you want the firm to process the monthly payments and deal with the tax reporting. For more information, go to NationalFamilyMortgage.com.

I saw the private mortgage as a good deal for both Hannah and me. She was in a stronger position when bidding on properties, because she was effectively a cash buyer. She also got the loan without a lot of hassle, her closing costs were low and she avoided taking out private mortgage insurance. Meanwhile, I'm earning a higher interest rate than I could get at the bank or from high-quality bonds. And, of course, I had the pleasure of helping Hannah buy her first home.

The rate we settled on was the current average rate for a 30-year fixed-rate mortgage. It's possible to charge less. But you need to charge at least a minimum rate of interest, as represented by the IRS's "applicable federal rates," or you could find yourself dealing with thorny tax issues involving imputed interest and gift taxes.

So how's our private mortgage working out? So far, so good.

343. REFINANCING

If interest rates have fallen since you took out your mortgage, you may find it's worth refinancing, which involves swapping your current mortgage for one with a lower interest rate. But check that it really is worthwhile.

To that end, you need to make an apples-to-apples comparison. Let's say you have had your current 30-year fixed-rate mortgage for six years, so what you now effectively have is a 24-year loan. If you refinance and replace that 24-year loan with a new 30-year loan, you will lower your monthly payment, even if the mortgage rate is exactly the same. The reason: You're taking your current principal balance and spreading its repayment over six additional years.

Instead, to see how much you are truly saving every month, compare your current payment to the payment on a hypothetical 24-year loan at the new, lower interest rate. You can calculate the latter by playing around with the Mortgage Calculator at Bankrate.com.

Next, take the expected closing costs for the refinancing and divide it by the reduction in your monthly payment. That will tell you how many months it'll take to break even. For instance, if the closing costs are $4,000 and you'll save $150 a month, it will take you some 27 months to break even. As long as you don't expect to move before the 27 months are up, refinancing probably makes sense.

When refinancing, consider taking out a mortgage that will be paid off by the time you retire, and preferably earlier. In the above example, where you have 24 years left on your current mortgage, you might opt for a 20-year or 15-year loan.

What if you find it isn't worth refinancing because your remaining mortgage balance is fairly small? Consider taking out a home equity line of credit—often called a HELOC—and using that to pay off your current mortgage. HELOCs are cheap to set up and the rates are typically low, in part because they are priced off short-term interest rates. There is a risk that the rate on your HELOC could increase. Still, if your mortgage is small and you expect to have it paid off within the next three or four years, that might be a risk worth taking.

344. HOME EQUITY LOANS

If you need to borrow, tapping into your home's value can be one of the cheaper options. The interest rate will tend to be low, because the loan is secured by your house, and the interest could be tax-deductible.

What sort of loan should you take out? You can choose between a home equity loan and a home equity line of credit. In terms of the interest rate, it's similar to choosing between a fixed-rate and an adjustable-rate mortgage.

The interest rate on a home equity line of credit, or HELOC, is pegged off short-term rates, just like an adjustable-rate mortgage. Usually, the rate charged by a HELOC is set at some discount or premium to the prime rate. Some banks have introduced HELOCs that offer low fixed rates for a year or more, hoping to encourage customers to use their credit lines. But after that initial period, the rate can change every month, and it could climb quickly if short-term interest rates rise. You won't be charged interest until you use the credit line. When you first apply for a HELOC, the bank will put a cap on how much you can borrow, such as $50,000 or $100,000.

Occasionally, a bank may cancel a credit line or reduce its size.

How does a home equity loan differ from a HELOC? The interest rate is typically fixed for the life of the loan, just like it is on a fixed-rate mortgage, and that rate will usually be higher than the rate on a HELOC. That extra cost buys you protection against rising rates. Unlike a HELOC, you have to decide how much you want to borrow. You would then need to repay the loan on a predetermined schedule, just as you would with a fixed-rate mortgage.

A HELOC can be useful both as a source of emergency money and for major expenditures, such as buying a car or remodeling the kitchen. You might also use a home equity loan for major expenditures, especially if you have a firm idea of how much you need to borrow.

345. PRINCIPAL AND INTEREST

Most mortgages are designed so that, with each payment, you not only pay the interest owed on the outstanding loan balance, but also you pay down part of the loan's principal balance. That means that, in the following month, the principal is slightly smaller, so you owe less interest and even more of your monthly payment can go toward reducing the loan balance.

As time goes on, the amount earmarked for principal starts growing by leaps and bounds. Suppose you borrowed $300,000 through a 30-year fixed-rate mortgage costing 5 percent. Assuming you didn't make any extra principal payments, it would take 15½ years to pay back the first $100,000 and another 8½ years to pay off the next $100,000. What about the final $100,000? That's paid off in the mortgage's last six years because, by then, most of your monthly payment is going toward principal and not interest.

This shifting mix of principal and interest often creates confusion among mortgage borrowers. One misconception: It isn't worth making extra principal payments when a mortgage is close to being paid off because, at that point, you aren't getting charged much in total interest.

That's true—except you are still getting charged the same interest rate. Suppose you have a fixed-rate mortgage costing 5 percent. Whether you make an extra principal payment in year one or year 30, the annual pretax return is still the same 5 percent. The only difference is that the extra principal payment early in the life of a mortgage saves you 5 percent in annual interest for more years.

346. PREPAYING A MORTGAGE

Is paying ahead on a mortgage a good investment? We have more on the "invest vs. pay down debt" question later in this chapter. But even if prepaying a mortgage isn't your best investment, retiring debt-free should be a priority. That way, you'll eliminate a major expense and potentially avoid the retirement tax trap described in Part XI. What if your last scheduled mortgage payment is after your likely retirement date? Consider making extra principal payments.

When you make additional principal payments on a fixed-rate mortgage, you pay off the mortgage more quickly. When you pay extra on an adjustable-rate mortgage, you trim the loan balance faster than scheduled, and that should result in lower monthly payments when your rate next adjusts—unless the interest rate adjusts higher and that swamps the impact of your extra principal payments.

Your mortgage lender might pitch you a "biweekly mortgage," where you pay half the mortgage payment every two weeks, rather than the full payment every month. That pays off your mortgage faster, because you end up making an extra month's mortgage payment every year. Alternatively, some dubious financial firms might offer "mortgage acceleration" services. Either way, don't bite. You can achieve exactly the same result, and avoid the fees charged for these services, by simply adding extra money to your monthly mortgage payment.

What if there's no way you will get your mortgage paid off by retirement or soon after? You might take the opposite tack. As you approach retirement, consider refinancing your mortgage with a new 30-year loan. That should sharply reduce your monthly payment, thereby trimming your retirement living expenses. Handling home loans in retirement is also discussed at the end of Part II.

347. MY STORY: PAYING OFF THE MORTGAGE

When my first wife and I bought a home in New Jersey in October 1992, we took out a $150,000 30-year fixed-rate mortgage at 7.7 percent. I had to remortgage the house in 1998, when we got divorced and I had to cash Molly out. At that juncture, I borrowed $148,500 using a 15-year fixed-rate mortgage at 7.125 percent.

Still, I was mortgage-free by 2005, thanks to regular—and occasionally large—additional principal payments. To some, this might seem like the height of foolishness: Mortgage rates are typically low and the interest is usually tax-deductible, making it perhaps the most desirable debt you can have. But even with all that, the after-tax cost of a mortgage is almost always higher than the after-tax return you can earn by purchasing high-quality bonds, so I viewed paying down my mortgage as a substitute for buying bonds.

Along the road to mortgage freedom, I took an interesting turn. By year-end 2003, my principal balance was down to $34,000. Interest rates, however, were also falling, and yet my loan was too small to make refinancing worthwhile. That's when I followed the advice of some *Wall Street Journal* readers and cooked up my own refinancing.

I took out a home-equity line of credit and used it to pay off the balance on my 15-year mortgage. At the time, lenders were competing fiercely for new customers, so there was just a onetime $40 fee involved and I was able to get a credit line set at half-a-percentage point below the prime rate, which meant an initial interest rate of 3.5 percent. There was some risk involved: If short-term rates had headed higher, I could have seen my monthly payments spike. But the risk seemed modest—and the problem was gone the following year, when I paid off the credit line.

With the mortgage gone, my fixed costs dropped sharply, and I was able to save significantly more every month and cover my children's college bills far more easily. There were, no doubt, investments that would have delivered a better return than paying off my mortgage. But making extra principal payments still strikes me as a great low-risk investment—and one that can buy you substantial financial freedom.

348. CREDIT CARDS

Credit cards have become so integral to American life that some folks almost never pay cash and instead charge even the smallest expenses. That's convenient, it can be safer than carrying cash and it could come with a monthly bonus, in the form of credit card rewards. Set against that is the well-known downside: If you aren't careful, you will charge too much, won't be able to pay off the balance in full and get walloped with finance charges.

There is no legal maximum interest rate that a credit card can charge, though many card issuers appear to charge no more than 29.99 percent. Minimum payments are typically set so that your balance should shrink over time, assuming you aren't adding more debt. That might mean the minimum payment is 1 percent of the balance plus that month's interest and fees, which all told might come to around 2 percent of the card's balance.

How many people carry a balance? Reliable statistics are surprisingly hard to come by, but it seems a little over half of all Americans carry a credit card balance and the average debt per cardholder is around $5,000.

Carrying a card balance, while sometimes unavoidable, isn't smart. Today, a credit card might charge an interest rate of 12 to 20 percent—an exorbitant sum, especially when you consider that today's savings accounts and short-term certificates of deposit pay 1 percent or less. Credit card debt is the classic example of bad debt: The interest rate charged is steep, the interest isn't tax-deductible and the money was typically used to buy nothing of lasting value.

Want to avoid charging so much that you end up with a bill you can't pay in full? Try deducting your credit card charges from the balance in your check book. That way, when the bill arrives, you won't be unpleasantly surprised—and you should have the money to pay off the entire sum owed.

349. CREDIT CARD REWARDS

If you use a credit card, you should use one that gives you rewards, whether it's cash back, rewards points, frequent-flier miles or some other bonus. Typically, these rewards are worth around 1 percent of the amount you spend, though some cards give as much as 2 percent and others have rotating categories where you can earn extra rewards, such as 5 percent cash back on restaurant purchases or at the grocery store.

Many rewards credit cards don't charge an annual fee. That isn't, however, true of cards that pay airline miles, so you need to weigh carefully the annual fee against the value of the frequent-flier miles you are likely to earn during the year.

While it is appealing to earn rewards, the value of those rewards pales next to the interest you'll pay if you carry a balance. Suppose you have a card that charges 18 percent in annual interest and pays you back 1 percent in cash. If you spend $1,000 and carry that balance, the 1 percent cash back on your $1,000 of spending will be less than one month's interest expense. And if you carry that balance month after month, the math only gets worse.

JONATHAN'S TAKE: Credit cards are a financial nightmare for many Americans because they make it so easy to overspend and end up in a financial hole. It doesn't have to be that way: If you funnel as much spending as possible through a rewards credit card and you're careful to pay off the balance in full every month, you will avoid the downside of credit cards, while collecting the equivalent of 1 percent back on every dollar you spend and perhaps more.

350. CREDIT CARD PERKS

Credit cards don't just offer rewards. They also offer a slew of perks, many of which aren't heavily promoted, so you may not be aware of them. Check to see whether your credit cards offer these benefits:

- Extended warranties on items you purchase with the card.

• Price protection if you buy an item and then see it advertised at a lower price soon after.

• Protection if an item you buy quickly breaks or is lost or stolen.

• Assistance if you have a dispute with a retailer over, say, the quality of something you purchased. A credit card representative may be able to help get your money back.

• Discounts if you buy items through the credit card's website.

• Accidental death and dismemberment insurance. The insurance may pay out if you are injured or killed in an accident that occurs while on a trip that was paid for with the credit card.

• Travel emergency assistance, including help with lost luggage and possibly even compensation for the items lost.

• Rental car insurance may be provided by your credit card. You may also be covered for rental cars by your auto insurer.

• Roadside assistance, including towing, tire changing and jumpstarting a battery, though you will likely pay a fee for these services.

• Concierge services, such as help getting tickets to shows or making restaurant reservations.

351. OVERDRAFT FEES

When you overdraw your checking account, you're borrowing money from the bank—and the effective interest rate could make carrying a credit card balance or taking out a payday loan seem like a bargain.

Banks typically charge around $35 for overdrawing an account. A common scenario: You buy a $2 coffee with your debit card, that overdraws your account, and suddenly the $2 coffee is costing you $37. To avoid getting hit with overdraft fees, you can decline overdraft protection. This is a particularly smart move if you're helping your teenagers open their first bank account. In all likelihood, your kids won't have much money in their account and won't keep close tabs on the balance. Declining overdraft protection will help them avoid a slew of $37 cups of coffee.

While declining overdraft protection will save on fees for ATM withdrawals and debit-card purchases, you'll still incur fees if you write checks or have recurring electronic payments that overdraw your account. Instead of an overdraft fee, you might get hit with a fee for non-sufficient funds, while also getting charged a fee by the merchant you failed to pay.

Want overdraft protection? You could opt for coverage, but keep money in, say, a linked savings account. If you overdraw your checking account, the bank will cover the withdrawal with money from your savings account. You will still be charged a fee, but it might be $10 rather than $35.

352. MARGIN LOANS

If you hold your investments in a margin account at a brokerage firm, you can typically take out a margin loan equal to 50 percent of the account's total value. This is the so-called initial margin requirement, and it effectively allows you to control investments worth twice as much as you could otherwise afford.

A margin loan doesn't have to be used to purchase additional investments. Some folks use margin loans to buy cars or pay the kids' college bills, in part because the alternative may be to sell winning stocks and thus trigger capital gains taxes. Your interest costs, however, are only tax-deductible if the margin loan is used to buy taxable investments.

Whatever your reason for borrowing, a margin loan has the potential to boost your returns if the market rises—and magnify your losses if it goes against you. Once you take out a margin loan, make sure your account continues to meet the margin maintenance requirements. Under FINRA rules, a margin loan must equal no more than 75 percent of your account's total value. But brokerage firms can impose their own stricter rules, often insisting the loan be no more than 70 percent of the account's value and sometimes less.

Suppose you deposited $10,000 in a brokerage account and then borrowed another $10,000 to buy additional stocks, so you controlled $20,000 of shares. If your stocks fall 29 percent, to $14,200, your $10,000 loan would equal more than 70 percent of the account's total value—and, depending on the brokerage firm's rules, you could receive a margin call.

At that juncture, you would need to reduce the loan as a percentage of the account's total value by either adding securities or cash to the account or by selling holdings to repay part of the margin loan. Be warned: Your brokerage firm may not call you before selling securities to meet margin requirements, so it's best to monitor the account carefully and take action before a margin call is a possibility.

Margin borrowing is often viewed as an indicator of investors' appetite for risk—and in late 2015 it's signaling that investors are cautious. As of September 2015, there was $453.9 billion in margin debt outstanding. That compares with $456.3 billion at year-end 2014, $444.9 billion at year-end 2013, $330.4 billion at year-end 2012 and $267 billion at year-end 2011.

353. LOANS FROM 401(K) PLANS

Many folks find 401(k) and 403(b) loans appealing, in part because the loans are easy to obtain and the interest that's charged goes back into their account, so they're effectively paying interest to themselves. But the loans can quickly lose their luster. A 2014 study by TIAA-CREF found that 29 percent of Americans who were participating in a retirement plan said they had taken out a loan from their plan. But 44 percent of those who had borrowed regretted doing so.

Why the regret? Borrowing has two costs. First, a 401(k) loan isn't really a loan. Instead, the money you're supposedly borrowing is actually removed from your account, which means you lose out on any investment returns the money might have earned. Second, while the money you originally contributed to your 401(k) plan came out of pretax dollars, you have to repay a 401(k) loan from post-tax income. In retirement, when you withdraw the money, you'll have to pay taxes on these dollars again, so they're effectively taxed twice.

Still like the idea of 401(k) loans? The good news is, they're typically easy to apply for, with no credit check required and often no loan application fee. You can usually borrow up to $50,000 or half your account balance, whichever is less, though plans can impose stricter rules and some don't allow loans. The money borrowed has to be repaid within five years, unless it's used to buy a home, in which case the repayment period can be longer.

If you leave your employer and don't promptly repay a 401(k) loan, it'll be considered a distribution and subject to both income taxes and probably tax penalties. Thinking of changing jobs? You should make a concerted effort to pay back the loan.

354. HARDSHIP WITHDRAWALS

If you have maxed out on 401(k) loans and you have an urgent financial need, you may be able to take a hardship withdrawal from your employer's plan. Hardship withdrawals are typically allowed for unreimbursed medical expenses, college bills and funeral expenses, to prevent foreclosure or eviction, or to buy or repair your principal residence. Similar rules apply to 403(b) plans.

While hardship withdrawals are legally permissible, your employer isn't obligated to allow them. Moreover, you may have to jump through various hoops, such as documenting your financial need.

With hardship withdrawals, the real hardship may be the cost involved. You will have to pay income taxes on the sum withdrawn, plus a 10 percent tax penalty if you are under age 59½. If you're in the 25 percent tax bracket, a $10,000 withdrawal could leave you with just $6,500 to spend after federal taxes and penalties, and even less if you have to pay state income taxes. In addition, you may be barred from making contributions to your 401(k) for the next six months.

355. LIFE INSURANCE LOANS

If you have a permanent life insurance policy and you've built up some cash value, you could potentially borrow against the cash value. The loans are easy to obtain, with no credit check required, because you're effectively borrowing from yourself.

Still, tread carefully. In theory, you don't have to repay life insurance loans. But any loan outstanding at the time of your death will reduce the policy's death benefit. Even if you don't repay the loan itself, think twice before skipping the interest payments. If you don't make the interest payments, those will get added to the loan balance—and you'll incur interest charges not only on the original sum borrowed, but also on any unpaid interest.

If the outstanding loan grows too large, so that the amount owed is greater than the policy's cash value, your policy could lapse, triggering a hefty tax bill. You would typically owe income taxes on the policy's cash surrender value, less the total premiums paid into the policy. That income tax bill would be avoided if you kept the policy until you died.

356. CAR LOANS

Need a car loan? Banks provide more auto loans than anybody else. Other major players include credit unions, auto-finance companies, car manufacturers and car dealers.

It might be convenient to get financing through the dealership. But you will likely get a better rate if you shop for a low-cost loan before you head to the car dealer. With a preapproved loan in your back pocket, you will be in a stronger bargaining position with the dealership, and you could parlay that preapproved loan into an even better deal.

The dealership might offer you the choice of a rebate or a 0 percent loan. To figure out which is best, simply compare the monthly payments on the 0 percent loan with the payments on the alternative loan, which would be a smaller amount borrowed—thanks to the rebate—but at a higher interest rate. That higher rate might not be so high if you bypass the dealership's financing department and get a low-cost loan elsewhere.

An auto loan won't necessarily be your best bet. Also consider whether it would be cheaper to buy the car with a home equity loan or line of credit. The rate may be lower than on an auto loan, plus the interest could be tax deductible. The downside: You put your home at risk if you fail to make the required payments on your home equity borrowing.

357. BUYING VS. LEASING

Today, around 30 percent of all new cars are leased—and the percentage seems to rise every year. Leasing can allow you to drive a car that you couldn't afford to buy. Historically, most leases have been for luxury cars. Lately, however, consumers have been leasing less expensive vehicles, as they struggle to make ends meet and as they grow more comfortable with monthly financial commitments for everything from cell phones to music streaming services to cable TV.

A good idea? With a lease, there's usually a mileage limit, such as 36,000 miles on a three-year lease, and insurance is typically more costly than it is for owners.

Still, leasing can be cheaper if you plan to get a new car every three years. Upfront costs on a lease, if any, should be far smaller than the down payment on a car loan, and the monthly lease payments ought to be less than a car loan payment. Because you might get a new car every three years, maintenance costs are likely to be modest and any major repairs could be covered by the warranty. And if you really like the car, you can usually buy it at the end of the lease at a preset price.

Problem is, getting a new car every three years is an expensive habit— and you'll likely fare better financially if you buy a car and hang on to it for longer. Remember, at the end of a lease, you don't own anything. But as a buyer, you could sell the car and use the proceeds to make a down payment on a new vehicle. Better still, you might keep the car until the loan is paid off, at which point you can enjoy driving the car with no monthly payments to worry about.

The bottom line: Over the long term, leasing every three years will be more costly than buying a new car and driving it for, say, six years. But before you rush out and buy a new car, keep in mind that there's an even cheaper option: Purchasing a used car that's maybe three years old and then driving it for another six years.

358. INVEST OR PAY DOWN DEBT?

Suppose you have $200,000 in bonds—and you also have $200,000 in mortgage and other debt. Arguably, your net bond position is zero. After all, your bonds are paying you interest, but your debts are costing you interest. In fact, the interest rate charged on your debts is likely greater than the interest you are earning on your bonds.

The implication: Instead of buying more bonds, you might use your extra savings to pay down debt. You may even find that, because your debts are costing you more than your bonds are earning, it makes sense to sell your bonds and use the proceeds to reduce debt.

But what if we're talking about mortgage debt, with its tax-deductible mortgage interest? Let's say you have a 5 percent mortgage and you're in the 25 percent federal income tax bracket, so the effective cost of your mortgage is just 3.75 percent. Fingers crossed, you should be able to earn more than that over the long term by purchasing a diversified collection of stocks.

What if the alternative is to buy bonds? Suppose you can buy bonds that yield 4 percent, which is higher than the 3.75 percent after-tax cost of your mortgage. That might seem more attractive. But if the 4 percent bonds pay taxable interest and you hold them in a regular taxable account, you might be left with just 3 percent after paying taxes—which means paying down the mortgage will give you a better return.

JONATHAN'S TAKE: Even if the potential gain from investing is higher, I still think there's great virtue in paying down debt, even low-cost, tax-deductible mortgage debt. The return is guaranteed, it makes your overall finances less risky and ridding yourself of all debt is a crucial step on the path to a comfortable retirement. Not sure whether it's a good time to buy stocks or bonds? When in doubt, you can do a lot worse than pay down debt.

359. STRUGGLING WITH DEBT

If you are well above the debt ratio used by lenders, which means you're devoting more than 36 percent of your pretax monthly income to servicing your debts, there's a good chance you have borrowed too much. But you probably don't need the debt ratio to tell you that because it's already painfully obvious.

What to do? The first step is to put yourself on a cash diet, which means not spending more than you earn and avoiding all new borrowing. Next, start to tackle your debts. Focus on paying down your highest-cost debt first, which will likely be your credit card balances. You might, however, take a slightly different approach if you have, say, student loans or car loans that are almost paid off. If you can get those paid off quickly, it might substantially improve your monthly cash flow, and then you can focus in earnest on paying off those credit cards.

Another possibility: If you have built up some home equity, set up a home equity line of credit or refinance your current mortgage. Either way, you could borrow against your home's value and use that money to pay off higher-cost debt. If you'll struggle to cope with the resulting monthly mortgage payments, refinance with a 30-year mortgage rather than anything shorter. That should help hold down the monthly payments.

As an added bonus, the interest on any home equity borrowing could be tax-deductible. Also consider other ways to consolidate debt, such as borrowing from your 401(k) plan or cash-value life insurance, and using that to pay off higher-interest debt. You might even apply for a bank loan, though that may be difficult to get if your finances are in rough shape.

Steer clear of debt-consolidation companies or other firms promising to help you pay off your debts. All too often, their loans come with exorbitant fees, high interest rates and other drawbacks. What if your debts are so great that you can't see any way to get yourself back on track? It may be time for more drastic action.

360. OVERWHELMED BY DEBT

Got so much debt that you can't see any way out? To find a reputable nonprofit credit-counseling agency, try the Financial Counseling Association of America (FCAA.org) or the National Foundation for Credit Counseling (NFCC.org). Identify a local credit-counseling agency and ask for a list of fees. If the fees aren't modest, you may have mistakenly contacted a for-profit credit counseling agency, debt-settlement firm or some other company hoping to profit from your misfortune.

If your debts are overwhelming, a nonprofit credit-counseling agency can help you settle on a debt management plan, which typically involves making loan repayments over a three- to five-year period. A debt management plan can lower your finance charges, reduce collection calls and help to repair your credit.

If part of your debt is forgiven, there could be tax consequences. You may receive a Form 1099-C for the amount of the cancelled debt, on which you might then have to pay income taxes. Talk to your credit counselor about whether there's an exclusion or exception that may allow you to avoid the tax on this phantom income.

Even before you contact a credit-counseling agency, you might be tempted to raid your retirement accounts to cover the mortgage or pay the credit cards. Don't do it. Not only would your retirement account withdrawals likely trigger income taxes and tax penalties, but you would also be spending money that would otherwise be protected from your creditors. If you end up in bankruptcy, you will probably be able to hang onto money you have in 401(k) plans and IRAs.

361. BANKRUPTCY

If your debts are too large to pay down and creditors are unwilling to forgive enough debt to make it manageable, you may need to file for bankruptcy. This isn't a step to be taken lightly. The bankruptcy will stay on your credit report for up to 10 years, and you will likely have little or no access to credit for a number of years.

If an individual files for bankruptcy, it's typically under either Chapter 7 or Chapter 13 of the bankruptcy code. With a Chapter 7 bankruptcy, your assets can be liquidated to pay off unsecured debt. In practice, any assets owned are often protected and thus nothing gets sold. Meanwhile, with your secured debts, such as your auto loan that's backed by your car or your mortgage that's backed by your home, you can either turn over those assets to the lenders involved or try to strike a deal where you keep the assets in return for making some sort of payment.

While a Chapter 7 bankruptcy deals with your debts through liquidation, a Chapter 13 bankruptcy tackles your debts through some form of payment plan. Chapter 13 bankruptcy is designed for those with regular incomes, who are then expected to complete a monthly payment program that lasts three to five years. How much you will be expected to pay will depend, in part, on how much you earn and how much you owe.

If you file for bankruptcy, you'll need an attorney's help. You can search for lawyers through NACBA.org, the website of the National Association of Consumer Bankruptcy Attorneys. Also check out BankruptcyResources.org and the "Get Informed" tab on Nolo.com.

PART XIII

GIVING
BEFORE YOU LEAVE,
LEAVE THEM SMILING

Most of us assume that buying items for ourselves is a sure path to happiness. But research suggests that we get far greater pleasure from buying gifts for others. In all likelihood, the same is true when it comes to our wealth. Amassing money may be comforting. But there's also tremendous pleasure in giving it away, whether to family members or to a favorite charity.

You'll want to consider how much you can afford to give away during your lifetime or whether you ought to wait until after your death. You should also think about whether you want to nudge the recipients to use the money in a particular way and what's the best gifting strategy, given your goals, and also the possible tax and other benefits.

For gifts to family members, that'll mean developing an estate plan, which might include making regular gifts during your lifetime. As you craft your plan, give some thought to end-of-life decisions, such as who will make medical and financial decisions on your behalf if you become incapacitated. These various estate planning issues are tackled in the pages ahead.

For charitable gifts, which we discuss toward the end of this chapter, you'll want to consider the potential tax savings. Your gifts may also be part of your retirement-income strategy: You might purchase a charitable gift annuity or create a charitable remainder trust, both of which can give you a combination of tax benefits and regular retirement income.

But whether the gifts are to charity or to family members, your primary motivation should be generosity, not the tax savings or other benefits. Yes, it's nice if you get a tax deduction in return for your charitable contribution. But you'll still end up with less money than you started.

362. DOS AND DON'TS FOR 2016

Looking to get your estate plan in shape? Here are some "to dos" for 2016:

• Get a will. According to a 2015 study by Caring.com, just 56 percent of U.S. parents have a will or living trust. The latter can be used as a substitute for a will.

• Talk to your adult children about your estate, including how much they will likely inherit, where key documents are located and what your wishes are regarding life-prolonging medical procedures.

• Consider what the embedded income tax bill in your traditional retirement accounts will mean for your heirs—especially if the "stretch IRA" disappears.

• Find out if your state imposes an estate or inheritance tax. A variety of websites keep a comprehensive list, including McGuireWoods.com (search on "state death tax") and Nolo.com.

And here are some things you shouldn't do:

• Don't worry about federal estate taxes. Thanks to today's $5 million-plus estate tax exclusion, just one out of every 600 deaths will likely trigger federal estate taxes. Indeed, you should review your estate plan if it was designed to avoid federal estate taxes—but your plan was drawn up before the sharp increase in the federal estate tax exclusion in the years since 2001, when the exclusion was just $675,000.

• Don't gift money to your children unless you're confident you have enough for your own retirement.

• Don't spend down your Roth IRA. If there's any asset you should keep for your heirs, that's the one.

363. NOW OR LATER?

As discussed in Part II, most of us are ill prepared for retirement. During our lifetime, we probably should be modest with our gifts to family and to charity. Instead, we might focus on how we'll disburse our wealth after our death. Our kids and other family members won't appreciate it if we give them a big hunk of our wealth today—and then ask for it back a decade later, when we're impoverished retirees.

What if you have done a fine job of saving for retirement and other goals, and you can afford to give away money now, rather than waiting until after your death? There are good arguments for giving away part of your wealth during your lifetime.

If you give money to family members while you're alive, you will get to share in their delight, and you might help them enjoy the sense of financial security you have achieved. In addition, you will get money out of your estate, including the future investment growth. That might reduce the potential bite from both federal estate taxes (though this won't be an issue for the vast majority of Americans) and your state's estate tax (which can be a big issue in some states).

Similarly, if you give to charity now, you will have the pleasure of knowing you are doing some immediate good. Whether you give money to charity now or at death, you will shrink your taxable estate. But by giving during your lifetime, you could also cut your federal income tax bill, assuming you itemize your deductions. By contrast, if you make a bequest upon death, there are no income tax savings.

364. ESTATE PLANNING

The primary goal of estate planning is simple: You want to make sure your assets end up with the right folks.

In all likelihood, you have already made a slew of estate planning decisions, perhaps without fully appreciating it. For instance, when you and your spouse bought the house and the car jointly with right of survivorship, you ensured your spouse would inherit both items should you die first.

Remember the IRA you opened years ago, with your sister named as beneficiary because you hadn't yet met your spouse? Unless you change the beneficiary, your sister will likely get that money after your death. Beneficiary designations also determine who will inherit trust assets, payable-on-death accounts and the proceeds from any life insurance.

What about your will? That determines who receives assets that go through probate. But as you might have gathered, assets like retirement accounts and property owned jointly with right of survivorship go directly to your heirs, and aren't subject to probate.

While estate planning is mostly about who gets what, you'll also want to give some thought to end-of-life decisions and to taxes. Federal estate taxes aren't an issue for 99.8 percent of Americans, thanks to 2016's $5.45 million estate tax exclusion. But your heirs could face state estate taxes, which can be owed on even midsize estates, and they will have to pay income taxes on any traditional retirement accounts you bequeath. With the latter in mind, you should think carefully about which assets to spend down during your lifetime and which ones to set aside for your heirs. Want to make sure your estate plan is fully fleshed out? You might start with our checklist.

365. ESTATE PLANNING CHECKLIST

If you're under age 50, you might focus on the first three items listed below. Those already retired or approaching retirement should probably consider every item on the list. Here are some key components of a well-thought-out estate plan:

• A will that specifies who should inherit those assets subject to probate. Drawing up a will becomes especially crucial once you have children, not least because you'll want to name guardians for your kids.

• The right beneficiaries listed on your life insurance and retirement accounts.

• Correct titling on major assets, such as your home and cars.

• Regular gifting to take advantage of the annual gift-tax exclusion.

• A revocable living trust if probate is a cumbersome process in your state or you own property outside the state where you have your primary residence.

• Trusts to control how your assets are disbursed, which could be crucial if, say, you are remarried but you want your assets eventually to go to your children from an earlier marriage.

• Steps to reduce federal and state estate taxes, if either could be an issue. You should also give some thought to the embedded income tax bills in your traditional retirement accounts, which could be the biggest tax headache your heirs face.

• Financial and medical powers of attorney in case you become incapacitated.

• A personal letter, or letter of last instruction, that provides additional details and spells out how your personal possessions should be disbursed.

For additional information, check out the "Get Informed" tab on Nolo.com, where you will find a host of articles on estate planning and other legal issues.

366. GIFT-TAX EXCLUSION

In 2016, you can give $14,000 to as many individuals as you wish, without worrying about the gift tax. This is the annual gift-tax exclusion. Do you and your spouse have three kids? You could together give each of them $28,000 this year, thus shrinking your estate by $84,000. As described in Part IV, there's even a special provision just for 529 college plans that allows you to contribute five times the gift-tax exclusion in a single year and count it as your gift for the next five years.

Even if you give more than the gift-tax exclusion, you likely won't pay gift taxes. Instead, the amount above the exclusion will reduce the sum you can leave to your heirs tax-free upon your death. Only if you manage to eat through your entire federal estate tax exclusion—$5.45 million in 2016— would you have to start paying gift taxes.

Let's say you are a single parent and you gave your only child a gift of $1,014,000 in 2016. That gift would be $1 million above the $14,000 gift-tax exclusion, so it would reduce the amount you can leave tax-free at death to $4.45 million. The super-wealthy sometimes make such large gifts because it gets the money, including subsequent investment growth, out of their estate, thus trimming the eventual estate tax bill.

An interesting wrinkle: While you can only give $14,000 to another person each year without worrying about the gift tax, there's no limit on the sum you can pay toward another person's medical or education expenses, as long as the money is paid directly to the medical provider or educational institution involved.

JONATHAN'S TAKE: Giving away money is perhaps the cheapest and easiest way to shrink an estate. There are no fancy estate planning techniques involved and no legal fees, which may explain why this strategy isn't given more publicity. If you can afford to make regular gifts to family members, seriously consider doing so.

367. SMART GIVING

If you give money to your children, either now or when you die, there's a risk they will quickly squander the money you so painstakingly amassed. Faced with this risk, some folks set up spendthrift trusts that parcel out the trusts' assets to the beneficiaries slowly over time. You could avoid that complicated and costly step if you raise money-savvy children, a topic we touch on in Part VII.

In fact, you might use your gifts to help your children, test how financially responsible they are and teach them about money. For instance, if your teenage children have earned income—perhaps from a summer job—you could fund a Roth IRA on their behalf, contributing up to the amount they earned. A Roth, with its tax-free growth, will likely make more sense than a traditional tax-deductible IRA, because the tax deduction won't be worth much if your children have only modest income.

When you fund the Roth, you might talk to your kids about how compounding works and perhaps use an online calculator to illustrate how much the money could be worth when they retire. An added bonus: The 10 percent tax penalty on early withdrawals may deter your children from raiding the account, though that penalty would only apply if they withdrew the Roth's investment earnings, not the original contributions.

Alternatively, once your children are in the workforce, you might encourage them to contribute to their employer's 401(k) plan by offering to reimburse 25 or 50 cents for every $1 they put in their 401(k). Similarly, to encourage your kids to save for a house down payment, you might offer to contribute $1 to their savings account for every $1 they contribute. With both strategies, you're encouraging good savings habits while also promoting worthy goals like saving for retirement and buying a home.

368. GIVING APPRECIATED STOCK

Instead of giving cash, you could give away investments that have appreciated in value. This can work well with charities, as we'll explain later in this chapter. But with your children or other family members, it can be a mixed blessing.

Let's say you give your children some shares you own. If you had paid $10 a share for the stock and it's now worth $50, your children will assume your $10 cost basis. If they sell, they'll owe taxes on the $40 per share in capital gains, assuming the stock is still worth $50. This isn't great—but if their tax bracket is lower than yours, there will be some tax savings. Your children will also assume your date of purchase, which will affect whether the gain is taxed at the short-term or long-term capital gains rate.

What if the stock has fallen in value? If, when sold, the stock is still worth less than your cost basis but more than the value when gifted, there's neither a gain nor a loss. In that situation, you would have been better off selling the stock first, taking advantage of the capital loss and then giving the proceeds to your children. If, however, the stock continues to fall in value, your children will be able to realize a capital loss, but only based on the difference between the value when gifted and the sale price.

If you hang onto the stock until you die, none of this matters. Your heirs inherit the stock at its current market value, thanks to the step-up in cost basis. At that point, any potential capital-gains tax bill disappears—but so, too, does the chance to use any unrealized capital loss.

369. WILL

There's a decent chance that your will won't determine what happens to the bulk of your wealth, because the fate of many assets depends on how they're titled and the beneficiaries named. Still, it's crucial to have a will that spells out who should receive those assets that are subject to probate.

Without it, you will die intestate. That means the disposition of your probate assets will be determined by state law—and your assets may not be divvied up the way you would have wanted.

In your will, you should also name a personal guardian for your minor children, which will be crucial if you and your spouse die prematurely. You will likely also want to specify that your wealth should be held in trust for your children until they reach age 18, 21 and possibly later, and also name someone to manage this money. That someone doesn't have to be your children's personal guardian.

As your life changes, you'll likely want to change your will. In particular, you will probably need to revise it if you marry, have children or divorce. You should also revise your will if the executor dies and possibly if one of your beneficiaries dies. Moving to a different state is another reason to revisit your will. While it may be acceptable in the new state, settling your estate could take longer. Revising your will is especially important if you're married and move from a community property state to a common law state, or vice versa.

370. DISCLAIMING

You can disclaim assets that are left to you in a will. At that point, the money disclaimed passes to the other heirs as though you had predeceased the person who had just died. A will might even have a disclaimer clause that specifies what will happen if money is disclaimed. When disclaiming, you can't specify who should receive your portion of the inheritance, so the wording of the will is critical.

What's the advantage of disclaiming? Let's say your mother leaves you $100,000. You don't need the money and, indeed, you fear the money will be subject to federal or state estate taxes when you die and leave it to your kids. Depending on how your mother's will is written, you may be able to disclaim the inheritance, with the money going directly to your children.

Similarly, you might disclaim part of the inheritance from your spouse, perhaps so the money ends up with your children now, while also reducing the risk that estate taxes will be due upon your death. You might do this if your spouse hadn't taken steps to use his or her estate tax exclusion—though you could also take advantage of the portable estate tax exclusion, discussed later in this chapter.

371. ESTATE PLANNING WHEN MARRIED

If you're married, you enjoy certain tax privileges, such as the unlimited marital deduction, which we'll tackle later in this chapter. But there is also a key obligation: You have to bequeath a minimum amount to your spouse. Exactly how much varies from state to state.

There are nine community property states: Arizona, California, Idaho, Louisiana, Nevada, New Mexico, Texas, Washington and Wisconsin. Puerto Rico is also a community property jurisdiction. In Alaska, spouses may create community property by entering into a community property agreement, but such agreements are optional. In a community property state, the wealth acquired during the course of the marriage—except gifts and inheritances—is considered equally owned by you and your spouse. That means you need to leave at least that much to your spouse.

The remaining states are common law states. In these other states, your spouse isn't entitled to an automatic 50 percent of the marital property. Instead, the minimum—typically a third of the deceased spouse's property—is specified by state law.

You are also required, under federal law, to name your spouse as beneficiary of your 401(k) plan and other "qualified" employer-sponsored plans, unless your spouse signs a waiver. This isn't true of an IRA. That said, if you live in a community property state, your spouse may be entitled to a portion of your IRA if you made contributions to the account while you were married.

372. BENEFICIARY DESIGNATIONS

When you open a retirement account or purchase life insurance, you usually name beneficiaries to inherit these assets. This is also true when you set up a trust.

Because much of your wealth may be in IRAs, 401(k) plans and similar accounts, it's crucial you have the right beneficiaries listed. Divorced? If you don't change the beneficiaries on your retirement accounts, your ex-spouse may get the last laugh.

Whoever inherits your retirement accounts has to follow special rules when making withdrawals. They will also have to pay income taxes on those withdrawals, unless the money is coming out of a Roth account. Still, even with an embedded income tax bill, a retirement account can make a fine inheritance—if Congress continues to permit the so-called stretch IRA and if your beneficiaries take advantage of it.

By contrast, your beneficiaries typically won't have to pay income taxes on life insurance proceeds. There could, however, be estate taxes owed, unless you arrange for the life insurance to be owned by somebody other than yourself. That somebody is usually not a person, but rather an irrevocable life insurance trust.

373. TITLING

Think about the assets you own that aren't in a trust or inside a retirement account. We are typically talking about items such as your home, car and taxable financial accounts. Will these assets pass directly to your heirs, or will they go through probate and be governed by your will? It will depend on how they're titled.

Assets held solely in your name will go to whomever you named in your will. One exception: If you title your bank and investment accounts as *payable on death*, those assets will bypass probate and go directly to the named beneficiaries.

What about jointly owned assets? If you own, say, a home with your spouse and you're listed as *joint tenants with right of survivorship*, your house will pass directly to your spouse, assuming you die first.

There's a variation on joint tenancy with right of survivorship that is known as *tenancy by the entirety*. Only spouses can use this ownership arrangement. It isn't recognized in most community property states and also some common law states. What's the advantage of tenancy by the entirety? Unlike with joint tenants with right of survivorship, you can't transfer your ownership stake without the consent of your spouse. This can provide protection from creditors if one of you is sued.

Finally, if you own property as *tenants in common*, there is no right of survivorship. While joint tenants are equal owners of a property, tenants in common can have ownership stakes that are different in size. If you own assets as a tenant in common, they would pass to whomever you named in your will.

374. FEDERAL ESTATE TAXES

You can leave any amount to a spouse who is a U.S. citizen without worrying about federal estate taxes, thanks to the unlimited marital deduction. But if you bequeath a total of more than $5.45 million to other folks in 2016, federal estate taxes kick in at a 40 percent rate. This $5.45 million is sometimes referred to as the unified credit—though this isn't strictly correct, because the credit is the tax you avoid, not the sum that avoids taxation.

Don't have anything close to $5.45 million? Taxes could still take a bite out of your estate for two reasons. First, your estate could be taxed at the state level. About a third of states levy either an estate tax or an inheritance tax, and sometimes both. Second, if you bequeath retirement accounts, other than Roth accounts, your heirs will owe income taxes as they draw down those accounts. The embedded income tax bill on traditional retirement accounts affects far more Americans than federal and state estate taxes, but it doesn't garner nearly as much attention.

What if you leave your heirs your home, which is worth far more than you paid? What if you bequeath regular taxable accounts where you hold, say, stocks with large unrealized capital gains? For those investments and for your home, there's good news: These assets enjoy a step-up in cost basis, which means their purchase price for tax purposes becomes the price as of your death. Result: Unlike with a retirement account, the embedded tax bill disappears. You may want to factor this into your planning as you consider which accounts to spend down during your lifetime and which to bequeath.

375. UNLIMITED MARITAL DEDUCTION

Spouses are free to give as much money as they wish to each other, both while they're alive and also upon death. In other words, as long as your spouse is a U.S. citizen, you aren't constrained by 2016's $14,000 gift-tax exclusion or $5.45 million federal estate tax exclusion.

Moreover, your federal estate tax exclusion is "portable." Let's say you die first and leave everything to your spouse, who is a U.S. citizen. Upon your spouse's death, the amount that can be bequeathed free of federal estate taxes would be twice as much, or $10.9 million, and probably more because of intervening inflation adjustments to your spouse's estate tax exclusion. Your unused exclusion amount, however, wouldn't increase with inflation after your death.

Portability isn't automatic, so it's important that your spouse and executor consult a qualified attorney. To claim the unused exemption, your spouse will typically have to file with the IRS within nine months of your death. Portability is claimed on Form 706, which is used for estate tax returns. Your spouse will likely have to pay an accountant to prepare the return, but it may be worth it, even if your combined assets are currently well below $5 million. The reason: Between your death and your spouse's death, the housing or financial markets might rise sharply, your spouse could receive an inheritance, or he or she might remarry someone with substantial wealth—and suddenly estate taxes are a big issue.

What if your spouse is a U.S. resident, but not a citizen? You can't take advantage of the unlimited marital deduction, but you could still benefit from the usual $5.45 million federal estate tax exclusion, so estate taxes shouldn't be an issue for most couples. While you're alive, you are also limited in how much you can give each year, without worrying about the gift tax, to a spouse who isn't a U.S. citizen. But again, the limit is high—$148,000 in 2016.

376. STATE ESTATE TAXES

Roughly a third of states have either an estate tax or an inheritance tax, and two of them have both. These taxes are separate from the federal estate tax—and they typically kick in at much lower asset levels.

Iowa, Kentucky, Nebraska and Pennsylvania all have inheritance taxes. An inheritance tax is levied not on the estate, but on those who inherit the money. Depending on the state, certain heirs may be exempt from the tax, such as your spouse and children.

State estate taxes are levied in Connecticut, Delaware, Hawaii, Illinois, Maine, Massachusetts, Minnesota, New York, Oregon, Rhode Island, Vermont and Washington, as well as in Washington, DC. Exclusions from state estate taxes are almost always much lower than the $5.45 million federal estate tax exclusion, which means your estate could avoid federal taxes, but still get hit at the state level. Tennessee had an estate tax in 2015, but it's slated to disappear as of 2016.

Finally, for the lucky residents of Maryland and New Jersey, there is both a state estate tax and an inheritance tax to contend with.

Some good news: A number of states are reviewing their estate tax, possibly with a view to raising their exclusion so it's more in line with the federal level.

377. STRETCH IRA

You might have heard financial experts claim that IRAs, 401(k) plans and other retirement accounts are terrible assets to bequeath, because the government will end up with more than 80 percent of the money. This is just a scare tactic by financial advisors trying to drum up business: Unless you're subject to federal estate taxes and the account's beneficiaries are in the top income tax bracket, the tax bill will be considerably smaller.

Still, a traditional retirement account could become a less attractive inheritance—if Congress kills off the so-called stretch IRA. We'll tackle that possibility in the next section. First, let's look at the current rules.

Today, spouses who inherit a retirement account can transfer the money into their own IRA, which allows them to postpone taking distributions until age 70½. Meanwhile, everybody else should consider taking advantage of the stretch.

That means moving the money into an inherited IRA and beginning distributions in the year after the original IRA owner's death. Spouses who are under age 59½ and need income right away might also choose this route, because it will allow them to avoid the 10 percent tax penalty on early withdrawals.

Each year's required minimum withdrawal is based on the beneficiary's life expectancy. That could mean a modest distribution. Meanwhile, the money remaining in the account can continue to grow tax-deferred. If handled correctly, an inherited IRA can provide beneficiaries with decades of tax-deferred growth, and that growth could more than compensate for a traditional retirement account's embedded income tax bill.

Three tips: First, it's crucial that beneficiaries follow the rules carefully—or they might disqualify themselves from using the stretch IRA strategy. Second, check whether the original owner of the IRA made nondeductible contributions. If so, you won't have to pay taxes on a portion of each year's withdrawals. Third, if the IRA was part of an estate that was subject to federal estate taxes, you may be eligible for a tax deduction known as "income in respect of a decedent."

Beneficiaries who inherit Roth IRAs will also need to take minimum distributions (unless you're the spouse and choose to treat the Roth as your own). But in the case of the Roth, the annual distributions and the growth of the remaining money will be tax-free.

378. DEATH OF THE STRETCH?

Because the stretch IRA can be such a financial bonanza for beneficiaries, there's been talk in Washington of forcing nonspouse beneficiaries to empty inherited retirement accounts within five years of the original owner's death. These proposals haven't become law, but the idea appears to be gaining currency and it could be part of the next tax overhaul.

Even if the stretch IRA is eliminated, there's no need for drastic action—but you may want to make four financial tweaks. First, you might draw more heavily on your traditional retirement accounts to pay your retirement living expenses, while setting aside taxable account investments for your heirs. Those taxable account investments would still benefit from the step-up in cost basis that will occur upon your death. That means your heirs would inherit your taxable account with no capital gains taxes owed.

Second, you might convert part of your traditional retirement accounts to a Roth IRA, and then leave the Roth to your heirs. If the stretch disappears, a Roth would also have to be emptied within five years—but your beneficiaries wouldn't have to pay taxes on it. By contrast, withdrawals from an inherited traditional retirement account would be on top of the other income that your heirs already earn, and thus those withdrawals could push them into a much higher tax bracket.

Third, you might name more beneficiaries for your traditional retirement accounts. That way, the withdrawals would be less per beneficiary—and hence less likely to force them into a significantly higher tax bracket.

Finally, if you plan to leave money to charity upon your death, you might leave your traditional retirement accounts, while saving your Roth and your taxable account for your children and other family members.

379. WHAT TO BEQUEATH

Your heirs will, most likely, appreciate anything you leave them. But some bequests may be more appreciated than others.

At the top of the list would probably be a Roth IRA. Yes, estate taxes could be owed if your overall estate is large enough and, yes, your heirs will have to draw down the account gradually over their lifetime—and possibly within five years if the stretch IRA disappears. But there will be no income taxes owed on those withdrawals, and the money that remains in the account can continue to grow tax-free.

Life insurance can also make an attractive inheritance, especially if you are subject to estate taxes. Why? The proceeds will be income-tax-free to your beneficiaries and, if properly structured, the policy won't be part of your taxable estate. Still, given how expensive life insurance becomes as you age, you probably shouldn't buy it solely to ensure an inheritance, unless estate taxes are an issue.

You might keep highly appreciated investments and bequeath those. That way, you'll avoid the embedded capital gains tax bill, thanks to the step-up in basis upon death, and that will leave more money for your heirs. In 2015, President Obama proposed eliminating the step-up. Even though the proposal didn't become law, it's an idea that may be revived at some point. Keep in mind that you should sell underwater investments, not bequeath them. You can use the tax losses to reduce your income tax bill while you're alive, but those losses have no tax value after your death.

What if you are faced with a choice between bequeathing a traditional retirement account and bequeathing money in a taxable account? If the stretch IRA survives, the traditional retirement account might make the better inheritance, especially for younger beneficiaries and those in low tax brackets. But if the stretch disappears, money in a regular taxable account will mean more after-tax dollars for your heirs.

Finally, your heirs will probably be less happy to inherit assets that are difficult to sell. At issue here are not only illiquid investments, but also time shares, antique cars and second homes. Clearly, if you're making full use of these assets while you're alive, you should keep them. But your heirs would probably prefer to receive cash.

380. TRUSTS

When folks hear that someone has set up a trust or is the beneficiary of a trust, one thought often comes to mind: We're talking about serious money. In the lexicon of wealth, the term "trust" is as evocative as "hedge fund," "private equity" and "overseas bank account."

In truth, a trust is just an estate planning tool, one that sometimes makes sense even for families with relatively limited wealth. Why would you use this tool? There are four reasons:

• Assets held in a trust can avoid probate. This is the reason some people set up revocable living trusts.

• A trust can allow you to control how the assets you bequeath are used after your death. For instance, folks will often use trusts when leaving money to children, including those with special needs, or to family members who are financially irresponsible. They might also use trusts if they're remarried and trying to provide for both a new spouse and children from an earlier marriage.

• Trusts can help if you fear you might be subject to estate taxes. Two popular tax-cutting strategies include using bypass trusts and setting up irrevocable life insurance trusts.

• For those worried about lawsuits, trusts can help with asset protection.

Depending on the type of trust, hefty costs can be involved. This shouldn't be an issue with, say, a revocable living trust used simply to avoid probate. But let's say you bequeath money to your children in a trust. The trust could pay substantial annual fees for administration and money management, and also need to file its own tax return.

381. REVOCABLE LIVING TRUSTS

Like a will, a revocable living trust is a way of detailing who should inherit your wealth after your death. But unlike a will, assets bequeathed via a living trust don't go through probate. It's also harder for disgruntled family members to challenge the terms of a living trust, and there isn't the potential publicity that accompanies the probate process.

Why are these trusts referred to as revocable? Assets placed in the trust can be removed at any time. Is it really that advantageous to avoid probate?

Much will depend on where you live. In some states, probate is a quick and easy process. In others, it's costly and cumbersome.

Even if probate isn't a great hassle where you live, you may want to establish a revocable living trust if you own a vacation home or other property in a different state from where you have your principal residence. If the trust holds this out-of-state property, your estate won't have to go through probate in two separate states. A living trust can also help if you become incapacitated. Depending on the terms of the trust, your spouse or successor trustee should be able to manage the trust's property without going to court to get the necessary authority.

If you have a living trust, you still need a will. Inevitably, there will be some probate assets that are outside the trust at the time of your death. Your will can specify who should receive those assets. Also keep in mind that a living trust, on its own, doesn't do anything to reduce estate taxes.

382. CHILDREN'S TRUSTS

While children can own property, they can't legally enter into contracts. That makes it difficult for them to manage an investment portfolio, because they can't buy or sell. This is the reason a child's investment account needs an adult custodian—and the reason substantial sums bequeathed to children who are under age 18 or 21 are often placed in a trust, with a trustee overseeing the assets involved. Trusts for children are typically testamentary trusts, meaning they're set up according to the instructions in your will, rather than being established before your death.

While your children could receive their trust assets once they reach the age of majority, which is typically 18 or 21 depending on the state, all the money doesn't necessarily need to be disbursed at that point. Instead, you might specify that the trustee should use the trust's assets to pay living expenses and education costs, with the remaining balance distributed when your children reach age 25 or even age 35. That will give them a chance to mature and, you hope, become a little more sensible about managing money.

While you may not want the trust to hand over great chunks of money to your children in their early 20s, you probably want the trust to disburse a little money every year for tax reasons. If a trust disburses its investment income, that income is taxable to the beneficiaries. But if the trust retains dividends, interest and realized capital gains, it can quickly find itself paying taxes at a steep rate. In 2016, a single individual needs taxable income of $415,050 before he or she is in the top 39.6 percent federal tax bracket, but a trust will be in that tax bracket if it retains more than $12,400 in taxable income.

You might be able to sidestep this problem by focusing the trust's investments on tax-efficient stock funds and tax-free municipal bonds. If you establish the trust while you are alive, you could also set it up as a grantor trust, which means that during your lifetime the trust's retained income would be taxable on your return.

383. SPECIAL NEEDS TRUSTS

If you have a child with a physical or mental disability who is unlikely to be self-supporting, you might set up a special needs trust, either during your lifetime or upon your death. By placing money in the trust, not only can you specify how the money should be spent, but also you won't disqualify the child from receiving means-tested government benefits.

Typically, if a child has more than a modest amount of cash in his or her name, the child will be disqualified from receiving Medicaid and Supplemental Security Income. The SSI program pays benefits to disabled adults and children with modest incomes and few assets. To avoid disqualification, you might encourage family and friends to make gifts to the trust, rather than directly to your son or daughter.

The trust shouldn't disburse money to the beneficiary, because that could also disqualify the child from receiving government benefits. Instead, the money should be used to pay directly for goods and services for the child, such as education costs, entertainment, vacations, a personal attendant and out-of-pocket medical expenses.

Make sure you use a qualified attorney to set up the trust. Carefully consider whom to appoint as trustees. You might pair a corporate trustee, such as a bank or trust company, with a family member. Look closely at the costs charged by the corporate trustee. Also ask the attorney whether the trust will be required to reimburse Medicaid after the beneficiary's death— and whether it's possible to sidestep this requirement.

384. SPENDTHRIFT TRUSTS

Suppose you plan to leave a healthy sum to your adult children, but you are worried they will quickly fritter away the money. Perhaps they have a problem with drinking, drugs or gambling. Perhaps they spend compulsively. Or perhaps you fear the inheritance will make them the target of scams and lawsuits.

One possibility is to leave money for their benefit in spendthrift trusts, from which the beneficiaries have no right to make withdrawals. Instead, money is only disbursed according to the terms you have drawn up. You can even specify that the trust shouldn't disburse money and instead should use its assets to pay certain living expenses for the beneficiary.

Because the beneficiary isn't allowed to make withdrawals, the assets should be protected from creditors if, say, the beneficiary is subject to a lawsuit or ends up in debt. Still, you will likely want the trust to disburse some money each year or purchase some goods and services for the beneficiary. As explained in the section above on children's trusts, a trust can find itself paying taxes at a steep rate if it retains even a modest amount of income.

385. IRREVOCABLE LIFE INSURANCE TRUSTS

Life insurance proceeds are almost always income-tax-free to the beneficiaries. But will estate taxes be owed? This is an issue for a small fraction of estates. If it is, you might consider an irrevocable life insurance trust. The insurance proceeds could then be used to cover estate taxes owed on other assets. Alternatively, the proceeds might provide an inheritance to children who don't want to be involved in the family business, thus avoiding the need to sell the business, possibly in a rushed sale at an unfavorable price.

Why use a trust to hold life insurance? If you own a policy when you die, the proceeds could be subject to estate taxes. But if insurance on your life is owned by somebody else—or some other entity, such as a trust—no estate taxes are owed.

If you buy life insurance within a trust, you might pay the premiums by making use of the annual gift-tax exclusion, which is $14,000 in 2016. To make use of the exclusion, your attorney will need to create a trust with so-called Crummey powers. That means the beneficiaries have the right to withdraw the money gifted—a right you hope they don't exercise.

If you transfer an existing policy into the trust, you need to live another three years beyond the date of the transfer for the change of ownership to be effective for estate tax purposes. Alternatively, you might cancel your current insurance and have the trust buy a new policy, assuming it makes financial sense and you can pass the necessary medical exam.

The tax advantages of life insurance are impressive, but so too are the premiums, especially as you get older. Still, for wealthy families facing estate taxes, it might be worth paying those premiums. If you're married, you may be able to trim the premiums by using your irrevocable life insurance trust to purchase second-to-die life insurance, which doesn't pay out until the second spouse in a couple dies.

386. BYPASS TRUSTS

Suppose you and your partner have substantial wealth, but you aren't legally married. To ensure you both take advantage of the federal estate tax exclusion, you might use a bypass trust, which is funded upon your death under the terms of your will or living trust.

Let's say you die first. Upon your death, your will might direct that a sum equal to the federal estate tax exclusion—$5.45 million in 2016—should go into a bypass trust, with the money perhaps earmarked for your favorite niece but with your partner still able to receive income from that money. This will use your estate tax exclusion. Upon your partner's death, another $5.45 million (though likely more, thanks to inflation adjustments) would pass free of federal estate taxes, for a total of $10.9 million.

Thanks to the portability of the federal estate tax exclusion, wealthy married couples have less need to use bypass trusts. Many couples—who built bypass trusts into their estate plan when the estate tax exclusion was far lower—should probably revisit their plan, and will likely need to revise their wills and living trusts.

Still, bypass trusts could make sense for some married couples. By stashing assets in a bypass trust upon the death of the first spouse, you sidestep the risk that those assets might appreciate substantially in the years between the first spouse's death and the second. If that happens and the bypass trust is not used, federal estate taxes may be an issue upon the death of the second spouse, even though the second spouse's estate gets to make use of both spouses' estate tax exclusions, thanks to portability.

On the other hand, if the assets are held in a trust and they increase substantially in value, your beneficiaries may have a different problem: capital gains taxes. That problem would be avoided if you simply leave the money to your spouse, because the assets would have their cost basis stepped up to the current market value upon your spouse's death. Your estate planning attorney can help you figure out whether capital gains taxes or estate taxes are the bigger issue.

The answer will hinge partly on the size of your estate and how assets are invested. A bypass trust could also help with state estate taxes, where portability may not be allowed. In addition, a bypass trust might make sense if you're remarried and have children from an earlier marriage. Even if the trust doesn't deliver big tax savings, it could ensure that your wishes are followed. The trust might provide income to your new spouse after your death, while ensuring that your children ultimately inherit the assets involved. Often, this is also the motivation behind setting up a QTIP trust.

387. QTIP TRUSTS

A Qualified Terminable Interest Property, or QTIP, trust can provide income for your spouse, while also naming the ultimate beneficiaries of the trust's assets. Sound like a bypass trust? It is—except a bypass trust makes use of your federal estate tax exclusion, while a QTIP trust takes advantage of the unlimited marital deduction.

This might seem unnecessary. After all, you could simply leave the money to your spouse, and that also would take advantage of the unlimited marital deduction. But let's say you were married before and you want to ensure that your wealth eventually ends up in the hands of your children from your earlier marriage or marriages. By using a QTIP trust, you can ensure that whatever assets remain in the trust after your spouse's death will go to them.

Unlike the money in a bypass trust, there may be federal estate taxes owed on the money in a QTIP trust.

388. ASSET PROTECTION TRUSTS

If you're worried about lawsuits, an asset protection trust could put your wealth beyond the reach of your creditors. For a trust to provide this sort of protection, it has to be irrevocable and needs to have spendthrift provisions. In other words, you can't reclaim the money put into the trust and you can't control how much the trust distributes each year. Instead, distributions would be at the discretion of an independent trustee, who might cease all distributions if you're the subject of a lawsuit.

An asset protection trust isn't necessarily a bulletproof defense against a legal judgment. But it's enough of a deterrent that plaintiffs may decide it isn't worth pursuing their case or they may settle for a modest sum. An overseas asset protection trust will likely be less vulnerable to legal challenges, but these are more expensive to set up and administer than domestic asset protection trusts.

Indeed, before you rush to set up an asset protection trust, carefully consider the costs involved. The initial and ongoing fees are likely to be substantial, including costs for legal work, administration and money management. Moreover, you are giving up control over your assets—not a step you want to take lightly.

389. DURABLE POWERS OF ATTORNEY

If you become incapacitated toward the end of your life, it may be difficult for your family to make financial and medical decisions on your behalf unless you have durable powers of attorney drawn up.

You will likely want two powers of attorney, one for health care matters and the other for financial decisions. These powers of attorney are often "springing," meaning they don't become effective until a doctor certifies that you are incapacitated.

With a durable power of attorney for financial matters, you specify what your "agent"—who might be your spouse or an adult child—can do on your behalf. This might include paying bills, making portfolio decisions, handling bank transactions and filing taxes. If you don't make such an arrangement and you become incapacitated or incompetent, your family may have to go through the cost and hassle of asking the court to appoint a guardian.

Meanwhile, a health care power of attorney (sometimes called a health care proxy) allows your agent to make medical decisions. As part of the health care power of attorney, or in a separate living will, you can detail your wishes concerning life-prolonging medical procedures.

390. LETTER OF LAST INSTRUCTION

A letter of last instruction isn't a substitute for a will. Still, it's worth drawing up, because it will help your family settle your affairs in the weeks and months after your death. In our paperless world, a letter of last instruction—sometimes called a doomsday letter—has become especially important, because you may not have paper statements lying around to help your family identify your assets and liabilities.

What should your letter include? It's up to you, but the more detailed it is, the better. You might include:

• Funeral instructions, who should be notified upon your death and which publications you would like your obituary sent to.

• A list of financial accounts, including credit cards, insurance, and bank and investment accounts, as well as the location of any safe-deposit box. Also include the names and contact information for your insurance agent, financial advisor, lawyer, doctors and any other professionals you regularly deal with.

• Details of where key papers can be found, such as your birth certificate, car registrations, will, trust documents, tax returns and financial account statements.

• The usernames and passwords for various email programs and websites you use.

• An inventory of household items and who you would like to receive them. You might specify who should inherit certain jewelry, furniture and paintings. If some items are particularly valuable, you may want to include them in your will, so your wishes are less likely to be contested.

Don't forget to tell your executor and other key family members where the letter is located—or all your hard work could go to waste.

391. GETTING ORGANIZED

As you look to get your financial affairs organized, start with that letter of last instruction. Do you find yourself writing a lengthy description of where all key papers are located and how you want matters handled after your death? That's probably a sign that you need to organize and simplify.

While folks are often advised to keep key documents in a safe-deposit box, this has a downside. After your death, the box may be sealed, and your family may not have access until they get a court order. A representative of the local tax authority may need to be present when the box is unsealed.

At a minimum, don't keep your will and burial instructions in the safe-deposit box. Your family will want immediate access to those—but it could take weeks to view these documents if they're in a safe-deposit box. Instead, keep them at home in a fireproof filing cabinet or metal box.

392. HAVING THE TALK

Many folks are uncomfortable discussing their finances. Still, you should seriously consider talking to your children and other affected family members about your financial situation and especially your estate plan.

Why? For starters, it'll give your family an idea of what they can expect to inherit, and they can then factor that into their own financial decisions. It can also give you a chance to explain your bequests, especially if you plan to give more to some family members than others.

In addition, you can talk about end-of-life medical decisions, what sort of funeral you want and where key papers are located. You might even discuss what you would like your children to do with their inheritance. Perhaps you are anxious for them to buy their own home or for your grandchildren to go to good colleges.

There could also be other nitty-gritty financial details you want to tackle. For instance, you might explain the benefits of doing the stretch IRA, especially with a Roth. Alternatively, perhaps you plan to bequeath appreciated stock, but you want to emphasize that this is simply to get the step-up in cost basis, and your children should sell the shares immediately and buy a more diversified portfolio.

JONATHAN'S TAKE: Most of us won't leave millions of dollars to our heirs. But we can all make sure that our affairs are well organized, that there's a detailed letter of last instruction, and that our families know our wishes regarding life-prolonging medical procedures. These steps—and more—can save our families from extra anguish during an already difficult time.

393. INVESTIGATING CHARITIES

Before giving to a charity, you want to be confident the money will end up helping your favorite cause, rather than being lavished on handsome salaries for the charity's staff and other administrative costs.

Doing an online search may turn up any complaints about the charity. Your state government or the Better Business Bureau might also have complaints on file. Check out the BBB website for charities and donors at Give.org. In addition, you might review the charity's Form 990, which it is required to file with the IRS and which might be available on the charity's website. This will give you details on its finances.

Make sure the organization is not just tax-exempt, but that it carries the Internal Revenue Service's 501(c)3 designation, which means your contributions will be tax-deductible. The charity's website should tell you. If you're uncertain, go to IRS.gov/charities and click on "EO Select Check."

As you investigate a charity, look for concrete results from the past year, rather than just a nebulous statement of purpose. You might try using CharityNavigator.org, CharityWatch.org, GiveWell.org, GuideStar.org and MyPhilanthropedia.org. CharityWatch.org and MyPhilanthropedia.org list top-rated charities by category. GiveWell.org tries to identify charities that do the most good per dollar spent. GuideStar.org allows you to download a charity's Form 990. Charity Navigator.org details how much of a charity's budget goes to administrative expenses and to fundraising costs—and how much to the charity's programs. The most efficient charities spend 10 percent or less of their revenue on administration and fundraising.

One tip: If a telemarketer calls seeking a donation for a charity, say "no," even if you're inclined to give. Telemarketers often take a large cut of any money they raise. If you want to contribute, give directly to the charity.

394. DEDUCTING CHARITABLE CONTRIBUTIONS

Charitable contributions should principally be motivated by generosity. Still, don't overlook the tax advantages.

If you give cash, you can deduct the entire contribution. For instance, if you're in the 25 percent federal income tax bracket, a $1 contribution will save you 25 cents in taxes. You only get this tax benefit if you itemize your deductions, rather than taking the standard deduction. If you usually take the standard deduction, you might bunch two or three years of charitable contributions into one tax year and see if that allows you to itemize. In any one year, the deduction for cash donations is capped at 50 percent of your adjusted gross income. Any excess can be rolled over and used during the subsequent five years.

Looking to save even more in taxes? Often the smartest strategy is to give appreciated assets that you have held for more than a year and which would otherwise be taxed at the long-term capital gains rate. Donating appreciated assets can have three tax benefits.

First, you can deduct the value of your contribution. That deduction, in any given year, is capped at 30 percent of your adjusted gross income. Second, you avoid paying capital gains taxes on the assets involved. To avoid the tax, don't sell the assets yourself, but instead let the charity do so. Third, you reduce the size of your taxable estate, which could ultimately mean paying less in federal and state estate taxes.

Want the tax savings today, but not sure which charities to support? You might contribute to a donor advised fund, such as those operated by FidelityCharitable.org, T. Rowe Price Group's ProgramForGiving.org, SchwabCharitable.org and VanguardCharitable.org. Your money can collect investment gains while you decide which charities to help. What if you have a loss on, say, a stock? Don't donate the shares. Instead, sell the stock yourself so you get the tax benefit from the loss, and then donate the cash proceeds.

If you're retired or approaching that stage, here's another option: In return for your charitable contribution, you could get a tax deduction and generate retirement income—by making use of charitable gift annuities and charitable remainder trusts.

395. CHARITABLE GIFT ANNUITIES

A charitable gift annuity is similar to a plain-vanilla, immediate fixed annuity purchased from an insurance company. You hand over a chunk of money to a charity, which then pays you income for the rest of your life. But there are five key differences from an insurance company's annuity:

• A charitable gift annuity can give you an immediate tax deduction, which is based on how much the charity estimates it will have left upon your death.

• The annuity can be funded with appreciated property, such as stocks or mutual funds with large unrealized capital gains. This saves you selling the property and paying the capital gains tax bill. But if you fund the annuity with appreciated property, you will have to pay tax on a larger portion of each annuity payment.

• These annuities typically treat men and women equally, which is beneficial to women. With a commercial annuity, women usually receive less income than men of the same age, because the insurance company factors in their longer life expectancy.

• Whether you are a man or a woman, a charitable gift annuity will typically give you less monthly income than a commercial annuity. Yes, this is a charitable gift, so a charitable gift annuity shouldn't be your first choice if you're looking for maximum retirement income.

• If you die young, your untimely demise will benefit the charity, not an insurance company. This may make it a little more palatable to plunk down a large sum, knowing you would collect scant income from the annuity if you go under the next bus.

For further information, check out the website of the American Council on Gift Annuities at ACGA-web.org.

396. CHARITABLE REMAINDER TRUSTS

A charitable remainder trust is similar to a charitable gift annuity, but you retain greater control over how the money is invested, who the trustee is and which charity ultimately benefits. The downside: A charitable remainder trust is more involved, and you'll likely need legal help to set it up.

How does a charitable remainder trust work? You transfer assets to an irrevocable trust, which then pays you income for a fixed time period or until you die. All the income you receive will likely be taxable. The money that's left in the trust then goes to the charity named.

A charitable remainder trust makes most sense if you can fund it with assets that have increased in value, such as stocks or real estate. By donating the assets, you avoid capital gains taxes and receive an immediate tax deduction, which is based on an estimate of the sum that the charity will eventually receive.

You have a variety of income choices. For instance, you might opt for a fixed annual amount, like you would receive from an annuity. Alternatively, your annual income might be set at, say, 5 percent of the beginning-of-year value of the assets you donated. That means your income will fluctuate from year to year—but, if the trust's investments perform well, it might rise over time.

Sound too involved? You could opt for a charitable gift annuity instead. Some charities also have pooled income funds, which operate like charitable remainder trusts, but the charity assumes the administrative duties in return for a fee.

397. QUALIFIED CHARITABLE DISTRIBUTIONS

In December 2014, Congress voted to allow so-called qualified charitable distributions, or QCDs, for the 2014 tax year. Many are hoping for a similar last-minute reprieve for the 2015 tax year. The QCD provision allows those age 70½ and older to contribute up to $100,000 directly from their IRA to a qualified charity and count the contribution toward their required minimum distribution.

The charitable gift isn't tax-deductible—but the IRA distribution also isn't included in your taxable income, which could have tax advantages. For instance, if your income is relatively high, the size of your itemized deductions and your personal exemptions may be curtailed. Alternatively, a QCD might help those who don't itemize their deductions or whose itemized deductions—even including any charitable gifts—aren't much higher than their standard deduction.

By making a qualified charitable distribution, you also lower your modified adjusted gross income. This may reduce your premiums for Medicare Part B and for Medicare's prescription drug benefit, and it could lower the tax you pay on your Social Security benefit.

While we wait to see what Congress does, you can always make a direct distribution to a charity. The check cut by your IRA custodian should be made payable to the charity. If the QCD provision isn't extended, you would treat the money sent to the charity as a regular IRA distribution and then include the gift among your 2015 itemized deductions.

398. CHARITABLE BEQUESTS UPON DEATH

If you decide to make a charitable donation upon your death, you won't get an income tax deduction, which you could receive if you made the gift during your lifetime. You will, however, shrink the size of your taxable estate.

You could simply name a charity in your will to receive some portion of your estate. But here's an intriguing possibility: Donate your traditional IRA. As mentioned earlier in this chapter, beneficiaries (other than a spouse) of a traditional or Roth IRA have to draw down the account, but they can do so over many years. Those who inherit traditional IRAs will have to pay income taxes on the taxable portion of the withdrawal. Still, if your beneficiaries are smart, they can draw down the account slowly and get the benefit of decades of tax-deferred growth.

What if you doubt your beneficiaries will take advantage of the stretch IRA? What if it looks like Congress will eliminate the stretch IRA and instead force most beneficiaries to empty inherited IRAs within five years? You might name a charity as beneficiary of your traditional IRA, while bequeathing your Roth IRA and other assets to your children or other family members. By giving your traditional IRA to charity, you'll shrink your taxable estate and get rid of the IRA's embedded income tax bill.

PART XIV

LIFE EVENTS
FROM BABIES TO BEREAVEMENT,
SOME FINANCIAL POINTERS

The first 13 parts of this book have tried to educate you about various personal-finance topics and then help you settle on the right strategy for tackling the financial task at hand. This chapter is a little different. Here the focus is on specific steps you might take at key turning points in your life:

- Graduating college
- Getting started as an investor
- Coping with market declines
- Moving in together
- Getting married
- Having a baby
- Sending children to college
- Getting divorced
- Changing jobs
- Losing your job
- Working for yourself
- Working abroad
- Nearing retirement
- Helping elderly relatives
- After a loved one's death

As you busy yourself dealing with these changes, keep an eye on the big picture. Moments of transition and turmoil are often a great time to reconsider your overall finances, and for that you'll want to turn to other parts of this book.

399. GRADUATING COLLEGE

As you leave college and enter the work world, money will likely loom large—or, to be more precise, the lack thereof. Still, don't let a modest paycheck deter you. With the right steps, you can put yourself on the fast track to achieve two of life's most important financial goals: buying a home and retirement.

Live beneath your means. As you consider what sort of place to rent and what other expenses to take on, aim to keep your cost of living low. That'll give you more financial breathing room, make your life less stressful and, as the pay increases come through, you can start socking away serious money for a house down payment and other goals.

Pay all bills on time. We're talking about things like rent, utilities, student loans and credit card bills. Where possible, set up automatic payments, so you are less likely to be late. Paying your bills on time is typically the biggest factor affecting your credit score. If you nurture your credit history and credit score now, you should be in good shape when you apply for a mortgage.

Take on debt cautiously. You likely already have student loans, and you might need to borrow to buy a car. If you can, avoid taking on other debts, so mortgage lenders won't have any concerns when you ask for that hefty home loan.

Use credit cards sparingly. To build a good credit score, it's helpful to charge a small sum every month and then pay off the credit card balance in full. Try not to let that small monthly charge become a large one. If you use too high a percentage of your available credit limit, it'll make you appear financially stressed and it could hurt your credit score. More important, if you charge too much, you may not be able to pay off the balance in full— and you'll likely incur steep finance charges.

Contribute to your employer's retirement plan. With retirement so far away, this might seem like a low priority. But be sure to contribute at least enough to get any matching employer contribution. You will soon get used to living without the money. The earlier you start saving, the more you'll potentially accumulate, and you could set yourself up for early retirement.

400. GETTING STARTED AS AN INVESTOR

If you don't have much money, it can be tough to get started as an investor. Many brokerage firms and mutual funds require an initial investment of $2,500 or $3,000, and sometimes more. What to do? Consider these steps:

Fund that 401(k). If you're in your 20s, there is a decent chance your first foray into investing will be through your employer's retirement plan. That's a great place to start, and not just because of the tax benefits and any matching employer contribution. You will likely find the plan includes a limited list of mutual funds, which makes the choice more manageable, and you don't have to worry about meeting some required minimum initial investment.

Look for low-minimum funds. For $100, you can buy one of the Charles Schwab mutual funds. Schwab's fund lineup includes index funds, fundamentally weighted index funds and target-date retirement funds. For $500, you can get into the Homestead Funds and some of the Nicholas Company funds. Artisan Funds, Buffalo Funds and Scout Investments will waive their regular minimums if you agree to a $50- or $100-a-month automatic investment plan.

For $1,000, you can purchase one of T. Rowe Price Group's target-date retirement funds in an individual retirement account, while $1,000 will allow you to buy a Vanguard Group target-date fund in either an IRA or a regular taxable account. If you have relatively limited savings, you won't be able to buy many investments, so you should probably stick with mutual funds that give you broad market exposure—which is what you get with a target-date fund.

Buy exchange-traded funds. Instead of mutual funds, you could open a brokerage account and purchase ETFs. Capital One Investing, Merrill Edge, TD Ameritrade and TradeKing have no required minimum to open a brokerage account. E*Trade will let you open an account for $500, while Charles Schwab requires $1,000, though Schwab will waive that minimum if you commit to adding $100 a month to your account. Some brokerage firms have a select list of ETFs that you can purchase without a commission.

Save for the house. To amass money for a future house down payment while also accumulating a pool of emergency money, try shoveling cash into a savings account or certificates of deposit. You won't earn much interest these days. But given that you can't afford to take much risk when pursuing short-term goals, a high return was never in the cards. Instead, your regular savings will be the key driver of the account's growth.

401. COPING WITH MARKET DECLINES

Most investors grow exuberant as share prices climb and fearful when they tumble. But to be a successful investor, you need to reverse those feelings, so you stand pat during market declines and, better still, seize the opportunity and invest more. That's tough to do—but these strategies may help:

Before selling stocks, talk to someone. That someone might be your spouse, a friend or colleague. Don't just talk about why you are fearful now. Also discuss why you're inclined to ditch the strategy in which you had so much confidence just a few months earlier. As you try to articulate what has changed, you may realize that not much has.

Think about value. Stocks aren't just pieces of paper. Rather, they represent partial ownership of corporations that often have growing profits and pay regular dividends. When share prices fall, stocks become better value relative to those profits and dividends—and the rational response is to buy more, not sell.

Look at the big picture. Your stock portfolio is likely a small part of your total wealth. While your shares may be falling in value, your other assets—including your bonds, your home and your income-earning ability—may be more valuable than ever.

Force yourself to rebalance. You should have a target percentage for your portfolio's allocation to stocks. A market decline will likely leave you underweighted. That means you ought to buy stocks as part of your regular rebalancing program. In fact, if the market drops severely, you may want to rebalance immediately, even if your next scheduled rebalancing is months away. If the market continues to fall, you can always rebalance again.

To read more about investors' mental mistakes, rebalancing and portfolio building, check out Part VIII.

402. MOVING IN TOGETHER

If you're in a relationship and decide to move in together, you may want to take things slowly—at least when it comes to your finances.

Rent a place you could afford on your own. That way, if the relationship doesn't pan out, you won't be saddled with a lease neither of you can afford.

Divide up financial responsibilities. Before moving in together, decide how you'll split the bills and who will be responsible for paying them. The more you discuss ahead of time, the less room there will be for misunderstanding.

Don't combine your finances unnecessarily. Initially, there's no need to entwine your finances by, say, opening a joint checking account or buying a car together. There just isn't much to be gained, except extra hassles if the relationship doesn't work out.

Gauge your partner's financial habits. Money is one of the biggest sources of tension in relationships, so it's important to get a handle on your partner's money habits. Is he or she careful about spending? Is your partner an aggressive investor? What's his or her attitude toward carrying credit card debt?

If your partner isn't careful about money, you will avoid financial headaches—and heated arguments—by keeping your finances separate. On the other hand, if it's clear you are both financially prudent and you believe the relationship will last, you might start marrying your finances, even if you don't envisage ever getting married. For instance, after a year or two, you might consider buying a home together and naming each other as beneficiaries of your retirement accounts and life insurance.

403. GETTING MARRIED

If you decide to marry, you'll have a lifetime of financial decisions ahead of you. But there are some items you should probably tackle right away:

Budget the wedding. Weddings are said to cost an average $25,000. Half of workers approaching retirement age have less than $50,000 in savings. An obvious question: Wouldn't it make more sense to opt for the cheaper wedding and save the rest for longer-term goals?

Get to know each other financially. Find out how much you each save regularly and have set aside for retirement, and how much you each have in debt. Also learn about each other's attitudes toward spending, credit cards and investment risk. It's worth checking out your future in-laws and how they handle money, because there's a good chance your future spouse has adopted many of his or her parents' financial attitudes.

Change beneficiary designations. You will likely want to name your new spouse as the beneficiary of your life insurance and retirement accounts. You both should also get new wills drawn up.

Rethink your life insurance. You may need to take out more life insurance, especially if you're planning to buy a home together, one of you plans to stop working or you intend to start a family.

Look for cost savings. You might save money by sharing phone plans and digital subscriptions, and by getting both of you onto whichever health plan offered by your respective employers is least expensive. Be warned: One cost could rise, which is the amount you pay in federal and state income taxes. In 2016, if you marry and your combined income is greater than $173,000 or so, your total federal income tax bill could be higher than if you remained single.

404. SAME-SEX MARRIAGE

Thanks to the Supreme Court's June 2015 decision, same-sex marriage is now legal in all 50 states. If you take advantage, you'll discover that there are some financial pitfalls to being married—but also some notable advantages:

Employee benefits. Many employers extended health and other benefits to their employees' unmarried partners, in part because gay and lesbian couples couldn't previously marry. Now that same-sex marriage is legal, some employers are expected to eliminate benefits for unmarried partners, making it financially beneficial to marry. If you are covered by a traditional employer pension plan and you opt to marry, you may also ensure that your spouse receives a survivor benefit, assuming you die first.

Social Security. A husband or wife may be eligible to receive both Social Security spousal benefits and survivor benefits based on the other spouse's earnings record. For more information, head to Part II.

Retirement accounts. If you bequeath your retirement accounts to your spouse, your husband or wife can then treat them as his or her own, rather than as an inherited retirement account. Result: Your spouse may not have to begin drawing down the accounts right away—and that means your husband or wife could enjoy a longer period of tax-deferred growth. This advantage will loom even larger if the so-called stretch IRA is disallowed for nonspouse beneficiaries, a topic we tackle in Part XIII.

Estate taxes. Married couples are able to make unlimited gifts to each other during their lifetime and leave unlimited sums to one another upon death. They can also take advantage of the portable federal estate tax exemption. You can learn more in Part XIII. Before same-sex marriage was legal, some couples made elaborate estate-planning arrangements, including the use of trusts. If you now choose to marry, these arrangements may be unnecessary. See a lawyer to discuss what steps you should take.

Bear in mind that marriage also has some financial drawbacks. If your combined income is greater than $173,000 or so, the so-called marriage penalty kicks in and you will pay more in federal income taxes than if you had remained single. In addition, if you have college-bound children and you marry, you may reduce financial aid eligibility.

405. HAVING A BABY

Once a baby arrives, you quickly discover two things are in short supply: time and money. According to the Department of Agriculture's Expenditures on Children by Families study released in August 2014, it costs $245,340 for a middle-income family to raise a child through age 17, figured in today's dollars. Costs in the first few years are pegged at $12,940 per year. How can you prepare your finances?

Stockpile cash. The more you have in a savings account, the easier it'll be to handle medical costs, buy all the baby paraphernalia, pay for babysitters and daycare, and more.

Assess living expenses. A pile of savings will help if one parent won't be working for a few months. What if one of you plans to stay home for the foreseeable future? You could quickly run through your savings, unless you take steps to cut back your living expenses. That isn't easy to do when you have an extra person to clothe and feed, and you might also need a larger home. Still, you will likely enjoy your new child more if you aren't financially stressed.

Check your employers' policies. See what the rules are regarding maternity and paternity leave. Find out what childbirth expenses will be covered, how much it will cost to get your new baby added to the health plan and what out-of-pocket medical costs you might face.

Revise your wills. Both of you will need to update your wills to name a guardian for your newborn, just in case you both die prematurely.

Boost life insurance coverage. You may have some coverage through your employer. But with the arrival of the baby, you will likely need a larger policy. Don't necessarily purchase this additional coverage through your employer. The premiums could be relatively high because they reflect the health of all employees, who on average may be older and some of whom will smoke. You will probably want coverage not only on the life of the employed parent, but also for the stay-at-home parent. A death in either case would mean significant additional ongoing costs.

406. HAVING A BABY WHEN YOU'RE A SAME-SEX COUPLE

What happens if you're part of a same-sex couple and you have a child—but you aren't the adopting or biological parent? Even though same-sex marriage is now legal in all 50 states, parental rights are likely to remain a tricky issue, so be sure to seek advice from a qualified attorney.

Apply for a second-parent adoption. If you aren't the adopting or biological parent, you may not have any rights if you get divorced, the other spouse dies or you simply want to visit your child in hospital. As a precaution, you might establish your rights by applying for a second-parent adoption.

Draw up a custody agreement. If a second-parent adoption isn't an option in your state, consult a lawyer who specializes in same-sex couples. The lawyer might suggest steps to secure your child-custody rights in case you get divorced or in case your child is hospitalized and the staff prevent you from visiting.

For instance, you might draw up a co-parenting or similar agreement. A co-parenting agreement is a declaration that you both consider yourselves parents of the child. While courts don't necessarily have to respect such agreements, they should help, as should any evidence that the nonadopting or nonbiological parent has behaved as though he or she is a parent to the child.

Name the other parent as guardian. Your lawyer might also suggest that the biological or adopting parent name the other parent as legal guardian in his or her will. This should secure the rights of the parent in the event the other dies prematurely.

407. OFF TO COLLEGE

When you send your teenagers off to college, you might include four tools in their financial backpack: a checking account, credit card, renter's insurance—and some sound advice.

Checking accounts. Favor checking accounts where your kids won't get charged a monthly maintenance fee and where they have access to a large number of fee-free ATMs at both college and home. Also make sure the account is set up so your children can't overdraw, and hence incur hefty fees, with ATM withdrawals or debit card purchases.

Credit cards. Many financial companies offer credit cards specially geared to students. This can be a good way for your kids to start building a credit history.

Alternatively, if your credit card company allows it, you might add your teenager as a joint accountholder to a credit card you already have. This can have a magical effect: You may discover that the card's entire history is added to your kid's credit report—and suddenly it will look like your teenager has been responsibly using a credit card for many years.

Instead of adding your student as a joint accountholder, you could add him or her as an authorized user. This, however, probably won't be as helpful in establishing your child as a good credit—and it may not help at all.

Renter's insurance. This is often recommended for college kids, so they're covered if their bicycle is stolen or their computer is destroyed in a fire. Would replacing your student's possessions cause real financial hardship? If the answer is "no," maybe you should skip the coverage.

Have the talk. Spend some time talking to your kids about the dangers of overspending. Discuss what they can charge to the credit card. Emphasize that they should tell you early on if anything goes awry—financially or otherwise—at which point the problem may be more easily fixed.

Not sure your teenagers will be financially responsible? You might keep them on a shorter leash by giving them spending money every two weeks or every month, rather than giving them a big chunk at the start of each semester.

For general information about paying for college, spend some time with Part IV.

408. GETTING DIVORCED

If you're getting divorced, be careful—but also try to be civil. Here are some steps to take in the initial weeks after the breakup:

Draw up a financial inventory. Make copies of financial account statements, tax returns, pay stubs and anything else that documents your collective income, assets and debts. Create a list of valuable household items. You might even photograph or videotape them. Don't discount the possibility that your spouse is hiding assets.

Disentangle your ongoing finances. Get your own checking account and credit cards, while cancelling joint cards. Your goal is to ensure you aren't responsible for any financial missteps that your spouse makes in the weeks and months ahead. At the same time, make sure the household bills get paid, or you may both see your credit scores plummet.

Find the right lawyer. While a courtroom battle is sometimes necessary, you don't want a lawyer for whom that seems to be the first option, not the last resort. The less time you spend in court and the more details you and your spouse can hash out on your own, the less costly your divorce is likely to be.

Avoid unnecessary arguments. Unfortunately, many divorces degenerate into needless bickering that leaves both parties worse off and the lawyers considerably richer. If you can manage to be civil, you will both benefit financially.

A modicum of civility is especially important if you have children. In the years ahead, you will need to make countless joint decisions regarding your children, plus you may need your ex-spouse's cooperation if, say, you suddenly need to work late and can't pick up the kids. Those conversations will be far easier if you haven't torn each other to shreds during the divorce proceedings.

Civility, however, doesn't mean you shouldn't be firm in seeking a fair settlement. The division of property, as well as the amount paid in child support and alimony, are crucially important. State law goes a long way toward deciding these issues. Still, think carefully about what's equitable and which assets to request.

409. SPLITTING FINANCIALLY

In a divorce, you should be able to keep any assets you owned at the time of the marriage, plus any gifts and inheritances you received while married. What about other assets acquired during the marriage? How those are divided will depend on state law, especially whether you live in a community property or common law state. Even then, it's important to pay close attention to the financial details:

Get all joint debts paid off. If you rely on your ex-spouse to continue making payments on loans that are in both your names, you're putting your credit history and credit score at risk.

Decide which assets you want. Many folks want to keep the family home, so they have a sense of stability and continuity. But if you do that, are you locking up too much of your wealth in your home—and could you afford the property taxes, maintenance and homeowner's insurance? If the property is worth more than you paid, you may want to sell it while still married. You can avoid taxes on $500,000 of home price appreciation if you're married, but that drops to $250,000 once you are single.

Consider embedded tax bills. Suppose you have two individual stocks valued at $20,000 each. One is worth less than the price paid and the other is worth more. The latter is less desirable, because you'll owe taxes when you sell, while the stock with a capital loss will give you a tax break.

Similarly, a traditional IRA or 401(k), with its big embedded income tax bill, is worth less than a comparable sum in a Roth account. Need to move retirement account money from one spouse to the other, so you equalize your assets? If done properly, you can avoid triggering an immediate income tax bill or tax penalty.

Think about the transition. If a divorce will compel you to return to work, you may want to seek taxable account money in the divorce, rather than retirement account money. This will give you savings you can easily draw on, should it take you longer than expected to find a job.

What if you're receiving money from your spouse's 401(k) or similar plan under a QDRO (qualified domestic relations order) and you think you'll need to spend it? You can take the money as a lump sum and avoid the usual 10 percent tax penalty on withdrawals before age $59\frac{1}{2}$, though you will owe income taxes. Be warned: If, instead of taking the lump sum, you transfer the 401(k) assets to an IRA and then try to spend the money, you will likely get hit with tax penalties.

410. DIVORCE AND STATE LAW

While divorces often trigger endless wrangling, there's less room for maneuver than you might imagine, because much depends on state law:

Community vs. common law states. There are nine community property states: Arizona, California, Idaho, Louisiana, Nevada, New Mexico, Texas, Washington and Wisconsin. Couples in Alaska can also create community property if they opt to enter into a community property agreement. In a community property state, the wealth acquired during the course of the marriage is considered equally owned by you and your spouse, and would usually be divided equally.

Other states are so-called common law or equitable distribution states. If you end up in court because you can't reach an agreement, a judge will order what he or she believes is an equitable division of the wealth acquired during the marriage. Equitable won't necessarily mean equal. You may not like the result, which creates a strong incentive to settle matters yourself. To learn more about divorce law in your state, head to DivorceNet.com.

In community property and most common law states, you should be able to keep the wealth you brought to the marriage, as well as gifts and inheritances received during the marriage. But if this separate property was mixed with marital property—let's say you put it in a joint account with your spouse—then you may lose a portion in the divorce proceedings.

Alimony. Today, stay-at-home and lower-earning spouses are less likely to receive alimony and instead are expected to return fulltime to the workforce unless, say, they are in their 50s. But it's hard to generalize. If the marriage lasted more than 10 years and one spouse will find it tough to support himself or herself, alimony might be awarded, but perhaps only for a limited time.

Child support. Unlike alimony, which is hard to predict, child-support payments are typically driven by state formula, so there's little room for contention. State formulas are based on the notion that one parent is the custodial parent, which can seem unfair when the parents have joint custody and want an equal say in how to spend money earmarked for the children's benefit. While alimony is tax-deductible for the payer and taxable to the recipient, child support is neither tax-deductible nor taxable.

If you have a child, negotiate who gets to claim the kid as a dependent for tax purposes. If you have two children, you might each claim one as a dependent. That will allow both of you to file as head of household, which will trigger a smaller tax bill than filing as a single individual.

411. MY STORY: HOW I HANDLED MY DIVORCE

My first marriage didn't turn out so well. But the divorce was surprisingly successful.

When Molly and I separated in 1998, we quickly agreed that we should make the divorce as amicable and inexpensive as possible. The math was obvious—every $100 we spent on legal fees meant $50 less for each of us—and figuring out a fair way to split our assets wasn't especially difficult. For $500, a local lawyer turned our plan into a formal agreement and helped us with the child support calculations. Molly and I then saw lawyers on our own. Those two lawyers each charged $200 to review our property settlement and suggest tweaks, bringing the total tab to $900.

At the time of our separation, Hannah was age nine and Henry was five. To make the upheaval less wrenching, I stayed in our current home and Molly bought a house around the corner. On their scooters, the kids could get from one house to the other in less than 60 seconds—and Molly and I avoided a lot of awkward pickups and drop-offs. In fact, we probably saw each other less than if we had lived farther apart and had to transport the kids back and forth by car.

In the years that followed, Molly and I had to deal with a slew of issues related to Hannah and Henry—everything from bedtimes to summer camps to college choices. But we rarely disagreed and were almost always civil. I tried to put aside the divorce's raw emotions and instead view our dealings as a business relationship, where the goal was to figure out what was best for our kids. But Molly and I also benefited, financially and otherwise. I would take the children if she needed to travel. Molly would cover if I had to work late. Even now, with both Hannah and Henry out of college, we occasionally swap emails, sharing tidbits of news about the kids or concerns that we have.

412. CHANGING JOBS

If you change jobs, it's likely for a more enjoyable or more senior position—and it may mean more money. But don't focus just on the size of your new paycheck. Also give some thought to your new job's health, life and disability insurance, as well as the retirement benefits.

Health insurance. If it will take a few months before you are eligible for health care coverage at your new job, you might be able to continue your old employer's health benefits by taking advantage of so-called COBRA coverage.

Life and disability insurance. You'll want to consider what sort of disability and life insurance coverage your new employer provides, and whether you should supplement this with individual policies. You can read more about life, disability and health insurance in Part V.

Your old employer's retirement plan. If your current employer has a vesting schedule for its retirement plan contributions, see if delaying your job change by a few weeks will garner you additional retirement money. Also, be sure to pay back any 401(k) loans—or you could find yourself facing income taxes and tax penalties.

Consolidate retirement accounts. Got retirement savings in your old employer's plan? You could transfer the money to an IRA, which will simplify your finances, give you more investment choice and may lower your investment costs. If you move your 401(k) to an IRA, be sure to do a trustee-to-trustee transfer or you could end up with a nasty tax conundrum.

Before moving the money, give some thought to how this will affect future Roth conversions, what it means for creditor protection, what's the best strategy if you have your old employer's stock in the plan—and whether your old 401(k) is so good that you shouldn't move the money. All of this is covered in detail in Part XI.

Your new employer's retirement plan. Your new employer may automatically enroll you in its retirement plan. But if you sign up yourself, you may get into the plan more quickly and at a higher contribution rate. If your new employer's plan is top-notch, you might even transfer your 401(k) balance from your old employer to the new plan.

413. LOSING YOUR JOB

If you lose your job, you may want to consolidate your 401(k) money in an IRA and you might continue your current health benefits by taking advantage of COBRA coverage, discussed in Part V, just like those who are changing jobs. But also consider taking these other steps:

Prep your finances for hard times. If you have an inkling that layoffs are in the works, save whatever you can, pay back 401(k) loans, and trim the balance on your credit cards and home equity line of credit. Don't, however, rush to pay off car loans and student debt. While you can always run up the balance again on your home equity line of credit and on your credit cards (though it isn't advisable), you can't "re-borrow" your auto and student loans.

Slash your living expenses. Instead of opting for COBRA coverage, see whether you can trim your health insurance premiums by purchasing a policy through your state's insurance exchange. Also, cut out discretionary spending, so you only have fixed costs to worry about. That way, you should be able to make your savings and any severance payment last longer.

Apply for unemployment benefits. Depending on state law, if you receive a severance payment from your employer, you may not be immediately eligible to receive unemployment benefits. Still, apply as soon as you lose your job, so payments start once you're eligible.

Manage your tax bill. Because you have lost your regular income, you may find you're in a surprisingly low tax bracket. To take advantage of your low bracket, think carefully about the timing of stock sales and any retirement account withdrawals. For instance, if you are laid off late in the year and you are compelled to dip into retirement accounts to pay living expenses, the tax bill may be lower if you delay any retirement account withdrawals until after Dec. 31, at which point it will be a new tax year—and your tax bracket may be far lower.

414. WORKING FOR YOURSELF

It may be appealing to work for yourself, but it also comes with a hefty price tag. Here are some of the costs you'll face.

Higher payroll taxes. If you're self-employed, you have to pay both the employee's 7.65 percent Social Security and Medicare payroll tax and the employer's 7.65 percent contribution, though you can take a tax deduction for the employer's portion.

Health insurance. You will need to purchase your own health insurance, though that has become easier, thanks to the health care exchanges. If you are younger without a substantial nest egg, you should probably also get disability insurance. It's best to buy disability coverage while you are employed by someone else, or you could struggle to get coverage. Both health and disability insurance premiums are tax-deductible if you're self-employed.

Funding retirement. Fulltime employees can often contribute to 401(k) plans using payroll deduction, and the money they sock away typically earns a matching employer contribution. But if you are self-employed, all this will be on your shoulders. You might fund a SEP IRA, where you could stash as much as 20 percent of your net self-employment income. Alternatively, consider a solo 401(k), which would allow you to save as much as $53,000 in 2016, or $59,000 if you're age 50 or older.

Larger emergency fund. Because you won't have a steady paycheck, you should probably follow the standard advice and keep the full six months of living expenses in conservative investments held in a taxable account.

No sick days or vacation time. That bigger emergency fund may come in handy if you don't have income for a while because of illness, a lack of customers or you take time off.

Accounting and legal issues. Depending on the complexity of your business, you may need to hire an accountant. You might also want to set up your business as an S corporation or limited liability company, which can protect your personal finances from claims against your business by creditors. Both options are described at the end of Part V.

415. WORKING ABROAD

If you're a U.S. citizen working in a foreign country, you will face all kinds of financial headaches. Many are unavoidable. But you will likely want to keep your finances as simple as possible by limiting the number of financial institutions you deal with and the number of investments you own, so you don't add to your headaches.

Even though you work abroad, you have to file a U.S. tax return each year declaring your worldwide income. The filing deadline is typically June 15, not April 15. You can avoid having your income taxed twice—by both the U.S. and the country where you live—by claiming a credit for foreign taxes paid and by taking advantage of the foreign earned income exclusion, which is $101,300 in 2016. Still, you could suffer some double taxation, because you might not receive credit on your U.S. tax return for all taxes you paid abroad.

To crack down on tax evasion, Congress passed the Foreign Account Tax Compliance Act (FATCA) in 2010, which requires foreign financial institutions to report U.S. account holders. Some foreign banks, which don't want to deal with the reporting requirements, have stopped opening accounts for U.S. citizens. Those moving abroad can also find it tough to get credit cards, cell phones, Internet service and mortgages, because they don't have a credit history in the country where they're now working. Because of the hassles of borrowing, you may find it easier to pay cash—assuming you can afford to.

Every year, if you have more than $10,000 in all foreign accounts combined, you have to file a Foreign Bank and Financial Accounts report, otherwise known as FinCen Form 114 and sometimes just Fbar, with the U.S. Treasury. The deadline was recently changed to April 15, from June 30, though you can request an extension to Oct. 15. There's also a requirement to report foreign financial assets under FATCA, though the threshold is $50,000 and sometimes higher, depending on your situation. The FATCA requirement is met by filing Form 8938 with your U.S. tax return.

U.S. citizens working abroad sometimes have difficulty opening a bank account in the U.S. because they don't have a U.S. address. Some U.S. banks have even taken to closing accounts owned by those living overseas, though there's no law that requires a U.S. citizen to have a U.S. address.

If you work for a foreign company, you may not be contributing to Social Security. That means you should probably save extra on your own to ensure a comfortable retirement. Even if you pay Social Security and Medicare payroll taxes, you likely won't benefit from Medicare coverage if you choose to remain overseas during retirement.

For further information, go to AmericansAbroad.org and check out the "Current Issues" tab.

416. NEARING RETIREMENT

You can learn more about preparing for retirement and generating retirement income in Part II. But here are some additional steps you might take in the year or two before you quit your job:

Check the employee handbook. By delaying retirement by just a few weeks or months, you may qualify to get cashed out on vacation days for the current year or to receive money held in the company's deferred compensation plan. You might also become vested for a portion of your employer's matching contribution to the 401(k).

Exercise employee stock options. You may have been awarded options years ago and never given them much thought, perhaps because the amount involved was small and the stock hasn't been much of a performer. Still, the options may be worth a modest sum, so be sure to exercise them before you quit.

See the doctor and dentist. If you have good medical and dental coverage through your current employer, get health issues tackled now, before you retire.

Refinance your mortgage. Ideally, you should get your mortgage paid off before you retire. But if that won't happen any time soon, it may be worth refinancing. It'll be easier to get approved for the loan if you still have a job and a regular income.

Set up a home equity line of credit. With any luck, you'll never have to use it. But it could come in handy if you suddenly need cash—and, as with a refinancing, it's a lot easier to get approved for a home equity line of credit while you still have a regular paycheck coming in.

417. HELPING ELDERLY RELATIVES

Looking after your parents or other elderly family members? In all likelihood, it's a team effort, with perhaps your siblings involved and others whom you have hired. To help matters run more smoothly, consider these steps:

Create a list of experts. Pull together the names and contact information for doctors, dentists, lawyers, tax preparers, financial advisors and anybody else who assists your parents. Make sure your siblings and other caregivers have the list.

Find a backup. If you and your siblings don't live near your parents, find somebody local who can check on your parents if you become concerned. Make sure that person has a set of keys to your parents' home.

Agree on how to share costs. If your parents don't have enough money for their own care, you and your siblings may have to pick up part of the cost.

Early on, discuss how much you can afford to spend and create a system of monthly accounting, so nobody ends up shortchanged.

Watch for abuse. There might be physical or emotional intimidation or, alternatively, perhaps someone is stealing from your parents. If you think something is awry, be quick to alert others.

Have a contingency plan. What if things deteriorate with your parents—and it's suddenly clear they can no longer live independently? Ideally, you should discuss this with your parents ahead of time. For instance, if the next step is an assisted living facility, it will be easier if you check out a few places ahead of time and get your parents' opinion.

Throughout, keep the focus on what your parents want. Emphasize that you're trying to help them maintain their independence. As we age, we have a sense that we're losing control. If you start making decisions without consulting your parents or you push them too hard to make changes, they will likely feel as if they're being forced to surrender yet more control—and the conversations could quickly turn contentious.

418. AFTER A LOVED ONE'S DEATH

Death, unfortunately, is often accompanied by a slew of practical details. Where to begin?

Look for funeral instructions. You may discover they're in the deceased's will or letter of last instruction.

Consider the cost. This is hardly the moment when most folks are up for price shopping, yet it pays to keep your wits about you. Funeral homes often nudge the family to spend more than is necessary. To read more about funeral expenses, check out the Funeral Consumers Alliance at Funerals.org. According to the National Funeral Directors Association, the median cost of a funeral with burial is $7,181, while the median cost of a funeral with cremation is $6,078.

Order death certificates. The funeral home may ask how many copies of the death certificate you want. Don't skimp. Depending on the complexity of the deceased's finances, you might order 10 or more. You'll need these certificates whenever you claim benefits or property on behalf of the deceased's beneficiaries. It's often cheaper and easier to order death certificates from the funeral home than to obtain them later.

Watch out for theft. Burglars occasionally target the homes of the recently deceased, so you might ask the police to keep an eye on the house. Perhaps more alarming, family members sometimes feel they're free to grab whatever they want without asking. If the deceased had valuables of any kind, consider getting them out of the house.

Locate key papers. In particular, find the will and see who is named as executor. What about other financial or legal papers? For now, set them aside. You don't want to throw anything away until you're confident you have identified all assets and have the account statements you need.

419. SETTLING AN ESTATE

Are you named as executor of an estate? Here are some steps you'll likely need to take:

Hire an attorney. Don't feel compelled to use the deceased's lawyer, especially if he or she doesn't specialize in settling estates. A lawyer might charge a flat fee, a percent of the estate's gross value or by the hour. Try to avoid an hourly fee, because it's hard to know what you will end up getting charged.

If the deceased has investments in a regular taxable account, ask the attorney whether you should sell the assets. That may be an especially smart move if the deceased's portfolio consists of large investments in just a few stocks. Thanks to the step-up in cost basis upon death, the capital gains tax bill should be little or nothing. You may also want to diversify the deceased's retirement account if the investments don't appear prudent.

Gather financial papers. Find the latest statements from the deceased's bank, credit cards, mortgage companies, mutual fund companies, brokerage firms, insurance companies and any other financial firms the deceased had dealings with. See if there's a safe-deposit box. Also study the deceased's most recent tax return and see what arrives in the mail. That way, you can make sure you've located all assets.

Check with financial advisors. If the deceased used a broker, financial planner, insurance agent or accountant, these folks may be helpful in locating assets and settling the estate. Ask the insurance agent about any life insurance. Talk to the accountant about filing final federal and state income tax returns for the deceased and, if necessary, federal and state estate tax returns. Even if federal estate taxes aren't owed, spouses may want to file a federal estate tax return to claim the right to use the deceased spouse's unused estate tax exclusion.

Call current or former employers. If the deceased was still working, he or she may be due a final paycheck and a payout on employer-provided life insurance. Even if retired, the deceased may have 401(k) assets at an old employer, or heirs might be eligible for survivor benefits from the pension plan.

Contact Social Security. You'll need to stop benefits and see about any survivor benefits. If the deceased served in the armed forces, also call the Department of Veterans Affairs.

Think before you spend. If you're the executor, you are likely also one of the estate's beneficiaries. It can take a few months before you receive a distribution from the estate. That's good news—because it will give you time to contemplate what to do with the money. This could be the windfall that puts you on track for retirement, so think twice before going on a spending spree.

As executor, you might want a quick education on estate planning. For that, check out Part XIII.

PART XV

YOUR FINANCIAL PLAN
CHARTING YOUR MONEY PATH IN 18 EASY STEPS

T hanks to the proliferation of online calculators, it's now possible for
ordinary investors to piece together their own lifetime financial plan.
Want a roadmap to guide you through the years ahead? Check out the 18
steps below. Depending on your situation and how much financial progress
you have already made, some steps may be unnecessary.

    1.   Estimate your retirement income needs. One rule of thumb says
that, once retired, you need 80 percent of your final salary to be financially
comfortable. But you might be fine with less if you're a prodigious saver
who regularly socks away 20 percent of income, rather than the often
recommended 10 percent. You might also make do with less if, by
retirement, your mortgage is paid off and the children are off the family
payroll.

    2.   Get a handle on Social Security and pension income. If you are
entitled to a traditional employer pension, check the latest benefits
statement from your employer or contact human resources. Meanwhile, to
find out how much you might receive from Social Security, go to
SocialSecurity.gov and click through to the Retirement Estimator. If you're
unable to use that calculator, try the Quick Calculator, also available at
SocialSecurity.gov.

    3.   Set a goal for your retirement nest egg. Take your answer from Step
No. 1 and subtract the sums from Step No. 2. Let's say you will need
$50,000 a year to retire in comfort and you'll receive $20,000 from Social
Security and nothing from an employer's pension plan. That leaves $30,000

a year that will need to come from savings. To generate that income using a 4 percent portfolio withdrawal rate, how much would you need to save by retirement? If you divide $30,000 by 0.04, you'll get your answer: $750,000.

4.   Calculate required monthly savings. To find out how much you need to save each month to amass your target retirement nest egg, use the Savings Goals calculator at Dinkytown.net. Err on the conservative side by plugging in a 5 percent annual return and 3 percent for inflation.

5.   Design your portfolio. Your investment return will depend on your basic mix of stocks and more conservative investments. To get some guidance on what mix you ought to hold, try the Investor Questionnaire at Vanguard.com.

6.   Prepare for financial emergencies. Get your latest paystub and see how much you take home each month, after taxes and any retirement-plan contributions are deducted. From that sum, subtract any additional monthly savings. That should give you a reasonable estimate of your typical monthly spending.

Experts often suggest holding an emergency fund equal to between three and six months of living expenses. Go for the full six months if your job is tenuous or you're self-employed. Opt for a smaller amount if your position is more secure, your spouse also works, you have a home-equity line of credit or you have other savings in a regular taxable account.

7.   Plug holes in your insurance coverage. There are seven types of insurance you potentially need: health, life, disability, long-term care, homeowner's, auto and umbrella liability. Here are some rough-and-ready rules.

Everybody should have health insurance, and you also need auto and homeowner's insurance if you own a car and a house. If you have less than $1 million in savings, you should probably have disability insurance if you're still in the workforce, and also life insurance if you have children still at home or a spouse who doesn't work. If you are approaching retirement and you have between $300,000 and $1 million in savings, consider buying some form of long-term-care insurance.

What if you have more than $1 million in savings? You can probably afford to self-insure for disability, life and long-term care. But consider getting umbrella liability insurance, in case you're sued.

8.   Decide how much house you can afford. Banks typically want borrowers to limit their monthly mortgage payments, including property taxes and homeowner's insurance, to 28 percent of their pretax monthly income. What does that mean in terms of house size? Try the calculator labeled "How Much House Can I Afford?" at HSH.com.

9.   Estimate college costs. Roughly speaking, it costs $20,000 a year for a state university, $40,000 for the typical private college and $60,000 for an elite private college. Make your choice, multiply by four and you'll have the

cost to send each of your children to college for four years.

10. Check financial aid eligibility. To get a handle on how much college aid you might receive, try the EFC Calculator at CollegeBoard.org. The calculator will give an estimate of your "expected family contribution"—how much you'll have to cough up for college costs each year. Colleges should then provide enough aid to cover the difference between your contribution and the college's annual cost.

11. Calculate your college fund's potential growth. If you won't receive much aid—and hence your expected family contribution is large—it probably makes sense to sock away some money for college. To find out how much you might amass by the time your children turn age 18, return to Dinkytown.net and use the Savings Goals calculator. Again, be cautious, opting for a 5 percent annual return and 3 percent for inflation.

12. Find a 529 college-savings plan. These plans are typically the best bet for college savers. Check out your choices at SavingforCollege.com.

13. Aim to retire debt-free. Probably the biggest debt you need to eliminate is your mortgage. If your home loan won't be paid off until after your expected retirement date, consider making extra-principal payments. To figure out how much you need to add to each monthly mortgage check, use the Mortgage Calculator at Bankrate.com.

14. Decide when to claim Social Security. You'll need to grapple with this issue as you approach retirement age. Often, the smart strategy is to delay benefits until age 70 if you're single. What if you're married? The spouse with the highest lifetime earnings should typically postpone benefits until 70, while the other spouse might claim benefits earlier. For further help, check out BedrockCapital.com's Social Security calculator, which has been revised to reflect the new rules introduced by the 2015 Budget Act.

15. Consider an income annuity. To supplement the income you'll receive from Social Security, you might purchase an annuity that pays lifetime income. How much income will you receive? Try the Guaranteed Income Estimator at Fidelity.com/gie.

16. Refine your retirement strategy. Social Security, together with any pension and annuity income, should provide you with a steady stream of retirement income. For additional spending money, you'll have your retirement savings, which you might draw down using a 4 percent withdrawal rate.

Those withdrawals, however, could run smack into a major market downturn. As a precaution, keep a sum equal to five years of portfolio withdrawals in money-market funds, savings accounts and other cash investments, which you can then draw on during rough spells for stocks and bonds. Also consider which expenses you would cut, should the market downturn prove to be especially severe.

17. Tap into home equity. Early in retirement, you might trade down

to a smaller home, thereby reducing your monthly costs and freeing up home equity, which you can then add to your retirement savings. Later in retirement, if you start to run out of savings, you might consider a reverse mortgage. To see how much cash that might provide, head to ReverseMortgage.org and play around with the site's calculator.

18.   Give some thought to your heirs. Estate planning can involve all kinds of legal documents and complicated strategies. But three steps are essential: Make sure you have a will, the right beneficiaries listed on your retirement accounts and the right beneficiaries named on your life insurance.

APPENDIX

KEY CONCEPTS
134 FINANCIAL IDEAS
EVERY INVESTOR NEEDS TO KNOW

Looking to refresh your memory about personal finance? You can always check the Internet—or the latest edition of the *Money Guide*—for current information on interest rates, market performance and tax rates. But to make smart decisions year after year, you also need a grasp of some timeless but crucial financial ideas. Below are 134 concepts that are discussed in the *Money Guide*—and which are critical to understanding the financial world.

SAVING FOR RETIREMENT

Human capital vs. financial capital. Your human capital is your income-earning ability. Early in your adult life, it's your most valuable asset. Academic economists view the income from human capital as similar to the interest earned from bonds. To diversify your human capital "bond," you might invest heavily in stocks when you're younger. During your working years, your goal is to convert your human capital into financial capital—meaning a huge pile of savings—so that one day you can retire. As you approach retirement, consider increasing your portfolio's allocation to bonds, so you have interest income to replace your human capital's earned income.

Stocks vs. bonds. When you buy a stock, you become a part owner of a business, and benefit from the dividends paid and any share price appreciation. When you buy a bond, you are lending money, and you receive interest in return for letting someone else have the use of your money. Stocks are sometimes referred to as "equities," while bonds are often called "fixed income."

Asset allocation. This is your portfolio's mix of the four major asset classes: stocks, bonds, cash investments such as savings accounts and money-market funds, and alternative investments like hedge funds and gold stocks. For instance, a portfolio might have 50 percent stocks, 35 percent bonds, 10 percent alternative investments and 5 percent cash.

Savings, investment returns and time. How much you amass for retirement and other goals depends on the interaction of three factors: the amount you save, the annual investment returns you earn and the number of years over which you save and collect investment returns. Want to accumulate more money for your goals? You might make use of one or more of these three levers—by aiming to save more, earn more or invest for longer.

Three-legged stool. Retirees have traditionally relied on three key financial resources: Social Security, traditional employer pension plans and personal savings, such as money in 401(k) plans and individual retirement accounts. With the disappearance of many traditional pension plans, most workers today rely solely on Social Security and personal savings.

Defined benefit vs. defined contribution plans. An employer's defined benefit plan pays you monthly income in retirement, with the size of that income typically hinging on your salary and the number of years you worked for the employer. These plans—which are increasingly rare—are funded by the employer. By contrast, defined contribution plans are typically funded partly or entirely by employees. Common types include 401(k) and 403(b) plans.

Individual retirement accounts vs. 401(k) plans. To fund an IRA or 401(k), you need earned income, and your annual contributions can't exceed the amount you earn. Both IRAs and 401(k) plans come in two flavors: traditional accounts, where you can get an initial tax deduction but all withdrawals are taxable as ordinary income, and Roth accounts, where there's no initial tax deduction but all withdrawals are tax-free.

You don't need to meet any special requirements to fund a 401(k) plan, beyond working at the employer in question. By contrast, to fund a Roth IRA or deduct your traditional IRA contributions, you need to meet the applicable IRS rules. Another difference: A 401(k) plan may offer a matching employer contribution—not something you can get with a traditional or Roth IRA.

Taxable vs. tax-deferred accounts. With traditional tax-deferred accounts such as 401(k) plans, IRAs and variable annuities, all taxes are deferred until money is withdrawn. This benefit comes with two costs. First, withdrawals before age 59½ typically trigger tax penalties. Second, withdrawals are taxed as ordinary income, which can mean a federal rate as high as 39.6 percent.

With a taxable account, there are no restrictions on how much you can invest or when you can withdraw, plus there's the chance to take advantage of the low tax rate on long-term capital gains and qualifying dividends. The downside with taxable accounts: You have to pay taxes each year on all dividends, interest and realized capital gains.

RETIREMENT INCOME

Longevity risk. This is the danger that you will live longer than you're financially prepared for, forcing you to cut back spending or take other drastic financial steps, as your savings start to dwindle.

Inflation risk. Over the course of a 20- or 30-year retirement, even modest rates of inflation can severely crimp the lifestyle of retirees who rely on income streams that are fixed in dollar terms, such as the interest payments from bonds, or the income payments from traditional employer pensions and immediate fixed annuities.

Four percent withdrawal rate. Studies suggest that retirees can withdraw 4 percent of their portfolio's value in the first year of retirement, and thereafter step up their annual withdrawals with inflation, and still make it through a 30-year retirement without running out of money. Let's say you retire with a $600,000 portfolio. You would withdraw $24,000 in the first year of retirement. If inflation runs at 3 percent a year, you would withdraw $24,720 in year two, $25,462 in year three and so on. Any dividends and interest you receive count toward each year's total withdrawal.

Sequence-of-return risk. Retirees face two potential drains on their nest egg's value: their own need for spending money and losses caused by market declines. Sequence-of-return risk refers to the danger that retirees suffer large investment losses early in retirement. Those losses—coupled with a retiree's annual withdrawals—can greatly damage a nest egg's value, sharply increasing the chance that the retiree may outlive his or her savings. By contrast, if retirees enjoy market gains in the first five years or so of retirement, they will often be in good financial shape for the rest of their lives, even if they later get hit with a large market decline.

Short-term vs. long-term investments. It's helpful to separate investments into two buckets: those where you're reasonably assured of not losing money— and those where you could suffer a large short-term decline. Investors with time horizons of five years or less should favor savings accounts, certificates of deposit, money-market funds, high-quality short-term bonds and similar conservative investments. Those with more than five years to invest might take the risk of owning stocks, and also longer-term or lower credit-quality bonds, with the goal of earning higher long-run returns.

Income vs. total return. Interest and dividend payments are one source of investment gain. But with bonds and especially stocks, your investment performance also hinges on what happens to the price of the investments you own. To calculate total return, you combine the investment income you receive with the gain or loss in an investment's price.

Social Security. To qualify for Social Security retirement benefits, you need to work and pay Social Security payroll taxes for 40 quarters, equal to 10 years. You can claim Social Security as early as age 62 or as late as age 70. By delaying, you can receive a benefit that's as much as 76 or 77 percent larger. Social Security benefits rise each year with inflation and are at least partially tax-free. In addition, your spouse and children may be eligible for benefits based on your earnings record.

Full Social Security retirement age. You can claim Social Security retirement benefits as early as age 62 or as late as age 70. Depending on when you apply, your monthly check will be calculated as a reduction or increase relative to the benefit you're eligible to receive as of your full Social Security retirement age, which is age 66 or 67, depending on the year you were born. Once you reach your full Social Security retirement age, you have the right to suspend your benefit and thereafter earn delayed retirement credits.

Social Security spousal benefits. A husband or wife is eligible to receive a spousal benefit that's equal to 50 percent of his or her spouse's full Social Security retirement age benefit. To receive the full 50 percent, the husband or wife must be at full Social Security retirement age. If the spouse applies before full retirement age, the benefit is reduced. A husband or wife can't receive spousal benefits until the other spouse applies for benefits based on his or her lifetime earnings record.

Delayed retirement credits. If you postpone claiming Social Security beyond your full retirement age, your benefit will be increased by 8 percentage points for each year you delay. For instance, postponing benefits from a full Social Security retirement age of 66 until age 70 would result in a 32 percent increase in your benefit. Keep in mind that spousal benefits are not eligible for delayed retirement credits, so there's no point in postponing spousal benefits beyond your full retirement age.

File and suspend. This used to be a strategy popular with married couples. At full retirement age, one spouse—typically the main breadwinner—would file for benefits. This allowed his or her spouse to claim spousal benefits. The main breadwinner then immediately suspended benefits until as late as age 70. This resulted in a larger monthly benefit, and also potentially a larger survivor benefit for his or her spouse. After April 2016, this strategy will no longer work. The reason: Under the new rules, if one spouse suspends benefits, the other spouse's spousal benefit is also stopped.

Immediate vs. tax-deferred annuities. Historically, immediate annuities have been used to generate retirement income, while tax-deferred annuities have been used to save for retirement. In recent years, thanks to "living benefits" riders, a tax-deferred annuity can now be used to generate retirement income. Insurers have also started offering deferred income annuities, sometimes called longevity insurance. These pay regular income starting at some future date.

Reverse mortgage. This is a way for those age 62 and older to tap into their home's value without selling. The proceeds from a reverse mortgage can be received as monthly income, a lump sum or a line of credit. The reverse mortgage is repaid after the borrowers die or if they move elsewhere. At that juncture, the amount owed can never be greater than the home's current value.

HOUSES

Land vs. dwelling. As you contemplate the potential return from owning a home, it's helpful to distinguish the dwelling from the land underneath it. You can be fairly confident the land will appreciate over time. By contrast, the dwelling itself will deteriorate, requiring regular maintenance and occasional upgrades if the property is to keep up with the broader housing market. The dwelling, however, also provides you with shelter—which is the key reason to own residential real estate.

Rent vs. imputed rent. The return from owning a home comes in two parts: price appreciation plus rent or imputed rent. Typically, the long-term price appreciation is modest. Instead, the biggest component of the return from homeownership consists of the rent you collect as a landlord or the imputed rent you enjoy if you live in the house yourself. To gauge the value of this imputed rent, consider how much you might receive each month if you rented out your home.

Winner's curse. If you get into a bidding war for a house and emerge as the winner, you may find you suffer from the winner's curse. This is the risk that you paid too much for the house, because you were willing to pay more than other potential buyers, who were perhaps more prudent. The winner's curse can also afflict buyers in other situations, such as those who make the highest bid at an art auction or corporations that come out on top in a takeover battle.

Down payment. This is the sum you put down when buying a house, and it represents your initial home equity. During booming markets, it's sometimes possible to buy a house with no money down, though typically you'll need to put down at least 3 to 5 percent.

Private mortgage insurance. If you take out a mortgage to buy a home and make a down payment that's less than 20 percent of the home's purchase price, the mortgage lender will likely require you to take out private mortgage insurance, or PMI. The lender should automatically stop charging

PMI once your regular mortgage payments cause the loan's principal value to fall below 78 percent of your home's original purchase price. You might ask the mortgage lender to remove the cost earlier if, say, home prices have increased substantially or you've made significant home improvements, and that means your home equity is now more than 20 percent of your home's current value.

Closing costs. The expenses incurred when purchasing a home can include legal fees, title insurance, a home inspection and mortgage application costs. One rule of thumb puts closing costs at 2 to 5 percent of a home's purchase price, but they can vary widely, depending on whether you're taking out a mortgage, whether there are transfer taxes involved and whether, in your state, you need a lawyer to complete the closing.

Home equity. To figure out how much equity you have in your home, take your home's current value and subtract all mortgage debt. Keep in mind that, if you sold your home, the proceeds would be somewhat less than your home equity, once you paid selling costs.

Leverage. If you have a home with a mortgage outstanding, you have a leveraged real estate bet. Suppose you own a $200,000 home with a $150,000 mortgage, so your home equity is $50,000. If your home's value rose 10 percent to $220,000, your home equity would climb to $70,000, a 40 percent increase. Conversely, if your home's value fell 10 percent, your home equity would shrink to $30,000, a 40 percent decrease.

Mortgage interest deduction. You can typically deduct the interest on $1 million of mortgage debt used to buy, build or improve a first or second home. You can also deduct the interest on $100,000 of home-equity borrowing used for any other purpose, unless you are subject to the alternative minimum tax.

Conflicts of interest. When selling a home, real estate agents have an incentive to get a higher price. But they also have an incentive to get the deal quickly concluded. For instance, if you hold out for a higher price and it takes longer to sell your home, that may mean substantially more money for you. But for your real estate agent, it may not mean a significantly bigger commission, but it could involve substantially more work.

Capital gains exclusion. This is the amount of price appreciation that isn't taxed when you sell a primary residence. Typically, if you have lived in a house for two out of the past five years, you can avoid capital gains taxes on $250,000 in price appreciation. This figure is increased to $500,000 if you are married filing jointly.

COLLEGE

Prepaid tuition 529 plans vs. 529 savings plans. A prepaid tuition plan is designed to let you lock in future tuition costs at today's prices. Often, the tuition credits can only be used at certain colleges. Meanwhile, a 529 savings plan allows you to amass money for college costs by investing in the financial markets, typically through mutual funds. Both 529 savings and prepaid plans will give you tax-free growth if the money is used for qualifying education expenses.

Kiddie tax. This can be an issue for families that save for college using custodial accounts. The kiddie tax can apply to children under age 19, or under 24 if they were fulltime students as of year-end. In 2016, the first $1,050 of a child's investment gains is tax-free and the next $1,050 is taxed at the child's rate. Above $2,100, gains are taxed at the parents' rate.

Expected family contribution. This is the sum a family is expected to contribute each year toward their child's college costs. If a college's total annual cost is greater than a family's expected family contribution, needs-based financial aid is typically provided to fill the gap.

Need vs. merit. Historically, most financial aid has been awarded based on a family's financial need. Over the past few decades, however, there has been a sharp increase in merit-based aid, which is awarded because the students are considered talented academically, athletically or in some other way.

Loans vs. grants. The two main types of financial aid are grants, which never have to be repaid, and loans. The latter may have a subsidized interest rate, but the money borrowed eventually has to be paid back. There is also a third type of financial aid: work-study jobs. Those jobs can be on or off campus and must pay at least the federal minimum wage.

Federal vs. institutional methodology. These are the two formulas used by the federal government and private colleges when determining a student's expected family contribution. The two formulas have two major differences. First, the institutional formula considers home equity, while the federal formula doesn't. Second, if the parents are divorced, the federal formula only considers the finances of the custodial parent and his or her new spouse, if any. By contrast, the institutional formula will consider the finances of both parents, and also those of their current spouses.

Parental assets vs. children's assets. Under the aid formulas, a child's assets are assessed much more heavily than the assets of the parents. This means that, if there are substantial assets in the child's name, the family will be expected to use most of those assets for college costs—and hence their aid eligibility will be significantly less.

Tax deduction vs. credit. Families with a student attending college may be able to take advantage of a variety of education tax deductions and credits. A tax deduction reduces the amount of income that's subject to taxation. For instance, if you're in the 25 percent tax bracket and have a $1,000 tax deduction, you would save $250 in taxes. By contrast, a tax credit reduces the amount of tax you owe dollar-for-dollar, so a $500 credit would trim your tax bill by $500.

Pay As You Earn. This is the name for the federal loan repayment program that caps student-loan payments at 10 percent of income and forgives all debt after 20 years.

PROTECTING YOUR FAMILY

Emergency fund. One rule of thumb suggests you should keep six months of living expenses in conservative investments, in case you lose your job, need to make major home repairs or have to handle other unexpected expenses. You might hold a smaller sum if you have a secure job, your spouse also works or you have easy access to borrowed money.

Credit lines. To help pay for financial emergencies, you might set up credit lines. Often the best option is a home-equity line of credit. With a credit line, you don't incur any interest expense until you borrow money, though you may have to pay a modest annual account fee.

Risk pooling. When you purchase an insurance policy, you are effectively joining with other policyholders to pool risk. Those who suffer misfortune collect from the pool of money that all policyholders have contributed to.

Self-insure. As you accumulate more wealth, you might drop some of your insurance policies or reduce the amount of coverage. Instead, you would "self-insure." For instance, those with seven-figure portfolios might eschew long-term-care insurance and instead plan on paying nursing home costs with their savings.

Property casualty vs. life companies. Property-casualty insurers provide protection for property through auto, homeowner's, renter's and similar policies. They also offer umbrella liability insurance. Life insurers, which focus on disability, life and long-term-care coverage, provide protection against the various misfortunes that can afflict individuals. Some insurers protect both property and individuals.

Premium. The amount you have to pay each month or each year for an insurance policy.

Deductible. If you have a claim on an auto, homeowner's or health insurance policy, your out-of-pocket cost is represented by the deductible, with the insurance company paying the rest. The higher the deductible, the lower your premium will be.

Elimination period. If you have a claim on a disability or long-term-care policy, the elimination period represents the amount of time you will have to shoulder costs before the insurer starts paying. The longer the elimination period, the lower your premium will be.

Co-payments and coinsurance. This is the sum you are expected to pay for each doctor's visit with a health insurance policy or with Medicare. A co-payment is a fixed dollar amount. Coinsurance is figured as a percentage of the medical bill. The coinsurance will be based not on the actual bill, but on the bill that reflects the discount the insurer has negotiated with the medical provider.

Managed care. In an effort to hold down costs, many health care insurance policies no longer allow you to see any doctor you wish. Instead, they offer some form of managed care. For instance, you might only be covered if you use the insurer's network of doctors. Alternatively, the policy might cover you if you visit an out-of-network doctor, but at a lower rate. You might also be required to get approval from the insurer before using some medical services.

Flexible spending accounts vs. health savings accounts. A flexible spending account (FSA) is funded with pretax dollars and used to pay medical expenses not covered by your employer's health care plan. A health savings account (HSA) is also funded with pretax dollars. It's used to pay for medical expenses not covered by a high-deductible insurance policy. Unlike an FSA, you aren't expected to largely or entirely empty an HSA each year—and, indeed, the account can be left to grow and then used to pay for medical expenses years later or even used for other costs.

Medicare vs. Medicaid. Medicare is the government-run health insurance program for Americans age 65 and up. Medicaid is the health insurance program for those with low incomes and few assets. Medicaid is run by the states, but funded by both the federal and state governments.

Rehabilitative vs. custodial care. You might require nursing home care when rehabilitating after an illness or injury. Alternatively, you might be in a nursing home because you can no longer handle your own daily needs and need custodial care. Medicare covers rehabilitative care for those age 65 and up, while Medicaid may pay for custodial care if you have few assets and limited income.

Cash value vs. term insurance. Cash-value life insurance combines pure insurance with an investment account. As the investment account grows in value, you purchase less pure insurance each year. By contrast, a term policy is pure insurance, providing a death benefit if you die while the coverage is in force, but nothing more.

Asset protection. This refers to the strategy of trying to protect your wealth from creditors who have a claim on your assets, either because you lost a lawsuit or because you took on too much debt and ended up in financial trouble.

Liability coverage. If you cause an auto accident or someone gets hurt at your house, the liability coverage that's part of your auto or homeowner's policy can help cover the medical costs of injured individuals and pay to repair damaged property. It can also help with any resulting legal claims.

For additional coverage, you might buy umbrella liability insurance.

Homestead exemption. If you lose a lawsuit or file for bankruptcy, your primary residence may be protected, depending on the state where you live. In some states, your entire home will be protected, while in other states the protected home value is capped at fairly modest levels.

SAVING AND SPENDING

Savings rate. This is the amount you save each year divided by your income. The savings rates advocated by financial experts are usually couched in terms of pretax income, but the official savings rate from the Bureau of Economic Analysis is expressed as a percentage of after-tax income.

Net worth. This is the value of your assets minus your liabilities. Assets could potentially include cars and collectibles. But it's more typical to limit the definition of assets to your investment portfolio and the homes you own. Liabilities include all your debts, including mortgages, car loans, student loans and credit card balances.

Fixed vs. discretionary spending. Fixed spending includes recurring costs such as mortgage or rent, property taxes, utilities, insurance premiums and groceries. Discretionary spending, by contrast, is easier to cut, and includes items like vacations, eating out and going to concerts. The lower your fixed costs relative to your income, the easier it will be to save and the more money you'll have for discretionary "fun" spending.

Hedonic adaptation. This is the surprisingly fast process by which we adapt to new developments in our life, both good and bad. For instance, we might quickly get used to a higher income or a larger home. This helps explain why money buys limited happiness.

Experiences vs. possessions. Academic studies suggest we get more happiness from experiences rather than things. Experiences—such as going on vacation—are not only enjoyable by themselves, but also offer months of anticipation beforehand and fond memories afterwards. By contrast, the pleasure from buying possessions can pass quickly, thanks to hedonic adaptation.

Flow. Our happiest times can include moments when we're engaged in activities that we're passionate about and find challenging. At such moments, we can be so engrossed that we lose all track of time. This notion of flow—as in "being in the flow"—was developed by psychology professor Mihaly Csikszentmihalyi.

Focusing illusion. When asked, those with higher incomes are more likely to describe themselves as happy, even though other studies have found that high-income earners are no happier on a day-to-day basis. This has been attributed to a focusing illusion: A question about their level of happiness prompts those with higher incomes to consider their fortunate position in the world. That, in turn, leads them to say they are happy.

Delaying gratification. This involves putting off immediate pleasure and instead focusing on longer-term goals. Good savers are able to delay gratification. This is also a hallmark of those who perform well in school, train to run marathons and successfully complete long-term work projects.

Compounding. In any given year, you can potentially earn investment returns not only on your original investment, but also on returns collected in prior years. For instance, if you earn 10 percent a year for 10 years, your cumulative gain wouldn't be 100 percent, but rather 159 percent.

Employer matching contribution. In an employer-sponsored 401(k) or 403(b) workplace retirement plan, the employee's contributions to the plan are often partially or fully matched by the employer. In a common arrangement, an employer will contribute 50 cents for every $1 that the employee contributes, up to 6 percent of pay. If employees contribute the full 6 percent, they receive 3 percent from the employer, bringing the total sum contributed to 9 percent.

Time-weighted vs. dollar-weighted returns. A time-weighted return reflects the gain you would have earned over, say, 10 years, assuming you bought at the beginning of the 10 years and never again bought or sold. By contrast, a dollar-weighted return takes into account when you bought and sold. If, say, the market fell sharply at some point during the 10 years and you invested more during the decline, these purchases would boost your dollar-weighted return.

Dollar-cost averaging. This is the strategy of investing the same sum on a regular basis, no matter what is happening in the financial markets. If you regularly contribute $300 a month to your 401(k) through payroll deduction, you're effectively engaging in dollar-cost averaging.

Value averaging. This is a variation on dollar-cost averaging that involves adjusting the amount you invest each month, depending on how the markets are performing. You start by establishing a target growth rate for your stock portfolio. If, because of poor returns, your stock portfolio doesn't achieve its target growth rate in any given month, you would increase the sum you save. If returns are better than expected, you would invest less. This somewhat contrarian approach can lead to better long-run results than dollar-cost averaging.

PORTFOLIO BUILDING

Time horizon. This is the length of time that your money will be invested, before you need to convert your investments back into cash to pay for your goals. The longer your time horizon, the more risk you can potentially take. Some goals, such as saving for a house down payment, have hard deadlines, with all money needed on a particular day. Other goals, like investing for retirement, involve softer deadlines, because you'll spend the money saved over time.

Risk tolerance. The amount of investment risk you can reasonably take is partly driven by factors such as your time horizon and the degree of risk in the rest of your financial life. For instance, those with longer time horizons and more secure jobs can arguably take greater risk. But you also need to consider how much risk you can personally stomach, including how unnerving you find market volatility and how likely you are to sell in a panic if there's a large market decline.

Loss aversion. While investors are often said to be risk averse, they're more accurately described as loss averse—meaning they hate to lose money. In fact, when faced with a loss, investors may increase risk in an effort to avoid the loss. One example: Investors will often double down on a losing stock, in an effort to recoup their loss more quickly.

Asset classes. The three major asset classes are stocks, bonds and cash investments. The latter includes savings accounts, certificates of deposit and money market funds. Alternative investments, such as real estate, gold stocks and hedge funds, are sometimes described as a fourth asset class. These various alternative investments, however, don't have many financial characteristics in common, except the hope that they will perform well when financial markets are struggling.

Diversification. To reduce the risk of owning any particular asset class, investors will buy hundreds and sometimes thousands of individual securities. Suppose you own just one or two stocks. You will have a lot of so-called idiosyncratic risk, and there's a danger that you won't be rewarded for the risk you are taking. As you add more stocks to your portfolio, you reduce this idiosyncratic risk and increase the likelihood that your results will track the broad market's performance.

Correlation. Investors often try to include uncorrelated investments in their portfolio, in the hope that some securities will post gains when others are struggling. The correlation among different stocks is typically quite high. Instead, to lower the volatility of a portfolio with significant stock exposure, investors will often turn to bonds, cash investments and alternative investments.

Volatility and investment compounding. The more volatile a portfolio's performance, the less efficient the process of compounding will be. Consider an example. Portfolio A gains 10 percent both this year and next. Portfolio B gains 20 percent in the first year and 0 percent in the second year. Portfolio C gains 25 percent in the first year and loses 5 percent in the second. The cumulative gain would be 21 percent for portfolio A, 20 percent for portfolio B and just under 19 percent for portfolio C.

Rebalancing. Investors often set target percentages for their various holdings, such as the amount they want to keep in bonds, real estate investment trusts, U.S. large-company stocks and so on. Once you've settled on such targets, you might periodically rebalance back to these target percentages, which will involve lightening up on recent winners and adding to lagging sectors. Rebalancing is mostly about controlling a portfolio's risk level, though it may also boost returns, especially when rebalancing among various stock market sectors.

Mutual funds vs. exchange-traded funds. Owners of mutual funds can trade shares through a brokerage firm or deal directly with the fund company involved. But either way, the ultimate buyer or seller is the mutual fund itself, with the share price established as of that day's market close. By contrast, exchange-traded funds are listed on the stock market, just like any other stock, and shares can be bought from and sold to other investors throughout the trading day.

Load vs. no-load funds. Load funds are sold through brokers and might charge a commission when you buy or a commission when you sell. These funds might also charge an ongoing commission, known as a 12b-1 fee. By contrast, a no-load fund won't charge a front-end or back-end commission, and any 12b-1 fee should be modest.

Expense ratio. This is a fund's annual expenses expressed as a percentage of fund assets. A fund that levies a 0.5 percent expense ratio is costing you 50 cents a year for every $100 invested.

Fees vs. commissions. Brokers are compensated by charging commissions when you buy and sell. Meanwhile, financial advisors charge fees. While a small number of financial advisors levy hourly fees or annual retainers, most charge a percentage of a client's portfolio value, such as 1 percent a year. In addition to this 1 percent for financial advice, investors will also incur the expenses charged by the mutual funds, annuities and other investment products that they buy.

Conflicts of interest. Different advisor compensation arrangements create different conflicts of interest. Brokers who charge commissions have an incentive to get you to trade and to buy high-commission products. Advisors who charge a percentage of assets have an incentive to manage as much of your money as possible. To that end, they might push you to roll over 401(k) assets to an IRA, even though the 401(k) has great low-cost investment offerings, and they might dissuade you from using your portfolio to pay down debt.

Market efficiency. The markets are often described as efficient, though what's meant by that phrase varies. Some academics think that stock and bond prices always accurately reflect all available information. Others argue that, while the markets aren't always efficient, they are efficient enough that very few investors will manage to earn market-beating returns over the long haul.

Index vs. active funds. An actively managed fund aims to pick securities that will outperform the fund's benchmark index, while an index fund buys many or all of the securities that make up a market index in an effort to match the index's performance.

RISK AND RETURN

Real vs. nominal. A nominal increase or decrease is an actual percentage change, without any adjustment for inflation. A real increase or decrease is the change after adjusting for inflation.

Dilution. As a company sells additional shares or compensates employees with stock, existing shareholders see their stake in the company diluted. Dilution also occurs at the macroeconomic level. As new companies spring up, existing corporations—and their shareholders—can see their claim on the economy's profits diluted. This macroeconomic dilution has been estimated at 2 percentage points a year.

Price-earnings ratio. This is a company's share price divided by its earnings per share. An example: If a company's stock is at $60 and its earnings per share are $4, the company's P/E multiple would be 15.

Dividend yield. To calculate a company's dividend yield, you divide the annual dividend by its stock price. For instance, if a company pays a dividend of 50 cents every quarter and it has a $40 stock price, you would divide the $2 total annual dividend by $40, giving you a 5 percent yield.

Book value. On a company's balance sheet, if you subtract the company's liabilities from its assets, you get stockholder's equity, which represents the amount invested in the company through both stock offerings and retained earnings. When stockholder's equity is computed on a per-share basis, it's known as book value. Some value investors favor stocks that trade at or below book value.

Beta. This is a measure of how much a stock rises or falls relative to a market index, typically the S&P 500. For instance, if a stock has a beta of 0.85 and the S&P 500 climbs 1 percent, you would expect the stock to rise 0.85 percent.

Value vs. growth. A growth stock is one that holds out the promise of rapid revenue and earnings increases, while value stocks may have a less promising outlook, but typically they are cheaper based on yardsticks such as price-earnings multiples, price-to-book value and dividend yields. Historically, value stocks have outperformed growth stocks.

Factor investing. Academic studies have attempted to identify which stock market characteristics—or "factors"—are associated with superior returns. Research has found that, historically, superior returns have been delivered by smaller-company stocks, value shares, stocks displaying short-term upward price momentum and stocks of companies with higher gross profitability.

Duration. This is a measure of a bond or bond fund's sensitivity to interest rate changes. A bond fund with a duration of five years would fall 5 percent in price if interest rates rose by 1 percentage point and climb 5 percent if rates declined by 1 percentage point.

Credit risk. When you buy a bond, you take on credit risk, which is the risk that the bond's issuer will default. This risk is negligible for Treasury bonds and modest for municipal bonds and large corporations. But defaults are a real possibility with so-called junk bonds, which are those that are rated below investment grade by the credit rating agencies.

Covered calls. Investors will sometimes sell call options against the stocks they own. This strategy generates extra income, thanks to the premiums received from the buyers of these options. In return for paying that premium, the buyers have the right to call away the stock at a specified price—which means the options' sellers could miss out on gains if the stock involved climbs sharply during the life of the option.

Cash investments. These are investments where there's little or no risk of losing money. Cash investments include savings accounts, bank money-market accounts, money-market mutual funds and certificates of deposit.

Alternative investments. This category includes a variety of investments, everything from timber to real estate investment trusts to gold stocks to hedge funds. The common element: These are all seen as investments that might fare well when stocks are performing poorly.

TAXES

Payroll tax. The Social Security and Medicare payroll tax is 15.3 percent of earned income. Half is typically paid by employers and half by employees, though the self-employed have to pay the entire amount. The portion that pays for Social Security—which is 12.4 percent in total, with 6.2 percent coming from employees—is levied on the first $118,500 of earned income in 2016. The Medicare portion—2.9 percent in total, with 1.45 percent coming from employees—is levied on every dollar earned.

Average vs. marginal tax rate. Your marginal income tax rate is the rate you paid on the last dollar of income that you earned. The average rate is the total income tax you paid divided by either your total income or your total taxable income.

Standard vs. itemized deductions. The standard deduction, which varies depending on your filing status, can be claimed by any taxpayer. It reduces the amount of income that's subject to income taxes. Instead of taking the standard deduction, some taxpayers itemize their deductions, which can result in a larger tax savings. These itemized deductions can include unreimbursed medical expenses, property taxes, mortgage interest, state and local income taxes, and charitable contributions.

Income vs. capital gains taxes. Income taxes are levied on wages, interest from bonds and bank accounts, short-term capital gains and retirement-account withdrawals, among other items. Capital gains taxes are paid on investments sold at a profit after holding them for more than a year. The capital gains tax rate can be as high as 20 percent—but it's still well below the tax rate on income, which can be as high as 39.6 percent.

Short-term vs. long-term capital gains. If you hold an investment for a year or less before selling, any profit would be considered a short-term capital gain and taxed at the higher income tax rate. If you hold the investment for more than a year, any gain would be taxed at the lower long-term capital gains rate.

Qualified dividends. If a stock pays a qualified dividend, it's taxed at the long-term capital gains rate, rather than at the higher income tax rate. Real estate investment trusts and some foreign companies don't pay dividends that are qualified. Even if a company pays a qualified dividend, you need to hold the stock for more than 60 days to receive the favorable tax treatment.

Traditional vs. Roth individual retirement accounts. A traditional IRA may give you an initial tax deduction, but withdrawals are taxed as ordinary income. A Roth IRA won't give you an initial tax deduction, but all withdrawals are potentially tax-free.

Tax-deductible contributions. When you fund a traditional IRA, you may be able to deduct your contributions, assuming you meet the income criteria or you aren't covered by a retirement plan at work. Contributions to traditional 401(k) or 403(b) plans are also effectively tax-deductible. Instead of receiving a tax deduction on your tax return, however, your employer takes your retirement-plan contributions out of pretax income, which results in comparable tax savings.

Earned vs. unearned income. Earned income is income earned from running your own business or working for others. This income is subject to payroll taxes, but also qualifies you to fund retirement accounts. Unearned income includes dividends, interest and capital gains. This income isn't subject to payroll taxes, and it may also be taxed at the preferential long-term capital gains rate.

Tax efficiency. When investors strive for tax efficiency, they aim to minimize the annual tax bill generated by their portfolio. This can involve placing investments that generate big annual tax bills inside a retirement account, buying tax-free municipal bonds in a taxable account and using a taxable account to buy and hold stocks and stock funds.

Asset location. To reduce a portfolio's annual tax bill, investors should pay careful attention to which investments they hold in tax-sheltered retirement accounts and which in taxable accounts. Investors might hold municipal bonds and long-term stock holdings in a taxable account. Meanwhile, they might use their retirement account to trade individual stocks and to hold actively managed stock funds, taxable bonds, real estate investment trusts and other investments that generate a lot of immediately taxable income.

BORROWING

Credit report vs. credit score. A credit report brings together details about your financial life. Many of those details relate to various ways that you've borrowed, such as mortgages, car loans and credit cards. A credit score is a measure of your creditworthiness based on the information in your credit report.

Debt ratios. This is the amount you pay to service your debts each month as a percentage of your pretax monthly income. Mortgage lenders typically don't want to see borrowers take on mortgage payments, including property taxes and homeowner's insurance, that are much above 28 percent of income. Lenders also prefer that borrowers limit total debt payments to 36 percent of income.

Secured vs. unsecured debt. If you take out a mortgage that's backed by your home's value or an auto loan that is collateralized by the car you bought, it is considered a secured loan. Because the lender has an asset it can seize if you fail to make your loan payments, the interest rate should be relatively low. By contrast, if you carry a credit card balance or take out a personal loan, there is no collateral backing the loan and hence the interest rate is typically higher.

Deductible vs. nondeductible interest. The interest paid on mortgages, margin borrowing and student loans may be tax-deductible. Interest on other debt, notably credit card balances and auto loans, can't be deducted on your tax return.

Fixed vs. adjustable-rate mortgage. A fixed-rate mortgage charges the same interest rate throughout the life of the mortgage, allowing the monthly payments also to stay the same. By contrast, the interest rate on an adjustable-rate mortgage changes periodically, often once a year, resulting in changes in the monthly payment. Hybrid mortgages combine features from both mortgages, charging a fixed rate for perhaps the first five years and then adjusting every year thereafter.

Principal vs. interest. On most mortgages, part of each monthly payment goes toward interest and part toward paying down the loan's principal value, which is the amount borrowed. As the loan balance shrinks, less of each monthly payment should go toward interest and more toward principal. Because the amount originally borrowed is gradually repaid over the life of the mortgage, these are sometimes called amortizing loans.

Loan vs. credit line. With a loan, the specified amount is borrowed all at once. With a credit line, the maximum amount that can be borrowed is set when the credit line is established. The borrower can then tap the credit line as needed.

Refinancing. If interest rates fall after you take out a loan, you might be able to refinance the loan, thereby taking advantage of lower rates. This is a particularly popular strategy among fixed-rate mortgage borrowers. The advantage of the lower rate needs to be weighed against the cost of the refinancing. Student loans are sometimes also refinanced.

Prepayment. To pay off a loan more quickly, borrowers will sometimes make extra principal payments. The return earned on these prepayments is equal to the loan's interest rate. Some lenders charge a prepayment penalty if you pay off a loan too quickly.

Debt consolidation. If you have high-interest debt, notably credit card debt, or you have an overwhelming number of loans outstanding, you might consolidate these debts into a single loan. For instance, you could consolidate your debts using a home equity loan, which should have a relatively low interest rate. The interest on the home loan may also be tax deductible. Similarly, students often end up with multiple federal student loans. To avoid having to pay so many loans every month, they often consolidate these debts into a single loan after they graduate.

Chapter 7 vs. Chapter 13 bankruptcy. These are the two main forms of bankruptcy for individuals. Chapter 7 bankruptcy deals with your debts by liquidating available assets or, if your debts are secured by particular assets, by returning these assets to lenders. Chapter 13 bankruptcy is for those with regular incomes. It deals with debts through monthly payments that might last three to five years.

ESTATE PLANNING

Probate. This is the legal review process, overseen by the local probate court, which occurs after your death. It's designed to ensure your assets are disbursed according to your will or, if there's no will, according to state law. Not all assets pass through probate, including assets held jointly with right of survivorship and retirement accounts with beneficiary designations.

Right of survivorship. If you own a house, car or other property jointly with right of survivorship, it passes directly to the survivor upon your death and doesn't go through probate.

Beneficiary designations. Assets in retirement accounts and trusts, and proceeds from life insurance policies, typically pass to the beneficiaries named on these assets—rather than to the heirs named in your will.

Trusts. A trust can be created while you're still alive or upon your death. Trusts are formed for a host of reasons, including protecting assets from creditors, saving on estate taxes, avoiding probate and controlling how assets are used after you die.

Gift-tax exclusion. This is the annual sum that you can give to another person, without worrying about the gift tax. In 2016, the gift-tax exclusion is $14,000. Got three grandchildren you want to help? You could give each grandchild $14,000, thus shrinking your taxable estate by $42,000. If married, your spouse could give another $42,000.

Federal vs. state estate tax. Federal estate taxes are levied on estates worth more than $5.45 million in 2016. Roughly a third of states have their own estate or inheritance tax. These typically kick in at lower asset levels than the federal estate tax.

Inheritance tax. While estate taxes are levied on the total sum bequeathed, inheritance taxes are levied on the recipients of the money. Six states currently levy inheritance taxes. Certain heirs may be exempt from the tax, such as your spouse and children.

Estate tax exclusion. This is the total sum, set at $5.45 million for 2016, that you can bequeath free of federal estate taxes. If, in any year, you give more than the gift-tax exclusion to someone, the amount in excess of the gift-tax exclusion will reduce the total sum you can bequeath tax-free upon your death. For instance, the gift-tax exclusion is $14,000 in 2016, so a gift of $1,014,000 to any one individual would reduce the credit available at your death by $1 million, to $4.45 million.

Unlimited marital deduction. Neither the gift-tax exclusion nor the estate tax exclusion matter when passing assets to your husband or wife. Both during your lifetime, and upon your death, you can give an unlimited sum to your spouse.

Step-up in basis. Under current law, if you own, say, a home or stocks in a taxable account that are worth more than the price you paid, the cost basis of these assets is stepped up to their current market value as of the time of your death, thus eliminating the potential capital-gains tax bill.

Stretch IRA. Beneficiaries who inherit a retirement account—other than a spouse—are required to begin drawing down the account almost immediately. The stretch IRA strategy involves doing this as slowly as legally possible. By drawing down the account gradually over the beneficiary's lifetime, the beneficiary can squeeze maximum gain from a traditional IRA's tax-deferred growth or a Roth IRA's tax-free growth. In recent years, Congress has considered putting a halt to this strategy and instead forcing beneficiaries to empty retirement accounts within five years of the original owner's death.

Power of attorney. In case you become incapacitated, you might draw up powers of attorney to designate others to make financial and medical decisions on your behalf.

Living will. This document specifies your wishes concerning life-prolonging medical procedures.

ABOUT THE AUTHOR

Jonathan Clements is a financial writer living just north of New York City. Born in London, England, Jonathan graduated from Cambridge University. He spent almost 20 years at *The Wall Street Journal* in New York, where he was a personal-finance columnist. Jonathan also worked at Citigroup for six years as Director of Financial Education for the U.S. wealth-management business.

Jonathan has written four earlier personal-finance books, and also a novel. His next book, *How to Think About Money*, is slated to be published in September 2016. Jonathan writes a monthly column for *Financial Planning* magazine and teaches personal finance at Mercy College in Dobbs Ferry, NY. He has appeared on ABC's *Good Morning America*, CNBC, CNN, Fox Business, Fox News, MSNBC, NBC's *Today Show*, public television's *Consuelo Mack WealthTrack* and National Public Radio. An avid bicyclist, Jonathan can, on many mornings, be found pedaling madly around town. He's married, with two children and two stepchildren—all a source of constant wonder.

You can learn more at JonathanClements.com or at the *Jonathan Clements Money Guide*'s Facebook page. You can also follow Jonathan on Twitter @ClementsMoney. Every few months, he puts out a free newsletter. You can see past issues at JonathanClements.com, and get on the distribution list by writing to ClementsMoney@gmail.com.

DETAILED TABLE OF CONTENTS